CONTENTS OF VOLUME IV.

HISTORICAL PAPERS—

I.	First Settlers of Tiverton, R. I.	5
II.	Rhode Island Colonial Paper Currency. *Welcome A. Greene.*	6
III.	New England Almanacs. *Amos Perry.*	27
IV.	The Hopkins-Ward Letters. II.—Letter of Samuel Ward. *Ray Greene Huling*	40
V.	Rebel Treatment of Tories during the Revolution. *The Sheriff Brown Papers*	77
VI.	The Revolutionary Movement in Rhode Island. *The Editor.*	81
VII.	Preaching on a Steamboat. *Rev. H. G. Perry.*	113
VIII.	Deposition of Andrew Willett. *Ray Greene Huling*	124
IX.	The Patriots of Hopkinton, 1776. *E. R. Allen.*	138
X.	Depositions, case of Hopkins and Ward. *Ray Greene Huling.*	143
XI.	Jamestown Record	149
XII.	Rhode Island Partners in the Susquehanna Purchase	150
XIII.	The Roger Williams Meeting-house, Salem, Mass.	152
XIV.	A Road Damage	168
XV.	Improved Order of Red Men. *Fred. J. Smith.*	186
XVI.	French Spoliation Claims. *Amasa M. Eaton.*	202
XVII.	Alexander's Deed to the Proprietors of Providence. *Fred. A. Arnold.*	238
XVIII.	Origin of Name, East Greenwich	249
XIX.	Ancient North End Landmarks. *An Old Resident.*	268
XX.	Deed from Wesauamog to the Proprietors of Providence. *Fred. A. Arnold.*	290
XXI.	Address *B. B. Hammond.*	300
XXII.	The Israelites in Rhode Island. *Rev. F. Denison.*	301
XXIII.	Address. *Rev. Myer Noot.*	318
XXIV.	Is America only East Greenwich?	327

GENEALOGICAL PAPERS—

    I. The South Kingstown Births. *The Editor.* ...45, 125, 169, 275
    II. The Record of Old Smithfield. *The Editor.*.....57, 100, 189, 257
    III. The Story of the Tablets. *James L. Sherman*..70, 116, 178, 283
    IV. Notes on the Tillinghast Family. *Mrs. E. H. L. Barker*.... 140
    V. The Wilcox-Wordell Marriage. *Ray Greene Huling*........ 142
    VI. Vision Casey. *Rev. Henry G. Perry*....................... 153
    VII. A Mythical Pedigree. *Ray Greene Huling*................. 235
    VIII. The Bull-Jenkins Family. *Steuben Jenkins*................ 250

POETRY—

    I. A Survey of Narragansett Bay, 1741. *One of the Surveyors*.. 1
    II. Our Forefathers' Song. 1630 147
    III. A Memorial of Rev. Mr. Lee. *Esther B. Carpenter*......... 151
    IV. Canonchet. *Albert G. Greene*............................ 161

HISTORICAL NOTES—

    The Bradford Durfee..................................... 26
    A Political Letter.. 39
    Letter from George Champlain... 56
    The Manor Livingstone Ladies........................ 69
    First Marriage in Bristol.................................. 80
    Commencing in time...80, 160
    Coggeshall Fiasco 99
    An Unfortunate Family................................... 115
    John DeWolf...... 137
    An Old Fashioned Name....... 139
    Burning the Pope.......................... 141
    For Lexington and Concord 142
    First Religious Worship in Burrillville.................... 146
    Powder Plot Day.. 157
    Mr. Malbone's Letter............................. 157
    The Wightman Bible.............................. 158
    Stone Splitting... 158
    Tornado.. 158
    The Rhode Island Colors................................ 159
    Register of Births in Kings Towne........................ 159
    Fisherman's Rights 159
    Telegraphic communications between Boston and Providence ....·........................... ... 160
    Site of the Davis House................................... 160
    The Only Turnpike.. 160
    First Freewill Baptist Church of R. I..................... 177
    An Old Bell.................... 234

A MAGAZINE

Devoted to the Antiquities, Genealogy and Historical Matter; Illustrating the History of the

State of Rhode Island and Providence Plantations

A Record of Measures and of Men
for Twelve Full Score Years and Ten

Volume 4: 1885–86

James N. Arnold, Editor

HERITAGE BOOKS
2015

HERITAGE BOOKS
AN IMPRINT OF HERITAGE BOOKS, INC.

Books, CDs, and more—Worldwide

For our listing of thousands of titles see our website
at
www.HeritageBooks.com

A Facsimile Reprint
Published 2015 by
HERITAGE BOOKS, INC.
Publishing Division
5810 Ruatan Street
Berwyn Heights, Md. 20740

Originally published by
The Narragansett Historical Publishing Company
Providence, Rhode Island

E. L. Freeman and Son, Printers
Central Falls, Rhode Island
1885-6

— Publisher's Notice —
In reprints such as this, it is often not possible to remove blemishes from the original. We feel the contents of this book warrant its reissue despite these blemishes and hope you will agree and read it with pleasure.

International Standard Book Numbers
Paperbound: 978-0-7884-0141-1
Clothbound: 978-0-7884-6168-2

HISTORICAL NOTES (Continued.)

 Change from Old to New Style............................ 248
 Marriage of Seth Arnold................................... 248
 The Antiquary's Pudding................................... 268
 A Rhode Island Man the Originator of our Postal System.. 328
 Ancient Highways.. 328
 Three Facts regarding Rhode Island........................ 336
 Usquepaug Patents... 336
 First Interments in Riverside Cemetery.................... 336

EDITORIAL NOTES—

 Death of Dr. H. E. Aylesworth.............................. 78
 Two Good Works... 79
 Correction as to the Perrys................................ 79
 Correction.. 155
 The Hall Family... 155
 A Favor Requested... 155
 Mr. Austin's Dictionary........................155, 167, 335
 Mr. Rider's Notes... 156
 Acknowledgments... 253
 Thanks.. 253
 The United Service Magazine............................... 253
 Proceedings of Wyoming, Pa., Historical Society........... 254
 Removal to Providence..................................... 333
 History of Providence Plantations......................... 334
 New England Magazine...................................... 335
 Genealogical Notes.. 335
 Query... 335
 Descendants of William Hannum............................. 335

QUERIES—

 Birth of Mercy Tillinghast................................. 78
 John Hampden.. 78
 Joseph Ballou... 78

SOCIETIES AND THEIR DOINGS................................ 254, 329

ILLUSTRATIONS—

 Roger Williams Meeting House, Salem, Mass................ 152
 To Alexander's Deed, (4 ills.)............................ 238
 The Gov. Elisha Brown House............................... 269
 To Wesauamog's Deed, (4 ills.)............................ 290

INDEX TO NAMES AND PLACES.

A.

Aaron, 325
Abala, 112
Aborn, 232
Abraham, 301 304 305
Absolom, 38
Adamstown, Mass., 260
Adams, 215 218
Adam, 235 236
Adda, 236
Addeman, 331
Adeira, 236
Adet, 210
Aedd Mawr, 236
Aeneas, 236
Affleth, 237
Africa, 92
Agenaria (ves), 231
Albany, N. Y., 43 78 248 311
Albee, 105 111 199
Albro, 252
Alden, 149 292
Aldrich Tavern, 272
Aldrich, 58 59 61 63 64 65 66 67 106 108 111 190 191 194 197 198 200 258 261 262 263 266 272
Alexander, 80 238 240 241 242 257 317
Alger, 62
Alice (ves), 231
Alison, 210
Allen, 28 45 58 112 115 138 139 159 181 191 192 193 196 199 200 201 231 232 250 261 262 265
Almshouse, 309
Almy, 5 35 45 110 111 143 144 258 261
Alverson, 106
American Colonies, 138 327
America, 42 95 141 147 203 209 213 215 219 220 293 327 328
Ames, Iowa, 79
Ames, 29 33 35 200
Amwerid, 237
Anchises, 236
Anderson, 32
Andrews, 63 107 190
Andrew, 236
Angell, 58 107 110 145 190 199 201 248 261 262 298
Anthony, 5 61 232
Antonius, 236
Aplin, 143
Appleby, 111

Aquetnett, 3
Archer, 223
Armstrong, 69
Arnold, 23 57 58 59 60 62 63 64 65 66 67 68 78 81 105 106 107 108 110 111 190 191 192 194 195 197 198 199 201 231 232 235 237 238 243 248 251 255 257 261 263 284 290 300 330 331
Arnholt, 237
Arthur, 237
Arthvael, 237
Asaph, 324
Ascanius, 236
Ashton, 196
Asia, 325
Askwbut, 291
Assaracus, 236
Assawomset pond, 242
Assonet, 4
Assowetough, 232
Aster, 69
Asylum for Ind. Boys, 307
Asylum for Orp. Boys, 310
Athens of America, 305
Athens, 82
Atlantic, 16
Attleborough, Mass., 241
Atwell, 66
Atwood, 231, 284
Auchmuty, 231
Austin, 62 155 156 157 192 255 325
Aylesworth, 78
Ayrault, 150

B.

Babcock, 45 46 47 138 139 158 169
Bachus, 93
Bacon, 108
Bagbere, 273
Bagnall, 329
Bailey, 255 263 332
Baker, 294
Balch, 200
Balcome, 61
Balford, 259
Ballou, 61 62 64 65 66 67 78 81 189 194 199 258
Baltimore, Md., 186
Bannister, 190
Barber, 47 48 139
Barden, 67
Barker, 140 181 182

Barnard, Vt., 193
Barnes, 68 112
Barrington His. Anti Soc., 256 332
Barrington, 3
Barrows, 295
Bartlett, 57, 59, 156, 192 295
Bassett, 138
Bates, 48 60 65 66 67
Batrap, 80
Battey, 330
Bayard, 69
Bayly, 224
Bay State, 335
Beach, 107
Beals, 60
Becca (ves), 231
Belcher, 48
Belford, 335
Beli, 236
Bellingham, Mass., 59 65 106
Bell, 195
Benedict, 293 295
Benefit St., 284
Beneman, 79 80
Benjamin, 305 313
Bennett St., Boston, 317
Bennett, 143 196, 258
Benson, 105 197
Bentley, 48 69
Berry, 48
Betsey (ves), 230 231
Betty Sasemore, 242
Bickerstaff, 32 33 34
Billings, 86
Billington, 48 67
Binney, 73
Bishop, 111 200 231 258
Blackheath, 249
Blackmar, 7 247 248
Blackstone, Mass., 62 67 108 111
Blackstone River, 243
Blake, 58
Blaxton, 239
Blenddut, 236 237
Blenheim house, Eng., 304
Bliss, 292 331
Block Island, 1 9 20 77
Blumenthall, 314
Bnai Berith, 317
Booker, 60 263
Bonaparte, 217
Borden, 5 64 128 129 194 261 273 294
Boston Neck, 2
Boston Tea Party, 328

Boston, Mass., 10 12 21 28 29 31 34 39 73 76 83 106 107 142 160 232 250 258 292 293 306 307 310 313 316 331
Bosworth, 105 232 261
Bourne, 200 231 332
Bours, 41
Bowen, 65 150 199
Bowne, 294
Boyden, 106 191 257
Boyd, 192 232
Boyleston, Mass., 69
Boyce, 64
Bradbury, 224
Bradford, Durfee, (stm.) 26
Bradford, 62 194 105 261 292 332
Braman, 109 139
Brandywine (ves.), 231
Brayman, 48
Brayton, 194 199
Brett, 58 262
Bricknell, 192
Brickwain, 237
Bridgeport, Conn., 331
Briggs, 5 48 168
Brinley, 329 332
Bristol Co., R. I., 9
Bristol, R. I., 3 80 151
Britain, 231 235
British Army, 315
British Colonies, 10
British Parliament, 327
Broadhead, 230
Broadway, 198
Brookfield, Mass., 241
Brooklyn, N. Y., 294
Brooks, 310
Brownell, 106 142
Browne, 238 256 290 291 298
Browning, 48 49 107
Brown University, 305 330 331
Brown, 34 49 50 51 58 59 61 62 63 70 72 73 74 75 77 110 116 118 119 120 122 123 139 145 150 192 194 195 197 198 200 201 258 260 262 269 270 271 273 274 286 289 294 297 302 330
Bruner, 308
Brutus Darianlas, 236
Brutus, 236
Bryam, 108
Bucklin, 150 331
Buel, 224
Buffalo, N. Y., 113 311
Buffinton, 191
Buffum, 195
Bullard, 259
Bullock, 231
Bull, 51 250 251
Bunker, 271
Burbank, 61
Burch, 139
Burdick, 51 138 139 189 329
Burguess, 60 61 194 197 263
Burial Hill, 331
Burik, 110
Burkett, 262
Burlingame, 62 68 192 331
Burlington, N. Y., 78
Burnside, 81
Burn, 62

Burrillville, R. I., 65 106 110 146 177 195 200
Burt, 150
Butler house, 273 274
Butler, 231 232 273
Button, 139
Buxton, 57 195 263
Byram, 58 60 62 189 192 257

C.

Caddell, 236
Cadfan, 236
Cadwalladr, 235
Cadwallan, 236
Cadwallan, 236
Cady, 57 190
Caffwallan Lawbis, 236
Cahoone, 57
Cain, 237
Calder, 330
Caldwell, 57 106
California, 329
Callum, 57 100 191 260
Calvin, 57
Caman, 57
Cambreling, 223
Cambridge, Mass., 28 75
Camden, N. J., 147
Campannell, 302
Campbell, 52 57 68 69
Canada, 12 13
Canal St., Prov., 315
Canonchet, 161 162 163 164 166 167 240
Canonicus, 188 239 241 291
Cape Cod, 10
Cape Verd, 10
Caph, 237
Capins, 236
Cappair, 237
Capron, 57 58 59 258
Caradoc, 235
Carddoc, 237
Carenaoe, 309
Carey, 58
Cargill, 58
Carlile, 231
Carlisle, Pa., 289
Carmicheal, 331
Carmout, 58 59
Caroline (ves), 231
Carpenter, 52 58 107 108 139 246 254 298
Carroll, 58 100 261
Carr, 35 194 332
Carter, 32 33 34 59
Cartright, 139
Carvin, 58 59
Casey, 51 153 154
Case, 51 52 59
Cass, 59 64 65 66 100 101 263
Castle Isle, 3
Castle, 59
Castine, 71
Cawcaunchewatchatt, 297
Cayenne, 209
Cenecome, 61
Centralia, Ill., 153
Chace, 5 59 60 191
Chamberline, 60
Chambers, 60 223 260
Champlain, 52 53 56 138 139 142 231

Chamton, 150
Channing, 231
Chapin, 60 65
Chapman, 60
Chappell, 53
Charleston, S. C., 157 310
Charlestown, R. I., 331
Charley, 60
Charter, 60
Chase, 331
Chatman, 60
Chatterton, 60 190
Checkery, 60
Cheseborough, 60
Chetim, 236
Chicago, Ill., 79 80 115 153 154
Chillson, 60 61 101 102 195 258 259
China, 92
Choate, 223 224
Church of the Redeemer, 274
Church, 5 80 138 231
Chritchley, 262
Cicero, 151
Cincinnati, Ohio, 310 311
Ciprius, 236
Clapp, 61 310
Clarke, 53 54 61 138 139 145 169 192 196 231 261 292 293 295 302 332
Clark, 61 192
Clayton, 219 224 250
Clay, 219 220
Cleveland, Ohio, 113 311
Cleaveland, 62
Clemence, 62 68 298
Clementina (ves), 231
Clifford, 331
Clingman, 224
Clinton, 69
Clough, 28 62 261
Clydan, 237
Clydawr, 237
Coats, 102
Cobb, 308
Coddington, 44 78 84 85
Coelus, 236
Coel, 236
Coe, 62 102
Cohen, 316
Coggeshall, 38 54 62 99 251
Colburn, 62 152
Colby, 5 177
Colegrove, 138 150
Cole, 59 62 102 105 106 107 108 139 190 191 197 231 251 263 294
Collins, 54 62 63 139 231
Collyare, 292
Colonial Assembly, 303
Colony house, 304
Columbia (ves), 231
Colwell, 63 112
Coman, 102
Commerce (ves), 231
Comstock, 54 59 60 61 63 64 65 66 68 102 103 107 108 111 196 258 263
Concord, Mass., 142
Conanicut, 9
Congden, 54 55 65 168 169
Congregation Shangaria Chased, 309

Index to Names and Places.

Connauicutt, 2 85 87 97
Connella, 65 111
Connelly, 77 78
Connecticut, 9 77
Constitution Hill, 296 297
Continental Congress, 328
Cooke, 55 77
Cooke, 5 59 65 66 67 78 104 106 107 155 191 194 231 262
Coombes, 67
Coon, 138 139
Cooper, 67 110 232
Copeland, 67
Corbett, 80 82
Corey, 67 104 191
Corlis, 181
Cornell, 67 68 143 246 263
Cort, 68
Cory, 5
Cottrell, 55 139
Coventry, R. I., 336
Cowen, 68 104
Coweset Bay, 9
Cozzens, 57 68 200
Crandall, 55 139
Cranston, R. I., 158 286
Cranston, 8 13 68
Cravin, 68
Crary, 231
Crittenden, 224
Crocker, 68
Crosbee, 68 105
Crosby St., N. Y., 316
Crossman, 62 68
Cross, 55
Crowell, 68 107 262
Crown Point, 145
Cruff, 68 105
Cruger, 69
Cudworth, 68 111
Culling, 69
Cumberland, R. I., 8 58 61 67 69 106 108 191 194 197 198 199 241 258 259 261
Cumstock, 190
Cunedda, 236
Curocoa, 302
Currie, 145 146
Curtis, 56 68 69 200
Cushing, 69 223
Cutchley, 61
Cutler, 69
Cutting, 69
Cybelyn, 236
Cynedda Weledig, 236
Cynwarch, 236

D.

Daboll, 29
Dailey, 68 105
Dalby, 105
Daley, 108 109
Dampney, 105
Danby, Vt., 190
Daniels, 109 111
Dan, 236
Danwell, 105
Darbin, 105
Dardau, 236
Darling, 66 105 106 109 191 197 260 263
Dartmouth, 5 63

Dauber, 105
Davenport, 35
David, 324
Davidson, 106
Davie, 215
Davisville, 160
Davis, 57 58 106 107 139 160 231
Davrond, 107
Day, 67 107 109
Deake, 107 242
Dean, 68 107
Dedford, 249
Deirk, 107
Delaware River, 186
Delaware, 79
Dempsey, 107
Denison, 255 299 300 324 329 330
Denmark, 233
Dennis, 5 256
Depforde, 249
Deptford, 249 250
De Regeters, 69
Derk, 107
Deseada, 209
Destitute Orp. Boys Soc., 309
Detroit, Mich., 113
Deweil, 292
De Wolf, 137
Dexter, 31 58 62 107 108 109 197 231 285 286 287 288 296 314
Dhu, 237
Diana (ves), 231
Dickens, 231 302
Dickinson, 56
Dillingham, 108 110 259
Dixon, 108 110
Dockray, 56
Dodge, 108 262
Dodion, 236
Doli, 237
Dorchester, Mass., 76 241
Dorrence, 150
Dorr, 79 108
Doten, 108
Dotey, 108
Douglass, Mass., 59 197 260
Douglass, 56
Dowell, 108
Drake, 241
Draper, 150
Drowne, 39 78 150
Duane, 69
DuBois, 69
Dufu, 237
Dungan, 294
Dunlap, 108 110 237
Durfee, 5
Dutch Island, 149
Dyer, 39 108 259 300
Dufnwall, 236 237
Dyndocthwy, 237
Dyre, 56

E.

Eaglestone, 139
Ealy, 252
Earle, 39 110 125 289
Earl of Bellomont, 124 142
Earl of Loudoun, 41 42

Earnest, 254
Easter, 39
East Greenwiche, 249 250 327 328
East Greenwich, 160 249 252 313
Eastman, 110
Easton, 79 110 125 250
East Providence, 8 243
East Windsor, Conn., 60
Eaton, 202 254
Eckert, 188
Eddy, 67 110 112
Edes, 32
Edmunds, 110
Edwards, 139 293 295
Edward (ves), 231
Eidiol, 237
Eineon Irth, 236
Eisylht, 237
Ekins, 111
Eldred, 124
Elidrmawr, 236
Elizar, 305
Eliza (ves), 231
Ellet, 111 195
Elliott, 111 194
Ellis, 111 232
Ellsbree, 68 111
Ellsworth, 215
Emerson, 111 197 333
Enches, 111 112
Englaud, 10 11 12 19 20 75 76 87 89 92 93 97 143 151 190 202 203 204 205 208 210 211 216 244 249 250 293 302 308 328 335
Ennis, 111 262
Enos, 236
Ephraim, 64 111
Ericthonius, 236
Estance, 299
Esten, 111 299
Estes, 111
Europe, 203 209 212 315
Evans, 63 105 111 112 113
Everett, 223 329
Evroc Cadarn, 236
Evule, 112
Exeter, R. I., 160
Eyre, 289

F.

Fairbanks, 189 260
Fairbrother, 189 198
Fairfield, 189
Fales, 189 192
Fall River, Mass., 26
Fanning, 189
Fanny (ves), 231
Farce, 105
Farnesworth, 32
Farnum, 59 64 67 68 190 193 194 199
Farragut, 256
Farrar, 190 194 198
Farrer, 60
Fauchet, 207
Favorite (ves), 231
Fayal, 10
Fayerweather, 335
Feathergill, 190 191

Felix, 242
Fells Point, Md., 311
Felsh, 190
Feltus, 190 261
Female Asylum, 307
Female Hebrew Ben. Soc., 310
Female Orp. Asylum, 310
Fenner, 189 190 243 245 297
Ferent, 190
Field's Point, 243
Field, 190 329
Fifield, 190 191
Finch, 193
Finsilever, 315
Fireman's Ch. Ass. 310
First Bap. Ch. Newport, 293 295
Fisher Island, 1
Fisher, 191
Fish, 105 125 257
Fisk, 67 191 193 336
Fitchburg, Mass., 40 143 200 235
Fitch, 69
Fitton, 191
Fitts, 191
Flagg, 76
Fletcher, 191
Flynn, 191
Follett, 191
Fones, 142
Foot, 66 191
Force, 191
Fords, 191 193
Ford, 57 193
Foredice, 125
Fort Du Quesne, 37
Fort Mifflin, 186
Fort Ninegret, 331
Foss, 192
Fossyth, 223
Foster, R. I., 262
Foster, 28 61 139 192 274 295 336
Fowler, 192
Foxboro, Mass., 58
France, 12 13 151 202 203 204 205 207 208 209 210 212 213 214 215 216 218 219 220 221 225 226 227 228 233 234
Francis, 119 120 121 122 123
Franklin (ves), 231
Franklin, 31 125 202 328
Frazer, 193
Freebetter, 32
Free Sons of Israel, 317
Freeman, 61 192 193
Freetown, Mass., 273
French Islands, 211 213
Frenchtown, 160
French, 158 256
Friends' Meeting House, 272
Friendship (ves), 231
Frinnecome, 192
Frost, 192 261
Froy, 151
Fry, 129 192 224 231
Fuller, 192 193 195

G.

Gage, 193
Gallia, 151

Gallington, 189
Gammell, 254 329
Gano, 179 243 258
Gansett Bay, 1
Garddufu, 237
Gardiner, Me., 263
Gardiner, 77 125 126 127 138 168 193 194 231
Garwst, 237
Gaskell, 59 194 196 201
Gaspee, 83 94 330
Gavitt, 127 128 194
Gazette, 271
Gee, 194
Genedawc, 236 237
General Assembly, 302 303 321 333 334
General Garcia, 234
General Greene (ves), 231
Georgetown, D. C., 183
George II., 1
George, 290
Geraint, 236
Gerry, 69 213
Gibbs, 231
Gibson, 142
Gifford, 63 194
Gilbert, 111
Giles, 223
Gile, 194 196 198
Gilliot, 256
Gillis, 194
Gills, 190 194
Gilmore, 67 194
Gilpin, 332
Gladding, 231
Glasie, 194
Glaumorgan, 235 237
Gleason, 195 196
Glocester, R. I., 57 61 62 64 67 110 112 198 200 259 260 262 286 291
Goddard, 33 39 328
Goff, 195
Goldwaite, 195
Gooding, 195
Good Intent (ves), 231
Gore, 195
Gorham, 188
Gorton, 38
Gorwst, 237
Gould, 128 195
Gourgand, 219
Graff, 195
Granada, 209
Grant, 195 336
Grason, 195
Graves, 273
Gray, 5
Great Bridge, 36
Great Britain, 83 94 138 202 203 208 216 220 303 327
Greene Towne, 249
Greene, 6 23 24 26 28 31 35 36 37 38 42 43 44 61 82 111 124 138 141 160 161 192 195 196 231 294 330 331 334
Greenville, 291
Greenwich Bay, 9
Greenwiche, 249
Greenwich (ves), 231
Greenwich, 2 9 17 249 258 328
Greenhalgh, 195

Grenawic, 249 250
Griswold, Conn., 57
Gross, 196
Grosvenor, 196
Guadeloupe, 209 230
Guilderland, 248
Guild, 79 196
Gully, 196
Gurley, 195 196
Gurgain, 237
Gurgan, 236
Gurgant, 237
Gwent, 237
Gwillaim, 237
Gwrtholi, 237

H.

Hachniach, N. J., 192
Hacker, 196
Hadley, 197
Hague, 31
Hakes, 105
Haley, 128
Hallowell, 197
Hall, 108 139 149 155 197 252 264
Halsey, 231
Hames, 197
Hamilton, 69 204
Hamlin, 224 272
Hammond, 99 128 299 300 330
Hammett, 149 197
Hamond, 197
Hampden, 78
Ham, 197
Hancock, 197 260
Handon, 197
Handson, 128
Handy, 197 198 199
Hannah, 128 190 198
Hannum, 335 336
Hanson, 57 60
Happy Return (ves), 231
Harkinson, 198
Harkness, 198 264
Harriman, 198
Harrison, 153 198 304
Harris, 60 63 69 108 112 150 189 190 194 197 198 199 200 201 261 264 265 266 286 298 332
Hartford, Conn., 310
Hartshorn, 200
Hartwell, 68 200
Hart, 200 305
Harwich, Conn., 261
Haskin, 200
Hastings, 201
Hathaway, 199 201 262
Hatherly, 292
Hautless, 194 201
Haverhill, Mass., 158
Hawkings, 298
Hawkins, 201 247 248
Hawks, 201
Haws, 201
Hayden, 201 251
Hayes, 128 257 313
Haynes, 257
Hays, 305 306 310 312 314
Hayward, 191 257
Hazael, 292
Hazard, 128 129 130 131 150 255

Index to Names and Places.

Healey, 131
Hearnden, 248
Heath, 257
Heaton, 258
Heavens, 258
Hebrew Ben. Ass., 309
Hebrew Ben. Soc., Gimeleet Chased, 310
Hebrew Ben. Soc., Mashebat Nafesh, 310
Hebrew Con. Adas Isreal, 311
Hebrew Con. Ashabat Isreal, 311
Hebrew Con. Beth el Isreal, 311
Hebrew Con. Beth Shalome, 310
Hebrew Con. Briai el Isreal, 311
Hebrew Con. Briai Isreal, 311
Hebrew Con. Briai Jeshurun, 311
Hebrew Con. Chachag Shalome, 310
Hebrew Con. Mikoe Isreal, 310
Hebrew Con. Shangarai Shumoyen, 311
Hebrew Con. Shangarai Tefila, 310
Hebrew Con. Shearith Isreal, 310
Hebrew Con. Tifereth Isreal, 311
Hebrew Con., 310 311
Hebrew Ed. Soc., 309
Hebrew For. Soc., 309
Hebrew Hospital, 308
Hebrew School Talmud Yeladin, 311
Hedden, 258
Helme, 131 132 133 169
Heman, 324
Hendrick, 58 258 266 267
Henry (ves), 231
Heury, 267
Herd, 258
Herendeen, 57 60 106 201 258 259 260 262 263 267 268
Herker, 197 260
Hester, 260 261
Hetock, 60 260
Hew, 237
Hewes St., Prov., 273
Hewes, 274
Hewitt, 189 260
Heyward, 69
Hicks, 260
Hide, 260
Higgins, 260
Higinbottom, 133
Hill, 59 62 138 139 190 199 259 260 261 268
Hines, 62
Hixon, 192 261
Hix, 5
Hodgeson, 261
Hoge, 260 261
Hogg, 261
Hog Island, 3
Holbrook, 61 261 268
Holburton, 261
Holden, 38 261 294

Holdoff, 140
Holland, 133 143 302
Holley, 133 200 261 262
Holliston, Mass., 69 111 257
Holloway, 251
Holman, 111 262
Holmes, 223 252 262 268 291 292 293 294 295
Holoway, 262
Holroyd, 141
Holt, 108 260 262
Holway, 133 251 252
Holy Land, 309 311
Holyoke, 28
Honduras Bay, 141
Honeywell, 77 78
Hooker, 61
Hopkins, 38 39 40 67 143 144 145 146 262
Hopkinton, R. I., 138 139 160
Hope Island, 2
Horswick, 61 262
Horton, 68 201 262
Hosea, 362
Hotchkiss, 262 268
Hough, 263
House, 332
House of Commons, 327
Howard, 59 150 188 189 223 263 268
Howell, 71 72 287
Howland, 5 149 231 263
Hows, 259 263
Hoxie, 331
Hoyle, 263
Hoyt, 330
Hubbard, 240 272 295
Hudson, N. Y., 272
Hudson River, 13 331
Hudson, 263
Hughes, 263
Huling, 40 124 142 143 169 235 237
Hullmes, 290 291
Hull, 133 134
Humane Society, 308
Humes, 62 67 263
Hunt, 105 263 330
Hutchinson, 141 157 256 263 268 328 329 331
Hyde, 107 262 264
Hyndeman, 105 264

I.

Iago, 236
Iags, 236
Idwallo, 236
Illinois, 78
Industry (ves), 231
Ingalls, 68
Ingersoll, 223
Inmau, 66 190
Ireland, 89 108 194 249
Irish, 134
Iros, 236
Irving, 256
Isaiah, 324
Ithel, 237

J.

Jackson, 231 308 329

Jacobs, 232 300
Jamaica, Vt., 111
Jamestown, R. I., 9 149
James II., 44
Janes, 331
Japheth, 236
Jaqueth, 258
Javen, 236
Jawger, 200
Jay, 69 208 209 210
Jeduthun, 324
Jeffers, 105
Jefferson, 204 206 218
Jeffries, 5
Jenckes, 19 41 57 60 64 74 105 106 107 178 192 198 199 262 263 293
Jenkins, 250 251 252 271 272 273
Jerusalem, 304 305 309 315 317 325
Jestyn, 235 237
Jewish Cemetery, Newport, 301 302 307 308 309 312 317
Jewish Cemetery, Prov., 316
Jewish Synagogue, Newport, 301 304 306 307 309
Jewish Synagogue, N. Y., 307
Jews Hospital Soc., 309
Jews Hospital, 310
Jillson, 58
Joanna (ves), 231
Johnston, R. I., 58 111 140 158 201 291
Johnson, 69 99 192 194 255 263
Jones, 195
Joperson, 260
Josephs, 309 311
Jupiter, 236

K.

Kay St., Newport, 302
Keais, 134
Keese, 299
Keith, 106 107
Kelleys Ford, Va., 331
Kelley, 195
Kelton, 200 201
Kenyon, 134 138 139
Kent Co., Eng., 249
Kent Co., R. I., 249 327 328
Kent, 249
Kerryn, 236
Kilahea, 331
Killingly, Conn., 61 297
Kimball, 61 192
King Charles II., 244
King David Lodge, 313
King George III., 26 93 94
King Phillip (stm.), 26
King Phillip, 4 84 187 188 240 245
Kings Co., 77 78
Kingsley, 191
Kingston, Jamaica, 306
Kingston, 9 17 249 328
Kings Towne, 124 142 150 159 160 249
King, 61 66 198
Kins, 65
Knight, 189 330
Knowles, 168 330

Kishershel Burzel, 317
Kurshudt, 309 311

L.

Ladies' Ben. Society, 309 310
Lafayette, Ind., 79 80
Lafayette, 98 217 272
Lake Champlain, 13
Lake Erie, 79 81 82 113
Lake, 5
Lameck, 236
Lancashire, Eng., 291
Lancaster, Eng., 293
Langworthy, 139
Lapham, 57 107 108 190 191 197 198 263
Larkin, 138 139
Latham, 65 106
Lawrence (ship), 153
Lawrence, 26 150
Lawton, 191 333
Leach, 194
Lee, 151
Leeser, 311
Leicester, Mass., 313
Leigh, 195 200
Leonard, 63 66
LeRoys, 69
Lever, 261
Leviticus, 325
Levy, 305 313 316
Lewistown, Del., 79
Lewis, 138 139 196 270 271 273
Lexington, Mass., 142
Leyden, 143
Lillibridge, 134 139
Lily (ves), 231
Lincoln, 57 60 63 100 189 195
Lindsey, 105 200
Lippitt St., 274
Lippitt, 37 110 231 245
Lisbon Port, 303
Lisle, Ill., 252
Little Compton, R. I., 9 144 336
Littlefield, 134 135
Littleton, Mass., 200
Livingstone, 69 223
Llanthony, 235 237
Lleon, 236
Lockwood, 59 198
Locrinus, 236
Lodi, N. Y., 197
Loge, 260
Lombard, 249
London, Eng., 83 249 250 309 311
Long Island His. Soc., 294
Long Island, 246
Long St., E. G., 313
Long Wharf, 99
Lonsdale Block, 272
Lookout Mountain, 331
Lopez, 303 305 306 308 313 314
Lord Byron, 114
Lord Chatham, 256
Lord Colville, 82 83
Lord Dartmouth, 141
Lord North, 141 157
Louisburg, 37 82 83
Louisiana, 227 308
Louisville, Ky., 311

Louisquiset, 239
Lowell, Mass., 110 197
Lowise, 69
Low, 37 38
Lucar, 290 295
Lucena, 305
Lunt, 135
Lydia (ves), 231
Lynn, Mass., 200 292
Lyn, 236
Lyon, 288 289

M.

Maccabees, 304
Maccavy, 195
Machpelah, 302
Madeira, 10
Madison, 220
Maelgan Gwynedd, 236
Maelwynoc, 236
Maidstone, 194
Main St., E. G., 313
Malavery, 64
Malbone, 56 158
Manchester, Eng., 293
Manchester, 5 231
Manning, 180
Mansfield, 59 60 65 68 190 197 241 262 263
Manton Village, 297
Manton, 238 246 290 296 297 298 299
Man, 57 58 60 61 62 64 65 68 75 76 105 106 108 191 192 196 199 200 201 258 259 261 262 263 292
Many Holes, 245
Marble, 106
Mariawn, 237
Mariegalante, 209
Marion, 223
Marriott, 327
Martha's Vineyard, 273
Martinique, 209
Martin, 38 67 231 262
Marshall, 138 204 213 220
Marvel, 201
Mary (ves), 231
Mashackqunt, 238
Mashapauge Pond, 245 246
Mashapaug, 244
Mashovsakit, 290
Mash, 135
Masipauge, 246
Mason, 75 79 116 301 329 330
Mass. Bay Co., 9
Mass. Colony, 9
Mass. Female Hos., 309
Mass. Gen. Hos., 307
Massachusetts, 13 85 87 97 158 226 238 241 335 336
Massasoit, 239 240 241 242
Mather, 241
Mathewson, 67 190 191 193 231 260 263
Mathews, 329
Mattapoiset, 240
Matteson, 150
Mawoin, 242
Mawney, 135
Mawr, 237
Maxson, 138

Maxwell, 31 231
McClintock, 232
McDanwell, 264
McGeer, 257 261 262
McKensie, 188
McSparren, 335
Medbury, 57 65 199
Mediterranean, 307
Medoc, 236
Medus, 302
Meere Bank, 243
Meesham, 139
Meeting St., Prov., 314
Meiric, 237
Melcome Horsey, 237
Membyr, 236
Memphis, Tenn., 311
Mendez, 299 314 315
Mendon, Mass., 59 67 100 101 194 197 200 263
Methusalem, 236
Mervey, 105
Mexico, 233
Miantonomah, 188
Miantonomi, 161 239 241 291
Middleboro, Mass., 242
Middletown, R. I., 293 295
Mikoe Isreal, 316
Milbury, Mass., 200
Milford, 60 139
Miller, 189 192 298
Mill River, 160
Mill St, N. Y., 316
Milsie Asylum, 310
Minerva (ves), 231
Miner, 139
Miquelon, 209
Mishouskit, 290
Mitchell, 58 106 111 135 199
Mobile, Ala., 311
Mobegan, 161 162
Monmouth Co., N. J., 296
Monogen, 237
Montauck Point, 1
Montauck, 77
Montefiore, 309
Montgomery, Ala., 311
Montgomery, 36
Mooanam, 246
Moore, 34
Moray, 150
Morehead, 224
Morey, 135
Morfortaine, 217
Morris, 69 206 207 208
Morudd, 236
Moses, 308 316 320 325
Moswansicut Pond, 291
Mount Hope, 3
Mowry, 59 61 62 63 64 65 66 67 68 105 108 110 111 112 190 191 193 194 195 196 198 199 200 201 260 261 262 263 266
Mumford, 135 136 251 336
Munroe, 203 210 231
Murray, 215 218
Musketo Cove, 246
Mussey, 59 67 190
Myers, 308 309
Mystic Bridge, Conn., 331

N.

Namumpam, 240

xii.   *Index to Names and Places.*

Nancy (ves), 231
Nanipsick, 290
Nathan, 311
Nantes, 254
Nantucket, 271 272
Napau, N. J., 58
Naples, 233
Napoleon, 217 218 219 233
Narragansett Bay, 1 9 13 82 84 85
Narragansett Country, 38 78 96 159 255
Narragansett, 124 161 163 164 166 168 188 239 240 241 250 251 331 333
Narrow River, 159
Nashua, N. H., 110
Nash, 191
Nason, 191
Nassau Hall, 180
Natick, 188 242
Nemaskets, 242
Neotaconckanitt, 297
Neptune (ves), 231
Neutecontenant Hill, 296
New Amsterdam, 302
Newbern, N. C., 82
Newell, 200
New England, 13 20 29 30 76 83 161 240 293 335
New Hampshire, 145
New Haven, Conn., 310
New Jersey, 180 252 294 330
New London, Conn., 29
Newland, 61
Newman, 31 292
New Orleans, La., 308 309 310 311 312
Newport Co., 143 144 145
Newport Harbor, 15
Newport His. Society, 256 332
Newport Med. Soc., 332
Newport Nat. His. Soc., 256 332
Newport, R. I., 8 9 10 15 17 20 25 31 32 33 34 36 39 44 45 56 77 79 83 84 124 128 142 143 144 145 146 157 188 211 230 240 250 251 256 268 292 293 294 295 296 299 301 302 303 304 305 306 307 308 309 310 311 312 313 314 315 316 317 329 332 333
Newtown, 36 38
New Shoreham, 9
New York Harbor, 137
New York, 20 21 26 30 39 43 69 139 160 234 263 294 301 302 308 309 310 313 314 316 320 335
Nicholas, 110 188
Nichols, 62 136 137 143 144 332
Nicolis, 150
Niles, 137 201
Nineteenth St., N. Y., 314 316
Nipuack, 241
Noahen, 236
Noah's Ark, 274
Noot, 255 299 300 216 318 326
North Am. Coast, 10
North Am. Rel. Soc., 309
North America, 21 203
Northampton Co., Va., 289

Northampton, Va., 288
North B. Ground, 116 283
North End, 273 274
North Main St., 272 273 274
North Kingstown, 2 9 38 158 170 194 252 328
North Providence, 58 195 268
Northup, 77 232
North Uxbridge, Mass., 194
Norton, Mass., 241
Norwich, Conn., 34 113
Noyes, 255
Nyc, 231.

O.

Oatley, 169
Ohabei Shalome, 317
Ohio (stm.), 113
Old Stone Mill, 309
Oliver, 328
Oliveyra, 305
Olney St., Prov., 274
Olneyville, 187
Olney, 182 184 185 201 238 243 244 247 274 290 296 298
Omwedd, 237
Oneco, 162
O'Neil, 169
Orange (ves), 231
Orphan Home Asylum, 309
Osborne, 169
Otis, 145
Owain, 237
Owen, 107 108 198 237 271
Oxford Uner., 293
Oyster Bay, 246

P.

Pacific, 92
Padarn Perfrydd, 236
Paddock, 139
Paine, 58 59 62 65 67 106 111 201 263 267
Page St., Prov., 315
Palestine, 309 311 317
Palmer, 110 138 139
Palmiter, 139
Panoquin, 240
"Parade," 306 314
Parmenter, 333
Parsons, 79 263 329
Paris, 206 207 213 215 218 227 229 230
Patience Island, 2
Patt, 69
Patton, 329
Patty (ves), 231
Pauchaset River, 246
Paukanawqut, 238
Pawcatuck, 1
Pawcatuck River, 9
Pawtucket, Mass., 192
Pawtucket River, 239
Pawtucket, 8 188 194 284
Pawtuckqut, 238
Pawtuxett Bridge, 2
Pawtuxet Neck, 246
Pawtuxet, 9 38 244 246
Payne, 255
Peace (ves), 231
Pearce, 5 68 273
Peckeckoe, 302

Peckham, 56 139 158 170 171 232 257
Peck, 181 231 331
Peeus, 195
Peirce, 140 141
Pelham St., 314
Penissel, 237
Pennington, 224
Pepewahim, 291
Pepewashim, 291
Pequoting, 164
Perry, 27 68 79 80 81 98 113 115 153 154 169 171 329 336
Perkins, 171 172 194
Perrin, 188
Peters, 259
Petonowowet, 240
Pettesquamoscutt River, 159
Pettes, 105
Peyton Randolph (ves), 231
Phelps, 231
Phenix, 188
Philadelphia, Pa., 115 119 120 121 295 309 310 311 316 328
Phillips, 32 57 59 69 77 108 172 191 192 195 198 200 240 241 242 258 259 260 262
Pickens, 223
Pickering, 66 189 213 219 220
Pickford, 198
Pierce, 222 224
Pigs' Eyes, 290
Pike, 296
Pinchbeck, 139
Pinckney, 213 220
Pine St., Prov., 315
Pirawesi, 217
Pitman, 170 243 255 274
Pittsburgh, Pa., 37 322
Pitt, 256
Place, 59 112 298
Plainfield, Conn., 57
Plimpton, 107
Plumer, 110
Plymouth Colony, 240
Plymouth, Mass., 85 239 240 241 242 292
Pocassett, 240
Pocasset, 240
Point Judith, 2
Pokanokett, 241
Polk, 222 224
Pollock, 172
Polly (ves), 231
Polok, 305 313
Polsey, 61 195
Pond, 191
Poppasquash, 3
Popple, 139
Porrex, 236
Porter, 67 69 160 195 200
Portsmouth, R. I., 8 36 58 67 84 98 142 239 251 294 299
Portuguese Syn., 301 314
Potowomut, 36 38
Potter, 6 77 106 138 172 173 174
Potts, 147
Powell, 235
Power, 174 183 297 298
Pratle Island, 3
Prence, 292
Preston, Eng., 291

Index to Names and Places.   xiii.

Preston, 219
Prince, 195
Proctor, 308
Proud, 145 146
Providence Co., 8 145 146
Providence Franklin Soc., 255 330
Providence Harbor, 9
Providence Plantations, 85 95 334
Providence River, 243
Providence, R. I., 2 3 6 8 11 17 19 26 32 34 35 36 37 38 44 62 63 70 76 77 81 116 118 119 120 122 140 145 146 155 157 158 159 160 161 178 179 181 182 183 186 188 189 192 197 200 201 202 211 230 238 239 243 244 245 246 247 248 254 255 257 260 269 271 272 273 283 285 286 289 290 291 294 295 296 297 298 299 300 313 314 315 318 321 326 329 330 333 334
Prudence Island, 2 7 115
Pyrr, 237

Q.

Quabauke, 241
Quackenboss, 248
Quashawaunamut, 238
Quebec, 157
Queens Co., N. Y., 246
Queen Anne, 11 88
Quianopen, 240
Quinsey, Mass., 308

R.

Randale, 150
Randall, 138 139 194
Ranger (ves), 231
Rankin, 332
Rathbun, 139
Ray, 58 260
Razee, 196
Read, 60 174 263
Red Bank, 99 159
Red Bridge, 243
Red Jacket, 188
Redwood Library B'ing, 304
Redwood Library, 310
Reid, 35
Rehoboth Church, 292
Rehoboth N. Purchase, 241
Rehoboth, Mass., 194 292 332
Regan, 236
Reid, 334
Reliance (ves), 231
Reservoir Av., Prov., 316
Reynolds, 138 139 150 174 175 239 254
Rhau, 236
R. I. and Prov. Plantation, 77 182 298
Rhode Island Bank, 313
Rhode Island Cavalry, 331
Rhode Island Colony, 6 143 144 145 146
Rhode Island District, 287
Rhode Island Ento. Soc., 256
Rhode Island His. Soc., 27 202 254 329

Rhode Island Vet. Cit. His. Ass., 6 81 255 329
Rhode Island Island, 4 8
Rhode Island, 6 8 9 11 12 14 19 21 30 31 38 39 75 77 78 79 81 82 83 84 85 86 89 90 91 94 95 97 98 99 150 152 155 156 157 158 159 160 162 177 183 187 202 225 228 230 232 235 237 248 249 250 254 255 296 299 301 302 304 306 312 317 318 321 322 327 328 329 330 331 332 333 335 336
Rhodes, 175 248 268
Richards, 44
Richmond, R. I., 59 160
Richmond, Va., 309 310 312
Richmond, 143 144 197
Rider, 6 156 157 244
Right, 77 78
Ringgold, Tenn., 331
Risley, 257
Riverside Cemetery, 336
Riviera, 305 213 216
Riwallon, 236
Roanoke, 82
Robbins, 175
Roberts, 223
Robie, 28
Robinson, 39 138 139 175 176
Rochester, N. Y., 124
Rochester, Mass., 262
Rocky Hill, 246
Rodman, 81 176 177 251 252
Rogers, 66 139 177
Roger Williams Park, 244 245
Rome, 82
Root, 329
Roseville, Ill., 78
Rose, 177
Rossiter, 288
Rottenberg, 316
Rounds, 191
Rover (ves), 231
Royal Spring, 4
Royce, 224
Rudolph, 139
Rum Caladr Cras, 236
Russell, 223 231 330 331
Ruth (ves), 231
Rytberick, 237

S.

Sabin's Inn, 330
Saffin, 171
Saint Arma's Asylum, 309
Saint Domingo, 209
Saint Francisco, 234
Saint Helena, 219
Saint James, 141
Saint John's Lodge, 313
Saint Lawrence River, 13
Saint Louis, Mo., 311
Saint Lucie, 209
Saint Mary's Cat. B. Asy., 310
Saint Paul's Church, 335
Saint Pierre, 209
Saint Rafael, 234
Saint Vincent, 209
Sakesakit, 290 291
Salem Church, 292

Salem, Mass., 152 200 291 294
Salisbury, 330
Sally (ves), 231
Sampson, 35
Samuel, 323 324
Sanborn, 32
Sandborn, 57
Sanders, 69
Sands, 275
Sandwich Island, 331
Sandwich, 250 251
Sanford, 144
Sanksuit, 243
Sansuwest, 242
Saratoga, N. Y., 98
Sasafrax Cove, 244
Sassamon, 241
Sasuman, 238 241
Satterly, 139
Saturnus, 236
Sauders, 139
Saunkussecit, 242
Savannah, Ga., 310
Sawsuett, 242
Sawyer, 194
Sayles, 59 61 63 64 65 66 67 68 105 107 110 111 189 191 192 194 198 199 200 201 238 239 245 246 258 259 260 262 263 265 294
Scaligor, 151
Scarborough, 330
Scholes, 197
Scituate, R. I., 195 291
Scotland, 89
Scott's Pond, 313
Scott, 57 62 65 66 143 190
Seabury, 278
Seacink, 3 158
Seager, 275
Seamans House, 310
Seconet Shore, 4
Seconet Town, 4
Secunk, 238
Seekonk, Mass., 7 295
Seecunk, 165
Seissyll, 236
Seissylt, 236 237
Seixas, 305 313 316
Sekesacutt Hill, 298
Sekesakit, 297
Sepauqut, 238 240
Seth, 236
Seville, 5
Shaw, 71 262
Shearith Isreal, 316
Sheffield, 5 150 169 275
Sheldon, 64 67 106 150 199 201 261 276 277 298
Sheperd Tom, 38
Sheperd, 31 260 309
Sherbourne, 142
Sherlock, 59
Sherman, 70 116 169 178 188 194 200 277 278 283
Shinson, 261 262
Shippee, 57 60 105 258 259 260 263
Shurrucks, 330
Silvius, 236
Slade, 261
Slate Rock, 7
Slater, 59

Index to Names and Places.

Slocum, 67 81 188 336
Sluman, 252
Sly, 59 64 66 67 111 189 198 200 259
Small, 244 247
Smithfield, R. I., 32 39 57 58 59 60 61 62 63 64 65 66 67 68 69 100 101 106 107 108 110 111 155 189 190 191 192 194 195 197 198 199 200 201 248 257 258 259 260 261 262 263 291
Smith, 60 65 66 68 69 107 108 110 111 118 169 186 189 190 191 197 199 224 256 259 260 261 263 274 278 292 295 298
Snell, 5
Snow, 198
Socks, 317
Sodom, 307
Soldiers' and Sailors' His. Soc., 256 331
Sons of Covenant, 320
Sons of Isreal, 315 316 318
Sons of Zion, 315
Sophia (ves), 231
South County, 160 329
South Ferry, 36
South Kingstown, R. I., 9 61 80 125 158 161 162 169 251 254 255 275 328
South Wales, 250
South Water St., Prov., 272
Southwick, 32 59 67 242
Spain, 90 91 233 302
Spanish Peninsula, 301
Spaulding, 199
Spear, 60
Spencer, 38 189 195 249
Sprague, 58 62 63 68 111 189 197 198 199 232
Springfield, 159 267
Spring Green, 120 121 122 123
Sprout, 266
Stafford, 5 28 150
Standish, 292
Stanley, 61
Stanton, 78 278 279
Staples, 63 64 68 201 257 261 263
State House, 304
Steadman, 279
Stearns, 262
Steele, 33
Steere, 60 62 63 66 68 105 107 110 197 201 259 298
Stewart, 149
Stiles, 28 139 306
Stillman, 138
Stillwell, 294
Stockwell, 30 34 39
Stone, 57 150 260 261
Stonington, Ct., 110
Storer, 332
Strange, 197 246
Stratford, 197
Streeter, 62 199
Streight, 262
Stuyvesant, 302
Sukey (ves), 231
Sumner, 207 220 224 228 233
Sunderland, 279
Surrenam, 141

Susquehanna, 150
Swain, 279
Sweden, 26
Sweet, 60 62 139 169 190 201
Swift, 33 250
Swining, 105
Sykes, 108
Sylvester, 144 145
Syssylth, 237

T.

Taber, 5 231 262
Taft, 61 62 190
Talbot, 107 108 111 190 198
Talcott, 78 335
Tallman, 5 314
Tallerand, 213
Talmuth Torah Sch. Fund, 309
Tanner, 138 139 144 279
Tatapanum, 240
Taunton River, 158
Taunton, Mass., 183 240 266
Taylor, 39 60 61 63 65 67 68 69 105 107 110 112 146 190 194 195 196 197 198 200 262 272 273 279 295
Tefft, 61 68 108 280
Tegid, 236
Ten Broecks, 69
Ten Mile River, 243
Thayer, 61 65 66 260
Thomas, 29 33 60 62 169 243 249 292
Thompson, Mass., 107
Thompson, 63 105 106 200
Thoms, 149
Thornton, 32 68 140 299
Thurber, 198 258
Thurston, 32 67 138 139
Tice, 252
Tilley, 332
Tillinghast, 38 78 140 141 160 183 189 256 283 284
Tilton, 188 332
Titus, 57 66 106 198
Tiverton, R. I., 5 9 128 129 140 143 200
Tobago, 209
Tobey, 58
Tom, 242
Tom Watchemoket, 238
Topham, 162
Torrey, 280 295
Tory, 292
Totten, 280
Touro Institute, 315
Touro St., Newport, 302 304
Touro, 304 305 306 307 308 312
Tower, 108
Trask, 63 64 106
Travis, 28
Trotter, 149
Truesdon, 258
Tucker, 63 65 67 190 192 331
Tulley, 28
Turgett, 107
Turner, 169 256 332
Twing, 310
Tyler, 59 111 198 200 201 232

U.

Uncas, 161

Underwood, 280
Union (ves), 231
United Colonies, 83 84 161
United Hebrew Ben. Soc., 310
United States Marshal, 287
United States, 6 14 75 157 159 183 186 187 202 203 204 206 207 208 209 210 212 213 214 215 216 217 218 219 220 225 226 227 228 233 308 317
Updike, 38 168
Upton, 331
Urien, 236
Usher, 63 231
Usquepaug, 336
Uxbridge, Mass., 61 107 190 192 194 199 200

V.

Valentine, 273
Vallett, 191
Valley Forge, 202
Van Duzer, 69
Van Dyke, 294
Vatel, 215
Venter, 296 297
Vermont, 28
Vernon, 231
Verrinder, 61 189 194 197
Vera Cruz, 81
Verry, 60
Vichan, 237
Vincent, 246
Vinton, 81
Viol, 3
Virginia, 309 237 327
Vncas, 241
Voorsanger, 316
Vose, 260
Vssamequin, 316
Vychan, 237

W.

Wachamoquitt Point, 243
Wachamoquitt, 243
Wachamoquott, 243
Waite, 5 280
Wakefield, 194 336
Waldron, 108
Wales, 235
Walker, 150 197 224 258
Wallace, 80
Walling, 111
Walmesley, 280
Walpole, Mass., 58
Wampanoag's, 242
Wampanoag, 164 167 188
Wamsitta, 239 241
Wamsuta, 188 240
Wanasquatucket River, 296 297 298
Wanskuckfields, 297
Wanskuck, 296
Wanton, 5 8 39 240
Wardwell, 231
Ward, 8 40 45 143 145 146
Warnerd, 244
Warner, 37
Warrenton St., Boston, 317
Warren, R. I., 32
Warwick Bay, 2

Warwick, R. I., 3 9 17 35 120 121 122 289 294 328 331
Washington, D. C., 229 231 232 249
Washington Hotel, 272
Washington, 82 159 182 202 206 212 213 219 307
Wasquadowisk, 238
Watchamoqut, 243
Watchemoket Cove, 243
Watchemoket, 242 243
Watch Hill, 1
Waterman, 190 200 243 248 297 298
Waterford, Mass., 62
Waterhouse, 39
Waterloo, 329
Watkins, 60
Watson, 168 195 281
Watuspaquin, 242
Wauchimoqut, 242
Waumsitton, 238 240
Wayland B'ing, 315
Wayunkege, 291
Wayvnkege, 290
Weatherhead, 194
Weathersfield, Conn., 260
Webb, 192 282
Webster, 215 216 220 223
Weeden, 282
Weetamoo, 240
Weight, 169
Weir, 282
Welch, 282
Weldon, 257
Wells, 138 139 189 282
Wesauamog, 290
Westcott, 272 273

Westerly, R. I., 9 17 142 282 329
Western Isle, 10
Westfield, Mass., 336
West Greenwich, R. I., 249 250 251 336
West Indies, 10 44 211 212 215 306
Westminster St., 300
West River, 297
West, 32 33 34 138 139
Wetherby, 105
Wetherhead, 258
Weybosset St., 272 315
Weybosset, 188
What Cheer Rock, 243
What Cheer, 243
Wheaton, 231 255
Wheeler, 34
Wheelock, 263
Whettemore, 28
Whipple, 57 66 76 106 108 110 201 246 248 258 273 296
White, 58 139
Whitman, 195 238 246 258 290
Wilbraham, Mass., 329
Wilbur, 106 107 259
Wickford, 9 32 249
Wightman, 158
Wilcox. 5 142 201 282
Wilkinson, 32 58 62 63 106 108 111 150 197 258 260 263 296
Wilkins, 223
Willard, 34 108
Willett, 124 139 142 239 241
Williamson, 69
Williams, 7 11 84 85 152 161 232 238 244 245 246 247 248 282 290 291 294 295 297 302 330
William (ves), 231
William, 238 239 240
Willis, 76
Willson, 149
Wilson, 282 283
Windward Isle, 204 230
Wing, 199 258
Winslow, 188 241
Winsor, 58 107 110 111 140 192 194 198 201 262
Winterbottom, 191
Winthrop, 295
Wipen, 192
Witter, 138 139
Wolcott, 111 274
Woodbury, 261
Woodle, 5
Woodstock, Conn., 61
Woodward, 68 231 235
Wood, 144 332
Wordell, 142
Worden, 283
Worcester, Mass., 68 69 111
Wrentham, Mass., 76 107
Wright, 195
Wyoming, Penn., 250 254
Wyoming, R. I., 150

Y.

Yale College, 306
Yeshuat Isreal, 304
Ynir, 237
Yorktown, 98
Young, 68 201 261

THE
Narragansett Historical Register.

NARRAGANSETT PUB. CO., PUBLISHERS. | Terms, $2.00 Per Annum. | JAMES N. ARNOLD, EDITOR.

VOL. IV.   HAMILTON, R. I., JULY, 1885.   No. 1.

A JOURNAL

OF THE

SURVEY OF THE NARRAGANSETT BAY, AND PARTS ADJACENT, TAKEN IN THE MONTHS OF MAY AND JUNE, A. D., 1741. BY ORDER OF THE HONORABLE COURT OF COMMISSIONERS APPOINTED BY HIS MAJESTY KING GEORGE THE SECOND. POETICALLY DESCRIBED BY ONE OF THE SURVEYORS.

These Lines below, describe a just Survey
Of all the Coasts, along the 'Gansett Bay;
Therefore attend, and quickly you shall know
Where it begins, and how far it doth go.
From *Pawcatuck*, we steer'd our Course away,
And to *Watch Hill* we went without delay;
Which gave a Prospect of the Neighboring Shore
And distant Isles, where foaming billows roar.
Here *Fisher's Isle* appears, and looks just by
And *Montauk Point* we plainly could descry;
Block Island also near us did appear,
We took our Course, and how each Place did bear.
From hence our Course did lead us on the Sands,
The utmost Bounds the Billows here Commands,
Whose raging Waves caress the Beach and Shore
With endless Motion, and a murmuring Roar:
Then passing o'er the Breaches in our way
Made by the Surges of the raging Sea.
Where in the Land Calm Ponds we here espy'd
Which rise and fall exactly with the Tide.
Within these Ponds are Fish of Various Kind,

Which much delight and please both Taste and Mind.
And many Fowls the Industrious Archer gains,
Which amply doth Reward his Time and Pains,
(Here in a Pond, our Caution to oppose
A Horse did launch and wet his Owners Cloaths,
The frightened Jade soon tack'd himself about
Which made us laugh as soon as he came out.)
Then round *Point Judith* which was in our way
The Courses there, and Length we did Survey,
Then *Boston Neck* along that pleasant Shore
We next survey'd, and found how each part bore;
(*Connanicutt* we also viewed full well,
And other Parts too tedious here to tell.)
Went on this shore, round points of Lands and Coves
Thro' various Fields and most delightful Groves,
From hence along unto *North Kingston* shore
Crossing the Meads, which Verdant Greens now wore.
And then for *Greenwich* next, we shap'd our way,
(Passing more Islands which lie in the Bay,
As *Hope* and *Prudence* that most pleasant Isle
And Patience also, a most fruitful Soil.)
Crossing a Harbour, we came to the Town
Which seems to be a Place of great Renown,
For Liberty of Conscience here they take
Here's Church and Baptist, also those that Quake.

From hence we went along with our Survey
By various Turns and came to *Warwick* Bay
And in that Town did of their Dainties eat
And in soft Slumbers pass'd the Night with Sleep.
Here neighbouring Orchards in their verdant Blooms
The gentle Air sweetens with their Perfumes;
Which pleasing Prospect did attract our sight
And charm'd our Sense of smelling with Delight.

From hence we went on our Survey again
By fertile Meads which join the wat'ry Main,
Turning more Points, and passing on our way
Came to a Place on which a Dead Man lay,
A dreadful sight it was, our Blood run chill
It damp't our joys and made our Spirits thrill,
Ah! what is Man? when he by Nature's Laws
Is fall'n a Prey to Death's relentless Paws
But vanity? His mortal Part I mean
But stop my Muse and quit this mournful Theme.

From hence by Fields, and now and then a Ridge
We came at length unto *Pawtuxett* Bridge,
The Southern Bounds which Providence does claim

And does divide fine *Warwick* from the same.
Passing along still by the flowing Tide
The famous Town of *Providence* we spy'd,
To which we came, viewing how Nature made
(With Art allied) this for a Place of Trade.
 This Pleasant Town does border on the Flood
Here's neighboring Orchards, & more back the Wood,
Here's full supply to chear our hungry Souls
Sr. Richard (strong) as well as Wine in Bowls.
Here Men may soon any Religion find
Which quickly brought brave Holland to my Mind.
For here like them, one with the greatest ease
May suit him self, or quit all if He please.
 Our haste in Business call'd us from this Town
By *Seaconk* shore, away to *Barrington*
Passing that Ferry, something did accrue
Which the next Lines, shall give unto your view,
Here jumping out our Horses from the Boat
One blundering sprang which rais'd up each Man's note
And tumbling o'er the Horse fell on his Back
Into the Deep and wet his Masters Pack.
 For Bristol Town we shap'd our Course away
And *Poppassquash* we quickly did survey,
But on this shore we turn'd a while to rove,
And went to *Vial's* and walk'd thro' his Grove.
This charming Place was neat and clean, a Breese
Attend the shade made by black cherry Trees,
On either side a Row of large extent
And nicely shading every step We went:
Methinks young Lovers here with open Arms
Need no young Cupids to inspire their Charms,
For what can raise the Nymphs or Swains to love
In sweet Caresses, sooner than this Grove.
 From hence (with Air) we pass thro' *Bristol* streets
Where Generous Hearts did give their liberal Treats,
Yet soon we found one of another Mould
For here a Crabbed Jade did at us Scold,
Her grevel'd Notes yet made some of us smile
Whose impeous Talk was near to *Prattle Isle*,
Which Place we named to memorise this Scold
And for her sake this story I have told.
 Now next we took our Course to *Castle Isle*
And pass'd away soon from this pleasant Soil
Finding exactly how *Hog-Island* bore
With Course and Distance to *Aquetnett* shore.
Mount Hope from hence we plainly now espy'd

Which was hard by, or near the flowing Tide,
To which we came taking the Courses here
To neighbouring shores, and Islands that are near.
  Turning aside we saw the Royal Spring
Which once belong'd unto an Indian King,
To chear our Hearts we drank the cooling stream
In memory of *Philip* and his Queen.
Next we ascended *Philip's* Royal Seat
Where he was slain, and all his Armies beat
We saw the Place where quartered he did hang,
Where joyful notes of Praise those Victors sang.
  Upon this Mount the wandering Eye may gaze
On distant Floods, as well as neighbouring Bays
Where with one Glance appears Ten Thousand charms
With fruitful Islands, and most fertile Farms.
Now from this Mount we went (like Men well skill'd)
By Flocks and Herds which verdant Pastures fill'd,
Unto *Assont* took the Distance here
And turn'd about new Courses now to steer.
From hence we went by various Towns in haste,
And by *Rhode-Island* shore we also past
Where every Turn and Cove We noted down
Shaping our Courses unto *Seconet* Town,
When we came near that pleasant place and soil
I heard a story which will make you smile.
A worthy Friend who lately had great Losses
Amongst his stock, but chiefly in his Horses,
By evil Men, who haunts his Fields by night
When he's from home and kills them out of spight,
This Friend relates (whose Daughter was before me]
With chearful Air the following Famous Story:
  " One Evening clear (said he) she took up Arms
" Laying aside a while her Virgin Charms.
" And walk'd abroad some of my Fields to view,
" The Flocks and Herds, to see what would ensue
" Then instantly with Courage being inspir'd
" She at an Armed Rogue her Pistol fir'd
" Crying aloud you Wretch begone from hence,
" Or stand and fight me in your own Defence.
" But guilty Creature, he took to his Heels
" And left this Maiden in the Conquer'd Fields
" Who joy'd awhile for this brave Action done,
" And then return'd unto her Peaceful Home.
  From hence we passed along *Seconet* Shore,
Unto its Point where Dreadful Billows roar,
Whose rolling Waves come tumbling from the main

And kiss the Shore and then retire again.
   Here may the Eye survey the tossing Sea
And sport the sight with Ships that sailing be
Upon this Coast, which come from distant Lands;
And then may turn and view the Beach and Sands,
True Gratitude forbids I should be mute,
Where Generous Souls, our Spirits do Recruit.
Now sure, this Town deserves our best of Praise,
Since none more strived our Spirits soon to raise.
   But stop my Muse, let's haste on our Survey
And stretch our Course along the Eastward Bay.
So then from hence we measur'd by the Sands
An Eastward Course along those Pleasant Lands,
And came to *Dartmouth* a most liberal Town
Whose liquid Treats their generous Actions crown,
   Here is the place where we did end our Works
Here we left off, (and did it with a jirk)
And then retir'd our Field Book for to scan,
And of this large Survey to make a Plan.

W. C.

THE FIRST SETTLERS OF TIVERTON.

The following named persons were inhabitants of Tiverton when it was made a town, by order of the General Court, bearing date March 2, 1692.

Major Church, John Pearce, John Cook, Gersham Woodle, Richard Borden, Thomas Cory, Joseph Anthony, Joseph Wanton, Daniel Howland, Edward Briggs, Amos Sheffield, Edward Colby, David Lake, Joseph Tollman, Christopher Almy, Stephen Manchester, Job Manchester, Edward Gray, Forbes Manchester, William Manchester, Daniel Wilcox, Joseph Taber, Thomas Waite, John Briggs, John Cook, William Almy, John Cook, Jr.

In 1698, I find the marks of cattle recorded, in addition to most of them mentioned above, the following named persons:

John Seville, Josiah Stafford, Benjamin Chace, Robert Dennis, Gersham Manchester, Samuel Hix, William Durfee, Jethro Jeffries, Samuel Snell, Thomas Cook.

Some of the "Whys and Wherefores" of the issue of the Rhode Island Colonial Paper Currency.

AN ADDRESS DELIVERED BEFORE THE RHODE ISLAND VETERAN CITIZENS HISTORICAL ASSOCIATION, FEBRUARY 2D, 1885, BY WELCOME A. GREENE.

Mr. President and Ladies and Gentlemen:

It is, of course, well known to you all, as a matter of historical fact, that at various times paper currency, of one form or another, was issued by the Colonial Government of Rhode Island; and that great suffering and loss was incurred by its citizens owing to the depreciation of such currency; notwithstanding which, so strong was the feeling that it was the right, power and even duty of the Legislature to issue such currency at proper times, that the denial of such power, by the Constitution of the United States, was one of the reasons why Rhode Island was the last State to accept and approve thereof.

I say it is well known to you; for the historical facts of the case have been ably collected and published by the late Hon. Elisha R. Potter and afterwards more fully commented upon and illustrated by Mr. Sidney S. Rider in his historical tract on the subject published in Providence and to be found in the cabinet of your parent society.

To this work I am much indebted for details of information which otherwise without difficult and laborious research I should have been unable to discover.

But it is not entirely by the examination of dry statements that the lessons of history are to be learned.

The mere facts that issues of paper money were made in 1710, and later—that "banks" so-called were issued in 1715, and at various times till 1750; that the money depreciated till in 1769—it required 29 shillings in currency to purchase one shilling sterling—do not teach us whether such issues were advisable or inadvisable, whether the depreciation and resulting losses that followed were the inevitable results of such issues, or of other circumstances.

Whether our ancestors were wise or not in the matter of such issues? Whether they were in such a position that they were the best steps that could be taken under the circumstances? are questions that can only be advantageously considered by grouping together many other facts and looking at all the circumstances surrounding the case—by taking a mental photograph, so to speak, of the colony at the time of the issues, and, from its study, learn the true lesson of the events.

We think that an hour may be pleasantly and profitably spent in reviewing the circumstances surrounding our ancestors when they performed their acts, and will help us to look at the facts as they looked at them; to feel the difficulties of their various situations as they felt them, and to appreciate the remedies (if remedies they were) as they appreciated them.

If it has no other good effect it will fix more vividly in our minds some of the details of the early history of the colony, for it is the side lights and local items in our view of historical scenes that fix them permanently in the mind. Those of us who can remember "Slate Rock" as it appeared 40 years ago projecting into the waters of the Seekonk, with the contour of the river's bank practically much as existed in the time of Roger Williams, can have a much more vivid conception of his approach and landing, than the youth of the present day who is shown a stone far above its natural level and far removed from the water, and is told that on that stone, then many feet below its present position, Roger Williams first landed in Providence.

Without meaning to criticise harshly or in any way disparage the able work above mentioned, we think it can justly be said in regard to it that the reader arises from its perusal with the impression on his mind.

What manner of men were these? Of what material

were our ancestors formed that they *could* make such colossal blunders in their financial management? Were they blind? Were they imbecile? or were they dishonest that they could go on making issue after issue of depreciated and depreciating currency, and could only be stopped by the strong arm of power reached forth by the British Government?

And yet we know that our ancestors were not dishonest. They were not weak; on the contrary, " there were giants in those days;" and when we find such men as Governors Samuel Cranston, William Wanton, John Wanton, Richard Ward, etc., favoring and advocating such issues, when we recollect that the control of the local government of the colony was then vested entirely in the hands of the freeholders thereof; that for years the issue or non-issue of this money was the leading political question of the day, and that a large majority of the voters must have been in favor of it. I think that we must come to the conclusion that there was something in the status of the people, in their commercial relations, or their pecuniary necessities, in one, the other, or all of them, that made those steps the march of wisdom which, when barely read of in their results, at a distance of more than a century, seem the tottering foot falls of imbecility or folly.

What that *something* was we shall strive to point out, and it seems to us that it can be found, if at all, only by taking a nearer view of the colony as it then existed.

At the period of its first issue of paper currency, 1710, the colony of Rhode Island contained about 7000 inhabitants.

Of them, a little over 2000 lived in Newport, the metropolis of the infant State, and were grouped mostly on the land to the eastward and north-eastward sides of the present inner harbor of the place.

In the town of Portsmouth, at the north end of the island of Rhode Island, resided some 600 inhabitants.

In the Providence of that day, which included the whole of the present Providence county (except Cumberland, East Providence and part of Pawtucket), resided some 1500 inhabitants, the dwellings of most of them being grouped on the eastward side of Providence harbor, which then extended half a mile further to the north than at present.

In Warwick there were some 500 inhabitants living on the south bank of the Pawtuxet, the western shore of Narraganset Bay and the northern and north-western shores of Coweset or Greenwich Bay.

At Greenwich, at the south-western end of the last named bay, there was a settlement of somewhat less than 300 inhabitants.

In Kingston (including the present N. and S. Kingstown and other towns) there were some 1200 inhabitants with the greatest concentration at Wickford.

In Westerly, on the Pawcatuck river (claimed by Connecticut as part of that colony but practically an integral portion of Rhode Island), there were about 600 inhabitants.

At Jamestown (Conanicut Island) there were about 200 inhabitants, and at New Shoreham (Block Island) there were some 200 more.

In addition to these, what is now the county of Bristol and the towns of Tiverton and Little Compton (then parts of Massachusetts colony), aggregated perhaps 800 inhabitants, whose principal trading connection would naturally be with Newport.

We notice that all these settlements, except Westerly, were on, or close to the shore of Narraganset Bay. There were no extensive settlements in the back country, and these settlements rather dotted than lined the shores of the bay. The rest of the colony was a wilderness, the home of wild beasts and haunt of Indians.

The natural emporium of these settlements was Newport, to and from which, over the surface of the bay, ebbed and flowed the feeble currents of what little internal trade existed in the colony.

As might be expected, the principal merchants of the colony congregated at Newport. Of the 29 vessels then owned by the colony, all but two or three belonged there. Thence were sent vessels over the sea to neighboring colonies and to foreign countries. There were received the return cargoes, whether merchandise or money, and thence distributed over the colony.

Outside of Newport the principal occupation of the inhabitants was agricultural; with the exception of saw mills and grist mills there was scarcely any manufacturing industry. In fact the colony was jealously watched by the English authorities, and all manufacturing "proper to England," on the part of the colonists, promptly and diligently discouraged.

Roads in the colony were few and poor. The ferries, by which access to Newport was obtained, apparently were considered of more importance than any other public means of communication—the roads simply ran to the ferries.

There was a foreign trade to the West Indies and to the Western Islands (Fayal, Madeira, Cape Verd, etc.) carrying the productions of the colony, agricultural and lumber, and bringing back the productions of those countries, also a trade with the British colonies on the North American coast.

There was no direct trade with England, but all trade of that kind was through the merchants of Boston, probably carried on by means of vessels sailing round Cape Cod. There was, however, a large consumption of English goods, for Gov. Cranston estimated that for many years previous to 1708 the colony had paid to Boston merchants annually £20,000 sterling in cash on account of such trade, and this represents only the balance of trade as concerned England, which all this time was heavily against the colony.

There does not seem to have been any source from which to obtain coin to supply this demand, except the balances of trade in favor of the colony on account of its foreign trade; and such trade was looked upon with a jealous eye by the British authorities, some of whom did not hesitate to charge the colony with being a nest of pirates and smugglers on account of the same.

While laboring under these adverse circumstances, the colony was obliged to protect itself from pirates who then infested the coast at all times, and, in time of war, from the more legitimate naval forces of the enemy, for while the English authorities were eagerly encouraging all enterprises that called money away from the colony to pay for English goods, they bitterly reproached it that it did not provide more adequate means of defence against the enemies of England, and even recommended to Queen Anne to take away its charter as a punishment for such remissness and other offences.

THE MONEY OF THE COLONY.

When Roger Williams first came to Providence, the Indians living in the territory now known as Rhode Island had a sort of currency used by them in trading, as a money of exchange, made of shells and known as "wampum" and "wampumpeag." There were two grades distinguished by their colors, one white, the other black—the latter being worth two times the former. In larger transactions it was strung and counted by the "fathom." Its value was continually fluctuating, but generally the black kind was worth about six shillings per "fathom." For trading with Indians this might serve, but at best it was but little if any improvement on the barter system, and it was clearly impractical on account of its bulk to use it in transactions involving large values.

With the increase of the settlements and their increasing trade arose the necessity of having more convenient means of exchange.

The settlers must have brought some money with them, but it was very little, and soon exhausted in paying for tools and supplies from England, and the drain that way as we have seen was very large.

That personal credit, in the form of notes of hand, was used largely is very clear, but that was of no avail beyond the small environment where a man's individual, financial and moral character was understood.

There were of course none of our modern banks and bank bills in the colony.

There was and had been no money coined in this colony, and but little in Massachusetts Bay Colony, and what little had been coined there had been jealously watched, and its continued issue finally stopped by England in 1668.

It would seem that, in Rhode Island at least, gold and silver coin was not in those days in the strictest sense a currency, but had rather a fluctuating barter value—sterling being the money of account, and the value of an ounce of silver or gold therein varying at different times; still silver coin came the nearest to being a currency, as the word is now used, of anything they had.

The only source the colony had of obtaining coin lay in the balances of trade, which might exist in its favor, on account of its dealings with other countries as above described; and we find that most of the coin circulated in its limits was Spanish silver thus obtained, and *that*, as we have seen, was largely drained away to Boston.

It is evident that this source of supply of coin was, to an extent, fickle and uncertain; that though its average might perhaps be reckoned on with some definiteness yet in case of a sudden emergency, calling for large sums at once, no dependence could be placed on getting relief from that source.

In such a case no help could be hoped for from England. The colonies were for England's benefit, not England for the colonists. At least it was so regarded by the English authorities.

Now, considering all these circumstances, let us look at the question squarely.

In 1710 an emergency arose. There was war between England and France in which their respective colonies participated.

An expedition against Canada was to be fitted out, and Rhode Island had her quota to raise, equip and pay.

The sea coast defences must be placed in a condition for effective defence immediately, for it was feared that a fleet would be fitted out in France to sail to the mouth of the Saint Lawrence River, thence down the coast of New England, capturing all its ports, and ascending the Hudson River, deliver reinforcements to Canada, *via* Lake Champlain.

This was an emergency that called for immediate action. Money, current money, was needed; £7000 was wanted in 1710, and perhaps an equally large sum might be needed the next year.

Where was it to come from ?

There were no merchants able to loan the needed funds to the Government, and if there were they had not available currency to loan.

Paper money issued by the Government was to our colonial ancestors of that date an untried measure, but some of them had seen it used in Canada, and it is probably from them that the suggestion came to adopt that mode of relief, and an issue of treasury notes had been made in a somewhat similar emergency by Massachusetts in 1690. It seemed as if no possible way was left to obtain the currency but to pledge the faith of the colony for the amount needed, and to issue it in bills of credit.

One hundred and fifty years later, when, instead of a few feeble settlements on the shore of Narragansett Bay, with about 7000 inhabitants, the country involved consisted of a cordon of wealthy states stretching across the continent, with an immense commercial fleet, with an inter-state commerce of thousands of millions of dollars annually, having all the advantages of steam power in its manifold uses, with the telegraph, with the most skillful (taken as a whole) manufacturing population on the face of the globe, with thousands of banks and loaning institutions scattered through the country, with the most effective gold and silver producing districts in the world within its limits, with capitalists by scores and hundreds who could count their millions of dollars where the wealthiest men of Rhode Island in 1710 could barely command thousands of pounds, another war emergency arose.

Four hundred millions of dollars in Bills of Credit (we called them greenbacks) were issued, and they still remain outstanding.

Is there? can there, be any good reason for the act of our day and generation but what justifies with tenfold force, the acts of our ancestors in 1710?

Does the fact that the greenbacks of 1860, after depreciating to about forty cents on the dollar, have since appreciated to par in gold, while the issues of the colonies never rose to par in gold or silver, make any difference as to the propriety or justification of the measure?

No. It was a war measure; it was that or destruction; and the colony chose as wisely, in making their issues of 1710–11, as the United States in 1860 and later.

This issue of 1710–11, in all £13,300, was evidently successful in meeting the wants of the people. It furnished a money that was considered as having the most available and considerable security then obtainable, viz., the resources, credit and good faith of the colony, which was receivable at a fixed valuation for debts due to the colony, and was free to a certain extent (for the time being, at least), from fluctuations in value among the people. In other words, it was considered more *as money*, and less as an article of merchandise than any other medium of exchange then to be found in the colony.

It is true that this money had at the time of its issue a less nominal value than English sterling, being valued at eight shillings, while the latter was then about five shillings to the ounce of silver, but it was received as and became both a money of account and currency within the colony, and in fact its use was so greedily adopted by the people of adjoining colonies that a large proportion was speedily absorbed by them. And in Oct., 1710, for the sake of giving the money a greater value in the colony than elsewhere, an act was passed authorizing the colonial treasurer to receive it for taxes at five per cent. advance. These bills of credit, as they were paid into the treasury, were intended to be destroyed by the General Assembly.

Under the influence of these measures the trade, population and wealth of the colony increased rapidly.

We now come to a different phase of the matter, viz., the issue of the "*Banks*," so-called.

In 1715 a large portion of the bills of credit issued in 1710-11 had been either paid in and destroyed or absorbed by other colonies; and there was again a scarcity of circulating medium, while owing to the increasing internal and external commerce of the colony, a greater demand for it existed than ever before.

There was also need of money in the treasury to build a jail in the "metropolis of the colony" (Newport), and to repair the fort in Newport harbor.

There was a feeling in the colony that those individuals who needed the money to use, who had the enterprise and energy to avail themselves of it in advancing their private interests as well as the public good, and were able to give proper security for it, should have it; paying interest on it and repaying the principal sum when due.

Thus the colony would draw from these people, in addition to other taxes, the interest due on the sums loaned, thereby obtaining funds for its extraordinary expenses, and at the same time the money would have the value supposed to be derived from the name, faith, and credit of the colony.

To carry out this plan the "Bank" of 1715 was issued, viz., £40,000 in bills of credit were issued by the colony and divided by the Legislature among the several towns, being delivered to certain of the freeholders upon their severally giving mortgages to the colony of their real estate in double the value of the bills received, they to pay five per cent. interest on the amount received, and to repay the loan in ten years. Who selected the favored ones to receive the loans, we have been unable definitely to discover, but the selection was probably made by the town councils of the several towns.

Why it was called a "Bank" we are unable to tell. It was certainly distinct from and unlike anything known by that name in modern times.

Whether this was a wise step or not, opinions may now well differ.

Probably in view of the subsequent history of the finances of the colony, most would now say that it was unwise. But we must recollect that we look through the telescope of history reversed; to see things as our ancestors saw them, we must get to the other end of the instrument.

That money, a circulating medium was needed by the people, there can be no doubt. They had "resources" but not "money."

The present system of banks and banking, and loaning associations, had not arisen. The present means of speedy and safe communication and transmission from one portion of the globe to another, whereby money readily flows to where it is needed did not exist.

No students of the science of government had drawn the distinction of our day, as to the proper sphere and scope of a governmental body.

The idea of incorporated bodies vested with powers of issuing bills or making loans was unthought of, or if thought of, was then considered as impracticable on this side of the Atlantic.

The Legislature itself was rather a patriarchal institution than a Legislature, as we know such bodies now.

It made laws, and it executed them. It acted as a high court of appeal and of chancery. It granted divorces, settled estates, and loaned money (belonging to the colony) to deserving individuals, sometimes charging, and sometimes not charging, interest on such loans.

With a government of that kind, and situated as they were, the most natural resort of the people in their difficulties was to the Legislature, and we find that, notwithstanding the fiery ordeal of political warfare to which, at a later day, the question of the issue or non-issue of paper money was subjected, the objection, that the General Assembly was acting beyond the proper scope of its powers in making the issue, was never raised or apparently thought of.

However it may seem to us, it is evident that the people of that day were in favor of the "Bank," for, notwithstanding the fact that upon the issue of the first one in 1715, the currency depreciated to twelve shillings per ounce of silver, no objections were made; and in 1721, a new "Bank" of £40,000 was called for and issued on the same terms, though the currency then depreciated to sixteen shillings to the ounce of silver.

In connection with this matter of depreciation, we must bear in mind that all circulating mediums in those days were fluctuating; thus, English sterling, which in this colony was almost a pure money of account, and therefore less liable to fluctuate, varied at times from five to seven shillings to the ounce of silver.

The colony was now fairly embarked upon a voyage of discovery over the sea of paper money, and apparently a prosperous one.

Between 1708 and 1730 the settlement at Greenwich sextupled its population. Westerly quadrupled, and Kingston trebled theirs. Warwick and Providence each nearly trebled, and Newport more than doubled their respective populations.

Commercial and agricultural wealth increased in enormous proportions, and such manufactures as the jealousy of England allowed them to attempt, were introduced as fast as they were deemed advisable.

Is it any wonder that the men of that day believed in the system?

Before its introduction, in nearly three score years, the population had only grown to about 7,000.

After its introduction, in one score of years, it increased nearly 11,000.

What had the opponents of the system to say against such facts and such figures as these?

Flushed with the success that had attended the issue of the first two "Banks," when the time came that the first of them should be paid, the Legislature extended the loan for three years, and in 1728 authorized the issue of a new "Bank" of £40,000, which was apparently intended to be loaned to the individuals who had taken the loan of the first "to prevent the individuals taking the first loan from the impoverishment and destruction that would follow if the Government exacted the payment of said first 'Bank' in one sum," the Assembly "judging it an infringement upon the liberty and privilege of the English subjects to enrich the one at the immediate ruin of the other;" though as a law was made that the first "Bank" should be paid in ten annual payments of ten per cent. each, instead of being paid in one sum, it practically made an increase in the amount of the currency. The depreciation then came to be eighteen shillings to the ounce of silver.

By acts of the General Assembly other special loans were sometimes made of the colony's credit to individuals.

In emergencies, bills of credit were issued by the colony in anticipation of the interest due on the "Banks," to be redeemed and retired when the said interest was paid. As an instance, £2,000 for repairs of the fort in 1728.

The unanimity that at first existed in regard to the advisability of these issues did not continue.

As the amounts outstanding became larger and the depreciation steadily increased, a strong party grew up among the freeholders of the colony in favor of curtailing these issues and calling in the old "Banks" promptly.

They saw, or thought they saw, in the near future nothing but destruction to the best interests of the colony, resulting from the then present course, and when, in 1731, a new "Bank" of £60,000 was called for and ordered by the General Assembly to issue, with a depreciation to 22 shillings to the ounce of silver, this party, headed by the then Governor, Joseph Jenckes, of Providence, made itself powerfully felt.

Its resistance was carried so far that the governor refused to give the law authorizing the "Bank" his sanction, and attempted to establish a veto power. That was revolution; and when the Legislature refused to recognize such veto power, he referred the question to the Crown officers of England. The officers of the Crown, however, decided that the governor, as a member of the Legislature, had only the power to cast one vote, and was concluded by the action of the Legislature,—which remains Rhode Island law to this day—

And now the question became an active political one, and for years remained one of the most exciting issues that the political history of the colony ever knew.

Those opposed to the issues of paper currency claimed that it was owing to the continued and increasing issue that the currency was depreciating.

They said: "We have seen the paper money drop in value from 8 shillings to more than 20 to the ounce of silver.

"If these issues are kept up, we will see it go down continually till the money loses all value.

"It is not honest towards the creditor class in the community, who have loaned money in the past at its higher value, to depreciate the currency and compel them to receive payment of their loans in money of less value.

"It is true that the community is apparently growing rich fast, but it is in appearance only; it is a hollow show. Reduced to a silver valuation, we are not rich.

"This depreciation of currency is disturbing the relations of both our internal and our foreign trade, and must end in ruin.

"It is only the borrowing class who want this money issued in order that they may pay old debts in really less money, and they hope to incur new liabilities which they will pay in future in further depreciated funds. All who have the true interests of the colony at heart are opposed to it; and, finally, it is contrary to the spirit of the orders of the English Government."

In reply to this, it was said by the advocates of the system:
"We need and must have a circulating medium.

"Without it, we struggled along in poverty; since we have had it, see the advances we have made in material wealth, commerce and prosperity.

"Before we had it, how few were the vessels belonging to the colony. Now we count them into the hundreds of our own, besides those we have meantime built and sold in other countries.

"Before we had it, we were the servants of Boston merchants in regard to English trade. Now we trade direct with England, selling the English vessels of our own construction and goods obtained by our own trade with other colonies and foreign countries.

"Look at our increase of population from a few thousands to scores of thousands.

"Look at the increase of Newport from an unknown village, till now it rivals New York and bids fair to eclipse even Boston.

"Look at our military situation. Before, the easy prey of any; the scoff and scorn of all. And now, with our fort splendidly equipped at Newport; our armed vessel, the finest on the coast; and our privateers that beard the enemy on the ocean,—all making our colony, instead of the helpless object of attack, the bulwark and defence of New England.

"Look at our hemp industries. Examine them; strain them, for it will do no hurt for some of your party to strain hemp.

"Look at our harbor of refuge at Block Island, and the

consequent growth of the cod and whale fisheries; at the growth of our various manufacturing industries; at our lighthouse, and our public buildings—all which came into being since the issue of paper money—and say, if you can, that we have had no real growth.

"It is not true that the fact of silver increasing in value as it has shows the fallacy of our currency.

"Silver is simply an article of trade. So long as Boston and other merchants can offer high prices in goods for it, it will be high. The way for us to bring it down is to get the goods here cheaply and offer as much for it.

"The prosperity of the country is not hollow, but real. The increase in population shows it; that in property, even if valued in silver, shows it. The increase is immense,—unprecedented; and it all became possible simply by the issue of paper money.

"What we have had, has placed us where we are. Let us have more of it, till we leave New York in the shade, and Boston hides its diminished head before our peerless Newport."

Such were the arguments used in that day. And, ladies and gentlemen, those were great times for the colony of Rhode Island. Perched on the rocket of apparent prosperity, she was whizzing aloft to the very zenith, illuminating the whole coast of North America with her glaring light.

With a majority of the freeholders actuated by arguments like these, the opponents of paper money were thrown out of office and a long series of administrations in favor of it elected.

"Banks" were issued in 1733, '38, '40, '43, and in 1750 the last "Bank" of the *colony* was issued. In *that* an attempt was made to fix a value to the issue by act of the Legislature, hoping to stop and turn back the tide of depreciation.

During the later years the party opposed to the currency was growing stronger, and it was through the influence of that opposition that this attempt to prevent, by act of legislation, the depreciation of the money was made.

The opposition, however, seems not to have been strong enough to prevent further issues, for they were finally stopped, not by local action of the freeholders, but by orders from the British Government.

Then came the question of caring for the depreciated paper, and *then*, all the gloomy forebodings of the anti-issue party seemed to be realized.

The paper went down, down, down! till, in 1769, it required twenty-nine shillings in paper to purchase one in sterling.

We have not time and it is foreign to our purpose to detail how our ancestors escaped from their financial difficulties.

It is a matter of astonishment that they *were* enabled to pass through such an ordeal, and the general development of the colony did not cease in its onward course. There was a *retardation* and *change in direction*, but not a *stop*.

Our subject was "the whys and wherefores of the issues of the *colonial* paper currency," and does not carry us to the issue of another "Bank" by the State in 1786. This was an act of a different day and generation, guided by different motives and acting from different experiences.

In conclusion, let us say that we have not attempted the solution of any of the vexed economico-political questions that arise out of situations such as we have described. We do not attack nor defend the issue of paper money as an abstract question.

We do not attempt to define money even. It would take hours to do it, and it is foreign to our subject.

We have only tried to place before you the circumstances under which our ancestors were placed from 1710 to 1750, the arguments by which they were convinced, and to recall facts and events showing that their course—however it may look to us now—was such that wise men and patriotic men might well have pursued it then.

Mr. James N. Arnold, after the delivery of the preceding address, commented upon the same as follows:

Mr. President, Ladies and Gentlemen: The paper that has just been read by Mr. Greene we think in excellent taste, and certainly he has presented excellent reasons for the measures noted in his paper, and his remarks are timely, and we think they round out more fully what has before been written upon this subject.

At the conclusion of Mr. Greene's paper, an unthinking opinion is, the system was bad, hence the decline, and finally its utter abandonment. With all Mr. Greene's reasonable arguments and apologies in its favor, the system would not and did not stand a practical test. Mr. Greene has followed the lawyers' rule of keeping to one point, and perhaps does not do full justice to his clients. A point omitted, Mr. President, we wish to call your attention to, and to speak of one cause that made this decline more marked, and this point has not been weighed as carefully as it should have been by those who have treated on this subject.

The point I am about to present can be illustrated by a fable, and we call the colony the artist and the home government the learned friend. The artist and his friend took a walk. They came to a delightful little nook. The artist said: " What a charming little picture; a pearly stream, a bank of flowers, a bird on a limb overhead, and a frog sitting on a stone in the water." The artist saw it all and said: " Beautiful! beautiful! beautiful!" "Beautiful," said his friend, "in what? Has that owl any music in him? and for a soul he has none. That stream of water runs from one mud-hole to another. That bunch of flowers—why, there are hundreds all around here as good as that one. And that frog—gracious! now, be honest, don't you think the creature's mouth is too wide and his nose too flat to look well?"

Moral: How easy to find fault when one has the will to do it.

That is just the case here presented. The colony could not perfectly please the English capitalist. They could never give satisfaction, and of course no system of finance could find favor with them, and did not.

You will please notice Mr. Greene has given the ratio of decline all the way through, and he is just like a boy on a sled sliding down hill,—the longer he slides, the faster he goes; until, had he not stopped, he would have his currency like a $20 Confederate note, which to-day can be had for a penny, and dear at that.

You will also observe that his decline is very moderate at first; and when we come to consider that it was a new system, and without a precedent, it showed a remarkable record, and has firmly proven its wisdom and its necessity at this time. Had it not been tampered with or disturbed, it would have ably vindicated its promoters and advocates.

The English capitalist, backed up by the government, saw that it must be broken down, and hence set up an opposition system; and, as this system was pushed and backed by the influence behind it, it accomplished its work. A shrewd plan, ably advocated and skilfully worked out.

The plan embraced these strong features:

(1.) To bind the victim in such a way as to make him advocate and work for it as warmly as the other party would work for the colonial system.

(2.) Based upon coin—a foundation that has stood a test, and was recognized by bankers and nations the world over.

(3.) To give seemingly as good terms as the colony.

(4.) To flatter and make believe that it offered safer means of loan and payment.

(5.) To give a wide choice in method of payment, and

(6.) To get the cream on the side of the capitalist.

In all these features the scheme was admirable and operated in this way:

The English capitalist sent to his agent at Newport a sum of money in coin. The agent lent this on real estate and crops to the planter, and he conditioned to pay interest, and make payments in grain, beef and produce. Had this clause been inserted in the colony plan, it would not have been carried out effectually, for the colony was not in position to handle to a profit the produce obtained; but you will notice during the Revolution this feature worked well, for the colony could use its produce to advantage, and did so, as you will readily call to mind.

This seemingly gold basis "tickled," to use a boy's word, and, as it came into practice, it rapidly formed two parties— "Hard Money," and "Paper Money." This was exactly the object sought—to divide, obstruct, yet make dependent upon the Home Government in every way possible, the colonies.

The result was it extended our commercial interests rapidly to foreign ports, and both systems aided this extension materially. As a result, the Spanish ports were visited for trade, and the trade, earning hard money, was profitable. As the English plan developed, it was seen, more or less, that the capitalist said "turkey" for himself every time. Hence Spanish money became popular, and, being more easily obtained, became the standard of value. The selfishness of the capitalist and the government becoming apparent, added popularity to the Spanish standard. The development of trade in this direction led the colony, in a measure, out of a bad position. The colony, by the two systems, was doing well. The Home Government, seeing this condition, contrived the "Stamp Duties," to get at the surplus means.

The colony had been victimized sadly by the English plan. Narragansett Records can show the historian a page of disaster that is fully equal, in proportion to the means risked, as any of the present day. They had not only ruined men by their scheming, but had demoralized the finances of the colony by creating a value of great uncertainty and very fluctuating.

It takes no deep thinker to see now the cause of that intense hatred that made our colony the most rebellious, and the first to openly insult the Home Government and chastise her authority on the sea.

Look at the Declaration of Independence, and note there the charges brought against King George. It is there charged repeatedly interference in our commercial, political and social affairs.

Mr. President, here is the grand cause of decline of our financial system. Not so much the defect of that system as from the effects of meddlesome outsiders.

We have read carefully when it was first printed the works to which Mr. Greene refers, and it came to us, as it did to him, that those facts wanted an explanation, and he has given part of it. It occurred also to us, Where is the scholar that can show the causes? The system was good; was timely; was a public necessity; and was so urgently demanded as not to admit of delay. It was projected in wisdom; it was measured with care; and it was intended to be conducted in a prudent way and manner, in every way honorable to both parties. A study of the whole proceedings shows that our Legislators were honest and conscientious men, and had studied deeply into the welfare of the colony and its needs.

THE BRADFORD DURFEE.—A new steamboat called the Bradford Durfee, built in New York, to run between Fall River and Providence, arrived at Fall River on Wednesday evening last. She was built by Lawrence & Sweden. Her engine is from the Allaire Works. She is said by the New York papers to be a splendid boat. She made her passage from New York to Fall River in twelve hours, including several stops. We understand she will take the place of the King Phillip on Monday next.—*Bristol Phenix, Nov. 1, 1845.*

NEW ENGLAND ALMANACS,

WITH SPECIAL MENTION OF THOSE PUBLISHED IN RHODE ISLAND.

A Paper read before the Rhode Island Historical Society, at the October Quarterly Meeting, 1884, by the Secretary and Librarian, Amos Perry.

ALMANACS constitute an interesting part of the collections of this society. These publications served in the early period of our history important purposes. They were consulted with care and often with a spirit of reverence and trust akin to that exercised in the perusal of the Holy Scriptures. Almanac-makers were reputed to be veritable seers. How they could read the heavens, determine the order of the sun, moon and stars, and foretell rain and sunshine, eclipses and dire events, was the wonder of multitudes who studied and pondered over their works.

Similar ideas are still entertained in some quarters of the globe, notably in oriental countries, where Jewish, Mussulman and Christian modes of designating the days, months and years are printed side by side for the convenience of merchants. But here all is changed. Science and art have produced a revolution in our modes of thought and action. Thrusting aside old-fashioned weather prophets and prophecies, we seek and will have for our guidance only the latest results of extensive scientific research and investigation. Our seers must lay no claim to supernatural wisdom, but must be diligent students of nature, observing the divine order in the material world, and giving the results of their observations.

Almanacs served our forefathers, not only as calendars, but as compendiums or rather medleys of astronomy, astrology, geology, meteorology, biography, history, tradition and science. They contained the dates of notable marriages, births and deaths; of many remarkable events; of college commencements, election days, cattle shows, the sessions of courts, together with enigmas, problems, quaint sayings, tables of distances, and practical information and suggestions of various kinds; and they often served at the same time as diaries and account books. Sea captains noted in them important facts connected with their voyages, as the dates of their departure and arrival, vessels spoken on the passage, and various striking occurrences. Farmers made notes about their cattle, hogs, sheep and crops. Clergymen made minutes, showing when, where and on what subject they preached and the complexion of their theology, as when the Rev. Ezra Stiles, D. D., wrote: "Feb. 13th, 1789. Gen. Ethan Allen, of Vermont, died and went to Hell this day." Inveterate chroniclers, like Theodore Foster, made their almanacs historical note books and literary curiosities for the instruction and amusement of succeeding generations.

The library of the Historical Society contains numerous collections of New England almanacs, together with some that were published in other parts of this country and in the old world. Yet it has but few extended series of almanacs that are complete. Until recently, no persistent effort was made to collect, classify and arrange these publications. The almanacs were scattered and unassorted, and were thus of no practical value to members of the society. As, however, the preparation of the catalogue progresses, the riches and the deficiencies of the society in this direction become apparent.

Though an almanac was printed in Cambridge, Mass., in 1639, and many almanacs were published in Boston before 1700, the oldest almanac belonging to this society was printed in Boston by B. Green, in 1701, and was edited by John Tulley. We have subsequent issues of almanacs by B. Green in 1703 and 4, that were edited by Samuel Clough; also an issue in 1709 was edited by Thomas Robie, A. B., and an issue in 1710 by Edward Holyoke, A. B., afterwards president of Harvard University. The names of N. Whittemore, Daniel Travis and Joseph Stafford appear as editors in almanacs published in Boston during the first half of the 18th century.

Of Nathaniel Ames's Almanacs, begun in 1725 and ended in 1775, the society needs, to complete its set, the issues of the following years, viz.: 1725, '7, '67, '8, '70, '1, '2, '3, '4 and '5.

Of Robert B. Thomas's Farmer's Almanac, begun in 1793 and continued to the present time, the society lacks only the first three, viz.: 1793, '4 and '5.

Of Isaiah Thomas's Almanacs, begun in 1775 and ending in 1818, the society wants the numbers for 1775, '6, '7, '8, '81, '2, '3, '4, '5, '6, '7, '8, '9, '91, and 1816.

Of Daboll's Almanacs, begun in New London, Ct., in 1772, to meet the special wants of seafaring men—particularly of the whalemen of New London—and continued to the present time, the society has only five numbers, viz., for 1793, 1801, '21, '66 and '76.

Of the American Almanacs, published in Boston, 1830 to 1861, the society has a complete set.

Of eleven numbers of the Clergyman's Almanac, published in Boston from 1809 to 1819, the society has all but the first three.

It has the Boston Almanac, each number bound in cloth and numbered from 1 to 44—1836 to 1879, inclusive.

It has also New England Anti-Slavery almanacs, temperance almanacs, and numerous medical, comical, denominational and newspaper almanacs, designed to promote some moral cause or advertise some medicine, food, newspapers or books. Some of these are now chronicles of olden times and much prized memorials of bygone scenes and events.

A series of almanacs published at the office of the New York Tribune, under the name of the Whig Almanac, from 1838 to 1855, and under the name of the Tribune Almanac from 1856 to the present time, is mentioned here, though published outside of New England, because these publications are more sought and consulted for their various statistics than any other almanacs in the library. Of the Whig Almanacs, the society lacks the first six and the numbers for 1847 and 1850. Of the Tribune Almanacs, the society has all the numbers; and most of them are the gift of Mr. John C. Stockwell, of New York city.

The above brief notices of comparatively few of the society's series of almanacs manufactured in New England, outside of our State, are given with the purpose of inviting friendly aid in making the improvements suggested.

Coming now to our special field of labor, we undertake the task of replying to the inquiries: "What series of Rhode Island almanacs has the State historical society in its archives? and what are some of the facts connected with this kind of publication in this State?"

Only partial and unsatisfactory replies can be here given. However much has been done to improve the looks and character of this cabinet, it should be understood that the confusion and chaos that once prevailed here have not yet given full place to order and light, and this happy result cannot be fully attained without facilities for classification, including due space for books, pamphlets, manuscripts, maps, charts, oil painted portraits, pictures of various kinds, Indian relics, interesting historic flags, and numerous other memorials, together with the means of defraying the expense of putting many of these things into a condition to be well preserved and of real service to the society and the State. It is enough here to say that loose papers, a few of which are deeds of real estate, last wills and testaments, and records of extinct societies and associations,—papers that would be choice morsels for genealogists and antiquarians,—nearly fill two trunks. These should be classified according to subjects or dates, put in book form and indexed; and over fourscore folio volumes of valuable manuscripts, already shelved and catalogued without an index, should all be indexed and carefully catalogued, to enable the student to readily refer to them. This is but one of a hundred matters of like moment that demand the attention of the librarian. Had he, like the fabled Briareus, fifty heads and a hundred hands, together with thrice the space of this building, and thousands of dollars at his command, all would be required to put this cabinet and library into a condition to worthily represent a veritable Rhode Island historical society—an object worthy the ambition of the noblest citizens of our State.

Though James Franklin published an almanac in Newport as early as 1728, the title page of the oldest Rhode Island almanac in the possession of the society reads thus: "Newport 1731. An Almanack for the year of our Lord 1731. By Samuel Maxwell, Newport, printed and sold by J. Franklin at his Printing House under the Town School-House." In bespeaking the favor of the reader, the editor refers to his youth, to his travels "in the more remote parts of the earth," and to his desire to "be serviceable to the Commonwealth."

The society's next Rhode Island almanac in chronological order was issued by the same publisher in 1732, entitled "The Rhode Island Almanac By Poor Robin." This was followed by almanacs with the same title and character in 1733, '5, '9 and '41. The issues of 1739 and '41 were printed and sold by Widow Franklin.

The society's next Newport almanac was entitled: "Poor Job. An Almanac for the year etc. By Job Shepherd, Philom." This was printed and sold by James Franklin in 1751, '2, '3, '4 and '5.

Regarding as a myth S. C. Newman's published statement in the Dexter Genealogy that "Gregory Dexter printed with his own hands the first almanac for the meridian of Rhode Island," and allowing the correctness of the statement made by the Rev. Dr. Wm. Hague, that this veteran printer went annually to Boston for several years to assist Benjamin Green in bringing out his almanac, it is clear that Newport led the State in making almanacs, as well as in printing books and in publishing newspapers. It is not probable that "the Rhode Island Almanac" of Newport was issued yearly from 1732, the date of the first issue, to 1805, the date of the last issue in the possession of the society, though it is probable that an almanac with some appropriate title has been published at

Newport each year since 1731, and the State historical society ought to have a full set of these publications.

In addition to the issues of the Rhode Island almanac already named, the society has the issues of 1772, John Anderson, editor, and Solomon Southwick, printer; 1791, E. Thornton, editor, and P. Edes, printer; 1792, editor and printer the same; 1793 and 94, the same editor, and Nathaniel Phillips, of Warren, printer. Phillips's United States Diary, or an Almanac, 1798, was printed at Warren, R. I., by Nathaniel Phillips. In 1801, Oliver Farnsworth, of Newport, was the printer; 1803, the same editor and printer; 1804, Benjamin West, LL. D., editor, and the same printer; and in 1805, the same editor and printer.

The society has other old Newport Almanacs, as follows: Anderson's Improved, by John Anderson, 1773-4-5. An almanac by John Anderson, 1776. In 1778, an almanac edited by Elisha Thornton, of Smithfield, and in the same year, another almanac edited by Daniel Freebetter, both printed and sold by Peter Edes, at Newport. In 1789 and '90, Thornton edited the Newport Almanac, and in 1797 he edited the New England Almanac, of the Bickerstaff series, for Carter & Wilkinson, of Providence.

In 1806, Remington Southwick, then teacher of mathematics in Washington Academy, at Wickford, edited and had printed for him at Newport "the Columbian Calendar or Almanac," and his son Alpheus Baker Southwick, who inherited and cultivated a taste for mathematics and scientific pursuits, died in Providence in 1884.

The society has a full set of the illustrated Mercury Almanac, printed by John P. Sanborn (the publisher of the Newport Mercury), from 1876 to 1885, except 1877, for which year no almanac was issued.

Though Providence was slow to make its first venture in almanac making, it has to-day an honorable record in this line of business. In 1763, Benjamin West made the astronomical calculations and selections for the first number of the

New England Almanac, and William Goddard printed and sold the work. This publication continued under the same editorial care till 1780. William Goddard was the publisher for three years; Sarah and Wm. Goddard for one year; Sarah Goddard & Co. for one year, and Sarah Goddard and John Carter for two years, and thence forward the name of John Carter appears on this almanac and its legitimate successor till 1815, which was the year after Mr. Carter's death.

In 1781 appeared the first number of what is termed a new series of almanacs. This series had for several years the same editor, the same publisher, and the same leading title as the last numbers of the first series. The noteworthy fact is, not that the character of the publication was changed, but that the editor and compiler played his part under the assumed name of Isaac Bickerstaff,—a pseudonym employed by Dean Swift a century before West's time, and by Richard Steele in the *Tatler* a half century before. The "New England" was the leading title of the old or West series, from 1764 to 1780, and of the new or Bickerstaff series, from 1781 to 1814. The new series (*i. e.*, the Bickerstaff series), was not styled "The Rhode Island Almanac" till 1815, when its original editor and publisher had departed this life, and the publication of the original Rhode Island Almanac, of Newport, had been suspended. Since that time it has been styled indifferently the "Rhode Island," the "Bickerstaff," and the "Bickerstaff Rhode Island." Its centennial with the name of Isaac Bickerstaff upon its title page would have been complete with the issue of 1880, but for the break of one year, 1797, caused either by the indisposition of the stated editor or by a misunderstanding between him and the publisher. The failure of this time-honored annual to make its appearance after 1880, caused regret on the part of many citizens.

Benjamin West gained reputation as an astronomer and an almanac maker. In the latter capacity he succeeded Nathaniel Ames and became a compeer of Isaiah and Robert B. Thomas, rendering services anonymously, as Benjamin West or as

Isaac Bickerstaff, in Newport, Boston, and Norwich, as well as in Providence. The Historical Society has all but ten numbers of the Bickerstaff series, viz., 1866, '7, '8, '9, '72, '3, '4, '5, '8 and '9, and an earnest appeal is made for assistance in completing the set.

After an interval of two years George A. Stockwell began (in 1883) a series of illustrated almanacs entitled "The Rhode Island Almanac," which, though claimed to be a continuation or legitimate successor of the Bickerstaff, promises to become a greater favorite at our homes than either the Bickerstaff, begun in 1781, and called the Rhode Island since 1815, or the original Rhode Island begun in Newport in 1732.

In 1780, Bennett Wheeler, who was a contemporary of John Carter and an enterprising printer, began the publication of the "North American Calendar" and continued it till 1805. The calendar, having the name of Benjamin West on the title page of many of its numbers, became a powerful rival of the Bickerstaff Almanac, published by John Carter; and hence arose an almanac feud which was in the doggerel of the day likened unto the "War of the Roses." Of this series of almanacs the society wants five numbers to complete its set, viz., for 1799, 1800, '1, '3, and '5.

B. F. Moore published the "Providence Almanac and Business Directory" from 1843 to 1845 inclusive, and John F. Moore from 1846 to 1850. Hugh H. Brown resumed this publication in 1855, adding to its attractions biographical sketches of distinguished men of Rhode Island, and issued three numbers. Ten of the eleven volumes with the above title are bound in cloth. The biographical sketches of several of the notable men of the State, contained in the volumes for 1855, '6 and '7, are sought and read with interest to the present time.

George O. Willard issued the "Providence Almanac" (illustrated) for the years 1874 and '75. An edition of this publication was also issued as "The Pawtucket Almanac."

Sampson, Davenport & Co. issued Volumes I. and II. "Providence Almanac and Business Directory" for 1880 and 1881, bound in cloth and gotten up after the fashion of the "Boston Almanac" before referred to.

In 1883 J. A. & R. A. Reid issued at Providence "The Artistic Almanac."

Having done thus much towards producing a list of Rhode Island Almanacs in the possession of this society, I propose now to call attention to one of many illustrations found in the Historical Cabinet, of the uses to which almanacs were put in the last century. The almanacs to which I refer are Nathaniel Ames's, for 1757 and 1758. They are inter-leaved so that with thirty pages of printed matter are forty-eight pages devoted exclusively to writing. The margins of the printed pages and every available space on the other pages are finely and closely written over. The almanac and record of 1758 are fastened with those of 1757, within a cover which is labelled:

"HISTORICAL SOCIETY, R. I.
FOR NORTHERN CABINET.
A. D., 1826——"

Who the author of this diary and "Memorandum of Remarkable Events" (the title standing at the head of each page) was, does not appear on record, and we find in the context at best, only clues to his real name. Yet we can trace the man, gain a clear idea of his characteristics and have reason to believe:

1. That he had been a physician inoculating for small-pox, though he did not practice medicine at the time of writing this diary.

2. That he or his wife (probably the latter) was related to the Greenes, of Warwick, the Almys, and the Carrs.

3. That though he used the vocabulary of the Friends, he was more intimately associated with the Baptists.

4. That he was an intelligent, benevolent and well-informed person, carefully observing the order of nature, and taking note of passing events in different parts of these plantations.

He does not state where he resided, and with my limited acquaintance with the places named I cannot satisfactorily settle this point. He buried his son at Newtown, and he often speaks of Newtown, thus leading me at the outset to think that he lived near a village of that name in Portsmouth. But this theory is inconsistent with other statements. After a violent rain storm he went to the Great Bridge to see the effects of the flood. His children went to Providence to witness a baptizing and returned home the same day, and repeatedly made this excursion between 10 A. M. and 7 P. M., stopping at Uncle Elisha Greene's once on his way back and forth. Once he went to Potowomut and waited there till the boat from Newtown came along and took him to Newport. On another occasion he set out at 10 A. M., reached the ferry at 2 P. M., and Newport at 6 o'clock. On his return at the close of the week, he left Newport at 2 P. M., reached the South Ferry at 5.30, and arrived home "through mud and mire" at 9 o'clock. Once he left Newport at 2.30 o'clock and arrived home at 6, and once he appends " L. D. P." to a brief request addressed to printers. Queries. Where was the ferry? Where the Great Bridge? Where the Newtown to which he refers? Where his home? and what was his name?

Here we are reminded of Montgomery's " Common Lot":

> " Once, in the flight of ages past,
> There lived a man, and who was he?
> Mortal, howe'er thy lot be cast,
> That man resembled thee.
>
> " Unknown the region of his birth,
> The land in which he died.
> His name has perished from the earth,
> This truth survives alone."

He has given a very full account of the weather for upwards of two years. On the first page of the pamphlet are noted the dates of thirty-one snow storms, from Nov. 3, 1756, to April 4, 1757. On the last page is a well-written treatise on the small-pox, showing that he had unbounded faith in the use of mercury and antimony and in the practice of bleeding. His records of marriages, deaths and funerals are numerous, and his remarks about them are interesting. Here and there may be found some detailed account of his petty farming business, as how many hills of beans he planted on certain days of the year, or when he began to pasture his horse in his neighbor's lot. His careful observations of wind and weather indicate the habits of a sea-faring man. His canoe, which was fastened to a wharf near his house, was manifestly his most important means of locomotion. Dire events and rumors of them were apparently caught up and recorded with as keen a relish as if he had been a modern newspaper reporter. He records the capture of Louisburg July 26, 1758 and, after the fashion of some modern poetasters, writes doggerel to express his respect for the mercy shown by the victorious English towards their captives on that occasion, and his abhorrence of the cruelty committed by the French at Fort Du Quesne (Pittsburgh).

The pamphlet bears evident marks of system, order and economy. Its headings and lines on each page are made with red ink. It contains a variety of observations on various subjects, and if printed word for word and furnished with explanatory notes, would in my opinion, interest meteorologists, genealogists and antiquarians. The diary begins on page two thus:

1757.
Jan. 16. Christopher Greene married to Esq. Lippits Daughter the same Day one of Coll. Lows Daughters married to Warner.
    17. Very Cold a woman froze to Death near Providence, by ye Post the advice came who See her Lye near a fence By ye Rhoad.

Jan. 20. Another of Coll. Stephen Lows Daughters married to B^n Spencer.
  23. Capt. Charles Holden married To Widdow Martin a Very agreeable match which is generally allowed by all.
  27. This Day about 4 P. M. my Son Thomas Died after a long Illness, aged 5 months & 11 Days I buried him a Newtown the Preachers were Unk^e E. Greene El^{dr} J. Gorton & Capt C. Holden."
Feb. 25. Capt. Esek Hopkins arrived with a prize.
  28. Now up as far as Pawtuxet."

The above is on the margin of the 10th page. On the margin of the 75th page is the following note:

"24th December 1758 a fire Broke out in the Court house at Providence by which means (I am told) consumed to the Ground and one more of ye houses near by Suffered the same fate—a Sadd affair for ye Government."

Falling stars, earthquakes, violent storms, and casualties of various kinds, including the hanging at Providence of an Indian named Absalom, are carefully noted. Among the deaths and burials mentioned, are Judge Benjamin Greene and his son, Gov. William Greene, Richard Greene, "Father" Greene, "Uncle" Fones Greene, John Greene of Potowomut, Abraham Coggeshall, Col. Daniel Updike of North Kingstown, and many other noteworthy Rhode Island citizens of that period. He mentions having attended a meeting at North Kingstown, where he met a multitude of people and saw Pardon Tillinghast, the son of his oft-named friend Philip, baptized.

His frequent use of local Indian names and of old colonial family names serves to carry our minds back to the middle of the last century, and his many incidental accounts of homely hospitalities, together with the mention of "Old Phillis," remind us of scenes in the Narragansett country depicted by Wilkins Updike and Shepherd Tom.

The leading objects of this paper are:

1. To awaken interest in almanac literature, with a view to save from devouring flames and remorseless paper mills the almanacs that may yet be found in the trunks, drawers and attics of various families in different parts of the State.

2. To acquire the means of completing imperfect series of almanacs, and obtain information about, if not a copy of, every almanac that has been either printed in Rhode Island or edited by a Rhode Island citizen.

3. To make a grateful acknowledgment of gifts for our almanac department, with special mention of the librarian of the Massachusetts Historical Society, the librarian of the Congregational Library, Boston, and Messrs. John C. Stockwell and Henry T. Drowne of New York city.

4. To prompt some persons to undertake the task of furnishing a list of all our city, town and State directories, church manuals, and gravestone inscriptions in church yards.

5. To urge the strict observance of the *common law* requiring every Rhode Island author or publisher to place a copy of his work in the archives of this society.

NEWPORT, 28th of ye 4th Mo., 1758.

DEAR FRINDS,

As we have bin informed that there is some of the frinds of Smithfield that has not yet proxed for Governor, we think it would be advisable at this time, for them to use their interest in favor of Governor Hopkins, as we have reason to think his opponent is not so moderate a man as we think is proper to sustain such a post at a time when there seems to be the greatest necessity to have a Governor that will act with clemency and moderation towards us as a people is the general sentiment of frinds this way and if frinds your way could find freedom to give him your votes hope it will prove to your and to our satisfaction who is your frinds.

SAMUEL DYER, *Capt.*   TIM WATERHOUSE,
JAMES EASTER, *Lieut.*   PETER TAYLOR,
DANIEL GODDARD, *Justice,* DAVID EARLE,
JOHN GODDARD,   THOS. ROBINSON.
JOHN WANTON,

THE HOPKINS-WARD LETTERS OF 1757.

CONTRIBUTED BY RAY GREENE HULING, FITCHBURG, MASS.

(*Continued from page 263, Vol. III.*)

THE REPLY OF SAMUEL WARD.

TO THE HON. STEPHEN HOPKINS, ESQ;

SIR,

You have lately printed a Piece filled with many severe and unjust Reflections on many Members of the lower House of Assembly; and as I had the Honor of being one of that House, I think myself oblig'd, in Justice to my own Character, and in Vindication of those other Gentlemen who were of the same Sentiments, to take Notice of that Performance.

EVERY Member of the General Assembly has a Right to make Use of his own Understanding, to form the best Judgment he can of public affairs, and to vote and act according to that Judgment. To charge then a great Part of the lower House with abusing their Power, in order to perplex and obstruct those Measures which were necessary for the public Good, only because they opposed the Raising of Men, when their being rais'd, could answer no other Purpose than putting the Colony to a vast Trouble and Expence, and to put Money into the Pockets of a few Men, is an Instance of great Want of Candor and Modesty in those who thus accuse them, and discovers how weak that Cause is, which is supported by such Means.

THE lower House was truly sensible of the Danger their Country was in, but as this Colony contains but an Handful of Men, they imagin'd our raising of Soldiers, unless in Conjunction with, and in Proportion to the neighbouring Governments, would be of no Service to the common Cause, but would greatly weaken and distress this Colony, and thereby disable us from hereafter effectually distressing the Enemy. Upon this Principle they oppos'd the Raising of Men. And what has been the Consequence of our raising so great a Number? By our extravagant Forwardness the last year, the Colony has been put to an intolerable Expence, and this year we are oblig'd to send an hundred Men more than our due Proportion.

YOU go on to charge them with misrepresenting every Step that has been taken, and as an Example, mention some Reflections that have been cast upon the Committee of War. That the Commissions granted that Committee are too large, is the Opinion of most Men who have no Connections with those Gentlemen: And that the Vote for allowing those Commissions was unfairly obtained, is very evident. There was a Debate in the lower House concerning the Allowance to be made to the Committee of War; some proposed One and an Half *per Cent.* and some *Two;* upon examining the Voices, it was a Tye-Vote, and the Speaker (who is one of that Committee) turn'd it for *Two per Cent.* But in Justice to Mr. *Bours* and Mr. *Jenckes,* I must observe that those Gentlemen generously declined voting in that Affair.

You positively assert, that "the Committee were always willing to leave to the General Assembly what Allowance they ought to have for their Trouble." This, Sir, I must tell you, is not true; for at last *February* Sessions, a Vote pass'd the lower House, that the Committee instead of *Two,* should have but *One per Cent.* for the future; but the upper House non-concurred with that Vote, and you in particular declar'd publicly, that they could not afford to transact the Business for less than *Two per Cent.* and offer'd to resign your Place; which plainly shews, that instead of submitting to the General Assembly what Allowance you should have, you chose to take Advantage of the Act already pass'd, tho' obtain'd in the Manner I have related.

You proceed next to the Raising the Four Hundred Men; and notwithstanding all your Misrepresentations of that Affair, I am of the Opinion, that every impartial Person will still think, that if you had done your Duty, this great Expence would have been sav'd to the Government.

When the Earl of *Loudoun's* Letter of the 20th of August was laid before the Assembly, they ordered Expresses to be sent to the neighbouring Governments, to acquaint them, that we would raise our Proportion of any Number of Men necessary for the general Defence. The Expresses return'd and inform'd us, that they believ'd that the neighbouring Governments would not raise any Men. Upon that, many Members thought that the small Number of Men we could raise, could do no Service against the Enemy: And as the Expense of raising them would be very great, they voted against it; but you press'd the Affair, and a Company of sixty Men was order'd. Now, had your Honor upon the Passing that Act, return'd an Answer to his Lordship's Letter, and acquainted him with what the Assembly had voted, as you might very easily have done, it is plain to a Demonstration, by his Lordship's Letters, that he would have made no other Demand, and consequently that extravagant Expence would have been sav'd to the Colony: But the not answering this Letter you endeavor to get rid of, by throwing the Blame upon the General Assembly for not ordering an Answer to be wrote. How trifling this Excuse is, will easily appear, by only observing, that this never prevented your answering other Letters; and that you, so far from waiting for Orders, have actually answer'd Letters during a Session of Assembly, without communicating the Contents to the Assembly. And how your Honor could say, "there was a Committee appointed for that Purpose," I can't conceive; for every Member of the Assembly well knew, that that Committee was appointed before the sixty Men were order'd, before you was chosen to wait upon his Lordship, and that they were to draw an Address, in which their Instructions were only to congratulate his Lordship upon his Arrival in America, and lay before him a State of the Colony; which (as the Vote says) they were to lay before that Assembly. And upon your being chosen to go, one of that Committee observed to the House, that 'as the chief Magistrate 'of the Colony was going in Person, it was unnecessary to draw 'up an Address,' to which the House acceded; and upon this, the Committee did nothing more in the Affair.

ANOTHER extraordinary Assertion is that you "did not press the Raising these Men." In what Manner can the Governor of a Colony give greater Encouragement to, and more strongly press the raising Men, than by offering to leave his Government to take the Command of them? And if you really thought, as you assert, that "it was too late in the Year for those Men to be of any Service," it was your Duty to inform the General Assembly of it, which would have entirely prevented this Expence. But to finish this affair, I think it fully appears, your Honor could have saved this Expence two Ways: *First*, by writing or ordering a Letter to be wrote to the Earl of *Loudoun*, which would entirely have prevented his demanding them. And, *secondly*, by opposing their being raised: To neglect then an Affair of so much Importance, and to encourage the Raising so large a Number of Men at a vast Expence, when you thought there was little likelihood of their being useful, discovers how little Regard you have for your distressed Country, and how little Reason you have to boast so much of your Diligence and Faithfulness to the Colony.

You observe, Sir, that "no Set of Officers, let their Pretentions "be what they will, can carry on the Operations of War without "Expences." I know of no Gentlemen who pretend to it. The utmost that can be expected from any, is, that all unnecessary Expences shall be avoided, and that they will not get all profitable Places into their own Hands, nor be influenced by any other motives than the Good of the Public.

You also observe, that "no civil Broils, Dissentions, and Dis- "putes, will make us more, but less able, to withstand the common "Enemy." This Observation is just; but pray, Sir, who is the Occasion of all these Broils?

When Mr. GREENE was at the Head of Government, there was no murmuring nor complaining in the Colony; but you propos'd yourself as a Candidate against him, and a vast Deal of Pains was taken to turn him out; but the People were so sensible of Mr. *Greene's* wise, just, and moderate Government, that he could not be remov'd. He served another year, and probably would have serv'd till this Time; for he resign'd not his Post because he was *worn out*, as you ungenerously, and very unjustly, insinuate, but because he saw a strong Party forming, and having nothing in View but the Good of his Country, did not choose to engage in Party-broils. Upon his Resignation, your Honor came in, and so many and so great are the Complaints against the Administration, that most of the principal Gentlemen in the Colony have applied to Mr. *Greene* to take the Government upon him again; he at first declined; but tir'd with Solicitations, and griev'd for the Distresses of his Country, he at length consented; not in order to raise civil Dissentions, but to suppress a violent Party, that have engrossed all the Power of the Colony into their own Hands; and by their bad Conduct, have brought the Colony to the very Brink of Destruction. But notwithstanding Mr. *Greene* behaved in this prudent Manner, you charge him, and all that oppose you, with acting upon Party Principles, and say, they ought to be looked upon as Enemies to their Country. Is not this a most ungenerous and ungentleman-like Reflection? But let the World judge who are the best Friends to their Country those who have maintained themselves and their Families out of the public Money, or those who have generously serv'd the Colony, without any Way consulting or promoting their own private Interest?

I SHALL take no further Notice of the high Encomiums upon your own Administration, which take up so great a Part of your Performance, than just observe, that those Gentlemen certainly stand in Need of Applause, who are forc'd to praise themselves; and that Administration must be very bad, which none commend, but those who are concerned in it.

You conclude, Sir, with saying, that "neither the Pleasure nor "Profit of the Office, but your Duty to God and your Country, "prevents your resigning your Post." But when a Man is seen to use every Art to gain for himself and his Family, Posts of Profit, and to make the most of every Employment, it is very natural to believe, such a Man is influenced by other Motives than those of Love to God and his Country. And lest I should be reproach'd, with "not having reduc'd my Complaints to any Certainty," you'll excuse my taking Notice, that your Honor is one of the Committee of War, and in that Capacity, receive a large sum from the Government: That the last Year one of your Sons was Commissary for the Troops: That Another, during great Part of the Campaign, was employed as his Assistant at *Albany;* and upon his Return, was sent by you to *New-York*, to bring Home the Sterling Money; and tho' so utterly ignorant of the Business he was to transact, that he never took a Bill of Lading, nor Receipt of any Kind, for the Money, yet was allowed double the Sum that Messrs. *Richards* and *Coddington* were, who had put themselves to an extraordinary Expence for Buoys and Buoy-Ropes, for the Security of the Money: And let me add to all this, that your Honor demands and receives *Fifty* or *Sixty Pounds* for a Letter of Marque, and demand much more for a Commission for a Privateer, when Mr. *Greene*, during the last War, was contented with *Five Pounds*.

And here I must not omit the Affair of those Frenchmen who were imprisoned last Summer, agreeable to an Act of this Colony. They petitioned the Assembly for Leave to go off in some Vessel bound to a Neutral Place, and prayed that they might in the mean Time be allowed to come out of Goal, and confine themselves at some private House, offering to give Bond for their good Behaviour. The first Part of their Petition was granted, to wit, that they might go off to some Neutral Port, but the latter Part the Assembly would by no Means grant. Notwithstanding which, in a few Days after the Assembly rose, your Honor took them out of Goal, allowed them to go up to *Providence*, and to live at Large without any Bondsmen. Upon Complaints being made of it to the Assembly, they voted that the Sheriff of the County of *Newport* should immediately go to *Providence* and bring them back, and confine them in Goal. This Vote, after lying some Days in the upper House, was return'd non-concurr'd, because you had promis'd in a Grand Committee of both Houses, that at your own Expence you would remand them to the Goal; which was never done, but they were sent off to the *West-Indies* soon after, and the Person who carried them, had several hundred Pounds for it. And here I must take the Liberty to ask you, whether breaking a Promise made to both Houses of Assembly, is consistent with your Duty to God? and whether treating our inveterate Enemies in such a Manner, discovers any great Regard for your Country? And is not taking Men out of Goal who were put in by Law, and continued in by the legislative Power of the Colony, acting in a tyrannical and arbitrary Manner, and actually subverting the Constitution of the Government, and assuming a Power not even pretended to by any King of *England* since *James* the Second?

MANY other Instances of your Conduct might be mentioned, which are inconsistent with the public Good; but enough has been said, not only to justify, but to shew the absolute Necessity of the Opposition which has been made: I shall therefore conclude, with observing, that when the Governor of a Colony has so little Regard to his Character, as to print absolute Falshoods, and is so fond of his Post, as to stick at Nothing to keep it, the World will judge what Sense he has of his Duty to God and his Country.

I am, SIR,

Your Honor's

NEWPORT, 12th *April*, 1757.

Most Obed' Serv',

S. WARD.

A LIST OF THE BIRTHS OF SOUTH KINGSTOWN, R. I.

From Records in Town Clerk's Office.

CONTRIBUTED BY THE EDITOR.

A.

Almy, Mrs. Abigail, servants.
    " Bristol, son of negro woman Phillis; Jan. 4, 1733.
    " Temera, daughter of negro woman Phillis; Feb. 2, 1748.
Allen, Christopher, of Samuel and Margaret; Feb. 8, 1748.
    " Deliverance, " " Mar. 17, 1751.
    " Mary, " " Feb. 3, 1754.
    " Deborah, of Benjamin and Waitstill; Mar. 10, 1753.
    " Waitstill, " " Sept. 26, 1754.

B.

Babcock, Mary, of Samuel and Bethiah; Dec. 18, 1721.
    " Jonathan, " " Nov. 26, 1723.
    " Samuel, " " Nov. 5, 1725.
    " John, " " Jan. 27, 1727–8.
    " Job, " " Jan. 20, 1729–30.
    " Simon, " " Jan. 6, 1731–2.
    " James, " " June 14, 1734.
    " Joseph, " " Oct. 4, 1737.
    " Mary, of Jonathan and Elizabeth; Sept. 1, 1724.

Babcock, Caleb, of Hezekiah and Mary ; Dec. 7, 1740.
" Peleg, " " April 18, 1742.
" Caleb, of Hezekiah and Mary ; July 10, 1741.
" Stephen, of Simeon and Elizabeth ; July 19, 1751.
" Bethiah, " " Dec. 1, 1752.
" Champlain, of Job (of Samuel) and Susannah ; Oct. 10, 1752.
" Elizabeth, " " " Feb. 27, 1775.
" George, of George and Mehitable ; Sept. 22, 1753.
" Lucy, " " Dec. 15, 1754.
" Cyrus, " " Dec. 11, 1756.
" Mary, " " Jan. 17, 1767.
" Frederic, " " Sept. 10, 1771.
" James, of James and Sarah ; Jan. 22, 1755.
" Sarah, of Jonathan and Amie ; Oct. 30, 1755.
" John, " " Aug. 18, 1757.
" Elizabeth, " " Nov. 28, 1760.
" Amie, " " July 2, 1763.
" Thankful, " " Feb. 15, 1766.
" Seager, " " May 8, 1769.
" Gideon, of John and Jemima ; April 28, 1757.
" Joseph, " " Aug. 19, 1759.
" Mary, " " Feb. 4, 1762.
" Ephraim, of George and Mehitable ; May 19, 1758.
" Susannah, " " May 2, 1760.
" Thomas Wheeler, of George and Mehitable ; Aug. 13, 1773.
" Mehitable of Peleg and Lucy ; Sept. 23, 1770.
" Esther, " " May 24, 1772.
" Peleg, " " July 14, 1774.
" George P., " " Oct. 19, 1776.
" Lucy, " " Dec. 2, 1778.
" Mary, " " Mar. 22, 1781.
" Joseph P., " " Jan. 17, 1783.
" Waity, " " Jan. 22, 1787.

Babcock, Susannah, of Peleg and Lucy; Jan. 22, 1787.
" Ethan, " " Aug. 7, 1789.
" Charles, " " Mar. 14, 1792.
" Abigail, " " Oct. 26, 1795.
" Frances Hazard, of Peleg and Lucy; Sept. 5, 1798.
" Amie, of Gideon J. and Hannah; Dec. 27, 1777.
" John, " " Feb. 1, 1780.
" Samuel, " " Mar. 22, 1782.
" Henry, " " Aug. 3, 1784.
" Hannah, " " July 1, 1786.
" John, " " Feb. 1, 1780.
" Samuel, " " Mar. 22, 1782.
" Henry, " " Aug. 3, 1784.
" Hannah, " " July 1, 1786.
" Charles, " " July 24, 1791.
" Lydia, " " Aug. 12, 1795.
" Joseph Browning, of Wm. Browning and Mary; Mar. 6, 1810.
" Frederic, of Frederic and Nancy; May 31, 1820.
Barber, Moses, of Moses, Jr. and Elizabeth; Feb. 25, 1705-6.
" William, " " Sept. 4, 1707.
" John, " " April 19, 1709.
" Elizabeth, " " Mar. 18, 1711.
" Nicholas, " " Dec. 23, 1713.
" Bridget, " " Jan. 23, 1715-16.
" Daniel of Moses and Susannah; April 22, 1715.
" Anna, " " Oct. 8, 1717.
" Sarah, of Samuel and Ann; Nov. 28, 1719.
" Mary, " " June 12, 1721.
" Benjamin, " " May 30, 1723.
" Martha, of Thomas and Avis; Oct. 9, 1726.
" Dinah, " " May 3, 1729.
" Thomas, " " June 5, 1731.
" Mary, " " Aug. 18, 1733.
" Zebulon, " " Jan. 22, 1736.
" Lydia, of Benjamin and Mary; April 16, 1730.

Barber, Henry, of James, Jr. and Eliza; Mar. 20, 1810.
Bates, Ruth, of Hezekiah and Elizabeth; July 4, 1746.
" Nathan, " " Sept. 18, 1750.
Belcher, Louis H., of Gideon and Eunice; Dec. 21, 1839.
Bentley, John, of William and Rachel; Sept. 24, 1755.
" Sarah, " " Oct. 11, 1757.
" Aggrippa, " " Oct. 14, 1759.
" Samuel, " " July 24, 1761.
" Charlotte, " " April 21, 1765.
Berry, Elizabeth, of Richard and Susannah, Aug. 18, 1727.
Billington, Jane, of Joseph and Abigail; Nov. 13, 1762.
" Elisha, " " June 24, 1768.
" Abigail, " " June 24, 1768.
Brayman, Jane; Oct. 28, 1695.
" James; Nov. 17, 1697.
" Mary; May 4, 1700.
" Joseph; Mar. 24, 1703.
" Benjamin; Apr. 3, 1705.
" John; Mar. 15, 1707.
" Freelove; Jan. 11, 1708.
" Abigail, wife of Joseph; Nov. 29, 1700.
" Sarah, of Joseph and Abigail; Feb. 19, 1725.
" Abigail, " " Dec. 23, 1727.
" Joseph, " " Feb. 23, 1729.
" Ann, " " Aug. 12, 1731.
" Thomas, " " Apr. 23, 1734.
" John, " " May 2, 1737.
" Paul, " " July 21, 1743.
Briggs, Charles W., of Palmer and Amie; July 21, 1813.
Browning, William, of William and Mary; Nov. 28, 1724.
" Wilkinson, " " July 14, 1731.
" John, " " July 26, 1733.
" Mary, " " June 10, 1735.
" Dinah, " " Sept. 10, 1736.
" William, of William, Jr., and Elizabeth; Apr. 21, 1756.

Browning, Christopher, of William, Jr., and Elizabeth, Sept. 25, 1758.
" Rebecca, of William, Jr., and Elizabeth, Mar. 13, 1762.
" Mary, of Joseph and Mary; Mar. 14, 1762.
" Susannah, " " Aug. 26, 1764.
" William, " " Sept. 5, 1767.
" Thomas K., of Thomas and Anne; Jan. 20, 1811.
Brown, Mary, of Samuel, Jr., and Sarah; Apr. 25, 1735.
" Anstis, of John and Ruth; Oct. 15, 1742.
" John, " " Jan. 14, 1744.
" Susannah, " " July 10, 1747.
" Penelope, " " Aug. 10, 1749.
" Ruth, " " July 5, 1751.
" Lucy, " " Feb. 24, 1755.
" Hannah, " " Apr. 6, 1757.
" Lydia, " " July 16, 1759.
" George, " " Sept. 27, 1761.
" Elisha, " " Nov. 24, 1763.
" George, of Robert and Sarah; Jan. 10, 1745.
" William, " " Sept. 13, 1747.
" John, " " Dec. 15, 1748.
" Franklin, " " May 25, 1750.
" Abigail, wife of Joseph; Nov. 29, 1700.
" Abiel, of Jeremiah and Hannah; June 17, 1746.
" Jeremiah, " " Jan. 7, 1747.
" Joseph, " " Sept. 29, 1749.
" Benjamin, " " Nov. 4, 1753.
" Joanna, of Hezekiah and Sarah (l. of Prov.); Oct. 13, 1746.
" Sarah, " " Jan. 16, 1748.
" Christopher, of Zephaniah and Alice; Feb. 16, 1756.
" Mary, " " Dec. 28, 1757.
" Alice, " " Feb. 17, 1761.
" Freelove, " " Mar. 4, 1763.
" Darius, " " Mar. 3, 1766.

Brown, Sarah, of Zephaniah and Alice; Aug. 13, 1768.
" Robert, of Robert and Elizabeth; Nov. 19, 1763.
" Susannah, wife of Robert, (Hopkinton); Dec. 14, 1770.
" Peter C., of Robert and Susannah; Mar. 15, 1792.
" Barker W., " " Dec. 8, 1793.
" Robert, " " Dec. 16, 1795.
" Phillip, " " Sept. 26, 1797.
" George Wells, " " Oct. 21, 1799.
" Henry, " " Jan. 17, 1803.
" Edmund, " " Feb. 10, 1805.
" David, " " Sept. 13, 1807.
" Benjamin, of Jeremiah, Jr., and Eleanor; June 6, 1777.
" Amie, " " Feb. 14, 1779.
" Hannah, " " Nov. 19, 1780.
" Jeremiah, " " Nov. 16, 1782.
" John, " " Nov. 19, 1784.
" Benjamin Brenton, of Silas and Frances; July 11, 1797.
" Silas, " " Jan. 2, 1800.
" Fannie, " " Feb. 18, 1803.
" Susannah, " " June 22, 1807.
" Elizabeth, " " Oct. 4, 1808.
" Sarah Ann, " " Apr. 2, 1810.
" Benj. Brenton, " " June 28, 1811.
" Lucy, of Palmer and Mary; Aug. 5, 1814.
" Robert Champlain, of Palmer and Mary; Mar. 24, 1816.
" Peleg, " " Oct. 29, 1817.
" Laura, " " Aug. 5, 1819.
" Palmer Armstrong, " " Apr. 17, 1821.
" Mary, " " Feb. 6, 1823.
" Sally Stanton, of James H. and Hannah S.; Mar. 20, 1822.
" James Dennis, " " Mar. 10, 1824.
" Hannah Maria, " " Mar. 2, 1826.

Brown, Mary Ann, of James H. and Hannah S.; Apr. 22, 1828.
Bull, Hannah, of Ephraim and Patience; Sept. 26, 1727.
" Ephraim, " " Sept. 6, 1729.
" Jireh, " " Jan. 15, 1731-2.
" Joseph, " " Feb. 18, 1733-4.
" Catherine, " " May 9, 1736.
" Hannah, 2d, " " Aug. 4, 1738.
" Thomas, " " Nov. 7, 1740.
" John, " " Feb. 19, 1742-3.
" Patience, " " Aug. 13, 1745.
" John, of Isaac and Rebecca; May 15, 1732.
" Elizabeth, of Timothy and Patience; Jan. 8, 1744.
" Aaron, of Nathan and Abijah; Aug. 27, 1746.
" Mary, of Joshua and Sarah; Jan. 15, 1766.
Burdick, George S., of Stephen and Mary; Dec. 28, 1861.
" Mary E., " " Dec. 28, 1861.

C.

Casey, Edmund, of Gideon and Jane; Aug. 16, 1747.
" Gideon, " " June 17, 1751.
" Sarah, " " Jan. 14, 1754.
" Mary, of Samuel and Martha; Feb. 7, 1754.
" Samuel, " " Feb. 4, 1758.
" William, " " July 15, 1760.
" Willett, " " Feb. 14, 1764.
Case, Mitchell, of Joseph and Elizabeth; May 29, 1722.
" Amie, of Emanuel and Hannah; Dec. 4, 1825.
" Hannah, " " Nov. 12, 1727.
" Mary, " " Aug. 19, 1730.
" Joseph, " " Jan. 27, 1732.
" Penelope, " " July 27, 1736.
" Emmanuel, " " Nov. 8, 1739.
" Susannah, of William and Mercy; July 30, 1733.
" William, " " June 22, 1735.
" Mercy, " " Oct. 11, 1737.

Case, Abigail, of Sanford and Mary; May 24, 1745.
" Hannah, " " Aug. 29, 1746.
" Alexander, " " Nov. 19, 1747.
" William, of Emmanuel and Ann; Aug. 17, 1762.
" Ann Maynard, " " June 23, 1766.
" John Peck, " " Dec. 18, 1774.
" Thomas Allen, of Emmanuel and Lydia; Mar. 30, 1783.
Carpenter, Samuel, of Solomon and Deborah; April 4, 1733.
" Joseph, " " June 22, 1736.
" Elizabeth, " " May 10, 1741.
" Jeremiah, of Daniel and Renewed; April 13, 1734.
" Sarah, " " Oct. 10, 1736.
" Jonathan, " " Aug. 2, 1739.
" Elizabeth, " " Oct. 2, 1741.
" Daniel, " " Sept. 8, 1744.
" Renewed, " " Aug. 4, 1746.
" Margaret, " " Sept. 1, 1749.
" Mercy, " " Dec. 8, 1752.
" Hannah, " " June 29, 1754.
" James, " " Feb. 26, 1756.
" Mary, " " Dec. 11, 1759.
" Stephen, " " May 31, 1763.
" Solomon, of Samuel and Deborah; April 21, 1754.
" Ephraim, of Jeremiah and Abigail; May 25, 1753.
" Dorcas, " " June 5, 1755.
" Sarah, " " Aug. 30, 1757.
" Esther, " " Jan. 1, 1760.
" Susannah, " " April 9, 1762.
" Jeremiah, " " June 23, 1764.
Campbell, Charles, of Charles and Martha; July 7, 1733.
" Mary, " " May 31, 1735.
" George, " " June 26, 1739.
Champlain, Stephen, of Stephen and Mary; Sept. 29, 1734.
" Hannah, " " Jan. 20, 1735.
" Sarah, " " Aug. 18, 1737.
" Mary, " " April 14, 1739.

Champlain, Susannah, of Stephen and Mary ; Mar. 26, 1742.
" Jeffrey, " " Mar. 21, 1744-5.
" Robert, " " April 12, 1747.
" Hazard, of Thomas and Hannah ; Sept. 13, 1754.
" Mary, of Stephen and Dinah ; June 26, 1760.
" Stephen, " " Aug. 3, 1763.
" Hannah, " " June 5, 1765.
" Susannah, " " Dec. 9, 1772.
" Thomas H., of Thomas and Hannah ; Oct. 9, 1768.
" Mary, of Jeffrey (of Stephen) and Mary ; April 7, 1769.
" Stephen Gardiner, of Jeffrey (of Stephen) and Mary ; Jan. 31, 1771.
" Robert, of Robert and Mary ; Nov. 1, 1769.
" Sarah, " " June 1, 1771.
" John, " " April 7, 1773.
" Robert H., of Stephen and Mary ; Oct. 18, 1796.
" Ann, " " Feb. 26, 1798.
" Mary, " " Oct. 7, 1799.
" Stephen, " " Mar. 12, 1801.
" Sarah, " " Mar. 4, 1803.
" George, " " Mar. 11, 1805.
" John B., " " Dec. 28, 1807.
" Abigail, " " Jan. 3, 1810.
Chappell, William, of Caleb and Sarah ; Nov. 25, 1757.
" Holley, " " May 15, 1759.
" Frederic, " " July 1, 1761.
" William, " " July 5, 1764.
" Susannah, " " Sept. 19, 1766.
Clarke, Emmanuel, of Benjamin ; April 4, 1697.
" Latham, of William and Hannah ; Nov. 19, 1724.
" John, " " Jan. 13, 1726.
" Benjamin, of Emmanuel and Margaret ; July 12, 1728.
" Mary, of Latham (of Samuel of Jamestown) and Mary ; Sept. 2, 1748.
" Wm. Case, of John, Jr. and Mercy ; July 21, 1756.

Clarke, Sarah, of John, Jr., and Mercy; Sept. 23, 1758.
" Hannah Niles, of Samuel and Sarah; Jan. 17, 1777.
" Latham, " " Mar. 31, 1778.
" Silas Niles, " " Feb. 10, 1780.
" Samuel, " " May 19, 1783.
" Mercy, of Wm. Case and Sarah; May 19, 1783.
" Mary Ann, " " July 18, 1785.
" John, " " Dec. 6, 1787.
" Nathaniel Helme, of Wm. Case and Sarah; Dec. 10, 1789.

Coggeshall, Hannah, of Joseph and Amey; Oct. 20, 1725.

Collins, Mary, of Hezekiah and Catherine; Sept. 6, 1736.
" Joseph, " " Apr. 18, 1738.

Comstock, Sarah, of Charles and Anne; Apr. 13, 1802.
" Joshua Perry, of Joseph and Sarah R.; Mar. 31, 1803.
" Mary, " " July 29, 1804.
" Esther, " " Feb. 12, 1806.
" Elizabeth, " " Mar. 16, 1809.
" Joseph Erasmus Darwin, of Joseph and Sarah R.; July 20, 1712.

Congdon, William, of Joseph and Mary; Jan. 1, 1724.
" Barberry, " " May 18, 1726.
" Mary, " " July 28, 1730.
" Samuel, " " Feb. 18, 1733.
" Mary, of William and Mary; June 5, 1729.
" Robert, " " Jan. 27, 1733.
" Sarah, " " May 9, 1735.
" Ann, of William (of Benj.) and Ann; Feb. 28, 1733.
" Hannah, " " Mar. 25, 1735.
" Joseph, of Samuel and Sarah; Mar. 1, 1758.
" Hannah, " " July 18, 1759.
" George, " " Dec. 9, 1760.
" Margeret, of Wm. (of James) and Rebecca; Oct. 24, 1759.

Congdon, Anne, of William and Rebecca ; Mar. 3, 1762.
" Thomas Taylor, " " Mar. 6, 1764.
" Sarah, " " Mar. 31, 1766.
" Stephen Champlain, of Sam'l and Susannah ; Dec. 9, 1805.
Cooke, Alice, of John and Elizabeth ; May 15, 1740.
" Sarah, " " June 14, 1742.
" George, " " Jan. 12, 1744.
Crandall, James, of Peter and Susannah ; Apr. 17, 1709.
" Mary, " " Feb. 17, 1711.
" Peter, " " July 4, 1713.
" John, " " June 18, 1716.
" Elizabeth, " " Feb. 1, 1718-19.
" Samuel, of Jeremiah and Elizabeth ; Sept. 18, 1750.
" Esther, " " Mar. 13, 1753.
" Jeremiah, " " Sept. 19, 1755.
" Dorcas, " " May 24, 1758.
Cross, Hannah, of Samuel and Ann ; Mar. 27, 1760.
Cottrell, Elizabeth, of Stephen, Jr., and Lydia ; Dec. 4, 1747.
" David, " " Apr. 7, 1752.
" Abel, of Thomas and Mary ; Oct. 22, 1747.
" Lydia, of Stephen and Lydia ; Apr. 6, 1755.
" Stephen, " " Aug. 20, 1758.
" Elizabeth, " " Sept. 3, 1761.
" William, of Thomas and Sarah ; Jan. 14, 1762.
" Thomas Paine, of John and Margeret ; June 28, 1768.
" Susannah, " " Oct. 29, 1770.
" Sarah, " " June 27, 1775.
" Susannah, " " Apr. 29, 1780.
" Abel, of Abel and Mary ; Feb. 9, 1771.
" Mary, " " Jan. 8, 1773.
" Silence, " " Apr. 11, 1775.
" James Arnold, of Abel and Mary ; June 22, 1777.
" Thomas, " " May 7, 1781.
" Margeret, " " Dec. 26, 1784.
" Benjamin Potter, " " May 30, 1788.

Curtis, Samuel, of Samuel and Amie; Aug. 14, 1747.
" Sarah, " " Feb. 25, 1752.

D.

Dickinson, Charles, of Charles and Mary; Feb. 27, 1716-7.
" Phillis, " " Mar. 17, 1718-9.
" Sarah, " " Jan. 18, 1722-3.
Dockray, Ann, of John Bigelow and Mary; Oct. 18, 1779.
" John Bigelow, " " Oct. 25, 1780.
" Mary, " " May 7, 1784.
Douglass, Maria, of George and Mary Ann; July 21, 1808.
" Eliza; June 30, 1811.
" William; May 10, 1813.
" Susan; May 12, 1816.
" Horace; Oct. 31, 1820.
" George Horace; Mar. 18, 1823.
Dyre, Hannah, of Charles and Penelope; Feb. 13, 1736-7.
" William, of William and Mercy; Oct. 11, 1749.

(To be continued.)

To William Peckham, Esq.

NEWPORT, 23 Aug. 1792.

SIR:—I passed your house yesterday with an intention to have called on you, but the Solemnity I was informed was about being performed in your family induced me to suspend the business I was pursuing of, as I may not have the opportunity to see you before the ensuing Election, I take the liberty to ask your interest in favor of Mr. Francis Malbone as a Representative to Congress. You may be assured he is a man of very good abilitys, and possesses a great share of Candour and Integrity and should he be elected I think he will do honour to the appointment. With due esteem

I am your friend,

GEO. CHAMPLAIN.

THE RECORD OF OLD SMITHFIELD FROM 1730 TO 1850.

From Records in Town Clerk's Office, Lincoln.

CONTRIBUTED BY THE EDITOR.

(*Continued from Vol. III., page 313.*)

MARRIAGES.

C.

Cady, Benejah, and Patience Shippee; m. by Thomas Lapham, justice, Sept. 13, 1759.
" Anne, and Gideon Man, recorded Jan. 30, 1792.
" Silvanus, of Benajah, and Sabra Whipple, of Gloucester, dau. of Thomas Shippee; m. by Edward Medbury, justice, Jan. 24, 1802.

Cahoone, Europe, and Walter D. Stone, Apr. 21, 1847.

Caldwell, George W., and Lucinda P. Davis; m. by Rev. C. H. Titus, Nov. 30, 1848.

Callom, Jemima, and William Ford, Mar. 26, 1749, Mar. 17, 1752.
" Daniel, and Lydia Buxton; m. by William Arnold, justice, Mar. 12, 1752.
" Hepsebeth, and Abram Harendeen, Aug. 2, 1786.
" Mrs. Roenna, and Daniel Bartlett, July 11, 1819.

Calvin, Aranda, and Stephen Sandborn, Apr. 13, 1840.

Caman, Joseph, and Peggy Jenckes; m. by Thomas Lapham, justice, Jan. 3, 1760.

Campbell, James H., of Plainfield, Conn., son of Bonaparte, of Griswold, Conn., and Amie M. Cozzens, of Charles, of Smithfield; m. by Rev. Mowry Phillips, May 20, 1849.

Capron, Margeret, and William Arnold, May 5, 1729.
" Charles, and Mary Scott; m. by William Arnold, justice, Dec. 16, 1742.
" Leah, and Joseph Scott, June 21, 1750.

Capron, Hannah, and Adam White, Jan. 25, 1767.
" Joseph, of Cumberland, son of Charles, and Sarah Arnold, of Thomas, of Smithfield, Feb. 22, 1776.
" Ruth, and Joseph Hendrick, Sept. 5, 1793.
" Lucy, and David Wilkinson, Apr. 9, 1809.
" Edwin, of Smithfield, and Deborah Angel, of Johnston, R. I.; m. at Johnston, by Rev. Elisha Sprague, Dec. 26, 1722.
" Dr. George, of North Providence, and Clariet Brown, of Smithfield; m. by Zalmon Tobey, justice, July 9, 1823.
Carey, Marvin, of Asa, of Portsmouth, R. I., and Desire B. Aldrich, of Amasa, of Smithfield; m. by Rev. Reuben Allen, May 11, 1840.
Cargill, James, and Sarah Aldrich; m. by William Arnold, justice, Feb. 23, 1743-4.
" Mary, and Seth Arnold, Oct. 25, 1750.
" Chloe, and Jonathan Jillson, Feb. 20, 1752.
" James, and Dorcas Arnold; m. by Thomas Arnold, justice, Dec. 7, 1752.
Carmont, Mary, and Robert Carvin, July 20, 1842.
Carpenter, John, and Mary Angel, widow of Daniel; m. by Rev. John Winsor, Feb. 13, 1796.
" Abigail, and Izreal Wilkinson, Dec. 9, 1813.
" William E., of Napau, N. Y., son of William, and Ely Loie Dexter, of Capt. John, of Smithfield; m. by Thomas Man, justice, Feb. 1, 1830.
" Ann F., and John C. Paine, Nov. 12, 1840.
" David, and Mary A. Davis, both of Foxboro', Mass.; m. by Rev. B. P. Byram, May 27, 1849.
Carroll, Joseph, of Walpole, Mass, and Abba Man, of John, of Smithfield, deceased; m. by Rev. Edward Mitchell, Nov. 2, 1786.
" Susan, and Samuel Ray, Apr. 8, 1813.
" James, and Mrs. Sally Blake; m. by Rev. Pliney Brett, Aug. 26, 1814.

Capron, James, and Nancy Hill; m. by Henry S. Mansfield, justice, Mar. 3, 1831.
" Sally B., and Stephen Slater, Jr., Dec. 23, 1839.
" Catherine, and William Gaskill, Feb. 17, 1850.
Carter, Eliza, and Albert Lockwood, Jan. 3, 1848.
Carvin, Robert, and Mary Carmont; m. by Rev. Asel D. Cole, July 20, 1842.
Case, Mrs. Susan, and John Place, Oct. 28, 1840.
" William S., and Cordelia Tyler, of Gardiner; m. by Rev. Mowry Phillips, July 12, 1846.
Cass, John, of Mendon, Mass., and Alice Brown, of Bellingham, Mass.; m. by Thomas Sayles, justice, Feb. 18, 1735-6.
" Mary, and Seth Cook, Apr. 5, 1739.
" Daniel, and Mary Cook; m. by William Arnold, justice, Apr. 7, 1744.
" Ebenezer, and Sarah Howard; m. by David Comstock, justice, Feb. 14, 1747.
" Oliver, and Amie Bartlett; m. by Stephen Sly, justice, Jan. 18, 1757.
" Hannah, and Jonathan Comstock, Feb. 19, 1761.
' Nathan, and Elizabeth Mussey; m. by Daniel Mowry, Jr., justice, Apr. 24, 1761.
" David, of John, of Richmond, R. I.; and Kezia Arnold, of Job, of Smithfield; m. by Welcome Arnold, justice, June 7, 1781.
" Marcy, and Heber Southwick, Dec. 14, 1804.
Castle, Nathan, Jr., of Douglass, Mass., son of Nathan and Apema Aldrich, of Sands, of Smithfield; m. by Caleb Farnum, justice, Nov. 28, 1816.
Chace, Joseph, and Mary Sherlock; m. by Stephen Sly, justice, Nov. 30, 1755.
" Coggeshall, and Amie Phillips; m. by Stephen Sly, justice, Jan. 31, 1765.
" Barnard, and Margery Pain; m. by Richard Sayles, justice, May 24, 1767.

Chace, Hannah, and David Read, May 16, 1790.
" Anna, and Izreal Arnold, Apr. 16, 1801.
" George, of Barnard, and Mary Smith, of Jeremiah; m. by Thomas Man, justice, Feb. 7, 1806.
" Adelia A., and Arnold Man, May 8, 1828.
" Alexander B., of John B., and Susan E. Bates, of Alice Esther Bates; m. by Rev. C. C. Taylor, June 4, 1842.
" George E., of Samuel, deceased, and Susan J. Phillips; m. by Rev. Warren Lincoln, Jan. 16, 1851.
Chamberline, George, of East Winsor, Conn., and Olive Beals, of Smithfield; m. by Rev. T. A. Taylor, May 3, 1848.
Chambers, William, and Hannah Hetock; m. by Rev. B. P. Byram, May 20, 1844.
Chapin, Moses Sanford, of Nathan, of Milford, Mass., and Martha Waite Comstock, of Henry, of Smithfield; m. by Arnold Spear, justice, Nov. 6, 1834.
" Nathan Tyler, of Milford, Mass., and Sarah Maria Comstock, of Smithfield; m. by Henry S. Mansfield, justice, Nov. 29, 1837.
Chapman, Oliver S., of Martin S. and Betsey, and Abbie D. Sweet, of Felix and Sarah; m. by Rev. J. J. Burguess, Dec. 23, 1849.
Charley, Abbie, and Sterry Jenckes, Sept. 2, 1821.
Charter, Rachel, and Hugh Thomas, Jan. 5, 1845.
Chatman, Olive, and Isaac Booker, Sept. 12, 1845.
Chatterton, Sarah, and Ellis Farrar, Apr. 2, 1846.
" Alfred, and Ellen Harris, both English; m. by T. A. Taylor, Sept. 17, 1849.
Checkery, Abigail, and Samuel Verry, Apr. 2, 1735.
Cheseborough, Phenia J., and L. S. Watkins, Jan. 27, 1847.
Chillson, Abigail, and Aaron Harendeen, June 10, 1734.
" Sarah, and Christopher Shippee, June 20, 1746.
" Jonathan, and Jane Harendeen; m. by Thomas Steere, justice, Feb. 9, 1757.

Chillson, John, and Sarah Newland; m. by Rev. Rufus Tefft, Oct. 20, 1787.
" Nancy, and Henry Peirce Greene, Feb. 23, 1815.
Critchley, Jane, and James R. Horswich, June 27, 1849.
Cinecome, Sarah G., and Charles Brown, Jan. 1, 1844.
Clapp, James H., and Alpha Maria Ballou; m. by Rev. T. A. Taylor, Feb. 25, 1841.
Clark, Sarah, and Peter Holbrook, Jan. 27, 1736-7.
" Robert, and Anna Taft, both of Uxbridge; m. by David Comstock, justice, Oct. 24, 1739.
" Tabitha, and William Hocker, Aug. 20, 1760.
" Ruth, and Daniel Aldrich, Nov. —, 1750.
" Mary, and Nebediah Brown, Sept. 4, 1757.
" Joseph, of Samuel, and Mary Foster, of Jesse; m. by Thomas Man, justice, Nov. 2, 1800.
" Anna, and Winsor Aldrich, Dec. 29, 1822.
" Alfred C., and Ann Thayer; m. by Ephraim Sayles, justice, July 12, 1840.
" Amie, and Thomas Burbank, June 8, 1841.
" Daniel S., of Daniel S., of Woodstock, Conn., and Amanda Malvina Freeman, of William; m. by Rev. William Verrinder, Apr. 5, 1846.
Clarke, Betsey, and Felix R. Kimball, Aug. 11, 1846.
" John, of John, and Cynthia Anthony, of Smithfield, dau. of Phillip, of Gloucester; m. by Rev. Junia S. Mowry, Sept. 10, 1846.
" Maria K., and Howard W. King, Jan. 11, 1847.
" Joshua S., (of Joshua and Mary, of South Kingstown, R. I.) and Cynthia A. Polsey, (of Adam and Lydia, of Cumberland); m. by Rev. J. J. Burguess, Dec. 7, 1848.
" Sarah, and John Balcome, Dec. 16, 1849.
" Daniel L., (of Daniel and Amie, born Killingly, Conn., now age 30,) and Lydia A. Stanley, (of William and Patience, of Cumberland, now age 26); m. by Rev. J. J. Burguess, Jan. 9, 1851.

Cleaveland, Moses, of Paris, and Julianna Nichols, of Joseph ; m. by Thomas Man, justice, Jan. 1, 1826.
Clemence, Richard, and Elizabeth Thomas; m. by Thomas Steere, justice, Feb. 4, 1749.
" Weight, of Richard, late of Smithfield, and Sarah Crossman, of Eleazer, late of Gloucester ; m. by Rev. Philemon Hines, Nov. 1, 1788.
" Laura Ann, and Willard Bradford, Mar. 29, 1841.
" Phebe S., and Francis Man, Dec. 25, 1843.
Clough, Freeman, and Phebe R. Hill, both of Providence; m. by Rev. B. P. Byram, July 29, 1849.
Coe, Benjamin, of John, and Mary Wilkinson, of Robert, deceased ; m. by Thomas Man, justice, Nov. 27, 1800.
" Ephraim, of John, and Deborah Mowry, of Jonathan ; m. by Samuel Man, justice, Oct. 27, 1808.
" Alden, of Benjamin, and Lydia Taft, of Brown; m. by Thomas Man, justice, Oct. 9, 1823.
" Robert W., and Nancy Pain, of Wilbur ; m. by Nathaniel Mowry, justice, Sept. 12, 1833.
Coggeshall, Sally, and Whipple Arnold, Feb. 26, 1839.
" Eleanor, and Leonard Scott Arnold, Aug. 12, 1839.
Colburn, Sarah, and Calvin W. Brown, May 8, 1836.
Cole, Mary, and Simeon Ballou, Apr. 1, 1762.
" Rebecca, and Elisha Sprague, Oct. 31, 1776.
" Samuel, and Permela Streeter, of George, Oct. 4, 1808.
" Precilla, and Benjamin Dexter, Nov. 28, 1840.
" Lucretia, and Alpheus Humes, Apr. 25, 1841.
" Amie Adelia, and Henry Austin, Dec. 30, 1841.
" Mason D., of Blackstone, son of Alpheus and Olive, and Betsey Burn, of Ezekiel and Esther ; m. at Waterford, Mass., by Rev. M. W. Burlingame, Jan. 14, 1849.
" Mary A., and Richard S. Burlingame, July 3, 1850.
Collins, Stephen, and Paulina Alger ; m. by Henry S. Scott, justice, Jan. 13, 1833.
" Thomas, of Thomas, and Almira Sweet, of James ; m. by Rev. Junia S. Mowry, Nov. 29, 1843.

Collins, Daniel S., and Sophronia Trask; m. by Rev. J. E. Gifford, May 1, 1850.
" Herman S., and Mary E. Trask; m. by Rev. J. E. Gifford, May 1, 1850.
" Rev. Barnabus, of Richard and Hope, of Dartmouth, Mass., and Thankful B. Leonard, of Nathan B. and Anstis, of Smithfield; m. by Rev. Warren Lincoln, Oct. 2, 1850.
Colwell, Anne, and Gardiner Aldrich, Mar. 22, 1789.
" Amie, and Robert Tucker, Jan. 28, 1798.
" Prudence, and Stephen Usher, Mar. 20, 1803.
" John, Jr., of John, and Sarah Mowry, of Jonathan; m. by Robert Harris, justice, June 6, 1813.
" Dianna, and Edward Evans, Mar. 26, 1840.
" Willard, and Laura Andrews, widow; m. by Rev. T. A. Taylor, June 12, 1845.
Comstock, Ichabod, and Zebiah Wilkinson, both of Providence, Sept. 13, 1722.
" Abigail, and Nathaniel Sprague, Oct. 1, 1733.
" Azariah, and Zerviah Sprague; m. by Thomas Sayles, justice, Apr. 20, 1735.
" Mary, and David Thompson, Nov. 18, 1735.
" Catherine, and Thomas Steere, May 16, 1736.
" Gideon, and Ruth Arnold; m. by Thomas Sayles, justice, Mar. 3, 1738-9.
" Daniel, and Martha Brown; m. by William Arnold, justice, Dec. 12, 1742.
" Anthony, and Mary Staples; m. by Thomas Sayles, justice, May 1, 1744.
" Mercy, and Amos Sprague, Apr. 7, 1745.
" John, and Ruth Comstock; m. by William Arnold, justice, Jan. 19, 1745-6.
" Ruth, and John Comstock, Jan. 19, 1745-6.
" Hezekiah, Jr., and Mary Arnold; m. by David Comstock, justice, Apr. 20, 1745.
" Rachel, and Anthony Steere, May 11, 1746.

Comstock, Ichabod, and Elizabeth Boyce; m. by William Arnold, justice, Mar. 26, 1746-7.
" Anne, and Joseph Comstock, June 7, 1747.
" Joseph, and Anne Comstock; m. by Thomas Sayles, justice, June 7, 1747.
" Deborah, and Enoch Arnold, June 23, 1747.
" Jeremiah, and Phebe Arnold; m. by David Comstock, justice, Oct. 25, 1747.
" James, and Mary Ephraim; m. by Thomas Steere, justice, July 6, 1750.
" Mirabah, and James Borden, Mar. 14, 1752.
" Lucy, and Moses Farnum, Dec. 17, 1752.
" Elizabeth, and John Malavery, Jan. 9, 1753.
" Martha, and John Farnum, Aug. 19, 1756.
" Ezekiel, of Smithfield, and Martha Arnold, of Gloucester; m. by Thomas Arnold, justice, June 30, 1757.
" Ichabod, and Sarah Jenckes; m. by Daniel Mowry, Jr., justice, Apr. 11, 1760.
" Jonathan, and Hannah Cass; m. by Stephen Sly, justice, Feb. 19, 1761.
" Nathan, and Abigail Arnold; m. by Ezekiel Comstock, justice, Jan. 2, 1763.
" William, and Rachel Aldrich; m. by Stephen Sly, justice, Feb. 21, 1765.
" George, and Catherine Arnold; m. by Stephen Arnold, justice, Mar. 9, 1765.
" Daniel, and Patience Jenckes; m. by Daniel Mowry, Jr., justice, Apr. 7, 1768.
" Anna, and David Ballou, June 9, 1770.
" Mary, and William Staples, Nov. 15, 1772.
" Jerusha, and Joseph Man, May 3, 1785.
" Rachel, and Trudiah Trush, Aug. 26, 1796.
" Enock, of Stephen, and Joanna Aldrich, of Samuel; m. by Benjamin Sheldon, justice, Dec. 25, 1800.

Comstock, Nathan, of Stephen, and Abi Paine, of Jonathan;
    m. by Edward Medbury, justice, Jan. 1, 1801.
"   Stephen, of Stephen, and Joanna Paine, of John;
    m. by Edward Medbury, justice, Jan. 1, 1801.
"   Isaac, of Dr. Ichabod, dec., and Mary Scott, of
    Jeremiah; m. by Thomas Man, Oct. 25, 1801.
"   Patience, and Elisha Arnold, Jr., Apr. 22, 1804.
"   Henry, of Ezekiel, and Clarissa Arnold, of Uriah;
    m. by Elijah Arnold, justice, Mar. 23, 1806.
"   Hannah, and James Aldrich, Sept. 25, 1808.
"   Welcome A., of Avisih, and Chloe Mowry; m. by
    Henry S. Mansfield, justice, Aug. 4, 1822.
"   Mary Elma, and Thomas J. Latham, May 14, 1829.
"   Martha Waite, and Moses Sanford Chapin, Nov.
    26, 1834.
"   Simon, of Smithfield, son of Stephen, and Phebe
    Thayer, of Burrillville, dau. of George; m. by
    Solomon Smith, justice, Mar. 19, 1835.
"   Abbie D., and David W. Aldrich, Oct. 13, 1836.
"   Sarah Maria, and Nathan Tyler Chapin, Nov. 29,
    1837.
"   Arnold, and Eliza C. Tucker; m. by Rev. T. A.
    Taylor, May 22, 1842.
Congdon, Sarah S., and Clovi H. Bowen, Apr. 30, 1840.
Connella, Hannah, and John E. Kins, June 10, 1849.
Cook, Benjamin, and Mary Cook; m. by David Comstock,
    justice, Mar. 26, 1739.
"   Mary, and Benjamin Cook, Mar. 26, 1739.
"   Seth, and Mary Cass; m. by William Arnold, justice,
    Apr. 5, 1739.
"   Elijah, and Joanna Bates; m. by David Comstock,
    justice, July 1, 1739.
"   Elisha, and Joanna Bates, July 1, 1739.
"   Joanna, and Ezekiel Ballou, July 3, 1740.
"   Peter, of Bellingham, and Elizabeth Bates, of Smith-
    field; m. by Thomas Sayles, justice, Sept. 24, 1741.

Cook, Peter, and Elizabeth Bates ; m. by do., Sept. 14, 1741.
" Nathaniel, and Martha Ballou ; m. by William Arnold, justice, Jan. 27, 1741-2.
" Aegal, and Keziah Titus ; m. by William Arnold, justic, Dec. 6, 1742.
" Josiah, Jr., and Sarah Atwell ; m. by William Arnold, justice, Dec. 23, 1742.
" Elisha, and Sarah Sly ; m. by David Comstock, justice, Jan. 27, 1742-3.
" David, and Hannah Ballou ; m. by William Arnold, justice, Feb. 3, 1742-3.
" Huldah, and Jeremiah Inman, Feb. 13, 1742-3.
" Abraham, and Mary Whipple ; m. by Thomas Sayles, justice, Dec. 15, 1743.
" Ebenezer, Jr., and Catherine Leonard ; m. by William Arnold, justice, Mar. 1, 1743-4.
" Mary, and Daniel Cass, Apr. 7, 1744.
" Thompson, and Joseph Ballou, Jr., June 7, 1744.
" Ebenezer, and Hannah King ; m. by William Arnold, justice, Feb. 13, 1745-6.
" Hezekiah, and Rachel Atwell ; m. by William Arnold, justice, June 6, 1746.
" Joseph, and Silence Mowry ; m. by Thomas Steere, justice, June 8, 1746.
" Samuel, and Sarah Smith ; m. by William Arnold, justice, Dec. 14, 1746.
" Daniel, and Elizabeth Scott ; m. by William Arnold, justice, Dec. 25, 1746.
" Elizabeth, and Abner Aldrich, Dec. 10, 1747.
" Margeret, and John Darling, Feb. 23, 1748-9.
" Presilla, and Peter Darling, Apr. 20, 1749.
" Mercy, and Benjamin Pickring, Mar. 29, 1750.
" Mary, and James Rogers, Nov. 2. 1750.
" Daniel, and Abigail Foot ; m. by William Arnold, justice, June 6, 1751.
" Abigail, and Joseph Thayer, Mar. 12, 1752.

Cook, Martha, and John Pain, ——, 1757.
" Benjamin, of Smithfield, and Huldah Mussey, of Mendon, Mass.; m. by Stephen Sly, justice, Jan. 18, 1758.
" Eunice, and William Sly, Nov. 5, 1761.
" Amie, and Stephen Mowry, May 20, 1762.
" Lillis, and Adonijah Blackmor, Apr. 22, 1768.
" Gideon, of Elisha, of Gloucester, and Jane Aldrich, of John, of Smithfield, Mar. 28, 1771.
" Temer, and John Sayles, 3d, Dec. 27, 1781.
" Patience, and Sylvester Mowry, Oct. 17, 1793.
" Destimoni, and James Southwick, May 24, 1812.
" Eliza, and George E. Hopkins, Oct. 11, 1840.
" Susan E., and Simeon G. Day, Aug. 31, 1843.
" Dr. Warner, and Elizabeth Arnold; m. by Rev. Emory W. Porter, Nov. 25, 1845.
" Mary S., and Stephen Y. Thurston, Oct. 15, 1846.
" Albert, and Phebe B. Gilmore; m. at Cumberland by Rev. John Barden, Jr., Sept. 24, 1848.
Coombes, Edwin, of Blackstone, Mass.; and Betsey M. Martin, of Smithfield; m. by Rev. T. A. Taylor, May —, 1844.
Cooper, Mercy, and Maturin Ballou, Feb. 28, 1759.
" Martha, and Daniel Mathewson, Mar. 2, 1764.
" Samuel, and Elizabeth Slocum; m. by John Farnum, justice, Apr. 20, 1766.
" Patience, and William Bates, Aug. 7, 1796.
" John, of Gloucester, son of Moses, Jr., and Unice Mowry, of Eleazur, of Smithfield; m. by Benjamin Sheldon, justice, May 24, 1801.
" Miriam B., and John M. Eddy, June 23, 1846.
Copeland, Abigail, and Joseph Billington, Dec. 27, 1840.
Corey, Martha, and Otis Tucker, Mar. 27, 1825.
" Sarah Ann, and Alvin E. A. Fisk, July 5, 1840.
Cornell, George, of Portsmouth, son of Hicks, and Abbie C. Humes, of Cogshall; m. by Rev. Junia Mowry, Nov. 5, 1843.

Cornell, Semanthe, and Nelson S. Mowry, May 29, 1845.
Cort, Alma A., and Nathaniel M. Ingalls, Mar. 2, 1851.
Cowen, Sarah, and Obediah Sprague, June 26, 1748.
   "   Sarah, and Esek Sayles, Dec. 30, 1776.
Cozzens, Mary E., and Geo. U. Hartwell, July 13, 1848.
   "   Amie M., and James H. Campbell, May 20, 1849.
   "   Eliza, and Alexander Smith, Apr. 13, 1851.
Cranston, Edward, and Louisa B. Pearce; m. by Henry S. Mansfield, justice, Nov. 28, 1822.
Cravin, Mary Ann, and Ezekiel Staples, June 18, 1846.
Crocker, Cynthia, and John Perry, Apr. 6, 1835.
Crosbee, Charles, resident of Smithfield, son of Benjamin, of Worcester, Mass., and Mary Dailey, of James, of Smithfield; m. by Ichabod Comstock, justice, Jan. 19, 1775.
Crossman, Eleazer, and Lydia Barnes; m. by Thomas Steere, justice, Apr. 29, 1747.
   "   Hannah, and Elijah Woodward, Jan. 30, 1763.
   "   Abiah, and Jerusha Young; m. by John Farnum, justice, Apr. 6, 1766.
   "   Sarah, and Weight Clemence, Nov. 1, 1788.
Crowell, Mary, and Darius Horton, Dec. 16, 1845.
   "   Paulina, and Wm. Henry Dean, Aug. 6, 1846.
Cruff, Thomas, Jr., and Sarah Man; m. by William Arnold, justice, July 1 or 2, 1745.
   "   Samuel, and Abigail Sprague; m. by William Arnold, justice, Mar. 15, 1746–7.
   "   Susannah, and Richard Thornton, Jan. 1, 1797.
   "   Artemus, of Samuel, and Anna Tefft, of Elder, Rufus; m. by Edward Medbury, justice, Aug. 14, 1800.
Cudworth, Sarah, and William Ellsbree, Jan. 27, 1846.
Curtis, Eliza Ann, and Sterry Smith, Oct. 16, 1842.
   "   Orin, and Elizabeth Burlingame; m. by Rev. T. A. Taylor, Aug. 7, 1843.
   "   Nathan J., and Dianna Young; m. by Rev. T. A. Taylor, June 2, 1844.

Curtis, Talcott, son of widow Huldah C., and Abigail Harris, of Jeremiah; m. by Rev. T. A. Taylor, Nov. 25, 1845.
Cushing, Louisa, and Arnold Smith, Feb. 27, 1834.
Cutler, Francis, of Holliston, Mass., and Mary A. Patt, of Cumberland; m. by Rev. E. M. Porter, Sept. 13, 1845.
Cutting, Joshua, of Worcester, Mass., son of Themial, of Boyleston, Mass., and Welthian A. Bentley, of Gardiner B., of Smithfield; m. by Rev. T. A. Taylor, Jan. 22, 1846.

(To be continued.)

THE MANOR LIVINGSTON LADIES.—Judge John Fitch, of New York, in an article in the *Home Journal*, says: Of the Livingston women, none will dispute me when I say (and I am a manor Livingston on the maternal line), that they are and have been among the most elegant, learned and refined women that this country has produced; wise and virtuous; devoted mothers, bringing up large families of children. They have married and intermarried with almost all the families of the State that fifty years ago held a conspicuous position in public esteem: the Jays, Clintons, Heywards, Astors, Armstrongs, Duanes, Campbells, Le Roys, Sanders, De Reysters, Ten Broecks, Johnsons, Crugers, Williamsons, Morrises, Bayards, Gerrys, Van Duzers, Du Bois', Cuttings, Lowises, Hamiltons, and they have perpetuated the characteristic marks of the manor Livingstons—the intellectual high forehead, massive brain, piercing black eye, with one eyebrow higher than the other; thick black hair. Invariably possessing fine conversational powers and a fund of general information, they have been, as a rule, vastly the superiors of the male descendants; polite, affable and high bred, ever ready to acknowledge modest merit and sterling worth; but difficult of approach by the vulgar upstart, as those who mingle in the refined society of New York, have so often seen.

THE STORY OF THE TABLETS.

I.

CONTRIBUTED BY JAMES L. SHERMAN, ESQ., PROVIDENCE, R. I.

THE editor of this Magazine, during his visits to the North Burial Ground, Providence, became deeply impressed with the beauty of the inscriptions on the Tablets erected here, and, also, with the fact how many distinguished persons they perpetuated the memory of. While here, he had the good fortune to find in Mr. Sherman a gentleman who at once entered heartily into his plans. Being familiar with the entire ground, he diligently set himself the task to copy accurately these inscriptions. Those presented in this paper give only a foretaste of what is yet to come, and we assure our readers they will find Mr. Sherman's paper very interesting reading.

In Memory of
THE HON. JOSEPH BROWN, ESQUIRE,
Who departed this Life Dec. 3, 1785,
In the 52d year of His age.
In the Course of his Life
He was a Representative for the Town of
Providence,
An Assistant to the General Court,
A Trustee of Rhode Island College,
A Professor of Experimental Philosophy, and
A member of the American Academy of
Arts & Sciences,
And of the Baptist Church here.
He descended from a Respectable line of Ancestors,
To which his Character added no inconsiderable luster.
The Faculties of his Mind were truly great & rare.
By the mere Force of Natural Genius,
He became an Adept in Electricity,

And well versed in Experimental Philosophy,
But his great Strength appeared in his favorite Study,
Mechanics.
He was a Patriot from Principle & zealous for His Country's
Freedom & Independence.
In his life were exemplified
Charity & Munificence Preëminently
With the other Virtues of an
Honest Man.
His disconsolable Widow, and Four Children
Have erected This Monument,
Of Conjugal & parental Tenderness,
And of their irreparable Loss.

In Memory of
Mrs. MARY HOWELL SHAW,
late wife of
Mason Shaw, Esq., of Castine,
and daughter of
David Howell, Esq., and Mary his wife.
She died at Castine, April 27, 1811,
Aged 31 years.
Her remains were interred here
May 22, 1811.
This Monument was Erected
by her affectionate Husband.
Here sweetly slumbers, 'till the just shall rise,
And God pronounce her welcome to the skies,
One, who, when ruined health found aid was vain,
Could nobly triumph o'er protracted pain.
In whom the charities of heart combined,
To meliorate the energies of mind,
When purest zeal, and liveliest fancy graced,
And reason wore the ornaments of taste.
With whom enthusiast—feelings warmest flame,
Consumed the selfish, in the social aim.

Her's the firm faith, that claim'd the fluttering breath;
And her's the holy hope, that lived in death.
Mother of babes, with every kindred grace,
An equal parent to an orphan race.
Each duty—bliss—of life within her call,
She felt—fulfilled—enjoyed—resigned them all.

Memoriâ in æternâ.
This Stone
Sacredly erected
by
His bereaved Widow
Anna Mauŕan Brown,
indicates the place of " final rest "
of what was mortal of
A. NICHOLAS BROWN,
eldest Son of the late
Hon. Nicholas Brown, Jr.
Born Sept. 16, 1832.
Died Aug. 12, 1864.
Requiescat in pace.

Also
An Infant Daughter, born Feb'y 5, 1859,
reposes here.
And a Son, born July 16, 1861.

In Memory of
MRS. MARY HOWELL,
The wife of
David Howell, Esquire,
And the daughter of
Jeremiah & Waitstill Brown.
She died July 6th, A. D. 1801,
In the 61st year of
her Age.

Unblam'd, unequall'd, in each Sphere of life,
The tenderest Daughter, Sister, Mother, Wife.
Her person lovely, good and great her mind,
In sickness patient, and in death resigned.
O Thou beyond, what Verse of Speech can tell,
My Guid, my Friend, my best Beloved, Farewell.

In Memory of
Mrs. Avis Brown,
Second Wife of
Nicholas Brown, Esquire,
And Daughter of
Captain Barnabas Binney
of Boston.

She possessed superior power of mind,
And was well versed in books,
And useful learning.
In the Holy Scriptures her knowledge
was preëminent, being an able
Defender of Gospel Doctrines.
She discharged with affection, every duty
To the children of her deceased husband,
Their extensive circle of friends,
And to the Ministers and Disciples
of her Divine Lord
And Saviour.
She died August 16, 1807,
Aged 58.

In Memory of
Mrs. Rhoda Brown,
Wife of Nicholas Brown, Esq.,
Who departed this Life
December 16th, 1783.
Aged 42 Years, 1 Month and 3 Days.

She was the Fifth Daughter of
The Hon. Daniel Jenckes, Esq.,
And Mrs. Joanna his Wife.
Given to Hospitality
She has often cheered the gloomy Mansions of
Poverty and Pain.
Nor was she less distinguished for the
culture of all those Virtues
Which add Dignity to the human Character;
Till her Tongue faultered in Death,
Her language was,
In my Distress I called upon the Lord my God,
Who enabled me to put my Trust wholly in Him,
And to declare what he had done for my Soul,
Now panting to be with Jesus.
My Flesh and weary Heart faileth
But God is the Strength of my Heart
And my Portion forever.
Whom have I in Heaven but Thee,
And there is none upon Earth
That I desire beside Thee.
Thou shall guid me by Thy Council
And afterwards receive me to
Glory.

HOPE BROWN,
Widow of
James Brown, Esq.
died June 8, 1792,
Aged Ninety Years, &
Six Months.
The mother of
Nicholas, Joseph,
John & Moses Brown.

The above is on a small slate stone in the Brown estate at North Burying Ground.

Sacred
To The Memory of
Mrs.
Alice Mason,
Relict of James B. Mason,
and daughter of the Hon. John Brown,
and Sarah his wife.
She departed this life Oct. the 3d, 1823,
in the 47th year of her age.
She has ta'en farewell!
Upon her hearth, the fire is dead,
The smoke in air has vanished;
The last, long, lingering look is given,
The shuddering start, the dying groan,
And the pilgrim on her way is gone.

Under this Monument
lie the remains
of the
Hon. James Brown Mason.
Having been a Trustee of Brown University
the place of his education,
Speaker of the General Assembly,
Major-General of the State of Rhode Island,
and a Representative in the Congress
of the United States.
He died August 31, 1819,
at the age of 44 years,
and 7 months.

In Memory of
William Man, who emigrated from
England, in 1636, and settled in
Cambridge.

Samuel Man, son of William, graduated
at Harvard College in 1642, and was
the first Minister in Wrentham.

Theodore Man, son of Samuel, died 1762
aged 82 years.

Thomas Man, son of Theodore, died 1809
aged 86 years.

AARON MAN,
Son of Thomas,
departed this life April 4, 1834,
in the 82d year of his age.
GRACE SPEARE WILLIS,
Relict of Aaron Man,
& Daughter of
Col. Josiah Flagg,
Born in Boston
Aug. 11, 1773:
Died in Providence
Oct. 29, 1843.

In Memory of Mrs. Sarah
Whipple ye Wife of Capt.
John Whipple. She was
Born in Dorchester in
New England, & Died in
Providence Anno Dom.
1666, Aged about 42
years.

In Memory of
Capt. John Whipple, who
was Born in England, &
Died in Providence Town
ye 16th Day of May Anno
Dom. 1,685, about 68
Years of Age.

The above are the two oldest stones in the North Burying Grounds, and are located 45′ W. of Eastern Ave., S. side of 1st Path S. of Lodge Ave.

REBEL TREATMENT OF TORIES DURING THE REVOLUTION.

No. V. INFORMATION AND TREATMENT OF SPIES.

From the Sheriff Brown Papers.

State of Rhode Island } To the Sheriff of the County of Kings
and Providence Plantations. } County or to his Lawful Deputy, GREETING.

Whereas, I have received undoubted information that a large fleet was seen yesterday afternoon between Block Island and Montauck steering for Newport, and most probably designed for to attack this state, I have therefore thought fit to call the Committee appointed to Act in the recess of the General Assembly to meet at the Court House in Providence this afternoon at four o'clock to Act and do whatever the Exigency of Affairs may require. You are therefore hereby in the Name of the Governor and Company of the State aforesaid to notify all the members of the Upper House of Assistants in your County, and such members of the lower house as you conveiently can to assemble together at the time and place and for the purpose aforesaid. Hereof fail not but make true return to me.

Given under my hand at Providence, in the State aforesaid this, third day of December, A. D. 1776 at two o'clock in the morning.

         NICH's COOKE, Gov'r.

Kings County, December ye 3d 1776, at 2 o'clock P. M.,

I received this warrant. I immediately sent an express to William Potter, Esq., to notify him to attend as within mentioned. I went to the house of Peter Phillips, Esq., who was in Connecticut that I could not notify him. I then notified John Northup and Sylvester Gardiner Esqrs to attend at the time and place within mentioned.   B. BROWN, Sher.

State of Rhode Island, &c. { In Council of War,
           {   August 3d, 1779.

Whereas this Council Hath received Information, that there are several persons lately landed from the Island of Block Island upon ye Mainland within this State (To Wit) Ann Right, Edward Connelly, and Abijah Honeywell, and it appearing to this Council their Intentions are to Collect Intelligence and Procure Provisions to carry to ye Enemy on Rhode Island.

It is therefore Resolved that ye Sheriff of ye County of Kings County, or his Deputy Proceed forthwith and apprehend ye said

Ann Right, Edward Connelly, and Abijah Honeywell, or any other person or persons whoever they may be, that he may have just grounds to suspect of being concerned in the same way, and them safely keep in his custody until ye meeting of ye Committee who are appointed by ye General Assembly to Examine all Suspected Persons who are thought to be Inimical to ye United States and them safely have before them to be dealt with as they may think Proper. Hereof fail not.

Given under my hand and seal by order of ye said Council of War.

Witness: WM. CODDINGTON, Cl'k.

King's County, August ye 14th, 1779.

Then apprehended the within named Anna Right, and have her before the Committee appointed by the General Assembly according to order.

SAM'L STANTON D Sher.

NOTES AND QUERIES.

Can any one give us the birth of Mercy Tillinghast, and the date of her marriage with Hon. Solomon Drowne. She was the daughter of Benjamin Tillinghast, and was the widow Mercy Arnold, at the time of the second marriage.

H. T. D.

Who can give us information regarding the English patriot, John Hampden, who owned land at one time in the Narragansett Country. Is there any evidence that he ever lived in this colony? W. K. W.

Joseph Ballou, Jr., married Thompson Cook, (see page 238.) This man's name was James Ballou, Jr. His wife's name was sometimes written Thomison. The date is right.

F. M. B.

We regret to announce to our readers that our friend and contributor, Dr. Homer E. Aylesworth, of Roseville, Ill., died there Jan. 30, 1885, aged 46 years, 4 months and 22 days. The doctor was born in Burlington, N. Y. He came to Illinois in 1863. The doctor was engaged in preparing a history of his family which once lived in Rhode Island, and where members of the family now reside. We trust this work will be preserved in its Mss. and that some other member of his family will carry it through to completion.

TWO GOOD WORKS.—Mr. S. V. Talcott, of Albany, New York, has forwarded us a copy of his Geneological Notes of New York and New England Families, a work of about 800 pages. We feel much flattered by being thus remembered, and we deeply enjoyed our study of its pages which show the work of a patient and pains taking author. Its historical value is great, and we believe the few copies yet undisposed of should be at once secured by the scholar. The $6.00 asked for it is a very low price for so much information. Another deeply interesting work is vol. VII. of the Collections of the Rhode Island Historical Society. A list of its contents is enough of itself to prove its value as a contribution history, which are: Early Attempts at Rhode Island History; The Narragansetts, by Henry C. Dorr; Early Votaries of Natural Science in Rhode Island, by Dr. Charles W. Parsons; The Commencement of Rhode Island College, by Dr. Reuben A. Guild; The British Fleet in Rhode Island, by George C. Mason, and also another paper by Mr. Mason, on Nicholas Easton, vs. Newport.

A CORRECTION AS TO THE PERRYS.—Rev. Henry G. Perry, of the Episcopal Church of Chicago, sends us the following, which explains itself:

To the Editor of the Chicago Journal:

In your issue of May 2, I notice the following: "Mrs. Mary Beneman, of Ames, Iowa, now visiting in Lafayette, Ind., is 112 years old. Her mind is strong and her health good, save that she is deaf. She is a sister of the famous Commodore Oliver Perry and is a native of Delaware."

This is wholly wrong, and doubtless the abbreviation of a so-called "special" dispatch from Lafayette which I saw in the *Times* of the 12th ultimo, stating that "Mrs. Beneman was born in Lewistown, Del., March 14, 1773, and is consequently 112 years of age;" and that "her father was Captain Christopher R. Perry, a Revolutionary soldier, while her brother, Oliver H., achieved a reputation as the hero of the Battle of Lake Erie."

The article concludes: "Altogether, Mrs. Beneman has about 120 children, grandchildren, great-grandchildren and great-great-grandchildren living." And "she still enjoys remarkably good health, although quite deaf. She will probably make her home in this city." [Lafayette, Ind., April 11, 1885.]

Relatives having written to me about this grossly erroneous statement requesting its correction, permit me to make such correction out of the family manuscripts of my father, the late Rev. Dr. G. B. Perry, who was as were Hon. Freeman Perry, grandfather of Commodore Oliver H. Perry and himself, and his father, Captain Christopher R. Perry, born in the same room at the original "Perry Homestead," South Kingstown, R. I.: Commodore Oliver Hazard Perry's father, Captain Christopher Raymond Perry, the second son of Hon. Freeman Perry, was born December 4, 1761. Captain C. R. Perry's wife was a Miss Sarah Wallace Alexander (of the Sir William Wallace blood), described as a very attractive, vivacious, accomplished lady, of uncommon conversational ability and pleasing address. By her Captain Perry had issue of six sons and three daughters, viz.: Oliver Hazard, Matthew Calbraith, Sarah Wallace, Raymond, Henry J., James A., Anna Maria, Jane T. and Nathaniel H.

From the foregoing it will at once be seen that not only was there no daughter "Mary" among Captain Christopher R. Perry's children, but notably—as the item of her says Mrs. Mary Beneman was born "March 14, 1773"—if Captain C. R. Perry was born, as the record shows, on the 4th of December, 1761, accordingly the Captain could have been but 12 years old in any case to be Mrs. Mary Beneman's father. As one would say in college days this is the *reductio ad absurdum*, and applies to the whole assertion complained of as fallacious, logically *falsum in uno falsum in omnibus*, including the "120 children, grandchildren, great-grandchildren and great-great-grandchildren, living," possibly, but unrelated to Commodore Perry. I can not imagine what could give rise to an item so wholly foreign to fact and delusive, as this now, which I *deny*, and, as others, have asked me, I have sought to *disprove*.

HENRY G. PERRY,
79 NORTH OAKLEY AVENUE, CHICAGO, May 5, 1885.

FIRST MARRIAGE IN BRISTOL.—William Corbett and Eleanor Batrap were married by Capt. Benjamin Church, Sept. 19, 1683. First wedding in town.

COMMENCING IN TIME.—The people of Bristol commenced to agitate the question of celebrating the 200 anniversary of the settlement of the town as early as 1837, nearly fifty years before that event would actually happen.

THE
Narragansett Historical Register.

NARRAGANSETT PUB. CO., PUBLISHERS. } Terms, $2.00 Per Annum. { JAMES N. ARNOLD, EDITOR.

VOL. IV.   HAMILTON, R. I., OCTOBER, 1885.   NO. 2.

The Causes of the Popularity of the Revolutionary Movement in Rhode Island.

A Paper read before the Veteran Citizens' Historical Society, Providence, April 6th, 1885, by James N. Arnold, Editor of the Narragansett Historical Register.

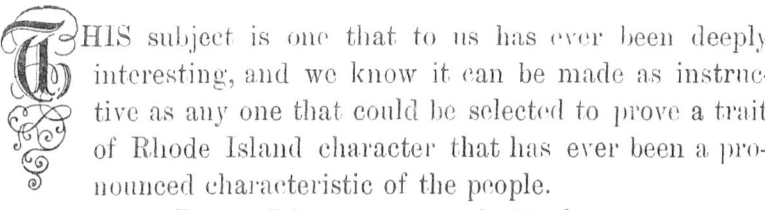THIS subject is one that to us has ever been deeply interesting, and we know it can be made as instructive as any one that could be selected to prove a trait of Rhode Island character that has ever been a pronounced characteristic of the people.

A true blue Rhode Islander is not afraid of an enemy, and needs no mere proof to substantiate the claim. The gallant Burnside by living in our State did not lose his soldierly qualities. Slocum, Rodman, and Ballou were certainly men that no one need be ashamed of. They died for their country and greater love than this no man can show, than to lay down his life for his friends.

The Mexican war produced the Rhode Island hero in Capt. Vinton, who yielded up his life at Vera Cruz.

The war of 1812 gave the noble Perry, who wrote from Lake Erie—" We have met the enemy and they are ours."

At Roanoke and at Newbern 50 years after, history again wrote, "Where the Rhode Island boys lead the fort is ours." The Revolution gave Greene, of whom the military critics have written, "Stood next in ability, and in every other commanding quality to the immortal Washington."

The old French war gave a naval power, of whom Lord Colville said, "Without whose aid the reduction of Louisburg was impossible."

We see by these examples that our people will compare with those of any of our sister States, and that our little commonwealth has produced heroes in each one of our historic contests that have made a fame broad as our land, and whose names will be recorded in our nation's history so long as it is read by man, even beyond the life of the nation itself, and in that same spirit we read to-day of those old heroes of Athens and of Rome.

It can be safely written—no people are more law-abiding than those of Rhode Island. None have greater respect for the laws of the land. But yet with all these qualities no people are more independent in thought and action, and none harder to subdue to tyrannic power.

William Corbett, the English Radical, was once in converversation with a naval officer, and was expressing his admiration of the character of the American sailor. "Pooh," said the officer, "I have been aboard their vessels and three-fourths of them are English." "Had you not all English on your vessels. The other fourth then being American must have made all the difference," was the keen retort of the Radical.

Lake Erie showed what could be done where Rhode Island blood had a fair show to display the hero. In the Revolution the same dauntless spirit was shown. Narragansett Bay has repeatedly seen conflicts that fully illustrate the spirit of her people, and she early taught the haughty Britton that here they could find a foe worthy of her steel, and one they could not safely despise.

In the Revolutionary struggle, and in the war of 1812, we see a courage displayed that went beyond the usual prudence of the soldier; went beyond the most hazardous phases of war, and to the extreme of one who fights the forlorn battle of despair. When one fights with such a spirit, there must be something deep and soul-stirring within. Something that has driven out all the usual qualities of soldierly prudence, and has educated a spirit of feeling, or emotion, and a peculiarity of character, that is rarely found on the pages of history.

These facts stand out boldly in our history as characteristic of the people. Great Britain had a powerful fleet and a large standing army at Newport during the Revolution. This was the last place to be given up to the victorious arms of the United Colonies. Boston had been given up early in the contest, and no attempt was ever after made at re-occupation. Newport on the other hand was taken, and maintained so long as they were able to hold a position in New England. The Home Government showed a bitterer spirit, and a more determined policy towards Rhode Island, than towards any other American Colony.

The expense of this military establishment was great. Did it mean nothing? No! It meant that Newport was the key to New England in the opinion of the Home Government. It meant that the Government dreaded the Narragansett privateers more than those of all the rest of New England. Lord Colville's testimony to the Rhode Island naval power at Louisburg had been a public document, and being corroborated by the testimony of other naval officers, had made the little colony famous at the Court of London.

The Gaspee affair gave the Government another surprise. Hence all this expense of a great military establishment at Newport during this historic struggle.

In short the Government had learned to dread the power of Little Rhody. They had been witnesses of her powers, and, as we have before remarked, they had in future years a chance to learn a few more lessons illustrating the metal of those gallant men that lived on the shores of Narragansett Bay. As the Indians of this historic region had given law to the other New England tribes, so the same spirit had been transferred to men of another race inhabiting this self-same place, and had again brought into prominence those noble qualities of heroic courage, of independence in action and commanding will, that had distinguished that race of men who had owned the soil from a period beyond the record of history.

Could this be learned in a day? Were this race of men bred by a phenomenal occurrence, and destined to pass away, or bloom flower like and pass with a generation? No! It was the work of generations. It was learned in a school of such peculiar discipline as has never fallen to the lot of any other American colony.

We have shown so far but a few characteristics of our people, and have named from the old French war to the present time but a few of our heroes. We have shown so far the opinion of English naval officers, and have, we think, proven that Rhode Island had early taught the Home Government a few lessons of warfare that caused her in the end to take extraordinary means to subdue the colony to her will.

Let us now commence at the other end of the line, and work up the causes that lead to the popularity of the Revolutionary movement in Rhode Island.

From the settlement to the end of King Phillip's war we shall condense our points rapidly. It has been well studied, and we perhaps may say the best studied of any Rhode Island subject, namely, the life and principles of Roger Williams, and the leading views of the Portsmouth and Newport settlers.

The Puritans had been disowned by the Church of England, as they were formerly disowned by the Roman Church. The Puritans in turn disowned Mr. Williams, Coddington and other companies of religious emigrants. Mr. Williams saw the logical conclusions in the future would be that men would take even wider views on religious subjects. Mr. Williams' judgment in this respect was clearer than that of any other religious teacher of his day, and he tried and did work out we think, successfully, the problem of religious liberty. It was not on the coast of Plymouth that the English emigrant learned those lessons, and enjoyed those beauties of religious liberty of whom the poet wrote,—

"Here they found freedom to worship God."

No, not here was it learned but on the shores of Narragansett Bay.

The liberal ideas of Williams at Providence, and Coddington and others on Rhode Island, called to their settlements men who we think made a pretext of religion in order to cover up their own selfish designs. It cannot be denied that both of our colonies (Rhode Island and Providence Plantations) suffered in a marked degree from these emigrations. The wisdom of our early settlers, and the strong ground they took that so long as they (the adventurer or erratic philosopher) did not do anything criminal in the eye of the civil law, to let the matter rest, and trusted the future to provide its own remedy; and time has shown this to have been deep wisdom.

Both the colonies of Massachusetts and Connecticut held stricter views in religious discipline, and made that influence felt here. It aroused naturally a spirit of opposition in our people. The Rhode Island idea was "*To mind their own business, and to insist that none others should mind it for them.*" This spirit early fostered a feeling that became intensified with years. As the government was purely democratic, all political and religious questions were canvassed and recanvassed by each freeman, both at home and in public, and in this way the seeds were sown that developed the Revolutionary spirit.

The battle with Connecticut and Massachusetts for life itself, and intensified by years and even generations of strife, had the result to cement solidly together the freemen of our colony. The pressure from without united the policy of our people, and the leading reasons for our course was a study that had come home to every freeman, and had been taught to each from the cradle. This spirit grew stronger as opposition continued to beat against it; and receiving so much of it from the adjoining colonies led our people to seek other alliances. This policy made our people early take to the water, and the produce obtained in this way finding a ready market, and at a profitable figure, was a strong incentive to enlarge the field of commerce. The continued policy of the adjoining colonies made strong a people on the sea that had first come to these shores for agricultural pursuits, and more peaceful and quiet purposes in life.

It looks indeed singular to us at this late day to see colonies of freemen in adjoining districts worshipping the same Christ, and drawing their rule of inspiration from the same book, and differing only in the interpretation thereof, and on minor points of doctrine at that, so bitter in spirit and action against each other. Singular indeed that such things should be carried into trade, and the more parties differed on some minor points of liberal interpretation, the further indisposed were they to tolerate each other's company. These little acts of christian or unchristian (as the word best pleases you) interchange of courtesies, in a great measure repelled trade, and led to another singular combination—that is, to rather trade with parties that differed far more radically on these same questions of theology. There can be at least one reason given for this, and that is the wide advariance between them would lead each to admit the impossibility of conversion, and so both prudently let the question alone, and attended to trade. As Josh Billings puts it, "They traded hosses and didn't ask each other about their soles."

It is clear now the cause that drew our early settlers in search of a new market, and also made a maritime people. Here were causes certainly that was educating a spirit of exclusiveness, and was in no way cementing the brotherhood of men. The Rhode Island idea being the most liberal, and wherever applied working to the best interests of the commonwealth became popular, and so ended, not in converting Rhode Island to Massachusetts and Connecticut, but bringing both of these States to Rhode Island. What a grand victory, to conquer such a powerful enemy with so small an army; but yet that little army was as the lion once said of her young, "It was a lion."

This victory of principle was a pride, and added an untold amount of energy to our people, and beyond an estimation. No sooner had she freed herself in a great measure from the crushing influence of Massachusetts and Connecticut, and when these colonies began to see their own interests in a better light, than the Home Government stepped in and commenced in a more decided manner that series of tyrannic measures that culminated in the Revolution.

When the colonies were first planted and weak, they would naturally be dependent upon the Home Government for supplies, and had that government been liberal in her policy towards them it would have perhaps made them more easy to govern. Yet had that government been more pleasing to her subjects, and they in turn been more interested in upholding her policy, there would have been no emigration. It is not the happiest families that break up soonest. Where parents strive to please their children, and the children love and respect their parents, they are loth to go away, and it would be great indeed those inducements that would decide the children to go to such a distance that never again would they see the loved one. A hated parent they would care less of seeing. It was not the love of England but the oppression therefore that planted these colonies.

As soon as these colonies could take care of themselves they did so, and the continued oppression of England strengthened this natural feeling of independence. This policy was felt in our colony decidedly. This interference wounded to the quick the spirit of our people.

Our finance system was all right when it was profitable to the English trader, and it was all wrong when it was not so. Whenever trade took another course than towards the English pocket, their interference became manifested. All the way from Queen Anne's time to 1760 selfishness is written above all things else.

The French war did the colonies great damage in at least two ways:

(1.) It put the colonies to such a test as to bring out their resources for waging successful war fuller than anything ever had before, and aroused the Home Government to jealousy at this display of unsuspected power.

(2.) It surprised the colonies themselves, and certainly created in the Home Government feelings more of envy than of real and generous satisfaction.

This state of feeling culminated in the series of stamp duties that lead up to the revolution that would naturally follow such circumstances.

Had the Home Government paid for all the extra expense caused by the French war, and had this war been caused in a measure by the colonies themselves, nothing would seem more natural than a recompense, and that means would have been proposed to accomplish it. The colonies had paid the war claim themselves, and the Home Government had therefore been put to no great expense in the prosecution of the war along the American coast. It was at best but the outcome of a selfish policy, and should not have taken place. There existed now no more reason why the colonies should be taxed more than had existed in the past. The colonies saw that this war had been caused by no fault of theirs. They therefore proposed to submit to the stamp duties imposed provided they could be represented in the Parliament. In short that they should have a voice in saying how the money so raised should be expended. This looks no more than right now and it was right then. They were by right entitled to this representation as loyal English subjects. That they never had been so represented did not in the least alter the justice of the claim. The occasion had never arisen for it until now. They had managed their own affairs and had paid their own bills. No direct tax had been levied by the Government upon the colonies. When, therefore, it was insisted that the colonies should be taxed as was Scotland and Ireland, then came the right to representation on the same principle as those two nations were taxed and represented. Nothing more fully showed the utter selfishness of the English government than this refusal of a just demand.

To the English charge that they were wealthy and now could be taxed, as before they were poor and could not so well afford it, was answered that the wealth had been created from other sources than English capital. They had traded in foreign lands and had so accumulated wealth, and England had no right to it. That the Home Government had got them into wars from time to time; had caused them heavy bills. If they were to furnish means for war they wanted a chance to express an opinion as to its necessity. This was the sentiment of all the colonies, and in none more decidedly than in Rhode Island.

They had been early driven to resort to maritime pursuits. In so doing had been exposed to untold perils. They had been so exposed for a long term of years. They had been obliged to adopt a system of finance that was as prudent and as safe as anything that could be thought of, and which had worked successfully when left alone. That had met all rea. sonable expectations. To have another system thrust upon them; to have it advocated by paid agents sent out to work it; to have it lead men into bad financial positions, and to prove fully as disastrous as the colonial system, was exasperating; and to have it tear down with it our own system finally, maddened and made desperate a band of men that had faced danger from their birth.

It is well known that there were several colonies sent out to other States from Rhode Island previous to the Revolution.

It is known, too, that these emigrants were intensely rebellious to the King. The reasons we have shown. They went from here broken in spirit and in purse, most of them, and feeling they had been swindled out of their hard earned toils. Right here could be written a painful story that has never been fully understood in Rhode Island. Many went from here vowing to utterly forget the past, and many did so in so successful a manner that to-day numerous are the cases that have come under our own observation where the descendants of these emigrants have tried to connect their name with those of early settlers of Rhode Island, and have failed so far, or have done so in a manner more or less imperfect. Here is another feature in the case before us of the English policy that claimed and grasped for all.

The English policy had been such a one as to be termed by our people the "robber" system, and the people of our State had it firmly believed that it had robbed them of their wealth, and that the Stamp Act was a bolder continuation of the same policy. One oppressive measure begets another, and drove the colony into the idea of robbing in their turn. The Revolution furnished the natural outlet. A privateer was just the thing to do it with. They were masters of navigation and naval warfare. It was the quickest way to reach the enemy, and our people were not slow to see all the strong points. Indeed so eager were they for the fray that they were rebellious before even the other colonies had thought of resisting by armed force the oppressions of England.

The history of privateering is interesting. It is germane to our text only how far it illustrates our subject of Rhode Island policy.

When Spain after the discovery of a new field for adventure and commencing a system of successful spoliation against the native tribes, and being wonderfully fortunate in so doing, she aroused in the bosoms of the nations around her the same spirit of cupidity she was so strongly educating among her own people. She first robbed the poor native of his little wealth, and her sister nations in turn robbed her. English cupidity saw no harm in warring against Spain. Privateering for such purpose was honorable, was patriotic, and was worthy of encouragement; was deserving of the blessing of the priest. When the colonies turned around and pursued the same policy towards her, then it was piracy and worthy of death. This was English logic. Verily, verily, I say unto you, it makes a mighty difference whose ox is gored.

The colony of Rhode Island being extensively engaged in navigation and naval pursuits, had learned the ox story well. Daily were the experiences they had encountered in foreign ports. They had found the English trader to be one that wanted all, and was like the lion of the fable who arranged with the dog and the fox to go hunting agreeing to divide the game. The result of the hunt was a fine deer. Now came the question of division, and the lion said, "One third is mine by natural right, one third as king of beasts, and as for the rest let him touch it who dares." This was the perfect Englishman of those days. The Rhode Island trader had experienced this for years. His credit had been impeached; his honesty doubted; his religious ideas ridiculed, and himself made infamous in every way possible.

The Colonial trader had a reverence for his flag and nation, and this bitterness between the rival traders was endured, even though it had extended over years and generations. Although they had been deluded, cheated, oppressed and over-reached in many ways by the English trader, yet his flag and nation he still held dear. It was not until the Government had enlisted on his rival's side that rebellion cropped out, and his nation's policy became hated and despised. The *Question* to bring this feeling out decidedly was the "*Tea Question.*" When the Home Government proposed to give this monopoly, and a monopoly it certainly was in every sense of the word, to a powerful company, and had barred out from participation in the profits the colonial trader, the Yankee was indignant thereat and he was mad all through. He was prudent enough to see he was not as strong as the Home Government. He was shrewd enough to see that the government had a right to make laws and grant monopolies, but his native independence came into play here and he said decidedly, "They can send the tea here if they choose, but they cannot make me use it." The English trader called this "Rebellion," and he insisted that the government should put this down, and that government was just weak enough to try it.

The question of liberty of trade had lead to the question of liberty of market, and the rights therein to buy or sell. Strictly speaking liberty of trade carries with it the liberty of the market. A just construction of this question by the colonies was named by the monopolist "Rebellion."

The English Government has been run by the traders for centuries. They have allowed their people to get a large lot of bad debts on hand by trading with an impoverished people, and have collected them at the point of the sword. Numerous are the witnesses of these atrocities on the pages of history. The most untutored savage in Africa has been her victim; India's clime testifies of her infamy; the smallest island setting upon the placid bosom of the gentle Pacific has a story of wrong to tell. Even the animals of the frozen north bear ample testimony to the cupidity so pronounced a characteristic of these modern Romans of infamy.

Liberty of trade is grand, and leads to grand results, but infamous measures such as has been pursued by the English traders backed up by the government, has caused misery and tears and woe wherever that flag has floated the wide world o'er. The cause of the Revolution was liberty of commerce, and the right to tax without representation. Take away these incentives and what is the result? China tells us that she has had no war of her own choosing in many centuries. All the wars she has had in modern times have been forced upon her. For example, England thrust the opium curse upon her at the bayonet's point. The French cause of war to-day is only for commercial advantage over a rival nation.

The whole subject turns now on this. The liberty of trade being the issue of course those colonies that were the most deeply interested in those pursuits, and the most extensively engaged in them would come in this case before the English trader and his tool the government, as the ones that needed the most meddling with. Those colonies that interfered the most with his own selfish pursuits, he would pronounce the most "rebellious" and the most "disloyal" to the king, i. e. himself.

Apologists for England have painted George as a maniac, and his private life has been viewed from every point. The essayist, moralist, historian, painter, poet and novelist, have each taken their turn at the picture. We believe this is no way to treat the subject, and no way to apologize for these measures. The executive departments were not maniacs if the king was. They were men who knew right from wrong, and could see a fault in another nation even of the minutest kind. They did see them and read the offender many a lesson on morality and right. When they talked theory they held the scales even and weighed accurately. When practice came in then the lion came out. Therefore we think the lion is a very appropriate and very fitting emblem of English authority. It stands out conspicuously and reads *Omnes capio*, or in English, "I take all."

Commerce and taxation being the leading causes of the revolution it follows naturally that our colony being the most extensively engaged in commercial pursuits in proportion to her means of any of the colonies, would naturally feel the most all those measures that sought to limit or to restrict her market. Hence in a war caused by interference in commercial pursuits, she would naturally be expected to take a conspicuous part in such a struggle, and history records she did take just such a part.

The American trader has insisted upon the liberty of the market. To the glory of our nation be it written she never as yet has made herself a tool of monopoly to rule a sister nation. She has always given even the humblest nations the right to buy or not of her as it pleased them, and has never declared war to collect trading debts.

The historian of Rhode Island says, (II. 373) "The Stamp Act produced the fusion of the rival factions three years later. The destruction of the Gaspee, the commencement of the Revolution, was the result of that fusion and its logical and premeditated conclusion was a practical declaration of independence. The Whigs had aimed at this from the beginning."

He says again, (II. 376) "The records of the colony had always closed with the words, "GOD SAVE THE KING." At the close of this session (May 4, 1776,) it was changed and "GOD SAVE THE UNITED COLONIES," appears for the first time. Rhode Island had become in form as well as in spirit an independent State. However reluctant other portions of the continent may have been to entertain the idea of a final separation from the Mother Country, in this colony the desire for final independence was early conceived and steadily followed."

It seems singular to us that our Fourth of July orators do not make it a point to mention in their addresses the declaration of May 4, 1776. So neglected has this been that the fact is not known to our people, and the knowledge therefore is confined to the students of history. If it was a long-winded document we should not blame them, but a document so short and decisive as this ought and should receive better treatment. Let me read to you: (Col. Rec. VII. 522.)

"Whereas, in all States, existing by compact, protection and allegiance are reciprocal; the latter being only due in consequence of the former.

And whereas, George the Third, King of Great Brittain, forgetting his dignity, regardless of the compact most solemnly entered into, ratified and confirmed to the inhabitants of this colony, by his illustrious ancestors, and till of late fully recognized by him, and entirely departing from the duties and character of a good King, instead of protecting, is endeavoring to destroy the good people of this colony, and of all the United Colonies, by sending fleets and armies to America to confiscate our property and spread fire, sword and desolation throughout our country, in order to compel us to submit to the most debasing and detestable tyranny, whereby we are obliged by necessity and it becomes our highest duty to use every means by which God and nature have furnished us in support of our invaluable rights and privileges, to oppose that power which is exerted only for our destruction.

Be it therefore enacted by this General Assembly, and by the authority thereof it is enacted, that an act entitled "An Act for the more effectual securing to His Majesty the allegiance of his subjects, in this Colony and Dominion of Rhode Island and Providence Plantations, be and the same is hereby repealed."

There is no mistaking these words for they breathe the spirit of a free people. The great declaration of July 4th following, goes more into detail and enumerates many of the causes that impelled us to the separation. We might sum up the whole as meaning, "We mind our own business and insist that none others shall mind it for us."

The Priests said the language of our revolutionary fathers was "heretical," and the Government called it "rebellion." In spite of those two old saws this has been the policy of our little commonwealth from the beginning, and is the controling American principle of to-day. From a small beginning what great results ensue.

Note in this great State paper the charges that are brought against the King. He is charged with *a long train of abuses and usurpations,* and that they were submitted to *so long as they were sufferable.* That when they showed a design to subjugate *a free people to despotic power* then it became a necessity *to provide new guards for future security.*

These declarations were not of a hasty, dynamic nature, but the facts had been laid before a prince whose oath at his coronation was to preserve, protect and watch over with all the care of a father his loyal subjects be they high or humble wherever fortune may have placed them, the wide world over. How had he kept his oath in regard to his American subjects? By spurning with contempt their humble petitions for justice. Among the many charges a few are these: Quartering armies among us in time of peace; cutting off our trade with all parts of the world; transporting us beyond seas for trial for pretended offenses; creating new offences and abolishing old ones as the whim dictated; interfering in our judicial and legislative proceedings; creating a tyrannic system of taxation; refusing our just demand to be represented. And so this grand old paper goes on and records in no uncertain manner these measures that called forth the energy of a free people, and which ended by floating on the ocean, that broad highway of commerce, the flag of another nation whose guiding principle was liberty.

Side by side of the National Declaration place that of our own little State, and note how beautifully they explain and harmonize each other. Both have the same lofty ideas of justice, of equality and of law; both breathe the same spirit of courage and soldierly qualities, and both rely on the same God of Nature and the Spartan courage born in man to maintain, uphold and protect our cause. How many have taken the two Declarations and placed them side by side? How many have read them in the spirit of historical enquiry? How many have noted the harmony between them? How many have noted the manly forbearance, the heroic courage and the firmness and determination to uphold the principles therein enunciated? What need is there of reading the heroic passages of old Grecian and Roman philosophers, while we have something as good nearer to our own time, more than to learn that those same old Grecian and Roman principles can be as tersely stated, as ably fought for, maintained, and died for in the Narragansett country as in those eastern climes.

The study of our State declaration need not end by reading this single State Paper, although there is fire enough of the hero engrafted to convince the scholar there was a daring spirit behind the hand that guided the inspiration. What our scholars should do is to study more carefully those State Papers that were drawn out by those contests with Massachusetts and Connecticut. They were models of diplomacy, and were so clearly written that even the authorities of those two States were compelled to acknowledge they plead their cause well. When these papers were contrasted with those they were designed to answer, at once was seen their beauty and the clearness of their construction. Whenever Rhode Island took a case before outside tribunals she won her cause. Englands king on more than one occasion conceded the justice of her claim and gave judgment in her favor, and whenever a cause was submitted to an outside and disinterested colony the same result followed. What produced this? She had justice on her side. She had the spirit of liberty in her bosom, and she had the courage to maintain her privilege as an American Colony, to mind her own business in her own way, and insisted sternly upon no outside interference.

These lofty ideas the Home Government saw must be uprooted, and when too late she tried to do it with a heavy hand, but then those roots of liberty had reached too deep into the souls of her people. They had become so interwoven there that no strength of tyrannic power was able to pull out or destroy. The more they were disturbed in these their natural elements, the stronger and the firmer they became. These roots run from colony to colony and drawing its nourishment from the souls of the people, and finally maturing into a perfect plant whose flower was called liberty and its perfume love.

Rhode Island has been called the "Peculiar Colony." We have no wish to dispute this judgment, but rather glory in her peculiarity. No other colony has had her experience, and as we have shown no other colony had such incentives to make, educate, and every way perfect a man of independent and self-relying qualities. Can it be wondered at then that our people are peculiar? Why it is just as natural for a

Rhode Islander to be peculiar as it is for a duck to take to the water.

We have shown that the causes of the Revolution were of such a nature as to call forth the very qualities of courage and endurance that had long been educated here, and of such a nature that developed to the extremist point all the resources of her people. In our humble opinion we believe that no careful historian who studies into the causes of the Revolution, can admit that its causes were of swift growth, and that they grew out of the Stamp Duties only. These Duties merely gave a greater impetus to movements already begun. It can be safely said that the causes reach back to the very commencement of these settlements. They were founded in independence, and they were taught to be dependent on themselves. As they grew stronger and these principles growing up also with the people, the final separation was only a question of time. It follows then from this reasoning that the colony who had learned this lesson best, and had experienced the most rigid discipline of such a school would naturally take the most active interest in such a struggle. Rhode Island had just such a discipline and the largest experience. She had learned her lesson, and the Revolution bears ample testimony to her patriotism, to her courage, to her heroic sacrifices and endurances, and finally to her glorious triumph along with her other sister colonies.

It is a historical fact that while we have had many a joke on us for the smallness of our territory and for our peculiarity, the pen has yet to write in disparagement of our courage. Not even a pin has been found yet to hang such an assertion on. At Portsmouth, General Lafayette remarked, was "The best fought battle of the war," and military critics concede the fact that had the naval power done as well as the land force, the British arms would have met a disaster fully as great as that at Saratoga and at Yorktown. Oh! had we but a Rhode Islander with a spirit like a Perry at the head of that naval armament, the British lion would have had cause enough for a growl. At Red Bank and on other bloody fields of that ever memorable and never to be forgotten contest, amid the smoke and carnage, amid the strife and where the smoke of conflict were swept aside by the hand of nature, the philosopher who was there to note the result could safely say in the language of the author of the "Star Spangled Banner," as he gazed from his prison towards the place where his flag was floating on the morning after the conflict. Yes, could say the sons of Rhode Island were still there, and the ghastly work around them would bear ample witness they had not been idle.

Such has been the outcome of such a discipline, and so firmly have these lessons been learned that it has not yet been forgotten, and, we may safely add, not likely to be for some time to come. It can be safely predicted that should another conflict in the future become a necessity, that our little commonweath can be depended on to do her duty without faltering. It can be safely written she will put forth those same heroic traits of character her sons have shown in the past, and in that grand historic time of which we have been treating; and she will fully vindicate those heroic characteristics that have made her sons illustrious in the past, and prove that she still has sons worthy and able to emulate the courage and the energy of their sires.

COGGESHALL FIASCO.—Early last Saturday morning one Coggeshall, being somhwhat drunk and crazy, went on the Long wharf and turned up his Backsides towards the Bum Brig in this harbour, using some insulting words upon which the Brig fired two four pound shot at: one of which went through the roof of Mr. William Hammond's store on the said wharf, and lodged on the distil house of Mr. Samuel Johnson at the N. E. part of the Cove within the Long wharf. The man was soon after taken up and sent out of town.— *Newport Mercury, Nov. 5, 1775.*

THE RECORD OF OLD SMITHFIELD FROM 1730 TO 1850.

From Records in Town Clerk's Office, Lincoln.

CONTRIBUTED BY THE EDITOR.

(*Continued from Vol. IV., page 69.*)

BIRTHS AND DEATHS.

C.

Cady,	Mary, of Benajah and Patience,				March 3, 1761.
"	Elias,	"	"	"	Sept. 8, 1763.
"	Phebe,	"	"	"	Nov. 10, 1766.
"	Anna,	"	"	"	May 2, 1769.
"	William,	"	"	"	Aug. 31, 1771.
"	Nicholas,	"	"	"	Jan. 20, 1774.
"	Sylvanus,	"	"	"	Oct. 15, 1777.
Callum,	Lydia, of Daniel and Lydia,				Dec. 5, 1752.
"	Anna,	"	"	"	July 27, 1754.
"	Sarah,	"	"	"	Dec. 22, 1755.
"	Eunice,	"	"	"	June 15, 1759.
"	Rachel,	"	"	"	April 3, 1762.
"	Elizabeth	"	"	"	March 16, 1765.
Carroll,	James, of Joseph and Abbie,				May 19, 1788.
"	Susan,	"	"	"	April 4, 1790.
"	Sally Blake, of James and Sally,				May 1, 1816.
"	Eliza Smith,	"	"	"	March 3, 1823.
"	Abbie,	"	"	"	Jan. 20, 1825.
"	Jesse, died, Jan. 13, 1844.				

Cass, Hannah, (Mendon), of Nathan and Hannah, Oct. 18, 1741.
" Joanna, (Mendon), of Nathan and Hannah, Dec. 21, 1743.
" Sarah, (Mendon), of Nathan and Hannah, June 30, 1746.

Cass,	Jonathan, (Sm.), of Nathan and Hannah,				May 16, 1748.
"	Lydia,	"	"	"	May 12, 1752.
"	Chloe,	"	"	"	April 6, 1754.
"	Samuel, (Mendon), of Daniel and Mary,				Aug. 10, 1746.
"	Joseph,	"	"	"	Mar. 31, 1748.
"	Hannah,	"	"	"	Jan. 10, 1749.
"	Mary, (Sm.)		"	"	Mar. 30, 1752.
"	Daniel,	"	"	"	Oct. 24, 1753.
"	Jonathan,	"	"	"	Mar. 3, 1756.
"	Josiah,	"	"	"	Sept. 24, 1757.
"	Sarah,	"	"	"	Nov. 9, 1759.
"	Amos, of Ebenezer and Sarah,				Nov. 7, 1749.
"	John,	"	"	"	April 10, 1752.
"	Luke,	"	"	"	Sept. 9, 1754.
"	Selve,	"	"	"	May 23, 1757.
"	Deborah,	"	"	"	May 14, 1761.
Chace,	Barnard, of Barnard and Margery,				Sept. 30, 1767.
"	Levina,	"	"	"	Jan. 31, 1769.
"	Anne,	"	"	"	Aug. 22, 1771.
"	George,	"	"	"	Feb. 19, 1774.
"	Nathan,	"	"	"	Nov. 17, 1776.
"	Urania,	"	"	"	Nov. 1, 1778.
"	Alpha,	"	"	"	Oct. 3, 1780.
"	Adeline, of George and Mary,				June 22, 1807.
Chillson,	Elizabeth, of Joseph and Sarah,				Sept. 28, 1747.
"	Mary,	"	"	"	May 1, 1748.
"	"	"	"	"	d. Dec. 7, 1749.
"	Joseph,	"	"	"	Dec 28, 1749.
"	Rufus,	"	"	"	Nov. 13, 1752.
"	John,	"	"	"	April 24, 1755.
"	Sarah, of John and Sarah,				Sept. 5, 1788.
"	Nancy,	"	"	"	Dec. 19, 1790.
"	Ethan,	"	"	"	May 2, 1792.
"	Betsey,	"	"	"	May 6, 1794.
"	Amie,	"	"	"	April 29, 1798.
"	John,	"	"	"	April 22, 1804.

Chillson, Eliza Anna, of John and Sarah, Aug. 12, 1807.
" Ruth, " " " Feb. 18, 1812.
Coats, Charles Newton, of James, June 15, 1849.
Coe, Allen, of Benjamin and Mary, Dec. 24, 1801.
" Mary Lapham, of Allen and Lydia, Oct. 20, 1824.
Cole, Sumner, of Samuel and Permela, July 13, 1809.
" Julian, " " " Aug. 4, 1811.
" Stephen, " " " Jan. 16, 1814.
" Alexander Burguess, of Ansel D. and Betsey Perry (Bowers), June 18, 1844.
Coman, Nathan, of Joseph and Peggy, Aug. 4, 1760.
" Isaac, " " " May 22, 1766.
Comstock, Ruth, of Ichabod and Zebiah, Jan. 20, 1723-4.
" Elizabeth, " " " Dec. 18, 1725.
" Ichabod, " " " March 17, 1727-8.
" Zebiah, " " " March 19, 1729-30.
" Abraham, " " " Dec. 30, 1734.
" Jonathan, " " " Sept. 7, 1737.
" Jemima, of Azeriah and Zeriah, Aug. 5, 1735.
" Moses, " " " Nov. 9, 1737.
" Lydia, " " " June 18, 1741.
" Aaron, " " " Jan. 13, 1745.
" Abener, " " " Aug. 1, 1747.
" Amie, " " " June 19, 1749.
" Azeriah, " " " Sept. 21, 1755.
" Mary, " " " Oct. 8, 1756.
" Adam, of Gideon and Ruth, Jan. 18, 1739-40.
" Alpha, " " " March 12, 1741-2.
" Ruth, " " " Sept. 11, 1755.
" True, " " " Feb. 14, 1745-6.
" Israel, of Daniel, Jr., and Martha, Nov. 6, 1743.
" Daniel, " " " Jan. 6, 1745.
" Jacob, " " " Nov. 1, 1747.
" Caleb, " " " Jan. 9, 1750.
" Chloe, " " " March 2, 1752.
" Martha, " " " March 13, 1754.

Comstock,	Esther, of Joseph and Anne,				Jan. 26, 1748.
"	Phebe,	"	"	"	April 13, 1750.
"	Chloe,	"	"	"	Aug. 15, 1752.
"	Laban,	"	"	"	March 9, 1755.
"	Luke,	"	"	"	Feb. 10, 1759.
"	Ezekiel,	"	"	"	Jan. 17, 1762.

" Stephen, of Hezekiah, Jr., and Mary, Aug. 13, 1758.
" Caleb, of Hezekiah, Jr., and Mary, July 28, 1763.
" Martha, of Ezekiel and Martha, Oct. 26, 1759.
" Rachel, of Jonathan and Hannah, Oct. 9, 1761.
" Anthony, b. March 26, 1762.
" Hannah, his wife, b. Oct. 4, 1773.

"	William, of Anthony and Hannah,				Mar. 25, 1791.
"	Phebe,	"	"	"	Feb. 7, 1793.
"	Anthony,	"	"	"	Oct. 7, 1795.
"	Hannah,	"	"	"	July 15, 1797.
"	Martha,	"	"	"	Nov. 17, 1798.
"	Ezra,	"	"	"	Nov. 1, 1800.
"	Olive,	"	"	"	July 10, 1803.
"	Eliza,	"	"	"	March 25, 1806.
"	Ezekiel Henry, of Henry and Sarah,				Mar. 8, 1788.
"	Caleb Greene,	"	"	"	Feb. 7, 1790.
"	Hannah,	"	"	"	June 5, 1792.
"	Job Scott,	"	"	"	April 18, 1794.
"	Mary Greene,	"	"	"	Feb. 17, 1807.
"	William Henry,	"	"	"	Mar. 20, 1809.
"	Martha Waite,	"	"	"	Aug. 8, 1811.
"	Sarah Maria,	"	"	"	Aug. 4, 1813.
"	Elizabeth Rense,	"	"	"	Nov. 5, 1815.
"	Clarissa Arnold,	"	"	"	May 5, 1818.

" Mary Elma, of Arooch and Joanna, July 17, 1808.
" Elisha, of Welcome A. and Chloe, June 1, 1823.
" Metcalf, " " " Dec. 21, 1825.
" Amanda Mariah, of Welcome and Chloe, Feb. 1, 1829.

Cook,	Eunice, of Elijah and Joanna,		Jan. 16, 1739.
"	Martha, " " "		Sept. 16, 1741.
"	Silvanus, " " "		Feb. 10, 1743.
"	Gideon, " " "		July 10, 1745.
"	Elijah, " " "		Jan. 16, 1754.
"	Joanna, " " "		Nov. 16, 1757.
"	Benjamin, " " "		April 10, 1764.
"	Sarah, of Seth and Mary,		March 26, 1740.
"	Hannah, " " "		May 12, 1741.
"	Mary, " " "		Jan. 21, 1742.
"	Seth, " " "		May 28, 1745.
"	Experience, of Seth and Mary,		Feb. 26, 1747.
"	Aaron, of Benjamin and Mary,		April 18, 1740.
"	Amie, " " "		July 4, 1744.
"	William, of Peter and Elizabeth,		Feb. 4, 1741.
"	Eve, of Samuel and Sarah,		July 22, 1748.
"	" " " "		d. Aug. 2, 1752.
"	Rest, " " "		Nov. 1, 1750.
"	" " " "		d. July 17, 1752.
"	Judith, " " "		Oct. 5, 1753.
"	Joseph, " " "		Dec. 25, 1755.
"	Tamar, " " "		April 30, 1759.
"	Eli, " " "		Jan. 18, 1762.
"	Lydia, " " "		May 1, 1764.
"	Jerah, " " "		March 28, 1767.
"	Philetus Henry, of Silvanus S. and Nolby R., March 9, 1738.		
Corey,	Adin Trask, of Taber and Prusha,		Feb. 25, 1780.
"	Leah, " " "		Sept. 14, 1783.
Cowen,	Mary of John and Sarah,		Feb. 28, 1719-20.
"	Sarah, " " "		May 22, 1721.
"	James, " " "		Feb. 19, 1722-3.
"	John, " " "		Jan. — 1724-5.
"	Joseph, " " "		May 1, 1727.
"	Alice, " " "		Feb. 26, 1728-9.
"	Hannah, " " "		April 25, 1732.
"	Benjamin, of John and Sarah,		Dec. 14, 1734.

Cruff, Mary, of Thomas and Hannah,				April 6, 1742.
" Ruth, of Samuel and Abigail,				June 21, 1747.
" Rhoda, " " "				Feb. 9, 1748-9.
" Elizabeth, " " "				Dec. 25, 1750.
" Joel, " " "				Feb. 1, 1757.

MARRIAGES.

D.

Dailey Mary, and Charles Crossbee, Jan. 19, 1775.

Dalby Mark, and Elizabeth Jeffers; m. by Rev. Ansel D. Cole, Nov. 28, 1844.

Dampney John, and Cynthia R. Swining; m. by George H. Mervey, justice, April 18, 1837.

Dauber Elizabeth E. and William Lindsey, Oct. 28, 1847.

Daniels James, and Martha Shippee; m. by Thomas Sayles, justice, Sept. 20, 1735.

" Abigail, and Ephraim Mowry, April 3, 1737.

" Mary, and Wetherby, Sept. 22, 1740.

" Naomi M. and Benjamin Evans, Jan. 21, 1787.

Danton Mary, and Andrew Man, Dec. 7, 1746.

Danwell Benjamin S. and Eliza T. Jenckes of Joseph; m. by Rev. C. C. Taylor, May 12, 1841.

" Sarah Mc, and Edward Hyndeman, May 18, 1847.

Darbin Deborah, and Henry Bosworth, April 25, 1732.

Darling Benjamin, and Elizabeth Farce; m. by William Arnold, justice, July 28, 1733.

" Joseph, and Mary Fish; m. by William Arnold, justice, Jan. 6, 1735.

" Susannah and David Thompson, Oct. 11, 1737.

" Keziah, and John Hunt, June 6, 1738.

" Ruth, and Joseph Albee, Nov. 8, 1744.

" Ebenezer, and Mary Hakes; m. by Thomas Steere, justice, Feb. 25, 1745.

" Samuel, and Sarah Benson; m. by Wm. Arnold, justice, March 5, 1746-7.

" Ruth, and John Pettis, Sept. 22, 1747.

Darling John, and Margaret Cook; m. by Wm. Arnold, justice, Feb. 23, 1748-9.
" Peter and Presilla Cook; m. by Wm. Arnold, justice, April 20, 1749.
" Enock, of Bellingham, Mass., and Lues Thompson of do.; m. by Thomas Arnold, justice, Nov. 26, 1751.
" Rachel, and Daniel Trask, Aug. 29, 1765.
" Henry, and Olive Herendeen; m. by Rev. Edward Mitchell, Jan. 23, 1784.
" Penelope, and Levi Aldrich, Nov. 13, 1786.
" Henry, Jr. of Henry, and Mary Wilbur of Daniel; m. by Thomas Man, justice, Dec. 13, 1805.
" Henry and Mercy Alverson; m. by Samuel Man, justice, Feb. 25, 1807.
" Roxanna, and Cyrus Marble, June 6, 1815.
" William Smith, of Henry, and Adeline Sheldon, of Charles; m. by Thomas Man, justice, April 20, 1832.
" George, of Boston, Mass., son of Samuel, and Susan F. Brownell, of Stephen F. of Smithfield; m. by Rev. John Boyden, Jr., Aug. 17, 1840.
" Maria, and William Darling, Oct. 4, 1840.
" William, of Burrillville, son of Henry, deceased, and Maria Darling of do., dau. of Elisha; m. by John Pain, justice, Oct. 4, 1840.
" Matilda W., and William B. Arnold, Dec. 31, 1840.
Davidson John, and Sabura R. Potter; m. by Rev. Asel D. Cole, Jan. 28, 1844.
Davis Benjamin, and Jemima Whipple; m. by Wm. Jenckes, justice, Dec. 2, 1744.
" Joseph, of Cumberland, and Hannah Wilkinson of Smithfield; m. by Thomas Latham, justice, Feb. 17, 1754.
" Harrison R., and Ruth Keith; m. by Rev. C. H. Titus, June 18, 1848.
" Lucinda P., and George W. Caldwell, Nov. 30, 1848.

Davis Mary A., and David Carpenter, May 27, 1849.
" Harriet P., and William H. Turgett, June 17, 1849.
Davrond Aaron, and Drusilla Owen; m. by Thomas Lapham, justice, May 19, 1748.
Day Samuel, and Amie Plimpton; m. by Thomas Lapham, justice, Nov. 17, 1754.
" Matilda, and Ora F. Steere, Aug. 1, 1822.
" Rosellana M., and Orrin W. Andrews, Feb. 25, 1841.
" Simeon G., a resident of Thompson, Mass., and Susan E. Cook of Smithfield; m. by Rev. Asel D. Cole, Aug. 31, 1843.
" Amie A., and Horace M. Beach, Oct. 15, 1849.
" Cynthia, and Dr. Avery F. Angell, July 31, 1850.
Deake John B., of John, and Martha Ann Smith; by Rev. T. A. Taylor, April 15, 1845.
Dean William Henry, of Eleazer, and Pailina Crowell, of Ebenezer; m. by Rev. Charles Hyde, Aug. 6, 1846.
Deirk Henry, of William of Uxbridge, and Amelia Keith, of Royal of Smithfield; m. by Rev. T. A. Taylor, Mar. 15, 1846.
Dempsey Neal, of Boston, Mass., and Ruth Smith of Wrentham; m. by Thomas Sayles, justice, May 3, 1743.
Derk William V., of William V. and Esther, and Mary S. Browing, of William and Phebe; m. by Rev. Baylis P. Talbot, April 13, 1848.
Dexter Anna, and Benjamin Arnold, Feb. 14 or 15, 1740-1.
" Gideon, and Martha Smith; m. by Wm. Jenckes, justice, Aug. 21, 1748.
" Andrew, and Lydia Jenckes; m. by Thomas Lapham, Sept. 25, 1748.
" Sarah, and Abraham Arnold, Feb. 25, 1768.
" Waterman, of Andrew, and Sarah Wilbur, of Daniel; m. by Ichabod Comstock, justice, Oct. 23, 1774.
" Phebe, and Eld. John Winsor, Jan. 23, 1777.
" Samuel, of William, deceased, and Candace Winsor of Elder John; m. by Rev. Samuel Winsor, June 14, 1778.

Dexter Hannah, and Job Arnold, Dec. 21, 1780.
" Christopher, of Jonathan of Smithfield, and Betsey Whipple of Cumberland, of Eleazer, dec.; m. by Rev. Rufus Tefft, Dec. 10, 1789.
" Clarissa, and Smith Dexter, Sept. 30, 1801.
" Smith, of Waterman, and Clarissa Dexter; m. by Thomas Man, justice, Sept. 30, 1801.
" Rebecca, and Isaac Tower, Feb. 4, 1802.
" Lydia, and Nathaniel Mowry, 3d, April 20, 1806.
" John, of Jonathan, and Mary Hall, of John; m. by Thomas Man, justice, May 11, 1806.
" Loie, and William E. Carpenter, Feb. 1, 1830.
" Ann Eliza, and Daniel T. Waldron, Aug. 3, 1839.
" Benjamin and Presilla Cole; m. by Rev. B. P. Bryam, Nov. 28, 1840.
Dillingham Elisha, and Huldah Wilkinson; m. by David Comstock, justice, June or Sept. 10, 1738.
" Hulda, and Nathan Herendeen, April 30, 1764.
Dixon Elizabeth, and James Sykes, Dec. 31, 1846.
Dodge Lucy, and George W. Holt, Sept. 3, 1839.
Dorr Aaron, and Presilla Owen; m. by Thomas Lapham, justice, May 19, 1748.
Doten Hope, and Samuel Smith, May 31, 1791.
Dotey Sarah, and William Phillips, Jr., dec., Dec. 23, 1745.
Dowell Alexander, of Blackstone, Mass., son of Francis and Bridget, and Ann Bacon of do., dau. of Jared and Sarah; m. by Rev. Bayles P. Talbot, May 27, 1849.
Dunlap Patrick, of Ireland, and Anna Man of Alfred; m. by Joel Aldrich, justice, July 3, 1814.
Dyer Jones, and Hannah Herendeen; m. by Jabez Harris, justice, Sept. 27, 1761.
" Ann F., and Curtis E. Willard, Dec. — 1846.

BIRTHS AND DEATHS.

Daley Mary, of James and Judith,   Oct. 25, 1748.
" Gideon, " "   June 15, 1751.

Daley Solomon, of James and Judith, April 13, 1754.
" Reuben, " " March 30, 1757.
" Thankful, " " March 30, 1757.
" Emor, " " July 25, 1760.
Daniels James, of James and Martha, Sept. 22, 1736.
" David, found dead in his bed, May 17, 1847.
Darling Henry, of Henry and Olive, March 20, 1784.
" William Smith, of Henry Jr., and Mary, June 2, 1808.
" Dennis Albert, " " Sept. 12, 1810.
" Sarah, of Henry and Mercy, Sept. 12, 1816.
" Lewis, " " June 17, 1818.
Day, Chloe, of Samuel and Amie, April 4, 1760.
" Jeremiah, " " Nov. 16, 1761.
" Amie, " " July 21, 1763,
" Samuel, " " Aug. 6, 1765.
" Loting, " " June 22, 1767.
" Mary, " " Feb. 18, 1769.
Dexter John, of James and Hannah, Feb. 11, 1716-17.
" Anne, " " Oct. 22, 1718.
" James, " " Feb. 24, 1720-1.
" David, " " Feb. 24, 1722-3.
" Hopey, " " Sept. 15, 1726.
" Marcy, " " Oct. 10, 1730.
" Amie, of Gideon and Martha, June 20, 1751.
" Phebe, " " June 7, 1753.
" Stephen, " " Dec. 1, 1755.
" Isabel, " " March 29, 1759.
" Martha, " " Jan. 20, 1763.
" David, " " April 18, 1765.
" Lydia, of Andrew and Lydia, Oct. 13, 1762.
" Anthony, of Christopher and Betsey, April 14, 1790.
" Amie, " " Nov. 24, 1791.
" Sukey, " " April 18, 1794.
" Polly, " " Feb. 8, 1798.
" Betsey, " " March 18, 1803.
" Maria, " " Feb. 11, 1807.

Dillingham Mary, of Elisha and Huldah, July 12, 1739.
" Hulda, " " March 9, 1740–1.
Dixon Robert, died June 18, 1839.
Dunlap, Gustavus Man, of Patrick and Anna, Feb. 13, 1815.

MARRIAGES.

E.

Earle Catherine, and Peleg Wilbur Lippitt, March 22, 1848.
Eastman Lyman T., of Lowell, Mass., son of Samuel, and Lydia A. Nicholas of Lowell, Mass., dau. of Holt of Nashua, N. H.,; m. by Rev. Charles C. Taylor, April 25, 1841.
Easton Dorcas, and Sylvester Mowry, Jr., April 2, 1801.
Eddy Daniel, and Mary Plumer; m. by Thomas Sayles, justice, Dec. 12, 1734.
" Joseph, of Gloucester, and Bethsheba Smith of Smithfield; m. by Thomas Sayles, justice, Nov. 23, 1735.
" Nathaniel, and Hannah Whipple; m. by Thomas Sayles, justice, Feb. 22, 1738–9.
" Zachariah, of Smithfield, and Mary Burik of Stonington, Conn.; m. by Joseph Palmer, justice, May 9, 1743.
" Hannah, and William Arnold, May 18, 1755.
" William, and Hadssah Angel; m. by Thomas Steere, justice, Aug. 12, 1756.
" Jerusha, and Eber Angel, Aug. 26, 1761.
" David of Nathaniel, and Naomi Arnold of Thomas; m. by Stephen Arnold, justice, Feb. 13, 1772.
" Mercy, and Darius Winsor, May 15, 1775.
" Desire, and Ezek Smith, June 19, 1794.
" Amie, and Aaron Arnold, Feb. 19, 1799.
" Abigail, and Benjamin Almy, Sept. 18, 1817.
" Phebe A., and Henry T. Brown, July 28, 1844.
" John M. of Gloucester, and Miriam B. Cooper of Burrillville; m. by Rev. T. A. Taylor, June 23, 1846.
Edmunds Lydia, and Stutely Arnold, Dec. 17, 1758.

Ekins John, of Worcester, Mass., son of George and Mary, and Hannah Connella of Blackstone, dau. of John and Bridget; m. by Rev. Bayles P. Talbot, June 10, 1849.

Ellet, Jonathan, of Thomas, and Amie Greene; m. by Peleg Arnold, justice, July 27, 1783.

Elliot Lydia, and Lyman Smith, March 26, 1863.

Ellis David, and Elvina Gilbert; m. by Rev. T. A. Talbot, Feb. 28, 1848.

" Henry A. of Holliston, Mass., son of Harvey of Jamaica, Vt., and Abbie Albee of Burrillville, dau. of Amos; m. by Joseph Almy, justice, May 26, 1849.

Ellsbree Williams, and Sarah Cudworth; m. by Rev. George Tyler, Jan. 27, 1846.

Emerson Ebenezer, and Elizabeth Wolcutt; m. by Jonathan Sprague, justice, April, — 1733.

" Catherine and Joel Sayles, June 23, 1813.

Enches Thomas, of Jesse, and Parley Sayles of Gideon, Feb. 14, 1820.

" William, of Jesse, and Levina Sayles of Benjamin; m. by James Wilkinson, justice, Jan. 3, 1823.

Ennis Susan C., and Benjamin F. Holman, July 20, 1848.

Ephraim Mary, and James Comstock, July 6, 1750.

Eston Jemima, and Benjamin Pain, April 30, 1751.

" Sarah, and Sterling Pain, July 28, 1808.

Esterbrook Susannah, and Jep Mowry, March 5, 1818.

Estis John, and Hannah Walling; m. by Stephen Sly, justice, Nov. 23, 1756.

Evans David, and Jemima Bishop; m. by John Aldrich, justice, March 27, 1755.

" Benjamin, of David of Smithfield, and Naomi Daniels of Johnston, R. I., dau. of Barrick; m. by Rev. Edward Mitchell, Jan. 21, 1787.

" William, and Nancy Appleby; m. by Daniel Winsor, justice, Feb. 20, 1803.

" Mary, and George Arnold, Nov. 6, 1808.

Evans John, and Sally Mowry ; m. by Robert Harris, justice, Oct. 17, 1816.
" Edward, of Benjamin, and Dianna Colwell, of William, dec.; m. by Rev. Reuben Allen, March 26, 1840.
" Burrill, of Benjamin, and Rhoda B. Place, of James; m. by Rev. Reuben Allen, May 28, 1840.
" Edward C. of Gloucester, and Abbie Emeline Mowry; m. by Rev. T. A. Taylor, Jan. 4, 1844.
" Elizabeth A., and Horace Barnes, Feb. 9, 1845.
Evule Mary, and Constantine Abala, Jan. 21, 1844.

BIRTHS AND DEATHS.

Eddy Mary,	of Nathaniel and Hannah,			Dec. 7, 1739.
"	Ruth,	"	"	Jan. 4, 1742.
"	Stephen,	"	"	May 18, 1745.
"	Daniel,	"	"	Oct. 23, 1747.
"	Mary,	"	"	Feb. 16, 17—.
Enckes Thomas,	of Jesse and Phebe,			April 8, 1798.
"	Gideon Sayles, of Thomas and Parley,			April 4, 1820.
"	Sally,	"	"	Sept. 16, 1822.
"	Wm. Sayles, of William and Levina,			Oct. 1, 1822.
"	Phebe,	"	"	Nov. 4, 1824.
"	Edward Smith,	"	"	Dec. 6, 1826.
"	Jeremiah Olney,	"	"	June 12, 1831.
Evans Edward,	of Daniel and Esther,			Nov. 27, 1710.
"	Anne,	"	"	Sept. 2, 1712.
"	Esther,	"	"	Dec. 17, 1714.
"	Thankful,	"	"	Feb. 17, 1718.
"	David,	"	"	May 16, 1721.
"	Zerviah,	"	"	Nov. 17, 1725.
"	Ruth,	of David and Jemima,		March 24, 1756.
"	Mehitable,	"	"	May 13, 1757.
"	Lydia,	"	"	May 4, 1758.
"	Sarah,	"	"	Sept. 9, 1759.
"	David,	"	"	May 11, 1761.
"	Benjamin,	"	"	Feb. 20, 1763.

Evans	Elisha,	of David and Jemima,		July 11, 1765.
"	Elizabeth,	"	"	Nov. 22, 1766.
"	John,	"	"	Feb. 29, 1768.
"	Edward,	"	"	May 8, 1770.
"	Gideon,	"	"	March 4, 1772.
"	Jonathan,	"	"	Dec. 8, 1773.
"	William,	"	"	Sept. 5, 1775.
"	David, Senior, died Oct. 6, 1800.			

(*To be continued.*)

PREACHING ON A STEAMBOAT.

AN INCIDENT OF RELIGIOUS WORK OVER FIFTY YEARS AGO.

THE following description of the effect produced by an occasional discourse delivered on board a steamboat on Lake Erie is extracted from a communication addressed to the editor of the Norwich (Conn.) *Courier*, 1835, and re-printed in the *Boatman's Magazine* of 1835.

"*In the morning sow thy seed, and in the evening withhold not thine hand; for thou knowest not whether shall prosper, either this or that.*"

About a year ago I passed on Lake Erie from Detroit to Buffalo in the steamboat Ohio. We stopped at Cleveland for passengers. Being alone and a Southerner I held little intercourse with any on board. We left Cleveland about 4 o'clock p. m. The afternoon was beautifully calm. I was much engrossed in thoughts upon the mighty achievements won by the gallant and lamented Perry, whose victory over a proud foe on those waters immortalized his name, and endeared his memory to all the Americans. Night closing in upon us, after partaking of an excellent supper, each one betook himself to his solitary pillow. The next morning presented to our view a clear sky, and there was just breeze enough to gently move the bosom of the vast lake. Our boat glided over the waters in grandeur, scattering the foam from before her proud breast, and leaving in her flight countless fire-sparks, like so many stars winging their way to the clouds. Though, experimentally, I knew nothing of the God of Redemption, or of the salvation obtained by the Savior, yet I thought much and often on nature. It was a luxury to contemplate the magnificence of what I deemed nature's mighty works. While sitting in the afterpart of the boat, indulging in one of these reveries, it was announced in my hearing that a religious lecture would be delivered in the cabin to such as desired to hear it. This was a proposal entirely new to me. I at once hastened to the place; I found all hands assembled and an interest of no ordinary nature seemed to be felt.

We sat a moment, and no one rising, I began to look around to see if I could select the speaker, upon which a gentleman of remarkably prepossessing countenance arose to address us. He was of middle stature, with full, deep, keen blue eyes—a noble, open, forehead, strongly resembling Lord Byron's—a prominent nose of the old Roman cast, light complexion, brown hair, which by nature was adjusted into many ringlets. He stooped a little on first rising, but soon elevated his person so as to stand perfectly erect. His voice was rich in tone. There was occasionally a catch or a choke in his speech, in consequence of an affection in the throat, under which I was told he was laboring. But notwithstanding he spoke with uncommon ease. No temerity, no extra effort, not a particle of ostentation. Words fell from his lips without labor, and were uttered with great distinctness. His style was smooth, beautiful and logically correct. His gestures were occasionally rapid, but always appropriate and natural. His ideas were not lumbered up with useless words, but had just enough to make the sentiment stay where he put it. The hearer was never plagued to comprehend his meaning. It seemed to me that the speaker possessed entirely a new art in communicating his ideas with power to instruct and please at the same time. It was perspicuity and rhetoric philosophically blended, so that every sentence became forcible and remarkable for plainness.

The subject was "The New Birth," one which to me had always wore a mystery. "Ye must be born again" I had read from my childhood, and had been taught to believe, though told I must not expect to understand it. And this I had been compelled to disregard, or rather to disbelieve the doctrine. But now the matter was presented to me in a perfectly intelligible form. Not a mystery hung over it. Said the speaker: "The mind of man is out of order. God in His holy word has caused to be written down His mind concerning the moral condition of the human family. He says He made man upright—made him good, made him in His own image; but man has rebelled and made himself a sinner. That is, he has become possessed of a mind hostile to his Creator's. The Divine Being has farther caused to be recorded his mind concerning Himself and His Son Jesus, and of man. Thus man is against God—is an alien—hates His ways, His will, and His word. Consequently God is opposed to man, who is the reverse. "Now," said the speaker, "man's mind must be turned to God's. His soul must sink into the will of his Creator. He must be changed in temper, in feeling, and in the spirit of his mind. This is to be born again—to be begotten again by the spirit of truth.

"It is grace that does this work; that grace which is the result of Christ's being crucified, in which we must have faith." I have given the preacher's words from memory, and, I believe, correctly. And what a moment it was to me! I began to discover the force and awful import of the doctrine. I felt its solemn truth, and must say, trembled in view of the consequences. I must be born again, I muttered to myself in my inmost soul. I must be like my God or never be happy with Him, was clearly and indelibly impressed upon my mind. I yielded to the conviction, for it was confirmed in my enlightened judgment. It was sufficient to say I entered the cabin a cold-hearted skeptic; I left it a firm believer in the reality of the Christian religion. I inquired who the speaker was, and judge of my surprise and delight when I was told he was the near kinsman of the illustrious Commodore O. H. Perry, his father's brother's son. It was the Rev. Gideon B. Perry, of Philadelphia.

I could then plainly discover the same calm, discerning, balanced spirit in the champion of the pulpit that marked the conduct and guided the champion of the lake which led him to victory and triumph. To the instrumentality of the Rev. Dr. Perry I am indebted for the first permanent religious impressions I ever received. I fondly trust they have resulted in the conversion of my soul to the truth as it is taught in the Scriptures.

The desire of my heart and my intentions now are to be the herald of salvation to others. To the accomplishment of this great and important object I am now devoting myself.

JAMES.

A copy of the *Boatman's Magazine* (of Buffalo), from which this letter was taken, is now in possession of the Rev. Henry G. Perry, of the Episcopal church of Chicago, son of the late Rev. Dr. G. B. Perry, formerly of Philadelphia, the subject of the sketch.

AN UNFORTUNATE FAMILY.—In the Newport Mercury under date of Jan. 29, 1770, mention is made of a collection for Thos. Allen, of Prudence, whose wife and 7 out of 11 children are blind.

THE STORY OF THE TABLETS.

II.

CONTRIBUTED BY JAMES L. SHERMAN ESQ., PROVIDENCE, R. I.

From the North Burial Ground, Providence.

In Memory of
OBADIAH BROWN, ESQUIRE,
Who departed this Life
The seventeenth of June,
MDCCLXII,
Aged Forty-nine Years, Eight Months, and
Four Days.
Descended of a good Family
He had strong natural Powers
Guided with exquisite Judgment —
Was honest, industrious, frugal,
Temperate, affable, benevolent;
A grave Magistrate,
A kind Husband,
Tender Parent,
A perfect Pattern for Masters
And illuseful Men.
As our country suffers when the useful die,
Heal up the Breach by following
their Example.

Sacred
To the Memory
of
MRS. ABBY MASON BROWN,
Consort of
Mr. Nicholas Brown, Jr.,
And Daughter of
The
Hon. James Brown Mason,

And Alice his Wife.
She Died
on the 7th November,
1822 ;
In the 23d year
of Her Age.
Her existence
Was touchingly beautiful and brief.
Gifted by nature
With a versatile, inquisitive, and
Brilliant intellect ;
Accomplished
By
Education
In those elegant acquisitions, which
Throw rich and enticing hues over the
Passing scenes of life ;
Animated by genius, and cherished
By affection
She experienced in these
Varied sources of happiness,
The benignity of
Heaven
Brightening her vernal years
with Joy and promise.
In the
midst of her hopes
and enjoyments, sickness made
its insidious approach, and left its blight
upon her brow.
She faded
From the earth, like a pale Autumn flower
Before the coming blast of winter;
Leaving for the
Contemplation of the young, an
Impressive instance of
Mortality
And
To the heart of affection,

The memory of her virtues.

"Though many a gifted mind we meet,
Though fairest flowers we see;
To live with others is far less sweet
Than to remember thee."

JAMES BROWN,
Son of
John Brown,
And Sarah His wife,
Born in Providence on the
22d day September 1761.
Died on the 12th of
December 1834.

He possessed a sound and highly cultivated mind, and closed a virtuous life in peace with all men.

SARAH BROWN
Relict of
John Brown,
& daughter of
Daniel Smith,
and Dorcas his wife.
Born in Providence on the
17th of May 1738
married to John Brown, on
the 27th of Nov. 1760,
died on the 27th Feb.,
1825.

Underneath this Stone
are deposited the mortal
Remains of
JOHN BROWN,
The enterprising
and accomplished Merchant :
the tried Patriot and
wise Legislator :
the universal Philanthropist
and sincere Christian.
Born January 27, 1736,
Died September 20, 1803.

1800

This Monument erected as a Tribute
of affection by
Thomas Willing Francis
Sacred
To the memory of his Brother
JOHN FRANCIS of Philadelphia,
who died in Providence
November 4th, 1796
aged 33 years 5 months
and 4 Days.
Also of
ANNE WILLING FRANCIS
and
SALLY BROWN FRANCIS
Daughters of
John Francis and Abby his wife.

ABBY FRANCIS
Daughter of
John Brown and Sarah
His wife.
Born in Providence
On the 20th of November
1766
Married John Francis
On the 1st of January
1788:
And Died on the 5th of
March 1821.

A most vigilant and affectionate mother:
and in every vicissitude of life a warm
and faithful friend.
Courteous, hospitable and benevolent:
She was distinguished by her uniform
practice of every social virtue and the
conscientious performance of every
christian duty.

JOHN BROWN FRANCIS,
Son of
John and Abby Francis.
Born in Philadelphia,
May 31, 1791.
Died at Spring Green, Warwick,
August 9, 1864.

" The path of the just is as
The shining light, that shineth more
And more unto the Perfect Day."
" Mark the perfect man, and
Behold the upright, for the end of
That man is peace."

"Therefore be ye also ready:
For in such an hour as ye think not,
The Son of Man cometh."

ELIZABETH FRANCIS,
Wife of
John Brown Francis,
Daughter of
Thomas and Dorothy Willing
Francis.
Born in Philadelphia,
January 27, 1796.
Died at Spring Green, Warwick,
June 14, 1866.

"This is my commandment,
That ye love one another, as I have
Loved you."

"For we believe that Jesus died and
Rose again, even so them also which sleep
In Jesus, will God bring with Him."

ABBY FRANCIS,
Daughter of
John Brown Francis,
and Annie his wife.
Born at Spring Green,
in Warwick, Sept. 8, 1823.

Endowed with
rare intellectual capacity,
unerring clearness of judgment,
and unfailing sweetness of temper,
as this world was spreading before her
its most attractive prospects,

She was suddenly arrested
by pining sickness.
During an illness
of more than three years,
She illustrated in a remarkable degree
all the graces of the Christian character,
and died October 19, 1841,
triumphing in the hope
of eternal life
through
Jesus Christ her Saviour.

To the Memory of
MRS. ANN CARTER FRANCIS,
Wife of John Brown Francis,
of Warwick,
And Daughter of Nicholas & Ann Brown,
of Providence.
She departed this life at Spring Green
on the 1st of May, 1828,
Aged 33 years and 5 months,
leaving two daughters of tender age.
The excellence of her character was exemplified
by her unpretending piety,
and the powers of a strong mind
she improved
by much practical observation & study
of the Scriptures.
In life, the source of comfort to her friends
and
her entire resignation to the will of God,
their only consolation in death.
Being suddenly removed from an affectionate
Husband,
and all that could make life desirable,

she is most sincerely lamented by her family
and sympathizing friends.
" Blessed are the pure in heart, for they shall see God."
" Blessed are the dead who die in the Lord."

Also
JOHN,
Infant son of John B. & Ann C. Francis,
who died at Spring Green previous to his Mother,
on the 10th of January, 1827,
Aged 10 months, and is buried here.

Sweet babe, reclining on its mother's breast.

In Memory of
NICHOLAS BROWN, ESQ.
who died Nov. 27, A. D. 1791, Ætat 62.
He descended from respectable Ancestors,
who were some of the first settlers in this State.
His stattue was large, his personal appearance
manly and noble.
His genius penetrating, his memory
tenatious, his judgment strong, his affections
lively & warm.
He was a daily persevering & liberal patron
of the College in the Town,
And a member & great benefactor of the Baptist Society,
His donations in support of learning and religion
were generous & abundant.
His occupation was Merchandize :
in which by industry punctuality & success,
he accumulated a large fortune.
He was plain & sincere in his manners, a faithful
friend, a good neighbor & entertaining companion.
His knowledge
of books, of men, of business, & of the world
was great ; and of the most useful kind.

He loved his Country,
and had an equal esteem of liberty & good government.
He had deeply studied the Holy Scriptures & was convinced
of the great truths of revelation.
He was a religious observer of the Sabbath,
and of Public worship, and
trained up his Household after him.
He was loved of all men, especially of good men,
The Ministers & Disciples of Christ,
who always received a friendly welcome under his hospitable roof.
As in life he was universally esteemed,
So in Death he was universally lamented.
The conjugal affections of a mournful widow
and the filial piety of an orphan son and daughter
have erected this monument.

DEPOSITION OF ANDREW WILLETT, 1699.

CONTRIBUTED BY RAY GREENE HULING.

When the Company of the Towne of Kingstowne, alias ; Rochester In the Narraganset, was Devided into two Companies by Maj^r John Green : I was then Chosen Capt: of the Southren Company of Said Towne, p. y^e : Souldires ; I Marched to the house of Mr John Eldred, were Maj^r Green was, and Desired of him to administer the oath, to Me, that his Majesty had Comanded for without takeing Said oath, I Could not, nor, would not accept of that place : Maj^r Green Made Answer, he had it not about him ; I told him wee had it here ; upon which I went and Brought it him ; and he Did administer the Said oath to me, and the Rest of the Comissiner of officers y^t: were there ; But as for ye association I set my hand not to it ; neither was it presented to Me p. Maj^r Green to Subscrib nor any other ; and that this is the trueth I have hereunto Set My hand this 26th of Sept: 1699.

ANDREW WILLETT.

NEWPORT, Septr 26, 1699.
   Jurat Cor Me.
      BELLOMONT.

[*From Mass. Archives, 2, p. 97.*]

A LIST OF THE BIRTHS OF SOUTH KINGSTOWN, R. I.

From Records in Town Clerk's Office.

CONTRIBUTED BY THE EDITOR.

(Continued from page 56.)

E.

Earl Benjamin, of John and Sarah,		Dec. 18, 1712.
" Susannah, " "		June 25, 1715.
" Abigail, " "		Aug. 7, 1724.
" Lydia, " "		Dec. 30, 1726.
Easton Sarah, of James and Waite,		Jan. 30, 1735.
" Mary of " "		July 17, 1737.
" Mercy, " "		Aug. 24, 1740.

F.

Franklin Sarah, of John and Elizabeth,		May 5, 1756.
" Mary, " "		Oct. 29, 1758.
" Frances, " "		Jan. 11, 1761.
" William, " "		Mar. 14, 1763.
" Robert, " "		Sept 26, 1765.
Fish Jeremiah, of Jeremiah and Mary,		July 4, 1724.
" Thomas, " "		Sept. 14, 1726.
" Patience, " "		Jan. 28, 1728.
" Mary, " "		Aug. 30, 1730.
" Isabel, " "		Feb. 2, 1732.
Foredice James, of James and Mary,		June 2, 1714.
" Abigail, " "		March 14, 1717–8.

G.

Gardiner Samuel, of Ephraim and Penelope,		Jan. 16, 1719.
" Christopher, " "		June 3, 1726.
" George, of George and Susannah,		July 25, 1720.
" Hannah, " "		May 27, 1723.
" Amie, " "		Aug. 15, 1725.

Gardiner	Anstis, of John and Mary,	March 23, 1721.
"	Hannah, " "	April 22, 1723.
"	Thomas " "	March 11, 1725.
"	Amos, " "	March 27, 1729.
"	Abigail, " "	Sept. 26, 1740.
"	William, " "	March 18, 1741-2.
"	Mary 2d, wife of above John, mother of two last children.	
"	Job, of Nathaniel and Mary,	July 23, 1723.
"	Edward, of Henry Jr. and Catherine,	Sept. 8, 1723.
"	Mary, " "	July 25, 1728.
"	Abigail, " "	March 9, 1732.
"	Henry, of William and Margaret,	Jan. 9, 1726-7.
"	Abiel, of Benjamin and Mary,	Jan. 20, 1727-8.
"	Nathaniel, of Nathaniel and Sarah,	May 18, 1735.
"	Paris, " "	July 28, 1743.
"	James, " "	May 30, 1746.
"	Sarah, of Caleb and Isabel,	April 29, 1736.
"	Dorcus, " "	March 16, 1739.
"	Nicholas, " "	Dec. 8, 1744.
"	Tabitha, " "	April 8, 1748.
"	Experience, " "	Nov. 1, 1751.
"	Christopher, of Henry and Anne,	Feb. 7, 1737.
"	George, " "	Jan. 3, 1739.
"	Jonathan, " "	Oct. 14, 1741.
"	Henry, " "	June 10, 1748.
"	James, " "	Sept. 30, 1749.
"	Desire, " "	Mar. 31, 1751.
"	Clarke, of William and Freelove,	Aug. 3, 1737.
"	Thomas " "	Mar. 7, 1738.
"	Stephen, " "	June 7, 1740.
"	Mary, " "	Feb. 13, 1744.
"	Desire, " "	Nov. 26, 1749.
"	Gideon, " "	Nov. 15, 1751.
"	William, of John and Mercy,	Aug. 1, 1743.
"	John, " "	June 17, 1745.

Gardiner	Alan, of John and Mercy,		June 3, 1748.
"	Mary, of Nathan and Catherine,		March 5, 1743.
"	Nathan, " "		May 15, 1747.
"	Sarah, " "		Dec. 29, 1751.
"	Susannah, of George Jr. and Sarah,		June 16, 1743.
"	George, " "		Mar. 18, 1745.
"	Rufus, " "		Mar. 9, 1747.
"	William, " "		Sept. 8, 1749.
"	Levi, " "		Sept. 29, 1751.
"	Mary, of Thomas and Mary,		Nov. 23, 1744.
"	Richard, " "		Feb. 3, 1745.
"	Thomas, " "		March 23, 1746.
"	Tabitha, " "		May 24, 1752.
"	Frederic, of Thomas (of John) and Martha, Aug. 24, 1751.		
"	Rowland, of George and Sarah,		Dec. 1, 1743.
"	Thankful, " "		Feb. 22, 1744–5.
"	Benoni, of Nathan and Sarah,		Nov. 5, 1753.
"	Cynthia, " "		Dec. 27, 1756.
"	Susannah, " "		Oct. 7, 1758.
"	Stephen Champlain, of Nicholas and Hannah, Dec. 3, 1755.		
"	George, of Nicholas and Hannah,		June 9, 1757.
"	Rowland, " "		March 18, 1759.
"	Hannah, " "		Oct. 7, 1763.
"	Jeffrey, " "		Nov. 12, 1765.
"	George Perry, of George and Elizabeth, June 14, 1793.		
Gavitt	Oliver, of Samuel and Ruth,		Dec. 23, 1766.
"	Daniel, " "		Oct. 20, 1768.
"	Mary, " "		Aug. 2, 1770.
"	Esther, " "		Feb. 26, 1772.
"	Elizabeth, " "		Nov. 12, 1773.
"	Samuel, " "		Nov. 10, 1775.
"	Hannah, " "		April 4, 1779.
"	John, " "		March 9, 1781.

Gavitt Ruth, of Samuel and Ruth, Nov. 9, 1784.
" Arnold, " " Jan. 9, 1787.
" Perry, " " May 19, 1789.
Gould Mary, of William and Penelope, March 11, 1731.
" Elizabeth, " " Dec. 23, 1733.
" Waite, " " June 10, 1736.
" Tabitha, " " July 12, 1738.

H.

Haley Joshua, of John and Mary, Dec. 27, 1721.
" Martha, " " April 7, 1723.
" Elizabeth, " " Aug. 17, 1726.
Hammond Nathaniel, of Thomas and Rebecca, Mar. 11, 1746.
" Mercy, " " Jan. 18, 1747.
Handsom Anne, of John and Mary, Feb. 4, 1720-1.
" Sarah, " " Nov. 6, 1722.
" John, " " Dec. 10, 1724.
" Abigail, " " Sept. 14, 1726.
Hannah Mary, of Robert and Catherine, Feb. 1, 1713-14.
" Sarah, " " Dec. 10, 1716.
" Tabitha, " " Feb. 21, 1717-18.
" George, " " March 26, 1719.
" Catherine, " " June 2, 1721.
" Hannah, " " Oct. 13, 1723.
" Elizabeth, " " March 17, 1725.
" Ruth, of Robert and Elizabeth, April 18, 1731.
" Desire, " " Feb. 11, 1732.
" Ann, " " Feb. 28, 1734.
Hatch Ezekiel, of Ezekiel (of Newport) and Mary, July 2, 1746.
Hayes Stove, (a dau.) of Moses M. and Rachel, June 29, 1779.
Hazard, Oliver of George and Penelope, Sept. 13, 1710.
" Mary, of Robert, of Thomas and Sarah, of Richard Borden of Tiverton, Feb. 23, 1716.
" Thomas, of Robert, of Thomas and Sarah, of Richard Borden of Tiverton, May 9, 1718.

Hazard Thomas 2d, of Robert, of Thomas and Sarah, of Richard Borden of Tiverton, Sept. 15, 1720.
" Jonathan, of Robert, of Thomas and Sarah, of Richard Borden of Tiverton, Aug. 17, 1726.
" Richard, of Robert, of Thomas and Sarah, of Richard Borden of Tiverton, Dec. 31, 1730.
" Sarah, of Robert, of Thomas and Sarah, of Richard Borden of Tiverton, June 27, 1734.
" Mary, of Hon. George, Esq. and Sarah, July 16, 1722.
" George, " " " June 15, 1724.
" Abigail, " " " March 12, 1726.
" Sarah, " " " Sept. 15, 1729.
" Penelope, " " " May 7, 1732.
" Carder, " " " Aug. 11, 1734.
" Arnold, " " " May 15, 1738.
" Robert, of Caleb and Abigail, May 1, 1723.
" Caleb, " " Jan. 21, 1724–5.
" Caleb, 2d, " " Sept. 22, 1726.
" Benjamin, of George (of Thomas) and Mary, May 22, 1723.
" Simon, of George (of Thomas) and Mary, Aug. 8, 1725.
" Mary, of George (of Thomas) and Mary, Nov. 23, 1727.
" George, of George (of Thomas) and Mary, April 16, 1730.
" Susannah, of George (of Thomas) and Mary, Dec. 18, 1732.
" Enoch, of George, (of Thomas) and Mary, Dec. 6, 1735.
" Thomas, of George, (of Thomas) and Mary, Oct. 11, 1738.
" Stephen, of Stephen and Mary, July 10, 1723.
" Mary, " " Sept. 18, 1725.
" Elizabeth, " " July 17, 1729.
" John, " " June 26, 1731.

Hazard	Jeremiah, of Jeffrey and Mary,		Aug. 13, 1726.
"	Thomas, of Jonathan and Abigail,		Feb. 22, 1727.
"	Susannah, " "		March 24, 1729.
"	Mary, " "		March 22, 1737–8.
"	George, " "		May 22, 1742.
"	Joseph, of Robert and Esther,		May 21, 1728.
"	Elizabeth, " "		May 31, 1730.
"	Esther, " "		Dec. 7, 1732.
"	Stephen, " "		June 13, 1736.
"	Robert, " "		June 13, 1736.
"	Penelope, of Capt. Thomas and Alice, Feb. 11, 1730.		
"	Hannah, " "		Aug. 5, 1732.
"	Sarah, " "		Jan. 23, 1734.
"	Alice, " "		Aug. 30, 1737.
"	Elizabeth, of Oliver and Elizabeth,		Sept. 13, 1737.
"	Sarah, of Samuel and Abigail,		Nov. 26, 1738.
"	Thomas, of Thomas (of Stephen) and Hannah, Nov. 30, 1741.		
"	Hannah, of Thomas (of Stephen) and Hannah, Dec. 22, 1745.		
"	Stanton, of Robert, Esq., and Esther,		June 8, 1743.
"	Martha, of Thomas and Elizabeth,		June 14, 1745.
"	Sarah, " "		Jan. 10, 1749.
"	Joseph, of William and Phebe,		Dec. 20, 1748.
"	Hannah, of Richard and Susannah,		April 14, 1753.
"	Robert, " "		April 11, 1755.
"	George, " "		Sept. 22, 1756.
"	Benjamin, " "		Dec. 26, 1757.
"	Susannah, " "		April 11, 1760.
"	Richard, " "		Nov. 14, 1761.
"	Abigail, of Dr. Robert and Elizabeth, Aug. 29, 1753.		
"	Esther, " "		July 26, 1755.
"	Elizabeth, " "		Nov. 28, 1757.
"	Sylvester Gardiner, of Dr. Robert and Elizabeth, July 27, 1760.		
"	Nancy, of Dr. Robert and Elizabeth, April 29, 1764.		

Hazard Charles, of Dr. Robert and Elizabeth, July 14, 1766.
" Alice, of George and Sarah, Nov. 15, 1754.
" Thomas, " " Oct. 3, 1757.
" George, " " April 8, 1762.
" Thomas, 2d, " " March 3, 1765.
" Robert Hull, of Carder and Alice, April 10, 1758.
" Peter Bowers, " " Dec. 5, 1759.
" Robert, of Joseph and Hannah, Jan. 31, 1762.
" Mary, " " May 29, 1764.
" Mary, of Enock and Mary, Sept. 6, 1763.
" Sarah, " " Aug. 13, 1768.
" Enock, " " Dec. 28, 1775.
" Alice, " " Jan. 11, 1778.
" Benjamin of Thomas (of Benj.) and Hannah, Nov. 4, 1784.
" Thomas, of Thomas (of Benj.) and Hannah, May 8, 1787.
" James Robinson, of Jonathan N. and Mary, Feb. 10, 1789.
" Alice Robinson, of Jonathan and Mary, Dec. 12, 1790.
" Stephen, of Jonathan and Mary, Sept. 20, 1792.
" Jonathan Nickols, of Jonathan and Mary, Jan. 16, 1795.
" Sylvester Robinson, of Thomas H. and Abigail, March 3, 1791.
Healey Horace Dighton, of Jonathan and Sally, Oct. 1, 1841.
Helme Benedict, of Christopher and Mary, March 22, 1723-4.
" Christopher, " " Jan. 31, 1725-6.
" Samuel, " " Sept. 7, 1728.
" Mary, " " March 9, 1732.
" Silas, of Rouse and Sarah, May 20, 1724.
" Sarah, " " May 16, 1727.
" Jonathan, " " Oct. 14, 1729.
" Oliver, " " June 17, 1731.
" Samuel, " " June 3, 1734.

Helme Robert,	of Nathaniel and Mary,		Aug. 12, 1739.
"	Esther, of James and Esther,		July 20, 1740.
"	Powell, "	"	June 17, 1742.
"	Rouse, "	"	April 10, 1744.
"	Sarah, "	"	Jan. 30, 1745.
"	Elizabeth, "	"	Feb. 15, 1747.
"	James, "	"	March 12, 1749.
"	Adam, "	"	Nov. 29, 1752.
"	Samuel, "	"	Feb. 7, 1755.
"	Sarah, "	"	July 6, 1757.
"	Gabriel, "	"	Oct. 26, 1759.
"	Nathaniel, "	"	Dec. 24, 1761.
"	Catherine, of Robert and Elizabeth,		April 25, 1764.
"	Nathaniel, "	"	Sept. 15, 1765.
"	Mary Hannah, of Robert and Elizabeth,		April 2, 1768.
"	Ann Harris, "	"	June 3, 1773.
"	Martha Perry, "	"	Jan. 25, 1781.
"	Robert Hanibal, "	"	Sept. 11, 1785.
"	Cyril Ray, "	"	March 18, 1788.
"	James, of James and Sarah,		Aug. 14, 1778.
"	Adam Powell, of James and Sarah,		April 5, 1780.
"	Mary, "	"	Jan. 6, 1782.
"	John Clarke, "	"	Sept. 30, 1783.
"	Esther, "	"	June 28, 1785.
"	Bernon, "	"	March 16, 1787.
"	Elizabeth, "	"	May 11, 1789.
"	Sarah, "	"	May 8, 1791.
"	Mary, "	"	May 20, 1794.
"	Nathaniel, "	"	Sept. 16, 1796.
"	Sarah Clarke, of James Jr. and Alice,		April 8, 1804.
"	Mercy, "	"	Aug. 28, 1805.
"	James, "	"	May 11, 1807.
"	Jonathan Perry, "	"	Jan. 13, 1809.
"	Adam, "	"	May 25, 1811.
"	Esther, of John Clarke and Susannah,		May 28, 1805.
"	Mary, " "	"	Sept. 24, 1807.

Helme Anne, John Clarke and Susannah,		June 14, 1809.
Higinbottom Mary, of Charles and Mary,		March 30, 1724.
" Charles, " "		March 27, 1726.
" Mary, " "		Oct. 19, 1727.
" Ann, " "		Sept. 15, 1730.

Holland Henry Hooper, of Henry Hooper and Susannah, July 24, 1767.
Holland John, of Henry Hooper and Susannah, Nov. 24, 1769.

" Louisa, of Stephen and Abbie,		April 20, 1852.
" Stephen, " "		May 14, 1855.
Holley Daniel, of Jonathan and Deborah,		Feb. 11, 1754.
" Henry, " "		Dec. 10, 1755.
" George, " "		Oct. 24, 1757.
" William, of William and Sarah,		Dec. 28, 1767.
" Benjamin, " "		Oct. 10, 1769.
" Penelope, " "		May 21, 1771.
Holway Silence, of Benjamin and Penelope,		Aug. 11, 1722.
" Daniel, " "		July 14, 1726.

" Robert Hannah, of Joseph and Catherine, April 12, 1742.

" Joseph, of Joseph and Catherine,		May 31, 1744.
" Joseph, of Joseph and Abigail,		Dec. 2, 1747.
Hull Joseph, of Tristam,		Oct. 1, 1706.
" Elizabeth, (Hull) wife of Joseph,		Aug. 23, 1715.
" Martha, 2d, wife of Joseph,		April 5, 1722.
" Sarah, of Joseph and Elizabeth,		Sept. 8, 1732.
" Tristam, " "		May 28, 1734.
" Hannah, " "		May 13, 1736.
" Elizabeth, " "		April 7, 1738.
" Elizabeth, of Joseph and Martha,		June 20, 1741.
" Joseph, " "		Feb. 23, 1742.
" Thomas, " "		Jan. 30, 1744.
" Benjamin, " "		Jan. 22, 1748.
" Thomas, " "		Jan. 23, 1750.
" Charles, " "		Sept. 20, 1752.
" Martha, " "		Oct. 26, 1755.

Hull Lydia, of Joseph and Martha,   Sept. 23, 1759.
" William, of William and Mary,   Oct. 7, 1737.
" James,   "   "   Aug. 31, 1744.
" Mary,   "   "   Oct. 8, 1746.
" Sylvester,   "   "   Oct. 18. 1757.
" Bathsheba, of Charles and Abigail,   June 13, 1738.
" Hannah,   "   "   June 23, 1740.
" Samuel,   "   "   May 20, 1742.
" Gideon,   "   "   March 6, 1744.
" Charles,   "   "   Jan. 26, 1755.
" Joseph, of Stephen and Martha,   March 22, 1739.
" Elizabeth,   "   "   May 15, 1741.
" Stephen,   "   "   Sept. 17, 1743.
" Latham,   "   "   Feb. 9, 1749.
" Samuel Dyre, of Stephen and Martha,   Jan. 20, 1745.
" Elias,   "   "   April 13, 1748.
" Sarah,   "   "   July 1, 1752.
" Hannah,   "   "   Aug. 22, 1754.

I.

Irish Thankful, of Jedediah and Mary,   Aug. 24, 1722.
" Joseph,   "   "   April 20, 1724.

K.

Keais Samuel, of William and Margeret,   Aug. 19, 1728.
" Sybil,   "   "   Jan. 10, 1729.
Kenyon James, of James and Ruth,   April 17, 1693.
" Elisha, of Thomas and Mary,   Oct. 26, 1716.
" Daniel,   "   "   June 24, 1721.
" Desire,   "   "   Nov. 24, 1723.
" Ellen L., of Thomas G. and Susan,   Feb. 12, 1859.

L.

Lillibridge Champlain, of John and Amie,   Sept. 15, 1739.
" Dorcas,   "   "   Aug. 27, 1747.
Littlefield Samuel, of Edmund and Martha,   Sept. 28, 1747.
" Sarah,   "   "   June 24, 1749.

Littlefield Penelope, of Edmund and Martha,	Jan. 1, 1753.
Lunt Mary, of William and Bethany,	Oct. 10, 1781.
" Joshua, " "	Aug. 29, 1783.

M.

Mash John, of John and Mary,	July 6, 1734.
" Rowland, " "	Aug. 16, 1736.
" Mary, " "	Oct. 19, 1741.
Morey Mary, of Joseph and Sarah,	Oct. 18, 1704.
" Robert, " "	Aug. 31, 1706.
" Joseph, " "	Aug. 24, 1708.
" Benjamin, " "	May 2, 1710.
" Roger, " "	July 2, 1712.
" Martha, " "	Dec. 5, 1714.
" Sarah, " "	Aug. 31, 1717.
Mitchell Mary A., of John R. and Mercy E.,	Aug. 4, 1858.
" Martha S., " "	April 8, 1860.
Mawney Mary, wife of Elisha R. Potter,	April 25, 1779.
Mumford James, of George and Mary,	Feb. 7, 1715.
" Robinson, " "	May 1, 1718.
" Mary, " "	Nov. 27, 1721.
" Rebecca, " "	May 2, 1724.
" Jirah, of Peleg (of Peleg) and Mary,	Aug. 5, 1717.
" Peleg, " " "	July 25, 1719.
" Abigail, " " "	Nov. 28, 1721.
" Samuel, " " "	Feb. 2, 1723.
" Content, " " "	March 23, 1725.
" Sarah, " " "	Sept. —, 1728.
" Peleg, " " "	Nov. —, 1729.
" Thomas, " " "	May 30, 1733.
" Stephen, of Joseph and Hannah,	March 2, 1718.
" Phebe, of Benjamin and Anne,	Nov. 25, 1721.
" Samuel, " "	Jan. 20, 1723.
" Thomas, " "	March 7, 1724–5.
" Peter, " "	March 9, 1727–8.
" Lucy, of William and Hannah,	Jan. 29, 1725.

Mumford William, of William and Hannah, Sept. 14, 1728.
" Nathaniel, of William and Ann, 2d wife, Dec. 29, 1729.
" Abigail, of William and Ann, 2d wife, Dec. 27, 1731.
" Paul, " " " Mar. 5, 1734.
" Sarah, " " " Mar. 26, 1737.
" Simon Ray, " " " April 25, 1739.
" Gideon, " " " Dec. 17, 1741.
" Augustus, " " " July 7, 1744.
" Waite, of Jirah and Mary, June 27, 1742.
" Gardiner William, of Jirah and Mary, Nov. 26, 1744.
" Jirah, " " May 30, 1747.
" Mary, " " Aug. 24, 1749.
" Mary 2d, " " June 17, 1751.
" Sarah, " " May 1, 1753.
" Hannah, " " Jan. 18, 1755.
" Paul, of Gardiner William and Elizabeth, Jan. 8, 1770.
" Dorcas, of Gardiner William and Elizabeth, April 8, 1772.
" Amie, of Gardiner William and Elizabeth, May 20, 1774.
" Silas G., of Gardiner William and Elizabeth, March 4, 1776.
" Oliver, of Gardiner William and Elizabeth, Jan. 12, 1778.
" Augustus, of Gardiner William and Elizabeth, Jan. 29, 1780.
" Elizabeth, of Gardiner William and Elizabeth, Feb. 4, 1782.
" Davis, of Gardiner William and Elizabeth, May 8, 1786.

N.

Nash Ann Engley, of Ruth Nash, Nov. 25, 1714.
Nickols Esther, of John and Elizabeth, Oct. 26, 1726.

Nickols Thomas, af John and Elizabeth,		Oct. 24, 1728.
" Jean, " "		Oct. 2, 1730.
" Martha, of Andrew and Rachel,		Oct. 24, 1741.
" Eunice, " "		July 6, 1745.
Niles Ebenezer, of Ebenezer and Abigail,		Mar. 4, 1709–10.
" Catherine of Nathaniel and Mary,		Mar. 5, 1724–5.
" Catherine of Nathan and Mary,		July 18, 1729.
" Mary, " "		May 19, 1731.
" Sarah, " "		Oct. 22, 1732.
" Silas, of Silas and Hannah,		Oct. 19, 1745.
" Nathaniel of Silas and Hannah,		Feb. 17, 1747.
" Mary, " "		Aug. 16, 1750.
" Sarah, of Jeremiah and Ann,		March 31, 1743.
" Ann, " "		Sept. 12, 1744.
" Martha, " "		April 21, 1746.
" Simon of Mingo and Dinah,		Nov. 23, 1776.

(To be Continued.)

John DeWolf died in this town Oct. 12, 1841, aged 82 years. He was the last survivor save one of a numerous family of brothers, all of whom began life without patrimony or patronage, and who by their own energy and attention to business accumulated a handsome fortune. Was many years Judge of the Court of Common Pleas. Held many offices of public trust both in his native town and of the State. Was in early life engaged actively in the War for Independence. Was among the sufferers of those imprisoned on the Jersey Prison Ship in New York Harbor. Perhaps it was his rough treatment here that gave his mind such a hatred of kingly rule and made him such an advocate and supporter of republican rule. His honesty was proverbial. His honor and integrity was never questioned. He stood high in the esteem of his fellow men.—*From Bristol Phenix, Oct. 16, 1841.*

THE PATRIOTS OF HOPKINTON, R. I., 1776.

CONTRIBUTED BY HON. EDWIN R. ALLEN, TOWN CLERK OF HOPKINTON,

Editor of the Narragansett Historical Register.

DEAR SIR :—Thinking your readers would be interested in knowing who were the patriots of Hopkinton during the struggle for independence, we have thought best to send you the following list which we believe comprises the brain and the best portion of our citizens at this time, together with the document to which they had affixed their ever to be remembered names.

HOPKINTON, Sept. 19, A. D. 1776.

I the Subscriber do solemnly and sincerely declare, that I believe, The War, Resistance, and Opposition in which the United American Colonies are Engaged, against the Fleets and Armies of Great Brittain, is : on the part of the said Colonies, Just : and nesesary ; and that I will not directly or indirectly afford assistance of any sort or kind whatever to the said Fleets and Armies during the continuance of the present war, but that I will heartily assist in the defence of the United Colonies.

Daniel Coon	Jesse Maxson	Benjamin Kenyon
Joshua Clarke	Samuel Champlain	William Tanner Jr
John Larkin	Phineus Maxson	Joseph Witter Jr
Amos Maxson	Hezekiah Babcock	Peter Kenyon
John Coon	William Coon Jun	Matthew Maxson
Thomas West	Elisha Stillman	Jonathan Coon
George Thurston	Caleb Potter	Stephen Maxson
Edward Wells	Elisha Coon	William Coon
Francis West	Joseph Maxson	William Greene
Zaccheus Reynolds Jr	Nathaniel Kenyon	William Bassett
William Thurston	Benjamin Colegrove	William Tanner
Samuel Hill	Stephen Potter	Thompson Wells
Benjamin Randall	Joshua Coon	Sylvanus Maxson
Benjamin Maxson	Ebenezer Hill	James Wells Jun
George Thurston Jun	Thomas Wells	Clarke Maxson
John Maxson	Abel Tanner	Caleb Church
Robert Burdick	John Robinson Jun	Elnathan Wells
Matthew Randall	Lawton Palmer	Zellemus Burdick
David Coon	Thos Potter Gardiner	Josiah Witter
William Witter	Eleazer Lewis	Nathan Burdick
Samuel Reynolds	John Mashall	Peter Kinyon Jun

John Cottrell	Henry Clarke	James Kinyon
Hubbard Burdick	William Meedham	John Maxson Jun
Francis Tanner	Francis Robinson	Jonathan Rogers
Moses Barber	Samuel Button Jun	Joseph Barber
Paul Burdick	Samuel Lewis	John Randall
Nathan Tanner	Barker Wells	John Satterly
Parker Burdick	Peter Wells	Ichabod Paddock
Moses Hall	John Millard	Jeffrey Champlain
Jacob Hall	Amos Langworthy	James Fry
Joseph Witter	James Braman	Cyrus Button
Rufhus Burdick	Hezekiah Carpenter	Thomas Cottrell
Abel Burdick	John Palmer	Fones Palmer
Daniel Peckham Jr	David Davis	Benjn Rathbun
Jonathan Wells Jr	Daniel Peckham Jun	Josiah Hill
William Burdick Jr	Ross Coon	Phineas Edwards
Asa Eaglestone	Stephen Crandall	Thomas Wells Jun
Jonathan West	Oliver Davis	Billings Burch
John Brown	Simeon Babcock	John Brown
Elnathan Burdick	Samuel Langworthy	Henry Wells
Amos Palmer Jun	Zebbeus Sweet	Joseph Cole Jun
Nathan Palmiter	Timothy Larkin	Amos Coon
Uriah Saunders	John Hall Jun	Hezekiah Babcock Sr
Elisha Wells	Amos Button	Izreal Stiles
Nathaniel Burdick	Bryant Cartwright Jr	Thomas Barber
Peleg Maxson	Rouse Babcock	Peleg Barber
Stephen R Burdick	Asa Miner	David Davis Jun
Bryant Cartwright	Clarke Reynolds	Elias Coon
Jesse Burdick	John Braman	Gideon Allin
Waite Burdick	Samuel Witter	Josias Lillibridge
Joshua Collins	Samuel Babcock	Joshua Wells Jr
John Vellett	Isaiah Maxson	Joseph Crandall
Joseph Thurston	Henry Foster	Elijah Crandall
William Popple	William White	Joseph Langworthy

The aforegoing is a true account of those that subscribed the Test in the town of Hopkinton.

Witness: ABEL TANNER, *Town Clerk.*

AN OLD FASHION NAME.—The Providence Gazette under date of Dec. 12, 1795, records the marriage of the following parties:

George Alexander Ceaser Augustus William Henry Soliman Obadiah Frederick Pinchbeck, and Miss Catherine Rudolph of New York.

A FEW NOTES ON THE TILLINGHAST FAMILY.

CONTRIBUTED BY MRS. E. H. L. BARKER, TIVERTON, R. I.

IN the *Newport Historical Magazine*, published January, 1881, pages 156–162, we find a very interesting paper upon "The Descendants of Pardon Tillinghast," and having in my possession some genealogical facts not printed in above mentioned paper. I send them to you believing they will interest some of your readers.

Elisha Tillinghast is mentioned as the thirteenth child of Philip Tillinghast, (said Philip was the second son of Pardon, the Baptist Elder.) Elisha is simply referred to as "born August 29, 1716. Married a Pierce, and died." He married Deliverance Pierce, by whom he had five children.

1. JOSEPH TILLINGHAST, born ———; died Dec. 18, 1780, "about two o'clock in ye morning. Married Harmona ———."

2. JOHN TILLINGHAST, "born in Providence, Monday the 9th of December, A. D. 1745;" died May 6th, 1810. "Married Elizabeth Thornton, of Johnston, at her home, one beautiful Sunday morning in May, 1770," the Rev. Samuel Winsor performing the ceremony. They lived happily together until separated by death, September, 1800. September 26th, Mrs. Tillinghast was stricken with yellow fever, as mentioned in your last magazine, and died after a brief illness of only three days. By this marriage the children were as follows:

   1. NANCY TILLINGHAST, born March 14, 1774; died unmarried March, 1848.
   2. SARAH TILLINGHAST, born Nov. 20, 1775; died ———. Married John Holdoff.
   3. MARTHA TILLINGHAST, born Wednesday, Aug. 25, 1778; died unmarried.

4. FANNY TILLINGHAST, "born Monday, Aug. 6, 1780;" died unmarried March, 1849.
5. AMEY TILLINGHAST, born Dec. 15, 1781; died Sept. 13, 1834. Married Hopkins Green, of Providence.
6. DANIEL PIERCE TILLINGHAST, born June 1, 1785. Lost at sea Sept. 13, 1834.
7. JOSEPH HOPKINS TILLINGHAST, born Monday, Oct. 1, 1786; died of yellow fever Aug. 22, 1800.
8. POLLY WILEY TILLINGHAST, born Sept. 20, 1788; died Sept. 17, 1800.
9. ELIZA TILLINGHAST, born Thursday, Sept. 15, 1789; died ———.
10. LYDIA HARRIS TILLINGHAST, born Wednesday, Jan. 6, 1791; died Aug. 6, 1796.

The 3d child of Elisha and Deliverance Pierce, was—

SAMUEL TILLINGHAST, born ———; "died at Bay of Honduras."

4. DANIEL TILLINGHAST, born ———; "died in Surrenam ye seventh day of May, A. D. 1763."

5. SARAH TILLINGHAST, born April 17, 1751. Married William Holroyd.

BURNING THE POPE.—Last Saturday there were two large Ropes, &c., carried about this town in commemoration of the gunpowder plot. On one of the stages besides the Devil and Pope, was exhibited the effigies of Lord North and that old traitor T. Hutchinson, which afforded great satisfaction to all friends of liberty in this place. In the evening the images were burnt, and with them a pamphlet with these words wrote on the cover:

"*Lord Dartmouth's pamphlet in justification of Popery, sent over to the Colonies.*"

This pamphlet was burnt to convince his Lordship that his patronage will by no means sanctify such villainous productions; the tendency of which the good people of America can see into as clearly as any of St. James' Cabal.—*From Newport Mercury, Nov. 7, 1774.*

THE WILCOCKS-WORDELL MARRIAGE.

CONTRIBUTED BY RAY GREENE HULING.

Whereas by an act said to be an Act* of assembly held by an adjournment at new Porte Mar. 23, 1696-7 there is in Said act Inserted as ffoloweth
      vizt,

    Voated, That the house of Majestrate is Resolved into A committie Mʳ Wᵐ Gibson assyᵗ being impeached by Capᵗ Jeffery Champlin assisᵗ for Marrying Daniell Wilcocks, and Mary Wordell of Kingstowne Contrary to the Law of this Colony said Gibson pleaded not Guilty but alsoe Confest the said parties were not published according to the Law of our Colony to his Knowledge.

    The Committie haveing heard both parties and upon serious Debate Doe find yᵗ the Mariage with Danˡˡ Wilcocks and Mary Wordell was done Contrary to the Law of this Colony therefore Doe Declare said Mariage to be Eleagal.

We Underwritten which have sett too our names Doe Declare that we belonging to the house of Debuties the Month and year abovesaid, and Did attend the house whilst they Sat upon the Makeing of acts untill they arose, Doe testify and affirme there was noe such bill or vote, Read Debated nor past in said house but Since we have seene the Said act past under the Seale of the Colony as an act of yᵉ assembly.

Newporte Sept. 26, °99.

                                  JOHN FONES.
                                  ANDREW WILLETT.

Jurat cor me.
    Bellmont.

---

* See R. I. Col. Rec. Vol. III, p. 323.

NOTE. The above is a copy of a paper on file in the office of the Secretary of the Commonwealth, Boston. The original was evidently intended to throw doubt on the validity of the records of the R. I. Assembly. The Daniel Wilcocks referred to was probably he of the Shannock Purchase, and a son of Stephen of Westerly. I should be glad to learn who were the parents of Mary Wordell.   R. G. H.

MORE TESTIMONY RELATIVE TO LEXINGTON AND CONCORD.—Last Thursday Major Henry Sherbourne and Capt. John Topham with one company Colonial Troops, also Capt. Brownell with Portsmouth company, marched for Boston.—*From Newport Mercury May 29, 1775.*

DEPOSITIONS PRESENTED IN THE CASE HOPKINS v. WARD, 1757.

CONTRIBUTED BY RAY GREENE HULING, FITCHBURG, MASS.

I. Deposition of Col. Job Almy.

I Job Almy of Tiverton, in the County of Newport, in the Colony of Rhode Island, &c. do testify, that at the Superior Court held at Newport in March, A. D. 1756, I brought a Writ of Review, against Joseph Scott, then high Sheriff of the County of Newport, for not levying an Execution, according to the Tenor of it, for 670 Pieces of Eight, &c. on John Bennett, who was Father-in-Law, and Gideon Cornell, who was Uncle to the said Scott, he insisting, that Bills of Credit were a lawful Tender. At which Court, the Jury gave me the Pieces of Eight agreeable to the Execution. After trying the said Case, I din'd at Mr. Jonathan Nichols's, Innholder in Newport, where were present, Stephen Hopkins, Esqr, then Governor of this Colony, and President of the said Court, Wm. Richmond, Esq., another of the said Justices of said Court, and Mr. John Aplin, with some other Gentlemen. And as in Conversation, I was blaming Mr. Aplin (who was my Attorney) for not insisting on the late Act of Parliament, wherein it is expressly declar'd, that no Bills of Public Credit should be a lawful Tender for any Money Debt, the said Stephen Hopkins, with some Warmth reply'd, What have the King and Parliament to do, with making a Law or Laws to govern us by, any more than the Mohawks have? and if the Mohawks should make a Law or Laws to govern us, we were as much oblig'd to obey them, as any Law or Laws the King and Parliament could make. I was somewhat surprised to hear him express himself in such a Manner, and after a short Pause told him, I believ'd it would be difficult for him to find a man who would go Home, and tell the King and Parliament such a Story. At the same Time, the said Stephen Hopkins further said, That as our Forefathers came from Leyden, and were no Charge to England, the States of Holland had as good a Right to claim us as England had.

JOB ALMY.

NEWPORT, SS.

TIVERTON, June ye 23rd, 1757.

This Day appeared the above-mentioned Job Almy, and made Oath to the above Deposition, which was signed by him at the same Time.

The adverse Party living above twenty Miles from the Place of Caption, was not notify'd.

Before me: RESTCOME SANFORD, Justice A. P^s.
The cost of takeing the above
Evidence is 15d.

II. Deposition of William Richmond.

William Richmond, of Little Compton, in the County of Newport, and Colony of Rhode Island, &c. Esqr. on Oath, declares, That being in Company with Stephen Hopkins, Esqr, then Governor of the Colony above-mention'd and Col. Job Almy, with several other Gentlemen, at the House of Mr. Jonathan Nichols, of Newport, Innholder, he heard the said Mr. Hopkins say, That they at Home had no more Right to make Laws for us, than the Mohawks, or any other Nation.

WILM RICHMOND.

NEWPORT, ss.

LITTLE COMPTON, June 22, 1757.

This Day appear'd the above-mentioned Wm. Richmond, Esqr and made Oath to the above Deposition, which he signed at the same time,

The adverse Party living above twenty Miles from the Place of Caption, was not notify'd.

Before me,

JOSEPH WOOD, Justice of Peace.

Cost allowed £0-10-0.

III. Deposition of John Tanner.

John Tanner of Newport in the County of Newport in the Colony of Rhode Island and so forth Goldsmith on oath deposeth & saith that the Current price for silver in the year One Thousand Seven hundred and fifty four was three pounds four shillings pr Ounce in the year One Thousand Seven hundred & fifty five Three pounds ten shillings, in July One Thousand seven hundred & fifty six from Five pounds Ten shillings to six pounds in the year One Thousand seven hundred and fifty seven from Six pounds ten shillings to Six pounds seventeen shillings and further this Deponent saith not.

JOHN TANNER.

NEWPORT, Aug. 2d 1757.

Sworn before Jos. Sylvester Just Peace. The adverse party was not present being more than twenty miles of———.

IV. Deposition of Jonathan Otis.

Jonathan Otis of Lawfull Age on oath Deposeth and Saith that he has keept an Account of the Currant price of Dolars for paper Bills this five or six year past, and that in the year fifty-five Dolars were sold Currant for three pounds fifteen and four pounds that in the year fifty-six and the last spring he the Deponent was obliged to give five pounds ten and six pounds in New hamp shire Bills and the Bills of the Old, Middle, and New Tenor of the Colony of Rhode Island, and further the Deponent saith that for those Bills that were emitted for the Crown point Expedition in the year fifty five when Dolars were about four pounds he the Deponent Rec'd of the General Treasury in exchange for some of the said Bills at the Rate of four pounds pr Dolar as when emitted taking the Treasurys note for One third for one year without interest, and further saith not.

Newport August 2nd 1757.

Jonathan Otis.

Sworn Before Jos Sylvester Just. Peace. The adverse party was not present living more than twenty miles of.

V. Deposition of James Angell.

James Angell of Providence in the County of Providence on Solomn Oath Testifieth and Sayeth that he being at William Proud's Shop in Providence Some Time in Aprill Last and the Honb^l Stephen Hopkins Esqr and Mr. Samuel Currie of Providence both being at said shop began a Dispute about a pamphilit which Mr. Samuel Ward had Published against the Said Hopkins, and In the Dispute Mr Hopkins Said To Mr. Currie that he Lookt upon Mr Ward No better then a Thiefe and a Robber for he had Published falsewood against him, and that he woold have Satisfaction of Mr Ward. Mr Currie replyed what you would not kill him for I heard that you Said you woold, yes Said Mr. Hopkins I think it would be no more of a Crime to Kill him then it woold be to kill a man that shoold brake my house open to Robb me for when a mans Good Name is Taken away and by such falsewoods as Mr Ward has published, and he not to Resent it he ought to be Treated As Mr Ward has Treated me. then Mr Currie asked Mr Hopkins wether it would not be murther in him to kill Mr Ward yes said Mr Hopkins it woold. but I Desire to give him this offer Either to Take a Pistle and I another and I will blow his braines out or he mine or that he shall give me satisfaction In Law, I likewise was pressant at Mr. Clarks Shop in Said providence when Mr Hopkins said much to the same purpote to Mr Elisha Brown.

James Angell.

The Deponent was asked whether the Words above mention'd Said to be spoken by Stephen Hopkins were the same, &c in the same order they were spoken by the Sd Hopkins.

Ans^r—Yes, to the best of my Remembrance.

Sworn in Providence the 23d Day of July A. D. 1757, in the action brought by Stephen Hopkins above s^d—against Sam^{ll} Ward

The S^d Stephen Hopkins Present

Before me.

GEO: TAYLOR, Just: Peace.

VI. DEPOSITION OF SAMUEL CURRIE.

Samuel Currie of Providence in the County of Providence & Colony of Rhode Island &c Gentleman on Solemn Oath doth Testify that on or about the Twenty Second Day of April last past, he the Deponent, was in Company, in Providence ab^{sd}, with the Honb^{le} Stephen Hopkins Esqr, at William Proud's Shop, after some Conversation, he, the s^d Stephen Hopkins, said he would sue Saml Ward, and if he could not have satisfaction in Law, he would take a Pistol & blow his Brains out; the Deponent replyed & said; Sir, that is wrong, he answered No, I look upon him as a Thief or a Robber, that should come to break my house open, he has Aspersed my Character; the Deponent replied again & asked whether that would not be murther; Seeing that he would Time to reflect after the Commencement of his action, Mr. Hopkins Answered Yes. And further the Depon^t Declares that he heard the s^d Stephen Hopkins at ye last Election at Newport speak Words to the same Effect.

SAML CURRIE.

Sworn in Providence the 23d Day of July A. D. 1757 in an action brought by Stephen Hopkins, Esq. against Saml Ward Esq.

The s^d Stephen Hopkins Present.

Before me.   GEO: TAYLOR, Just. Peace.

The Deponent was asked whether the Words above mentioned, said to be spoken by Stephen Hopkins, are the same, and in the Same Order they were spoken by the s^d Hopkins.

Ans^r. Yes to the best of my Remembrance.

Sworn at the same Time.

Before me.   GEO: TAYLOR, Just. Peace.

FIRST RELIGIOUS WORSHIP IN BURRILLVILLE.—The Quakers were the first to hold religious service within the limits of the town, commencing to hold service here about 1786.

OUR FOREFATHER'S SONG.

Editor of American Historical Record:

In a copy of "The Massachusetts Magazine" for the month of January, 1791, I find the accompanying song, which is probably the oldest of American origin. Though the poetry is of but little merit, the high antiquity of the song entitles it to preservation in the *Record*. As the magazine from which it was taken is a scarce work, I presume it is entirely unknown to a large majority of your readers.

WILLIAM JOHN POTTS.

Camden, New Jersey.

" To the Editors of the Massachusetts Magazine.

GENTLEMEN: The following song is upwards of one hundred and sixty years old. The British are passionately attached to the remains of their ancient poetry. I wish to encourage a similar spirit in America.

Yours,   J. F."

> New England's annoyances you that would know them,
> Pray ponder these verses which briefly doth show them.

OUR FOREFATHER'S SONG.
[Composed about the year 1630.]

I.

The place where we live is a wilderness wood,
Where grass is much wanting that's fruitful and good;
Our mountains and hills and our valleys below
Being commonly covered with ice and with snow;
And when the north-west wind with violence blows,
Then every man pulls his cap over his nose;
But if any's so hardy and will it withstand,
He forfeits a finger, a foot or a hand.

II.

But when the spring opens, we then take the hoe,
And make the ground ready to plant and to sow;
Our corn being planted, and seed being sown,
The worms destroy much before it is grown;
And when it is growing some spoil there is made,
By birds and by squirrels that pluck up the blade;
And when it is come to full corn in the ear,
It is often destroyed by racoon and by deer.

III.

And now our garments begin to grow thin,
And wool is much wanted, to card and to spin;
If we can't get a garment to cover without,
Our other in garments are ¹clout upon clout;
Our clothes we brought with us are apt to be torn,
They need to be clouted soon after they're worn;
But clouting our garments they hinder us nothing,
Clouts double, are warmer than single whole clothing.

IV.

If fresh meat is wanting to fill up our dish,
We have carrots and pumpkins and turnips and fish;
And is there a mind for a delicate dish
We repair to the clam-banks, and *there* we catch fish.
Instead of pottage and puddings and custards and pies,
Our pumpkins and parsnips are common supplies;
We have pumpkins at morning and pumpkins at noon;
If it was not for pumpkins we should be undone.

V.

If barley be wanting to make into malt,
We must be contented and think it no fault;
For we can make liquor to sweeten our lips,
Of pumpkins and parsnips and walnut tree chips.
Now while some are going let others be coming,
For while liquor's boiling it must have a scumming;
But I will not blame them, for birds of a feather
By seeking their fellows are flocking together.

VI.

But you whom the Lord intends hither to bring,
Forsake not the honey for fear of the sting;
But bring both a quiet and contented mind,
And all needful blessings you surely will find.[2]

—*American Historical Record, February, 1874, Vol. 3, No. 26.*

---

[1] "Clout, signifies patching."

[2] "The above was taken memoriter, from the lips of an old lady, at the advanced period of 92. There is visibly a break in the sense, commencing at the fifth line of the sixth verse. We conceive that four lines have been lost; and are also of opinion that the four last lines of the fifth verse, and all of the sixth belong together. Perhaps some poetical antiquarian may favor us with a correcter edition."

JAMESTOWN RECORDS.

May 15 1732 Voted that liberty be granted to any of the freemen of the Town to build a School house on the Artillery lot

Voted that John Hammett be paid ten pounds for his last years cost for his services as Schoolmaster

Voted that £20 be allowed towards building the schoolhouse

May 21 1733 John Hammett as Schoolmaster is allowed £10 for his services

Jan 15 1739-40 Voted and Ordered that John Hall shall procure bords timber shingles and nails to buld a hous on Duchisland 16 foot Long 14 foot wide and 7 foot Stud and land them on sd Duchisland and he to be paid out of the Town Treasury

Voted that John Willson and Job Howland shall overse and buld said house as soon as possible

Sept 17 1727 Quarterly meeting Voted by the major part of this meeting That if the Colony will have another ferry on ye east side of Jamestown then the Deputies of this town shall Put in a Petition in the Towns behalf for to have the benefit of the same. Apr 16 1728 ordered renewed

Oct 17 1727 Ord that John Thoms and family be warned by the Searjeant to Depart this Town within one month after the date hereof or get sufficient security to be transported by ye Constable

Ordered that if George Steward and family doath not depart this town in six weeks after ye date hereof he shall be transport by ye Constable.

Ordered that James Trotter be warned to appear at ye next Councill

20th of 1st Month 1704-5

John Alden sen being called before the Councell and questioned aboute hiss being in this Town without leave (of this

Town) and likewise why he didn't Life with his wife and provide for her as an honest man ought to doe. hee not giving a Sattisfactory account the Councill thought him no fitt person to remaine in this Town, but that he ought to go live with his Wife and provide for her; Shee living at this Time as hee sais at Kings Towne. Did warn him to depart out of this Town within one weeks time or seven dais from the Date of this meeting

RHODE ISLAND PARTNERS IN THE SUSQUE-HANNAH PURCHASE.

Among the six hundred men who for £2000 on the 11th day of July, 1754, purchased of the chiefs of the Five Nations the large tract on the Susquehannah where Wyoming now is, were the following from Rhode Island:

Jabez Bowen Esq	Michael Dorrance
Jonathan Randale Esq	Elnathan Walker
Rob Randale Esq	Amos Stafford Jr
Jonathan Nicolls	Simeon Draper
Robert Hazzard	Thomas Mattison
Benjamin Bowen	Daniel Lawrence
Francis Colgrove	Amos Stafford
Martin Howard	Samuel Drown
Philip Wilkinson	John Bucklin
Daniel Ayrault	Thomas Burt
George Dorrance	Jonathan Moray
Samuel Dorrance	Charles Harris
William Sheldon	John Reynolds
Eliakim Walker	John Reynolds Jr
Richard Chamton	Jonathan Reynolds
Beriah Brown	Benjamin Sheffield

Jonathan Hamilton.

—*From the Poetry and History of Wyoming, by William L. Stone. Page 387.*

[ANNO DOMINI 1691.*]

* These lines, the rude effusions of the Puritan muse, were penned by John Saffin of Bristol, in praise of his deceased father-in-law, Rev. Samuel Lee, the scholarly Congregational divine. E. B. C.

A MEMORIALL

Of the Deplorable death of that most Excellent Super-Eminent and Profound Divine the Rv^d Mr. Samuel Lee, who Expired some few days After he was taken Prisoner by the French, as he was going to England in Capt. Jno. Froy's ship, and carried into France on or about the   of   Anno 1691.

Great Lee is gone! whose copious pregnant Braine
A Magazine of Learning did containe:
So Universall his Trancendant parts,
He seem'd to Appropriate the liberall Arts
And sciences so profound so Innate to him
That scarcely in an Age, one could out doe him
The languages t' him so familiar were
That he with Scaligor or Cicero might compare
So Florid was his stile, so full of sence
So fraught with Rhetorick, and with Eloquence
With all accomplishments of every sort
That famous Oratours of him fell short:
And in the Sacred Text was so Profound
That He the Hereticks did all Confound
And like the great Apostle highly prise
Did Search into the Deepest Misteries
And studied hard the Darkest Prophesies
Such was his worth, such was his true desert
That all the Universe hath lost a Part
Yea the whole world in him, lost such a Treasure
Which none can estimate by weight or measure,
Then cease my Muse, time may A POET Raise
Born under better stars to sing his Praise.

EPITAPH.

Here Samuel that famous Prophet lyes
Who was Profoundly Learned grave and wise
Samuel our Reverend Seer surnamed Lee
Alas! in Gallia inter'd is Hee
More Learning Rare both Humane and Divine
United in his heaven-born soul did shine

Elustriously in splendour then in them
Like Ignorant Fools who did his worth contem.
Lament then may the Race of all Mankind
Even all that priz'd his parts yet left behind
Especiall in those places where he shin'd.

ROGER WILLIAMS MEETING HOUSE, SALEM
MASS.

This historic place needs no further description, as the story is already familiar to every Rhode Islander. In this building Williams preached those sermons that resulted in his banishment in the year 1635, and the settlement of Rhode Island in May, 1636. We only add that the Essex Historical Society has built over it another building to save it from the weather, and every means of safety are taken to preserve it for future generations.

We are indebted to Mrs. Isabella W. Colburn for the pencil sketch from which the above was copied.

VISION CASEY.

NOT THE LAKE ERIE HERO'S GREAT-GRANDDAUGHTER.

To the Editor of the Inter-Ocean:

CHICAGO, July 7.—In regard to an account in your issue of the 20th ult. as to " the great-granddaughter of Commodore Oliver Perry " being adopted into Colonel L. F. Casey's family at Centralia, Ill., etc., the story appeared so novel and surprising to me as of the Perry family identified with that of the well-known naval officer named, I wrote the Colonel as follows:

"CHICAGO, ILL., June 22, 1885.
COLONEL L. F. CASEY, Centralia, Ill.

Dear Sir: In *The Inter-Ocean* of last Saturday I notice as special correspondence to that paper under head-lines of 'Singular Incident in the Life of the Granddaughter of Commodore Perry,' etc., calling her ' Vision Casey, a girl of eight summers,' etc., that her father was the grandson of that renowned character in the history of our independence as a nation—the man who in 1813, on board the good ship Lawrence, wrote to General Harrison, ' We have met the enemy and they are ours,' closing with the assertion : ' I have given you the facts as related by Colonel Casey himself, and they cannot be questioned,' after speaking of the young Miss ' as the great-granddaughter of Commodore Oliver Perry, etc.' May I now as a relative of the officer in question, ask you for the full name of said Vision's father, the alleged 'grandson of Commodore Oliver Perry,' as designated in the article dated ' Centralia, Ill., June 19th,' and appearing in *The Inter-Ocean* next day as described. Expecting to hear from you at an early date, I am yours truly,

HENRY G. PERRY."

In response to which, as of equal interest, doubtless, to those who read the printed account, the following under date of July 1, was received:

"CENTRALIA, ILL., July 1, 1885.
To the REV. H. G. PERRY, Chicago.

Dear Sir: I have not answered your letter to me of June 22, mainly for the reason that I was trying to get facts so that I could correctly answer your inquiries. The question you ask is for the full name of Vision's father, and I have been diligently searching and inquiring among those who were acquainted with Mr. Perry to try and get his full name. "The best information I can get is that he was called 'Commodore,' and those that I have talked to on the subject think that Commodore was his Christian name. They knew him by no other. They further say (what I had often heard before) that he claimed to be a relative, they think a direct descendant, of Commodore Oliver Hazard Perry. Two years ago this day we took the little girl, and that day he was at my residence, and I saw him once or twice shortly afterwards. I saw him on the street, and he promised to call at my office, but failed to do so, and I have not seen him since. My information was, and is, that he left here to go somewhere north of this, but where I have not been able to learn. I heard a rumor sometime afterward that he was dead, but never could trace it to any reliable source. I did not ask nor did he tell me his full name. I only knew him as Mr. Perry. The facts stated in the slip you sent me of my wife being impressed with the child's face, and how we came to take her to raise, are substantially true, and that he was understood by his acquintances to be a relative of O. H. Perry, and perhaps a direct descendant and a grandson, is also true. I have inquiries on foot by which I think in a short time I will be able to learn his full name, and perhaps something of his faiher's name. As Christopher Raymond Perry, the father of O. H. and Matthew Calbraith Perry, a brother of O. H., and O. H. himself, were all naval officers, and I believe each a commodore—this Perry could hardly, if he descended from that family, fail to be the descendant of a commodore. This child we have is named Mary Eliza Perry, as her father gave it to me, and was aged eight years the 5th of May last.

Respectfully yours,

L. F. CASEY.

This correspondence, of course, upon such point in print explains itself. It not only seems wrong for such stories to pass undenied, but justly *a living kinsman's duty so far as possible to keep the family record that remains clear and true.* No granddaughter nor "great-granddaughter of Commodore Oliver Perry" (or daughter of any "grandson" of his), consequently, to my knowledge and belief, or so far as I can learn of such lineage, is with other than relatives, kindred of the family, or at their respective residences.

HENRY G. PERRY.

79 North Oakley Avenue, Chicago.

EDITORIAL NOTES.

CORRECTION. In the hurry of the proof reading the following errors have crept into the text of the Smithfield record: Elijah Cook, son of Elijah and Joanna, born Jan. 16, 1750; not Jan. 16, 1754. See page 104. Philetus Henry Cook, of Sylvanus S. and Nolby R., born Mar. 9, 1838; not Mar. 9, 1739. See page 104.

THE HALL FAMILY OF RHODE ISLAND.—Mr. Herbert A. W. Hall, No. 18 Potter Avenue, Providence, R. I., has been for some time engaged in compiling material for a history of the Hall family of Rhode Island, and he earnestly invites all those belonging to or in any way connected with the family (who have not already done so) to furnish him with such items of interest either of family register, town record, wills, deeds, occupation, &c., as they take pleasure in collecting for this interesting branch of family history.

A FAVOR REQUESTED.—Our patrons who have not already done so, will do us a great favor by remitting to us the price of their subscriptions to the present volume. We need the money most urgently. The Register cannot live nor no other historical work for that matter, unless the Patron and Editor work and help each other. The Register feels that it has done its part and still stands pledged to continue so doing. Therefore if our patrons will aid us in this way, or in getting new names for us, we shall be greatly obliged to them. We need all the aid we get and more in order to keep the Register up to its present high standard. We have several interesting articles ready for publication and shall print as fast as our means will allow.

We take this opportunity to speak of Mr. Austin in connection with his great work, "The Genealogical Dictionary of Rhode Island." Mr. Austin has worked on this matter in a way to convince us that he means business. We have no doubt that more will be found after Mr. Austin publishes, that could and should have been added in its place, but if it does not get into its appropriate place, the reader may feel sure it never came under his eagle eye. It is a work that has been honestly written and for a purpose. It has great value of its own. It will become any library and it merits a rich patronage from the people of our State. We are aware that there are a great many book buyers that have been often cheated in a subscription work, and have vowed never to subscribe for another. We have nearly come to that place ourselves, yet we hold a reservation; we want a guarantee of honesty. In this every man can rely in dealing with Mr. Austin. A subscription will do him far more good than a sale will afterwards, and no one will lose anything by subscribing. Mr. Austin will never compel a man to take his work if it is not satisfactory to his patrons. The Register has seen enough of Mr. Austin and of his work to feel safe in making these remarks and we wish the readers to know that we are to have a work that can be relied on to be what it claims to be—a record of the founders of Rhode Island.

In Mr. Rider's book-notes of June 6, 1885, is a critical essay upon the last volume of the Rhode Island Historical Society's publication. It is refreshing to find one man who has the courage to show these martinets on the classic hill that they are not near so severe to themselves as they are towards one whom they foolishly conceive their inferior, yet often far their superior in what may justly be termed solid historical inquiry and in its publication.

In his notes of July 18, 1885, Mr. Rider gives special attention to Mr. Bartlett's Bibliography of Rhode Island. This work was written and the proof read to suit Mr. Bartlett, not the people or scholars of the State. Mr. Bartlett made this work for his own especial use and study, and of course no one else has any right to its use. We consider it a very neat thing for the author's use but entirely worthless for us. We never could see why the author put that work together save on the reasons above given.

Mr. Rider is a sharp critic, and the Register stands by him in demanding that there be less careless publishing of our State annals hereafter. It is the purpose of the Register to get things exact, but when wrong stands ever ready to correct. It therefore comes out squarely for Mr. Rider and joins him in the demand that a reprint be printed as it is as far as possible, and that a Bibliography of our State be written in a fair and impartial manner, and in a spirit of historical inquiry.

The Genealogical Dictionary of Rhode Island is completed, and comprises the record of *four hundred and sixty-five* families. The author will endeavor to make arrangements for printing immediately. Additional subscribers should send their names at once to

J. O. AUSTIN, P. O. Box 81,
Providence, R. I.

HISTORICAL NOTES.

On the 5th of November being the Powder Plot, in the morning there appeared on a stage fixed on the axletree of a coach the effigies of Lord North and Gov. Hutchinson with the Devil and Pope. North had in his left hand the Quebec Bill, and the Devil a cannister of tea, spitting fire at North, and after being exposed to view the whole day through the principal streets, they were burnt with seventy-five (75) barrels of tar.—*Extract from a letter from Charleston, S. C., in Newport Mercury, June 23, 1775.*

NEWPORT, 4th Oct., 1790.

SIR:—From inclination as well as advice of friends, I shall be a Candidate for the office of Senator in the Congress of the United States, to which should I have the honor of being appointed my Constituents may depend that my services will be honestly and faithfully performed.

Should I be so happy as to be favoured with your interest, which I earnestly request, I shall not only esteem it a favour but the highest honour that can be conferred on him who is with Sentiments of Esteem and Regard,
Your most Obd't H'ble Serv't,

JOHN MALBONE.

To William Peckham, Esq.

The Bible once belonging to George Wightman of North Kingstown, now in possession of Horace H. Wightman, Haverhill, Mass., has the following memorandum:
George Wightman in 1715 age 83 yrs born June 1632

    1 Elizabeth b July 26 16—
    2 Aylle b Dec 9 16—
    3 Daniel b Jan 2 1665
    4 Sarah b Feb 25 1671
    5 George b Jan 8 1673
    6 John b Apr 16 1674
    7 Samuel b Jan 9 16—
    8 Valentine b Apr 16 1681
    Will proved Feb 12 1722

STONE SPLITTING.—Joseph Babcock got out mill stones. He had got out a stone that proved too hard to break in the ordinary way. Mr. Cyrus French told him that in Massachusetts where he came from they broke stones with iron wedges, and gave him the idea which Mr. Babcock put into execution with success. This is the first case of stone splitting by this method in South Kingstown that has come to our knowledge.

A tornado passed over the towns of Johnston, Cranston and southwesterly part of Providence, thence across the river Seekonk and on towards Taunton river, unroofing buildings and doing damage generally, Aug. 30, 1838.

PROVIDENCE, Jan. 15, 1784.

Major William Allen, of this town, who has served with reputation as an officer in the Rhode Island battalion in the army of the United States, through the whole of the late War, arrived last week from head quarters, bringing with him the standard of the Regiment to be lodged with his Excellency the Governor. This battalion having served with distinguished honour and reputation ever since the commencement of hostilities in 1775, and having repeatedly received the public thanks of their illustrious General for their good conduct in various points of danger, particularly at Red Bank and Springfield, was, pursuant to General Orders, finally and totally disbanded the 25th of December last. As a mark of affection for this Regiment, General Washington ordered, that no detachment should be made from it, altho' a considerable number of troops are and will be continued in the field till the peace establishment takes place.

(KINGSTOWN) March 15, 1696.

Voted That ye Berths of Children Borne in this towne shall be Entred upon Register in the Clerks Office then Every freemans child may hereafter Claim Birth Right in the place of his or hers name and know the time of their Births and age at any time hereafter.

Voted That all marriages solemnized in this Towne and Entered upon the towne Register Likewise That all Burialls within this towne Be Likewise Entred upon Register as aforesaid. R. G. H.

FISHERMEN'S RIGHTS.—The right to the shore for the purpose of fishing and clamming was distinctly bought up in the great purchase (so called) in the Narragansett Country in 1659, the Indians not selling the shore of the Pettesquamcutt or Narrow river.

Mr. R. Porter of Providence, has established a line of telegraphic stations between Boston and that city, by which intelligence may be communicated from one place to the other, in clear weather, in less than two minutes. Mr. P. is about to extend the line to New York, which when put in operation will enable him to communicate any intelligence from New York to Boston and receive an answer in twenty-five minutes.—*From Bristol Gazette and Companion, Jan. 14, 1837.*

Some of our citizens have suggested the propriety of celebrating the 2d centennial anniversary of the settlement of this town. This will be perfectly proper when the proper time comes. This town was settled in September, 1680, and the 2d centennial anniversary of course will not occur for almost half a century as may be found by an examination of our records.—*From Bristol Gazette and Companion, July 8, 1837.*

SITE OF THE DAVIS HOUSE.—On June 14, 1712, Joshua Davis Bought of John Greene, his wife Deborah, and mother Ann, a tract of land near "Mill River" in Kingstown. We suppose this to have been the beginning of the present prosperous village of Davisville. The purchaser owned one hundred and three acres on the opposite side of the river in the town of East Greenwich, and his dwelling house was a few rods east of the present residence of Mrs. Mumford D. Tillinghast in "Frenchtown," where a depression in the hillside marks the site.

R. G. H.

THE ONLY TURNPIKE.—The only turnpike ever built in Rhode Island that ever touched the South County, was the Providence and London which passed through Exeter, Richmond and Hopkinton.

CANONCHET.

BY ALBERT C. GREENE.

Re-published by special request of our South Kingstown patrons.

THE early history of New England contains no narrative of deeper interest than the story of the brave and unfortunate Canonchet, the "Great Sachem" of the Narragansetts, and the last who exercised actual supremacy over that powerful tribe. He was the son of Miantonomi, the noble and generous friend of Roger Williams, and the protector of the infant colony at Providence.

Miantonomi had been defeated and captured by the Sachem of the Mohegans, who has been well described as the "Cannibal Uncas;" and after the ceremony of a trial before the Commissioners of the United Colonies, was, by their order, delivered to his captor to be put to death; and was, by the latter, murdered in cold blood.

At his father's death, Canonchet became, by inheritance, Chief Sachem of the tribe, and held that station at the time of the celebrated battle between them and the whites, familiarly known as the "Great Swamp Fight." This desperate conflict occurred in December, 1675, on a spot within the present town of South Kingstown, in Rhode Island, and was long sustained on both sides with terrible energy, and great loss of life. The fort occupied by the Indians, contained a great number of cabins, (probably five or six hundred,) which had been erected as a shelter for their wives and children, and as places of deposit for their entire stock of provisions for the winter. During the battle the cabins were fired, many of the wounded, and of the women and children perished in the flames, and the whole of the corn and other stores of the tribe was utterly destroyed. Their defeat was disheartening and irretrievable. They lingered through the remainder of the winter; and, in the April following, Canonchet, having rallied the remnant of his broken forces in a distant part of his territory, intended there to commence a new plantation. The distressing circumstances arising from these events induced him, soon after his removal, to engage personally in a daring and romantic expedition to procure means of relief for his suffering followers.

That expedition resulted in his death. He was intercepted and seized by the whites — delivered to the Mohegan Sachem Oneco, the son of his father's murderer, and by him put to death, by order of the English captors. The last scenes of his life form the subject of the following imperfect sketch.

In the variety of incident contained in the whole record of Greek and Roman heroism, there is not a more noble picture of high and unbending honor, of stern and enduring firmness, of proud elevation of soul, than was exhibited during the last hours of this " untutored savage." His character has already given beauty to the page of the historian; and it will, in future time, furnish to the poet who can fully comprehend and delineate it, a rich and inspiring theme.

To those who are fully acquainted with the historical narrative on which the following poem is founded, it perhaps need not be said, that the most characteristic expressions in the language, which in the latter, is attributed to the hero, are words which are recorded as having been actually uttered by him. These are given as literally as it was possible to give them in a metrical composition.

> The last great battle had been fought,
> The fatal strife was o'er,
> And the haughty Narragansett power
> Had sunk to rise no more.
>
> The bravest warriors of the tribe
> In death were cold and low,
> And its proud hopes, and gathered might
> Had perished at a blow.
>
> The old, the mother with her babe,
> The wounded and the weak,
> Had left their spoiled and wasted land
> Another home to seek.
>
> Through forests heaped with drifted snow
> That weary band had passed,
> With wasting strength till they had found
> A resting place at last.
>
> And there, around the council fire,
> The nation's aged men,
> In sad and sorrowful debate,
> Once more were gathered then.
>
> Long had they sat, the winter's night
> Was drawing to a close,
> When in the midst their noble chief,
> The young Canonchet rose.
>
> "Fathers, I've listened to your talk;
> Your words are good," he said;
> "But words of council will not give
> My hungry people bread.
>
> Our women cry aloud for food,
> I hear them night and morn,
> And in our baskets there is not
> A single ear of corn.
>
> We have no seed to plant the ground
> Around our cabins here;
> How shall my famished people live
> Through all the coming year?

Fathers! Before the sun shall rise,
Canonchet must be gone,
To ask the Wampanoags to give
His starving people corn.

The English warriors are before,
The Pequots are behind;
But the Great Spirit for his feet,
A ready path will find."

The word was said; the Council rose;
And ere the morrow's dawn
Upon his brave and daring task
The youthful chief had gone.

And with quick eye and heedful step,
Throughout the toilsome day,
Kept through the trackless wilderness
His solitary way.

At length in view, beside his path,
A friendly cabin rose;
And there he entered wearily,
For shelter and repose.

But scarcely had a watch been set
His resting place around,
When from the hill above was heard
A low and warning sound.

And then a shout, a rush of feet,
A wild and hurried cry,
" The bloodhounds are upon the track,
The English foe is nigh!"

He heard that sound, that cry — and like
A lion from his den,
Made, with a giant's strength, his way
Through a host of armed men.

Then came the word for hot pursuit.
The answer quick and short,
The dry leaves crash 'neath the flying feet
And the musket's sharp report.

He darts through the brushwood, he springs through the brake,
The earth gives no sound to his tread;
But when e'er for an instant he turns on his heel,
His foremost pursurer is dead.

Across the wide valley and o'er the steep hill,
Like an arrow just loosed from the string;
As if in the speed of his flight he would vie
With the bullets around him that sing.

His eye is on fire, every sinew is strained,
His bosom is panting for breath;
But each time that the fire flashes forth from his gun,
It carries a message of death.

His foes are gathering fast behind,
He feels his failing strength;
But onward strains until he gains
A river's bank at length.

Where the deep Seekonk's winter's stream,
Like a cloud of feathery snow,
From the wave worn edge of the river cliffs,
Rolls down to its bed below.

The eager host rush wildly on —
Where is the warrior — where?
Beside the swollen river's brink —
Why stands he silent there?

With firm set foot and folded arms,
He views his coming foes;
But heedless sees the gathering crowd
That fast around him close.

" Now yield thee, Narragansett," cried
The youngest of the band;
The captive slowly turns his head,
And proudly waved his hand.

" You are a child; — for war
You are too young and weak;
Go, let your chief or father come,
And I to him will speak."

Then silently he turns to gaze
With fixed unmoving eyes,
Where stained with blood, and blacked with smoke,
His useless musket lies.

To seize their unresisting foe
None yet among them dare,
For his proud bearing overawes
The bravest spirit there.

That he now stands within their grasp
Can hardly gain belief;
Is this Canonchet — can it be
The dreaded Indian Chief?

" It is Canonchet that you see,
Let every one come near,
And listen, that you all may know
What brought the Sachem here.

You burned my people's villages,
And quenched the fire with blood;
My tribe were driven forth to starve,
I sought to bring them food.

I came to find them corn to plant,
To save the wasting lives
Of all our helpless, weak, old men,
Our children, and our wives.

Unhurt I passed your warriors though,
Your crowded warpaths passed
Until you tracked me to the bank
Of this deep stream at last.

I sprang among the hidden rocks,
To gain the other side;
I slipped, and with my gun I fell,
And sank beneath the tide.

Canonchet's aim is very true,
He can outrun the deer;
And to a Narragansett Chief,
Who ever spoke of fear?

But when he found that he had wet
The powder in his horn,
His heart was like a rotten stick,
And all its strength was gone.

He had no hatchet in his belt,
He could not fire his gun,
Then he stood still — because he knew
That his last fight was done.

The Narragansett's bow is broke;
The nation's power is dust;
Its Sachem stands a captive here,
And you may do your worst.

All whom he loved are dead and gone,
His people's hour is nigh,
Let all the white men load their guns;
Canonchet wants to die."

" Thy prayer is vain; the punishment
Our righteous laws decree
To rebels and to murderers,
Must be the doom for thee.

Thou to the white men's council fire,
A prisoner must repair;
And there thou must abide the fate
Which justice will declare.

But send back now thy messengers,
And let there forth be brought
The Wampanoag fugitives
Who thy protection sought.

They were thy nation's enemies;
Let them thy ransom be;
Deliver them unto our hands,
And thou again art free."

" No, not one Wampanoag, no!
My promise shall not fail;
Not one, no, nor the paring of
A Wampanoag nail!"

He threw a bitter glance of scorn
Upon the throng around;
And stilled was every motion there,
And hushed was every sound.

" 'Tis good; the Sachem then will die;
He understands it all;
His spirit hears it and is glad;
He's ready when you call.

He's glad, because he'll die before
His heart grows soft and weak;
Before he speaks a single word
Which he ought not to speak.

The Sachem does not want to talk;
His answer you have heard;
No white man from Canonchet's lips
Shall hear another word."

Around his tall and manly form,
He wrapped his mantle then;
And with a proud and silent step,
Went with those armed men.

The third day when the sun had set,
The deed of guilt was o'er;
And a cry of woe was borne along
The Narragansett shore.

Through the Narragansett land, a cry
Of wailing and of pain,
Told that its Chief, by English hands,
Was captured and was slain.

He bore the trial and the doom,
Scorn, insults, and the chain;
But no man, to his dying hour,
E'er heard him speak again.

A ROAD DAMAGE.

The price to every man here under subscribed is as to their several names annexed, is allowed by us, the Jurors, for land taken from them for country roads already laid out by us and the damage thereon accruing.

To Nicholas Gardiner,	£2, 10s.
" Samuel Watson,	£6, 00
" Benjamin Congdon,	£10, 00
" Capt. Lodowick Updike,	£10, 00
For the hummock by the watering place,	
To John Briggs,	£5, 00
And the old highway that is to lay the bog adjoining to him,	£33, 10s.

To Henry Knowles the remaining part of the highway to the north and east of his land. Laid way to be and remain six rods broad. He allowed remainder of said highway he is to have in lieu of the land taken from him and the highway laid out by us.

And upon further consideration we do order and allow ye highway to ye eastward of within mentioned Benjamin Congdon, shall be and remain eight rods wide, and the remainder of said highway on the west side of said highway from the house that was built by James Congdon, and so on to extend westward until it meets with the fence or line that is between the said Benjamin

Congden and the land that was his brothers, James Congden's, to lie and remain to him, the said Benjamin Congden, his heirs and assigns forever.

In witness whereof we have hereunto set our hands this 10th day of February, 1715-16.

Joseph Smith, *Foreman*,

Alexander Huling,	Samuel Weight,	Jonathan Turner,
Samuel Perry,	Ichabod Sheffield,	Jos. Sheffield,
Benoni Sweet,	George Thomas,	Samuel Helme,
Jeremiah Clarke,	Job Babcock,	Abiel Sherman.

A LIST OF THE BIRTHS OF SOUTH KINGSTOWN, R. I.

From Records in Town Clerk's Office.

CONTRIBUTED BY THE EDITOR.

(*Continued from page* 137.)

O.

Oatley Samuel, of Jonathan,		Oct. 23, 1726.
" Rebecca,	"	Sept. 10, 1728.
" Rhoda,	"	Dec. 29, 1730.
" Benedict,	"	Dec. 25, 1732.
" Joseph,	"	Mar. 14, 1739.
O'Neil Abbie Randall, of James and Mary,		Jan. 18, 1851.
" Mary Ann,	" "	April 8, 1853.
" Susan,	" "	Dec. 19, 1858.
" James Daniel,	" "	Sept. 2, 1861.
Osborne Hannah, of Nathaniel and Hannah,		Aug. 23, 1703.
" Nathaniel,	" "	Nov. 20, 1708.
" William,	" "	Sept. 30, 1711.
" Ann,	" "	Sept. 13, 1714.
" John,	" "	Dec. 30, 1715.
" Abigail,	" "	Feb. 25, 1718-9.
" Joseph,	" "	May 31, 1724.

P.

Pitman Sarah Ann, of George B. and Peggy D., Dec. 19, 1815.
Peckham Peleg,   of Benjamin and Mary,   June 28, 1723.
"   Joseph,   "   "   Jan. 14, 1725-6.
"   Isaac,   "   "   Dec. 23, 1728.
"   Mary,   "   "   May 28, 1730.
"   George Hazard, "   "   April 14, 1733.
"   Timothy,   "   "   July 19, 1737.
"   Josephus,   "   "   Feb. 21, 1742.
"   Peleg,   "   "   Jan. 11, 1762.
"   Sarah, of William and Mercy,   Nov. 28, 1777.
"   Alice,   "   "   Jan. 19, 1780.
"   William,   "   "   Nov. 11, 1781.
"   Mercy,   "   "   July 11, 1783.
"   Dorcas,   "   "   Feb. 7, 1787.
"   Perry,   "   "   June 30, 1789.
"   Elizabeth,   "   "   Nov. 9, 1792.
"   Elizabeth, of Peleg, Jr., and Desire (N. K.) July 25, 1786.
"   Rufus Wheeler, of Peleg, Jr., and Desire (N. K.) Sept. 27, 1789.
"   Peleg Brown, of Peleg, Jr., and Desire (N. K.) July 17, 1792.
"   George, of Peleg, Jr., and Desire (N. K.) Feb. 24, 1796.
"   Mary, of William and Mary,   Aug. 27, 1795.
"   Josephus, of Josephus and Mary,   May 26, 1788.
"   George,   "   "   Feb. 15, 1785.
"   William Robinson, "   "   July 4, 1791.
"   Hannah,   "   "   May 17, 1795.
"   Susannah Stanton, of William and Susannah, Jan. 3, 1804.
"   Sarah, of William and Susannah, June 23, 1805.
"   Benjamin,   "   "   Nov. 18, 1806.
"   William Stanton, "   "   Sept. 22, 1808.
"   Mercy Perry,   "   "   April 29, 1810.

Peckham Dorcas, of William and Susannah, June 5, 1812.
" Jane Hazard, " " June 8, 1814.
" George Hazard, " " Feb. 18, 1816.
" James Perry, " " March 25, 1819.
" Edwin Alexander," " Dec. 10, 1820.
" John Cross, " " Nov. 30, 1822.
" Alice Rathbone, " " March 8, 1826.
" Carder, of Benjamin and Mary, Jan. 22, 1800.
" Henry Waud, " " July 22, 1804.
" Renewed, " " Jan. 19, 1805.
" Edward Hazard, of George and Elizabeth, Jan. 2, 1809.
Perry Benjamin, of Benjamin and Susannah, Nov. 7, 1729.
" Edward, " " March 28, 1731.
" Freeman " " Jan. 23, 1733.
" Mary, " " Nov. 19, 1735.
" Mercy, of James and Mary, Feb. 24, 1754.
" Anna, " " March 16, 1756.
" James, " " May 26, 1758.
" William, " " June 19, 1759.
" John, " " July 28, 1760.
" John, of John and Hannah, Aug. 7, 1784.
" Robert N., of John B. and Susan, Dec. 27, 1805.
" Susan, " " March 16, 1810.
" John B., " " Feb. 14, 1814.
Perkins Nathaniel, of Nathaniel and Elizabeth, Jan. 1, 1739.
" Susannah, " " Jan. 13, 1742.
" Elizabeth, " " Dec. 25, 1745.
" Abraham, " " March 9, 1747–8.
" William, " " Nov. 20, 1754.
" Sands, " " May 12, 1757.
" James, " " March 13, 1760.
" Jenckes, " "
" Ebenezer, of Edward and Elizabeth, April 4, 1741.
" Ann, " " May 19, 1743.
" Brenton, " " March 23, 1745.

Perkins Edward, of Edward and Elizabeth, May 20, 1747.
" Joseph, " " Sept. 24, 1749.
" Abram, " " Jan. 19, 1752.
" Hannah, " " Nov. 19, 1753.
" Benjamin, " " Feb. 7, 1756.
Phillips Joseph, of Bartholomew and Mary, Aug. 11, 1703.
" Elizabeth, " " Sept. 10, 1705.
" Mary, " " Feb. 7, 1710.
" Abigail, of Joseph and ——— Jan. 26, 1729.
" Dorcas, " " Dec. 15, 1731.
" Bartholomew, " " Nov. 10, 1734.
" Joseph, " " May 8, 1737.
Pollock John W., of Wm. Wilson and Mary, March 28, 1785.
" Samuel Holden, of William and Lydia, Sept. 28, 1787.
" Sally S., of Sam'l Holden and Sarah, Oct. 27, 1809.
" Abbie C., " " April 14, 1811.
" Simon S., " " April 11, 1813.
Potter Rouse, of Ichabod and Margaret, Feb. 13, 1702–3.
" William, " " March 4, 1709.
" Margaret, " " Oct. 11, 1714.
" Samuel, of John and Sarah, July 28, 1715.
" William, of John and Mercy, Jan. 21, 1722–3.
" Samuel, " " Jan. 20, 1724–5.
" Mercy, " " Aug. 15, 1727.
" Sarah, " " Aug. 11, 1730.
" John, of Ichabod and Sarah, July 29, 1724.
" Simeon, " " Sept. 25, 1726.
" Ruth, " " Jan. 19, 1727–8.
" Rouse, " " Dec. 10, 1729.
" Joseph, of John son of Thomas, Sept. 24, 1724.
" Benjamin, " " Sept. 24, 1724.
" Mary, " " Feb. 4, 1726.
" Robert, of Ichabod and Deborah, Nov. 26, 1726–7.
" Elizabeth, " " Dec. 18, 1728.
" Deborah, " " Feb. 15, 1732.
" Ichabod, " " Sept. 13, 1734.

Potter Ruth, of Benjamin and Ruth, Nov. 8, 1728.
" Thomas Benjamin, " " March 8, 1732.
" Lydia, " " Sept. 13, 1734.
" Joshua, of Joseph and Abigail, March 7, 1730-1.
" Abigail, " " Jan. 7, 1732.
" Robert, of Robert and Judith, March 6, 1732.
" Martha, " " May 15, 1736.
" Hannah, " " Aug. 24, 1738.
" William, " " Jan. 5, 1742.
" Judith, " " July 16, 1745.
" Rouse, " " Jan. 3, 1748.
" Elizabeth, " " Oct. 3, 1750.
" Marberry, " " June 17, 1753.
" Samuel, " " March 6, 1757.
" Christopher, of Ichabod (of Ichabod) and Sarah, Nov. 15, 1732.
" Nicholas, of Ichabod (of Ichabod) and Sarah, Aug. 31, 1735.
" Mary, of Ichabod (of Ichabod) and Sarah, Sept. 26, 1737.
" Thomas, of Ichabod (of Robert) and Margaret, July 2, 1738.
" William, of Ichabod (of Robert) and Margaret, Nov. 14, 1739.
" Margaret, of Ichabod (of Robert) and Margaret, June 11, 1743.
" Mercy, of William and Penelope, Nov. 26, 1741.
" Thomas Hazard " " Dec. 8, 1753.
" Alice, " " April 20, 1756.
" Susannah, " " April 25, 1758.
" William Robinson, " " July 13, 1760.
" Benedict Arnold, " " Sept. 12, 1761.
" Penelope, " " March 7, 1764.
" William Pitt, " " April 10, 1766.
" Edward, " " Feb. 15, 1768.
" Simeon, " " April 25, 1770.

Potter Sarah,		of William and Penelope, Dec. 13, 1771.
"	John,		"		"		May 24, 1774.
"	Pelham,		"		"		Dec. 7, 1776.
"	Mary, of Benjamin and Margaret,	Jan. 2, 1747-8.
"	Susannah, of Thomas, Jr., and Elizabeth, Aug. 21 1759.
"	Margaret,	"		"		May 23, 1761.
"	Thomas,		"		"		Dec. 2, 1762.
"	Elisha Reynolds, "			"		Nov. 5, 1764.
"	Asa,		"		"		Sept. 4, 1766.
"	Elizabeth,	"		"		June 21, 1770.
"	Peggy,		"		"		May, 1778.
"	Benjamin, of William and Lydia,	Aug. 20, 1763.
"	James of Ichabod and Deborah,	July. 26, 1764.
"	Robert, of William (of Robert) and Mary, Dec. 28, 1766.
"	Stephen, of Stephen and Abigail,	May 31, 1775.
"	John, of George and Sarah,		March 25, 1789.
"	Alice, of John and Mary,		April 8, 1792.
"	William,	"		"		March 4, 1794.
"	Mary,		"		"		Aug. 30, 1795.
"	Elisha Reynolds, Elisha R. and Mary, June 20, 1811.
"	Thomas,		"		"		May 4, 1813.
"	Thomas Mawney,	"		"		Aug. 12, 1814.
"	William Henry,	"		"		Nov. 2, 1816.
"	James B. Mason,	"		"		Oct. 1, 1818.
"	Mary Elizabeth,	"		"		Aug. 11, 1820.
"	James H., of Frederic A. and Esther,	Oct. 28, 1850.
"	Sarah A., of Frederic A and Anna A.	Aug. 31, 1853.
Powers Samuel Hoxie, of Sam'l and Anne.	June 2, 1785.
"	Mary,		"		"		April 20, 1787.
"	Martha.		"		"		June 4, 1789.
"	Annie,		"		"		June 29, 1791.

R.

Record Virtue, of John and Deborah,		May 19, 1746.
Reynolds Elizabeth, of Elisha and Susannah,	June 30, 1729.
"	Mary,		"		"		April 11, 1731.

Reynolds	Ichabod, of Elisha and Susannah,	Sept. 5, 1732.
"	Susannah, " "	May 16, 1734.
"	Elizabeth, " "	Sept. 11, 1737.
"	Henry, " "	Oct. 13, 1741.
"	Sarah, " "	Nov. 9, 1748.
"	Benjamin, of Job and Abigail,	Sept. 5, 1746.
"	Abigail, " "	Nov. 27, 1749.
"	Phebe, " "	March 20, 1731.
"	George, " "	Oct. 7, 1753.
"	Mary, " "	Aug. 31, 1760.
"	Alice, of Henry and Mary,	April 17, 1749.
"	Sarah, " "	March 28, 1751.
"	Stephen, of John and Abigail,	Dec. 5, 1749.
"	Henry, " "	July 23, 1751.
"	Mary, " "	April 20, 1753.
"	Elisha, of Henry and Mary,	April 19, 1762.
"	Sarah, " "	June 29, 1764.
"	Mary, " "	Oct. 18, 1766.
"	James, " "	Jan. 7, 1769.
"	Thomas, " "	Jan. 13, 1771.
"	Henry, " "	Jan. 13, 1774.
"	Jessie, " "	April 1, 1780.
"	Lydia, of Lydia Seerant, of Col. Elisha,	Aug. 24, 1773.
"	Jennie, " "	April 14, 1775.
"	Nancy, " "	March 21, 1777.
Rhodes	Annie, of James and Annie,	Oct. 20, 1755.
"	Joseph, " "	Sept. 10, 1758.
Robbins	Thomas, of Thomas and Elizabeth,	Oct. 6, 1771.
Robinson	Rowland, of William and Martha,	Oct. 8, 1719.
"	John, " "	July 23, 1721.
"	Marah, " "	Jan. 27, 1722–3.
"	Elizabeth, " "	June 16, 1724.
"	Martha, " "	Nov. 11, 1725.
"	Christopher, of William and Abigail,	Dec. 31, 1727.
"	William, " "	Aug. 1, 1729.
"	Mary, " "	Oct. 8, 1736.

Robinson James,   of William and Abigail, Dec. 31, 1738.
"   John,   "   "   Jan. 13, 1742–3.
"   Christopher,   "   "   Dec. 31, 1747.
"   Hannah, of Rowland and Anstis,   May 10, 1740.
"   Mary,   "   "   Aug. 15, 1751.
"   William,   "   "   Sept. 13, 1758.
"   Hannah, of William and Sarah,   Feb. 21, 1751.
"   Abigail,   "   "   Aug. 24, 1753.
"   Phillip,   "   "   Oct. 6, 1755.
"   James, of Sylvester and Alice,   Oct. 3, 1756.
"   William,   "   "   Dec. 20, 1760.
"   Abigail, of Christopher and Ruhamah, Jan. 20, 1755.
"   Christopher,   "   "   Nov. 26, 1756.
"   George,   "   "   Aug. 3, 1758.
"   Elizabeth,   "   "   June 14, 1760.
"   Benjamin, of John and Sarah,   Aug. 5, 1763.
"   Sarah,   "   "   Dec. 10, 1764.
"   William,   "   "   April 25, 1766.
"   John,   "   "   Dec. 16, 1767.
"   Sylvester,   "   "   July 12, 1769.
"   Thomas,   "   "   May 5, 1771.
Rodman Thomas, of Thomas and Catherine,   March 9, 1707.
"   Patience,   "   "   March 22, 1709–10.
"   John,   "   "   Dec. 26, 1711.
"   Joseph,   "   "   Oct. 1, 1713.
"   Samuel,   "   "   March 22, 1716.
"   Ann,   "   "   April 20, 1718.
"   Robert,   "   "   June 11, 1720.
"   William,   "   "   May 3, 1723.
"   Joseph, of Joseph and Tabitha,   March 23, 1733.
"   Mary,   "   "   Feb. 7, 1736.
"   John,   "   "   March 24, 1737.
"   Thomas,   "   "   July 1, 1740.
"   Benjamin,   "   "   July 22, 1726.
"   Hannah, wife of Benjamin,   Oct. 26, 1723.
"   Catherine, of Benjamin and Hannah, Dec. 29, 1753.

Rodman Mary, of Benjamin and Hannah,		Dec. 16, 1755.
" Anne, " "		Dec. 11, 1757.
" Luceanna, " "		April 28, 1760.
" Ruth, " "		Aug. 12, 1763.
" Deborah, " "		Aug. 5, 1766.
" Isaac P., eldest son of Samuel and Mary, Aug. 18, 1822.		
" Sally, his wife, daughter of Lemuel H. Arnold, Feb. 25, 1826.		
" Isaac P., of Isaac P. and Sally,		April 21, 1848.
" Sally Lyman, " "		Feb. 10, 1850.
" Mary Peckham, " "		March 25, 1852.
" Samuel, " "		Feb. 6, 1854.
" Thomas, " "		March 23, 1856.
" Samuel, " "		April 11, 1858.
" Elizabeth Arnold, " "		July 24, 1860.
Rose Samuel, of John and Elizabeth,		Oct. 21, 1734.
" Abigail, " "		July 1, 1736.
" Thomas, " "		Jan. 30, 1739.
" John, " "		June 13, 1742.
" James, " "		Dec. 19, 1744.
" Phebe, " "		Dec. 4, 1746.
" Phillip, " "		Dec. 11, 1748.
" Stephen, " "		March 1, 1750.
" Mary E., of George P. and Harriet P.,		Sept. 3, 1853.
" George A., " "		July 25, 1856.
" Thomas, " "		Dec. 3, 1858.
Rogers Mary, of James and Mary,		Jan. 20, 1743.

(*To be continued.*)

FIRST BAPTIST CHURCH OF RHODE ISLAND.—This church was established in Burrillville, and was formed Dec. 15, 1812, with Elder John Colby as pastor. It was organized with nine members. The first church meeting was held Feb. 11, 1813. The first quarterly meeting was held here, March 12, 1814, in the old Burrillville meeting-house.

THE STORY OF THE TABLETS.

III.

CONTRIBUTED BY JAMES L. SHERMAN, ESQ., PROVIDENCE, R. I.

From the North Burial Ground, Providence.

In Memory of
JOHN JENCKS, ESQ.,
who departed this Life
January 2d, 1791,
Aged 61 Years.
Suffice it to say
That he was,
A Firm Patriot,
A Sincere Friend,
A Real Christian, and
An Honored Man.
Mark the perfect Man, and behold
The upright, for the end of
That Man is Peace.

In Memory of
MRS. FREELOVE JENCKES,
The Amiable Consort
of
John Jenckes, Esq.
She died on the 18th Day of June,
Anno Domini MDCCLXXX,
In the 42nd Year of Her Age.
She was of Honorable Descent, and
In her shone conspicuous
Piety and Benevolence.
With such other Virtues and Graces,
As exalt and adorn Human Nature.
She was given to Hospitality,
And the Poor daily experienced
Her liberality.

Above all she was a sincere Christian,
And died in the blessed Faith and Hope
of a glorious immortality
through Jesus Christ
Our Lord.

In Memory
of
JOANNA JENCKS,
Consort of the late
Daniel Jencks, Esq.
A Woman truly respectable & worthy
of imitation so long as the
Filial, Maternal or Conjugal Character
well supported are held in affection.
A Member of a Christian Church in the
Town of Providence more than 50 years,
which Church she adorned by her steady
Firm Faith, her humility, sobriety & Piety.
She was well-known for her
general benevolence, she was
equally distinguished for her diffusive
Beneficence.
As she lived, so she died,
a Christian filled with those hopes which
the Gospel of Christ only can inspire.
Obït 13th March, A. D., 1796,
Ætatis 92 Years and 3 Months.

In Memory of
the
Reverend STEPHEN GANO,
Pastor of the First Baptist Church
in Providence,
who departed this life, August 18,
A. D. 1828

in the 42d year of his ministry,
and 66th of his age.
As a Preacher,
he was evangelical, devout and impressive.
As a Pastor
faithful and vigilant:
In the duties of private life, exemplary.
His sound Judgement,
mild and conciliating manners:
fidelity in friendship:
integrity of heart:
ardent and elightened piety:
and indefatigable labors in the cause of
Christianity,
have left indelible impressions
on all who knew him.
"This Memory of the Just is Blessed."

In Memory of
the
REVEREND JAMES MANNING, D.D.,
President
of Rhode Island College.
He was born in New Jersey, A. D. 1738;
Became a Member of a Baptist Church, A. D. 1758;
Graduated at Nassau Hall, A. D. 1762;
Was ordained a Minister of the Gospel, A. D. 1763;
Obtained a Charter for the College, A. D. 1765;
Was elected President of it the same year;
And was a member of Congress, A. D. 1786.
His person was graceful,
And his countenance remarkably expressive,
of sensibility, cheerfulness and dignity.
The variety and excellence of his natural abilities,
Improved by education & enriched by science,
Raised him to a rank of eminence among literary
Characters.
His manners were engaging, his voice harmonious,

His eloquence natural and powerful,
His social virtues, classic learning, eminent patriotism,
Shining talents for instructing & governing youth,
And zeal in the cause of Christianity,
Are recorded on the tablets of many hearts.
He died of an Apoplexy, July 29, A. D. 1791,
Ætat. 53.
The Trustees and Fellows of the College
Have erected this Monument.

G. ALLEN, Sculp. Jan., 1793.

In Memory of
MRS. EUNICE PECK,
Wife of
Col. William Peck
of Providence,
and Daughter of
Capt. George and Mrs. Wailhill
Corlis.
She died the Twenty-fixth Day
of April *Anno Domini*
One Thoufand, Seven Hundred
and Eighty-four,
In the Twenty-ninth Year
of her Age.
She's gone ; fhe's paff the gloomy fhades of Night.

Sacred
to the Memory of
MRS. PHEBE P. BARKER,
the beloved and affectionate wife of
Col. William C. Barker,
and third daughter of
Mr. Isaac & Mrs. Phebe Peck:
She was born the 23d day of Nov., 1797,
and departed this life on the 1st day
of July, A. D. 1827.
While memory holds a seat, the

cherished remembrance of
her virtues will live in the
heart of her relatives and
friends, and the tender
recollections of her
unspotted life, operate
as a linient balm to
their lacerated
feelings.

Also PHEBE ANN,
daughter of
Col. Wm. C. & Mrs. Phebe P. Barker,
Died June 27th, 1827,
Aged 7 days.

Sacred to the Memory of
COL. JEREMIAH OLNEY.
A Patriot Soldier of the Revolution.
Late Collector of the Customs for the District
of Providence,
and President of the Society of Cincinati
of the State of Rhode Island
and Providence Plantations.
He closed his honorable and useful Life,
with Christian Serenity,
on the 10th day of November, 1812,
in the 63d year of his Age.
As a Citizen
he was virtuous and public-spirited.
As an Officer
he was ardent, judicious and intrepid.
The unqualified Approbation
of Washington, his immortal Chief,
is a Demonstration of his Worth,
which will transmit his Name
in the Annals of his Country
with Reputation

to Posterity.
To his natural elevation of Soul
were signally united
the purest Honour and Integrity,
from which no Interest could swerve,
No Danger appal him.
His Conscience was his Monitor,
Truth and Justice were his Guides.
Hospitality and Benevolence
were conspicuous Traits in his Character,
and his Relatives and Friends,
will cherish the Remembrance of his Virtues
while Memory holds a seat.

The Grave of
JOSEPH L. TILLINGHAST,
Counsellor-at-Law,
Born in Taunton, Massachusetts,
1790.
Died in Providence
Dec. 31, 1844.
He was for ten years a Representative
from this city in the General Assembly
of Rhode Island; and for six years, a
Representative from this state in the
Congress of the United States.
In silence and in hope
he rests.

Also
Sacred to the Memory of
REBECCA POWER,
his wife,
interred at Georgetown, D. C.,
where she died October 18,
1860.

This frail Memorial
is the last sad Tribute of
Affection to the Memory of
Miss SARAH ANN OLNEY,
Daughter of the late
Col. Christopher Olney.
She departed this Life the
16th Day of April, A. D. 1815.
Aged 30 Years.
While Memory holds a seat, the
cherished Remembrance of her
Virtues will live in the Hearts
of her Relatives and Friends,
and the tender Recollection
of her unspotted Life
operate as a Leinint
Balm to their lacerated
Feelings.

Here repose the remains
of
CHRISTOPHER C. OLNEY,
who on the 12th day of April,
A. D. 1809,
in the 36th year of his Age,
surrendered his soul to God,
in the full hope of a glorious
resurrection through the
merits of his Redeemer.
His Brother Nathaniel G. Olney,
as a tribute of his affection,
has erected this stone.
The brilliant star of faith arose and shed
Celestial comfort on the dying bed.

Sacred to the Memory of
MR. JAMES HUNNIMAN OLNEY,
son of Col. Christopher Olney &

Mrs. Minah his wife,
born April 7, A. D. 1767.
From his earliest youth
He was remarkably obedient & attentive
to his Parents,
kind & obliging to his relations & friends.
His person was graceful,
His manners, modest & unassuming,
conveying at once
an idea of an ingenious mind
and a feeling heart.
He sustained a fair moral character,
adorned with a display of those dispositions,
which endeared him to all his acquaintances.
He was educated a Merchant
was industrious, persevering & successful
in business,
till oppressed with a lingering disease,
which he bore with fortitude & resignation.
He closed his bright prospects,
and went out of the World
satisfied with the goodness of that God
who sent him into it,
& departed this life July 29, A. D. 1796,
in the 30th Year of his Age.

This frail Memorial
is the last sad tribute of
Affection to the Memory of
Mrs. SARAH ANN OLNEY,
Daughter of the late
Col. Christopher Olney.
She departed this Life, the
16th Day of April, A. D. 1815.
Aged 30 Years.
While memory holds a seat, the
cherished remembrance of her
Virtues will live in the Hearts

of her relatives and friends,
and the tender recollection
of her unspotted Life
operate as a lenient
Balm to their
lacerated
Feelings.

IMPROVED ORDER OF RED MEN.

CONTRIBUTED BY FRED. J. SMITH, PROVIDENCE, R. I.

THIS organization, known as the Improved Order of Red Men, is a fraternal and benevolent institution, of purely American origin. The exact date of its origin is not known, as evidence can be traced back to a period previous to the Revolution. But documents in possession of the Great Council of the United States, tell us that in the year 1813, a society of Red Men was formed at Fort Mifflin, on the Delaware River, then garrisoned by American troops; after peace was declared, members of the society became widely scattered, but being much impressed with the customs and habits, also the pleasant memories of its existence, formed new Societies, under the same laws and with the same intentions of the Society at Fort Mifflin. In the year 1835 we find many council fires kindled throughout the country, and in May of the same year, delegates from different jurisdictions convened at Baltimore, and adopted substantially the Ritual, Laws, and Regulations that govern it to-day. Since which time the organization is known as the Improved Order of Red Men. Its growth has been slow but sure, until now nearly every State in the Union contains Tribes and Great Councils, in full fellowship with the Great Council of the United States. The order is founded on the manners and customs of the Indian Race, and its Ritual perpetuates the memory of the forms and religious ceremonies peculiar to that unfortunate people. They believe in a Great Spirit who governs the world, so any one joining this Order must declare his belief in the Great Spirit, the Creator and Preserver of the universe. The subordinate branches or primary assemblies of the Order are denominated Tribes. The Ritual is divided into four Degrees: Adoption, Hunter's, Warrior's and Chief's; and for beauty and originality they are unsurpassed. The Supreme Body of a State is known by the title of Great Council, and the Supreme Body over all as the Great Council of the United States. The forms, ceremonies and lectures used in the adoption of members and confering of degrees are interesting and instructive, and free from anything frivolous or disagreeable. The meetings are held for the transaction of business of a moral, benevolent and charitable character, and everything partaking of levity, or political or sectarian tendencies, is excluded therefrom.

Its objects are to promote among men the exercise and practice of the true principles of benevolence and charity; the care and protection of the Widow and Orphans and the cultivation of friendly relations among mankind, in short the Motto—"Freedom, Friendship and Charity"—indicates quite clearly the objects and aim of the Brotherhood, whilst the preservation from oblivion of much that relates to one of the declining Races of mankind, and which will prove interesting to the student and antiquarian, may not be considered unimportant results of the organization, and it now has an existance in more than thirty-five jurisdictions; in some of these it equals the strongest of kindred societies in zeal and prosperity, and in many of them has a nucleus both healthy and promising.

The Order is not very strong in the Eastern States. It was first introduced into Rhode Island on the 4th day of September, 1871, at which time   instituted King Philip Tribe No. 1, at Olneyville, when the following Chiefs were raised up to their respective stumps: Sachem, Sr. Sagamore, Jr. Sagamore, Chief of Records, Keeper of Wampum, First Sanop, Second Sanop, Guard of the Wigwam, Guard of the Forest.

The Tribe increased rapidly in membership and in a very short time numbered over a hundred members.

Canonicus Tribe No. 2, of Phenix, also Miantonomah Tribe No. 3, of Providence, was instituted the following year. On the 5th day of August, 1872, Great Incohonie William B. Eckert, assisted by Morris H. Gorham, instituted the Great Council of the State at Miantonomah Wigwam No. 41, Weybossett Street, when the following Great Chiefs were raised up to their respective Stumps:

Great Prophet,	JOHN L. PERRIN.
Great Sachem,	W. V. SLOCUM.
Great Sr. Sagamore,	ANDREW MCKENZIE.
Great Jr. Sagamore,	N. R. TILTON.
Great Chief of Records,	H. B. WINSLOW.
Great Keeper of Wampom,	A. R. SHERMAN.
Great Sanop,	S. R. NICHOLAS.
Great Guard of Forest,	H. L. HOWARD.
Great Guard of Wigwam,	

Shortly after the institution of the Great Council the following Tribes were instituted:

Wampanoag No. 4, of Pawtucket; Narragansett No. 5, of Natick; and Red Jacket No. 6, of Newport. In 1874 Wamsutta Tribe No. 7, was instituted, but owing to the financial depression of the times they did not prosper, and in 1876 they surrendered their Charter to the Great Council.

There is six Tribes in the State at the present time (1878) with a membership of a little less than four hundred, the most prosperous of which is King Philip No. 1, of Providence, Canonicas No. 2, of Phenix, and Narragansett No. 5, of Natick.

The following are the present Great Chiefs of the Great Council of the State:

Great Prophet,	FRED. J. SMITH No. 1.
Great Sachem,	HIRAM L. HOWARD No. 4.
Great Sr. Sagamore,	H. C. BURDICK No. 6.
Great Jr. Sagamore,	FRED A. KNIGHT No. 3.
Great Chief of Records,	JOHN WELLS No. 5.
Great Keeper of Wampum,	O. D. TILLINGHAST No. 5.
Great Sanop,	JOHN GALLINGTON No. 1.
Great Mishenawa,	A. E. SPENCER.
Great Guard of Wigwam,	EARL FENNER.
Great Guard of the Forest,	S. A. BALLOU.

THE RECORD OF OLD SMITHFIELD FROM 1730 TO 1850.

From Records in Town Clerk's Office, Lincoln.

CONTRIBUTED BY THE EDITOR.

(*Continued from Vol. IV, page 113.*)

F.

MARRIAGES.

Fairbanks Joseph Orville, of James, and Rachel Hewitt, of Rhoda; m. by Rev. Wm. Verrinder, March 13, 1845.

Fairbrother Elizabeth, or Esther, and Christopher Harris, April 15, 1753.

Fairfield Skipper, and Rose Sly; m. by Thomas Sayles, justice, Sept. 1, 1736.

Fales David G., and Parthenia C. Sprague; m. by Rev. David Pickering, May 3, 1829.

Fanning John M., of Providence, and Amie Ann Miller, of Smithfield; m. by Rev. B. P. Byram, May 19, 1842.

Farnum Mary, and Silas Tuft, Jan. 26, 1748.
"   Moses, and Lucy Comstock; m. by Thomas Arnold, justice, Dec. 17, 1752.
"   John, of Uxbridge, and Martha Comstock, of Smithfield, widow of Daniel, Jur.; m. by Thomas Arnold, justice, Aug. 19, 1756.
"   Jonathan, of Uxbridge, and Urania Harris of Preserved, of Smithfield; m. by Stephen Arnold, justice, Sept. 29, 1765.
"   Mary, and Capt. Wm. Waterman, Nov. 27, 1777.
"   Lydia, and Benjamin Tucker, Mar. 23, 1786.
"   Mary, and George Smith, March 11, 1804.
"   Lydia, and George Angel, Nov. 25, 1810.
"   John, of Noah, and Lydia Mathewson, of Joseph; m. by Robert Harris, justice, Aug. 16, 1812.
"   Freelove, and Asahel Aldrich, April 10, 1817.
"   Ruth, and Daniel Mowry, 3d, Dec. 6, 1818.
"   Emily, and Henry S. Mansfield, Sept. 12, 1844.
Farrar Ellis, of Daniel F., and Sarah Chatterton, of Nathan C., both of England; m. by Rev. T. A. Taylor, April 2, 1846.
"   Mary, and Joseph Hansom, Dec. 21, 1846.
"   William, of Dan., and Sarah Gill, of John; m. by Rev. Bayles P. Talbot, —— 1846.
Feathergill Mrs. Mary, and Jonathan Armitage Fifield, Nov. 11, 1743.
Felsh Walton, of Attleboro, Mass., and Lydia Inman, of Smithfield; m. by Elijah Arnold, justice, June 7, 1815.
Feltus William H., and Olive L. Hill; both of Danby, Vt.; m. by Rev. David Andrews, Jan. 15, 1852.
Fenner Lydia A., and Isaac M. Sweet, March 18, 1849.
Ferent John Billings, and Julia Ann Latham; m. Rev. Asel D. Cole, May 15, 1843.
Field Phebe, and George Bannister, Feb. 19, 1754.
"   Mary A., and Charles A Scott, Dec. 2, 1844.

Fifield Jonathan Armitage, and Mrs. Mary Feathergill; m. by Thomas Sayles, justice, Nov. 11, 1743.
Fisher Daniel, and Mary Pond; m. by William Arnold, justice, Oct. 9, 1741.
" Joseph, and Rebecca Nason; m. by William Arnold, justice, Sept. 8, 1746.
" Susan L., and David Buffinton; Dec. 24, 1840.
Fish Mary, and Joseph Darling; Jan. 6, 1735–6.
" Ruth, and Samuel Hayward; July 13, 1743.
" Esther, and Ebenezer Albee; Feb. 28, 1750.
" Chloe, and Augustus Mowry, Nov. 30, 1780.
Fisk Alvin E. A., of Smithfield, son of Willard, and Sarah Ann Corey, of Cumberland, dau. of Christopher H.; m. by Rev. Reuben Allen, July 5, 1840.
" Abbie Ann, and Benjamin Kingsley; May 6, 1849.
" Mrs. Jenette, and James Lawton, Apr. 22, 1850.
" Hopesey B., and Levi Phillips; July 4, 1850.
Fitton John, and Martha Winterbottom; m. by Rev. Asel D. Cole, Oct. 14, 1844.
Fitts Elizabeth Ann, and Rev. Daniel Rounds; Apr. 1, 1840.
Fletcher Matilda, and James F. Smith; Mar. 25, 1850.
Flynn David, and Rachel Aldrich; m. by Thomas Arnold, justice, Mar. 22, 1752.
Force Elizabeth, and Benjamin Darling, July 28, 1735.
Fords William, and Jemima Callum; m. by Thomas Lapham, justice, Mar. 26, 1749.
Ford William and Jemima Callum; m. by Thomas Lapham, justice, Mar. 17, 1752.
Follett Lewis, of Cumberland, son of George, and Rebecca Mathewson, of Smithfield, dau. of Joseph; m. by Thomas Man, justice, June 10, 1824.
" Leonard Jenckes, of Leonard, and Phebe H. Vallett, of Wanton; m. by Simon A. Sayles, Nov. 24, 1842.
" James, and Mary A. Aldrich; m. by Rev. John Boyden, Jr., Apr. 16, 1845.
Foot Abigail, and Daniel Cook; June 6, 1751.

Foss Charles M., and Susan N. Miller; m. by Rev. B. P. Byram, June 25, 1848.
Foster Mary, and Joseph Clarke, Nov. 2, 1800.
" Samuel, and Angelina Arnold, of Olney; m. by George F. Jenckes, justice, Apr. 23, 1843.
Fowler John M., of Uxbridge, and Jane Burlingame, of Smithfield; m. by Rev. Reuben Allen, May 3, 1840.
Freeman Willard, of Whipple, and Olive Wipen; m. by Thos. Man, justice, Mar. 27, 1825.
" Margaret, and Benjamin Bartlett, Jan. 25, 1830.
" George Van Rensselaer, and Nacy V. Webb; m. by Asa Winsor, justice, Dec. 28, 1834.
" Truman, Jr., of Providence, and Margaret Boyd, of Pawtucket, Mass.; m. by Rev. B. P. Byram, Mar. 10, 1844.
" Amanda Melvina, and Daniel S. Clark, Apr. 5, 1846.
" Mary E., and Stephen Kimball, May 16, 1846.
" Lattice P., and Hiram B. Tucker, Nov. 29, 1847.
" Susan M., and Alfred Allen, May 3, 1848.
Frinnecome Mary Ann, and William A. Brickell, Sept. 18, 1845.
Frost Eliza, and Samuel Hixon, Jr., Dec. 22, 1846.
Fry Hannah G., and William R. Johnson, Sept. 27, 1841.
Fuller Barnabus S., of Smithfield, son of Hezekiah, of Hachniach, N. J., and Elizabeth Phillips; m. by Thomas Man, justice, Sept. 4, 1823.
" Lorenzo D., of Zachariah, and Martha A. Greene; m. by Ephraim Sayles, justice, Oct. 3, 1839.
" Thomas P., of Zechariah, and Robey Austin; m. by Ephraim Sayles, justice, Oct. 25, 1840.
" Martha J., and Stephen P. Brown, Oct. 29, 1846.
" Candace C., and Nathaniel T. Arnold, Oct. 13, 1850.

BIRTHS AND DEATHS.

Fales Elizabeth K., of David G. and Parthenia, Dec. 3, 1830.
" John R.,   "   "   Mar. 5, 1833.
" Geo. Stephens,   "   "   Dec. 25, 1836.

Farnum Mary, of John and Martha, Dec. 12, 1757.
" Rachel, " " Nov. 14, 1759.
" Stephen, " " Jan. 19, 1762.
" John, " " June 14, 1764.
Fisk Annsilia, of Jonah and Sarah, May 12, 1735.
" Jonah, " " June 15, 1737.
Finch Hopestill, of Henry and Abigail, Mar. 23, 1751.
" Stephen, " " Mar. 6, 1754.
" Peter, " " Oct. 8, 1756.
" Rebecca, " " Sept. 11, 1758.
" Henry, " " July 16, 1760.
Ford William, of William and Jemima, Sept. 12, 1749.
" Jean, " " Nov. 2, 1750.
" Ladoc, " " Sept. 21, 1752.
" Richard, " " Dec. 13, 1753.
" Joseph, " " Aug. 18, 1755.
" Anne, " " Apr. 21, 1757.
" Bathsheba, " " Nov. 25, 1758.
" Richard, " " Dec. 6, 1760.
" Prudence, " " Jan. 8, 1763.
Frazer William J., of Wm. H. and Isabella, May 9, 1845.
" John H., " " Sept. 28, 1850.
" Isabella, wife of William H., died Oct. 14, 1852.
Freeman Thomas, son of Joshua, b. Barnard, Vt., d. Mar. 1, 1848, aged 51 years, 11 months, 17 days.
Fuller Ezekiel, of Ezekiel and Abigail, Jan. 1, 1751.
" Isaiah, " " Mar. 19, 1753.
" George, " " Sept. 27, 1755.
" Abigail, " " Dec. 29, 1757.
" Abigail, of William and Sarah, Apr. 2, 1780.
" William, " " Apr. 12, 1782.

G.

MARRIAGES.

Gage Joan, and Isaac Mathewson, May 30, 1840.
Gardiner Samuel E., and Alice Mowry, of Nathaniel; m. by Rev. Reuben Allen, Feb. 3, 1831.

Gardiner William H., and Sarah H. Bradford; m. at Mendon, by Rev. Adin Ballou, Dec. 20, 1837.
" Nelson, and Jane Sayles; m. by Nicholas S. Winsor, justice, July 25, 1839.
" Vincent C., of Smithfield, and Mary Leach, of Cumberland; m. by Rev. Wm. Verrinder, Oct. 7, 1844.
" Erastus G., of North Kingstown, age 25, son of William H. and Patience, and Ann E. Sherman, age 25, dau. of John B. and Ann E. of Pawtucket; m. by Rev. I. J. Burguess, Jan. 16, 1851.
Gaskill Mary, and Adam Hautless, Dec. 28, 1741.
" Patience, and Jonathan Aldrich, Mar. 17, 1742-3.
" Libbeus, of Cumberland, and Philena S. Sawyer, of Smithfield; m. by Rev. John Borden, Jr., Oct. 19, 1841.
" William, of Smithfield, son of Edward, of Maidstone, Vt.; and Catherine Carr, of Ireland; m. by Rev. Junia S. Mowry, Feb. 17, 1850.
Gavitt Lucy, and William P. Perkins, Aug. 1, 1839.
Gee Henry, and Vesta Ann Randall; m. by Rev. T. A. Taylor, July 3, 1844.
Gifford Farnum, of Seth, of Uxbridge, and Robey Brown, of Seth, of Rehoboth, Mass.; m. by Caleb Farnum, justice, Aug. 31, 1815.
" Seth B. and Roxa Weatherhead; m. by Rev. Leonard Wakefield, Oct. 24, 1841.
" Elvina, and David Ellis, Feb. 28, 1848.
Gile Joseph, and Tabitha Harris; m. by Daniel Mowry, Jr., justice, Sept. 13, 1756.
Gillis Mercy, and Moses Aldrich, Feb. 16, 1758.
Gill Sarah, and William Farrar, ———, 1846.
Gilmore Sarah J. and Balsa Fisk Johnson, Jan. 26, 1843.
" Phebe B. and Albert Cook, Sept. 24, 1848.
Glasie Isaac, of Jacob, of North Uxbridge, and Lucy Brayton, of James of Smithfield; m. by Elisha Arnold, justice, Dec. 19, 1800.

Gleason Urziel, of North Providence, and Emily Kelley, of Smithfield; m. by Rev. E. W. Porter, Sept. 29, 1846.
" Charles, and Mary Ann Gurley; m. by Rev. Thomas C. Brown, July 2, 1848.
Goff Sarah, and Henry Wright, May 1, 1848.
Goldwaite Sarah, and Joseph Buxton, Feb. 10, 1752.
" Pelatiah, of John, and Charity Buxton, of James; m. by Elijah Arnold, justice, Dec. 5, 1799.
" Sally, and Thomas S. Brown, Dec. 8, 1844.
Gooding Susan M., and Thomas Bell, Oct. 30, 1848.
Gore Mehitable, and William Maccavy, June 27, 1740.
Gould William, of Burrillville, and Eliza Buxton; m. by Rev. T. A. Taylor, Mar. 21, 1844.
" Mary D. and Henry Polsey, Nov. 11, 1747.
Graff Philadelphia and James Peets, Aug. 1, 1793.
Grant James, and Thankful Arnold; m. by Rev. S. S. Bradford, Apr. 12, 1846.
Grason William, of Richard, and Urania, of Scituate, dec., and Hannah Mowry, of Darius and Lydia, of Smithfield; m. by Rev. Warren Lincoln, May 14, 1850.
Greenhalgh Mary, and William Prince, ——, 1846.
Greene Patience, and Welcome Arnold, Feb. 11, 1773.
" Mary, and Stephen Arnold, Jan. 5, 1783.
" Ruth, and Richard Buffum, Feb. 23, 1783.
" Amie, and Jonathan Ellet, July 27, 1783.
" Ebenezer, and Mary Jones; m. by Ananias Mowry, justice, Oct. 2, 1808.
" Henry Peirce, and Nancy Chillson; m. by Elijah Arnold, justice, Feb. 23, 1815.
" Martha A. and Lorenzo D. Fuller, Oct. 3, 1839.
" Sarah, and Joseph S. Whitman, Sept. 17, 1843.
" Benjamin P. and Lucy Ann Spencer; m. by Rev. Edwin Leigh, Nov. 30, 1843.
" Minerva A. and Augustus Phillips, Jr., Nov. 29, 1846.
" Hannah A. and Champlin L. Watson, Feb. 6, 1848.

Gross Samuel, of Henry, and Susan B. Ashton, of Samuel; m. by Rev. Reuben Allen, June 29, 1840.
Grosvenor Caroline Hall, and Rev. Timothy Alden Taylor, Sept. 2, 1840.
Guild Caroline M. and James E. Lewis, Dec. 3, 1846.
" Melinda Jane, and Wm. H. Bennett, July 8, 1849.
Gulley Phebe, and Elisha Mowry, Jr., Jan. 28, 1757.
" Thomas, of Jonathan, and Mrs. Hannah Mowry, of David; m. by Samuel Man, justice, Dec. 14, 1809.
" Sarah, and Simeon B. Razee, July 27, 1829.
Gurley Mary Ann, and Charles Gleason, July 2, 1848.

BIRTHS AND DEATHS.

Gaskill Levina, of Benjamin and Amie,   Sept. 27, 1765.
" Joanna,   "   "   Jan. 19, 1768.
" Ezekiel,   "   "   Dec. 12, 1769.
Gile Joab, of Joseph and Tabitha,   Aug. 16, 1761.
" Dorcas,   "   "   Nov. 27, 1763.
" Amie,   "   "   Dec. 7, 1766.
" David,   "   "   Mar. 16, 1770.
Gleason Cynthia A., of Smithfield, b. Mar. 27, 1799; d. Aug. 3, 1847.
Greene William, of Ebenezer and Mary,   Aug. 27, 1809.
" Mary,   "   "   Nov. 5, 1811.
" George, of Henry P. and Nancy,   June 23, 1816.
Gulley Stephen, of William and Martha,   Feb. 9, 1731–2.
" Jonathan,   "   "   Feb. 6, 1733.
" Christopher,   "   "   Feb. 24, 1735.
" Phebe,   "   "   Jan. 25, 1737.
" Mercy,   "   "   Jan. 9, 1740.
" William,   "   "   Mar. 2, 1743–4.
" Hannah,   "   "   July 4, 1748.

H.

MARRIAGES.

Hacker William, and Tabitha Clarke; m. by David Comstock, justice, Aug. 10, 1740.

Hadley William E., of Providence, son of John of Cumberland, dec., and Lucinda Benson, of Providence, dau. of Aaron of Lodi, N. Y.; m. by Rev. Wm. Verrinder, Apr. 13, 1845.
Hakes Mary, and Ebenezer Darling, Feb. 25, 1745.
Hallowell Richard, and Hannah Scholes; m. by Rev. Warren Emerson, Mar. 1, 1848.
Hall Joshua, Jr., of Cumberland, and Susannah Sprague, of Smithfield; m. by Thomas Lapham, justice, June 2, 1751.
" Lucina, and Reuben Aldrich, May 6, 1802.
" Mary, and John Dexter, May 11, 1806.
" Delia, and Paris Richmond, Aug. 13, 1829.
Hames Aaron, son of Robert of Douglass, Mass., dec., and Lydia Walker, of Reuben; m. by Peleg Arnold, justice, Feb. 17, 1785.
Hamond Parley, of Douglass, Mass., and Elizabeth B. Mansfield, of Smithfield; m. by Rev. Timothy A. Taylor, May 15, 1839.
" Mary A. and William Brown, Dec. 16, 1844.
Ham Phebe J. and Joseph Wilkinson, Sept. 23, 1846.
" George W. of Isaac L. of Lowell, Mass., and Diana Isis Steere, of Arnold, of Smithfield; m. by Rev. I. J. Burguess, Oct. 13, 1847.
Hancock Guy, of Mendon, Mass., and Rosanna Herker, of Smithfield; m. by Rev. Asel D. Cole, July 12, 1842.
Handon Mary W. and Edwin L. Smith, July 4, 1848.
Handy Kezia, and Simeon Harris, May 19, 1791.
" Lucy, and Nicholas Harris, Aug. 10, 1797.
" Waitey, and James Arnold, Aug. 10, 1826.
" Mary E. and Simon Strange, July 4, 1841.
" Jedidah, and Emer C. Smith, June 4, 1844.
" Asabiah, and Hamilton P. Aldrich, July 8, 1844.
" Benjamin W. and Lucy A. Stratford; m. by Rev. Asel D. Cole, Mar. 4, 1845.

Handy Silas, of Cumberland, and Caroline Snow, of Smithfield; m. by Rev. C. H. Titus, Dec. 31, 1848.
" William H. of Mason H., and Emeline F. Arnold, of Alvira A., dec.!; m. by Rev. T. A. Taylor, September 17, 1849.
Hanson Joseph, of John, and Mary Farrar, of Daniel; m. by Rev. B. P. Talbot, Dec. 31, 1846.
Harkinson Ellen, and John Pickford, May 20, 1849.
Harkness Rachel, and Hezekiah Thurber, Nov. 6, 1767.
" James T. and Julia A. Arnold; m. by Rev. Timothy A. Taylor, June 20, 1839.
Harriman Martha H. and Charles M. Lockwood, July 3, 1847.
Harrison Harriet M. and Jesse T. Mowry, Nov. 11, 1849.
Harris John, and Elizabeth King; m. by Thomas Sayles, justice, Nov. 1, 1739.
" Preserved, and Martha Mowry; m. by Wm. Jenckes, justice, Apr. 26, 1744.
" Capt. Enock, of Smithfield, and Alice Brown, of Gloucester; m. by Thomas Owen, justice, Feb. 23, 1751.
" Christopher, and Elizabeth (or Esther) Fairbrother; m. by Thomas Lapham, justice, Apr. 15, 1753.
" Tabitha, and Joseph Gile, Sept. 13, 1756.
" Jabez, and Mercy Arnold; m. by Benjamin Arnold, justice, Oct. 13, 1757.
" James, of Gloucester, and Anne King, resident of Smithfield; m. by Stephen Sly, justice, Nov. 18, 1757.
" Amity, and Henry Jenckes, Oct. 7, 1759.
" Anthony, and Ruth Broadway; m. by Daniel Mowry, Jr., justice, Jan. 1, 1761.
" Mary, and Thomas Lapham, June 25, 1761.
" Uriah, and Amie Tyler; m. by Jabez Harris, justice, July 5, 1761.
" Dinah, and Wanton Mowry, June 25, 1762.
" Capt. Richard, and Sarah Phillips; m. by Rev. John Winsor, Oct. 12, 1762.
" William and Marcy Sprague; m. by Daniel Mowry, Jr., justice, Oct. 16, 1763.

Harris Urania, and Jonathan Farnum, Sept. 29, 1765.
" Izreal, of Preserved, and Ruth Mussey, of Thomas; m. by Daniel Mowry, Jr., justice, Dec. 9, 1770.
" Lydia, and Nathaniel Spaulding, Oct. 27, 1774.
" Elethan, and Oliver Arnold, Dec. 3, 1778.
" Jesse, of Preserved, and Naomi Jenckes, of Thomas; m. by Stephen Brayton, justice, Nov. 1, 1781.
" David, of Abner, and Rachel Jenckes, of Thomas; m. by Stephen Brayton, justice, Sept. 19, 1782.
" Jonathan, of Abner, and Mary Jenckes, of Thomas; m. by Stephen Brayton, justice, Oct. 3, 1785.
" Jeremiah, of Jeremiah of Smithfield, and Rachel Hathaway, of Silvanus of Cumberland; m. by Rev. Abner Ballou, May 29, 1788.
" William, of Abner, dec., and Barberry Allen, of Waterman, dec., of Cumberland; m. by Rev. Edward Mitchell, Dec. 24, 1789.
" Mary, and Michael Sprague, Feb. 11, 1790.
" Simeon, of Smithfield, and Keziah Handy, of Uxbridge; m. by Rev. William Bowen, May 19, 1791.
" Mary, and Stephen Angel, Dec. 23, 1792.
" Mary, and George Hill, Nov. 11, 1793.
" Welcome, of David, Jun., and Zeriah Sayles, of John; m. by Benjamin Sheldon, justice, May 26, 1796.
" Achzah, and Ephraim Mowry, Jan. 8, 1797.
" Nicholas, of Richard of Smithfield, and Lucy Handy, of Benjamin of Uxbridge; m. by Edward Medbury, justice, Aug. 10, 1797.
" David F., of Joseph, and Lydia Streeter, of Rufus; m. by Thomas Man, justice, Dec. 31, 1800.
" Jabez, of Stephen, and Waite Wing, of Joshub; m. by Thomas Man, justice, May 1, 1803.
" Betsey, and Silas Smith, May 25, 1806.
" Farnum, of David, dec., and Olive Mowry, of William; m. by Thomas Man, justice, Mar. 12, 1809.
" Martha, and Thomas Mowry, June 9, 1811.

Harris Keziah, and Benjamin Lindsey, June 7, 1818.
" David, 2d son of Welcome, and Lavina Mowry, of Abial ; m. by Thomas Man, justice, Mar. 13, 1823.
" Thomas J., of Nicholas, and —— Holley, of William ; m. by Thomas Man, justice, Jan. —, 1830.
" Mason, of Burrillville, son of Simeon of Uxbridge, and Abigail Scott Aldrich, of George 4th, of Smithfield ; m. by Nathaniel Mowry, justice, July 4, 1833.
" Eliza J. and Allen Bishop, July 28, 1840.
" Albert Tillinghast, and Frances Amanda Sherman ; m. by Rev. William S. Balch, Feb. 25, 1841.
" Joanna, and George Tyler, Feb. 5, 1843.
" Hezekiah S. and Susan M. Jawger ; m. by Rev. Edwin Leigh, Aug. 27, 1843.
" Waity Ann, and Richard Mowry, Nov. 30, 1843.
" Abigail, and Talcott Curtis, Nov. 25, 1845.
" Mehitable, and Proctor Ames, Mar. 8, 1846.
" Caroline R. and Sayles C. Newell, May 10, 1846.
" Ellen, and Alfred Chatterton, Sept. 17, 1849.
" Ralph, and Elizabeth Thompson, both of Salem, Mass.; m. by Rev. T. A. Taylor, Aug. 21, 1850.
Hartshorn Sylvester, of Providence, son of Charles, and Amie Waterman, of Smithfield, dau. of Thomas, Dec. 7, 1820.
" Wellington P. of Lynn, Mass., and Phebe M. Kelton, of Smithfield ; m. by Rev. Edwin C. Brown, May 28, 1849.
Hartwell George M., of Fitchburg, Mass., son of Nathan, of Littleton, Mass., and Mary E. Cozzens, of Smithfield ; m. by Rev. Mowry Phillips, July 13, 1848.
Hart Wellington S. and Celista E. Phillips, both of Mendon, Mass.; m. by Rev. T. A. Taylor, Aug. 26, 1844.
" Joseph S. of Milbury, Mass., and Harriet Bourne ; m. by Rev. Emory W. Porter, Mar. 20, 1845.
Haskin Nicholas, of Tiverton, R. I., and Lydia Sly, of Gloucester ; m. by Thomas Sayles, justice, Apr. 30, 1744.

Hastings Mary Elizabeth, and Jeremiah Niles, May 17, 1842.
Hatch Harriet Celinda, and Joseph Colwell Allen, Jan. 12, 1841.
Hathaway Rachel, and Jeremiah Harris, May 29, 1788.
" Mrs. Abigail, dau. of Dr. Peleg, and Simon Horton, June 30, 1811.
" Joseph R. of Smithfield, and Phebe Ann Caroline Wilcox, of Providence; m. by Rev. Reuben Allen, June 17, 1839.
Hautless Adam, and Mary Gaskill; m. by William Arnold, justice, Dec. 28, 1741.
Hawkins Sarah, and Richard Sweet, June 19, 1733.
" Abigail, and Richard Sayles, Jr., Sept. 2, 1742.
" Zephanah, and Mary Marvel; m. by Thomas Steere, justice, Nov. 26, 1752.
" Lydia, and James Young, Nov. 19, 1755.
" Sarah, and William Pain, Nov. 23, 1757.
" Charles, and Sarah Olney; m. by Samuel Winsor, justice, Sept. 4, 1760.
" Mary, and Abraham Angel, Dec. 13, 1761.
" Jeremiah, and Ruth Mowry, dau. of Joseph; m. by Daniel Mowry, Jr., justice, Aug. 13, 1772.
" Mary, and Asa Sheldon, May 6, 1804.
" Harris, of John, of Smithfield, and Mrs. Mehitable Angel, of William, of Johnston, R. I.; m. by Samuel Man, justice, Nov. 19, 1809.
" Clarissa D. and Ephraim M. Staples, Jan. 30, 1840.
" Elnora, and Arnold H. Whipple, May 26, 1841.
" Smith B., of Charles, and Susannah Y. Tyler, of Providence, dau. of Abner; m. by Obed Pain, justice, June 29, 1843.
Hawks Lucretia, and Charles Brown, Feb. 8, 1795.
Haws Anne, and Obediah Herendeen, June 11, 1750.
Hayden Susan, and Jenckes R. Kelton, Dec. 23, 1838.

(To be continued.)

THE FRENCH SPOLIATION CLAIMS AND RHODE ISLAND CLAIMANTS.

A paper read before the Rhode Island Historical Society, December 1, 1885, by Amasa M. Eaton, Esq., of Providence.

THIS subject is but a memory of the past to those of the present generation. But the passage by Congress of the act for the relief of the descendants of claimants has awakened general interest in the subject, and it will prove interesting and instructive to examine its history.

In December, 1776, the United States, recognizing the benefit of an alliance with France, offered to the French Government a subsidy of two millions of dollars worth of provisions and six frigates, our assistance in the recovery of certain islands and rights then in the possession of England, and any other assistance which might be in our power, as good allies, if France would help us by an offensive alliance against Great Britain (*Secret Journal of Congress, vol. ii., pp. 30, 38, 39, 40.*) Then came the darkest hour of our struggle with Great Britain,—when, in the midst of gloom and suffering, our soldiers at Valley Forge, hungry, barefoot and in rags, Washington wrote to Congress that, "unless some great and capital change takes place the army must be inevitably reduced to one or the other of three things—starve, dissolve or disperse."

The great and capital change did come, and to the great rejoicing of this country the news was received during the darkest hours of our struggle with England that a treaty of alliance had been signed by Franklin and the other plenipotentiaries on the 6th of February, 1778, between France and the United States (*Statutes at Large, vol. viii., p. 6.*) On the same day another treaty, called the treaty of amity and commerce, was also entered into between the same States (*Statutes at Large, vol. viii., p. 13.*)

By Article 11 of the first named treaty the contracting parties guaranteed " mutually from the present time and forever against all other powers, to wit, the United States to His Most Christian Majesty, the present possession of the crown of France in America, as well as those which it may acquire by the future treaty of peace. And His Most Christian Majesty guarantees on his part, to the United States, their liberty, sovereignty and independence, absolute and unlimited, as well in matters of commerce, and also their possessions and the additions or conquests that their confederation may obtain during the war from any of the dominions now or heretofore possessed by Great Britain in North America," &c.

Article 12 provided this reciprocal guaranty should take effect the moment war should break out between France and England, and by Article 17 of the second treaty each country agreed to open its ports to the ships of war and privateers of the other, and to close them to those of the enemy of either, except when driven in by stress of weather.

And by the Consular Convention, so called, of November 14, 1788, between the United States and France, it was agreed that the consuls of each nation should have jurisdiction in the ports of the other in all civil cases relating to the vessels and crews of their own nation.

But after the successful issue of our Revolution, it was felt in the United States that we had promised too much. Public sentiment, which gradually took shape in the Munroe doctrine, now an accepted principle of every political party, gradually but definitely recognized the fact that we should not entangle ourselves in the affairs of Eruope nor allow any foreign power to restrict our dealings with other nations. Hence, when difficulties arose between France and England, and France turned to us for that help which she felt she had a right to expect, great was her disappointment to find our statesmen inclined to neutrality and a withdrawal from our treaty obligations with her.

Under the leadership of Jefferson, who hated the English, and the tendency of the Federalists, headed by Hamilton, to further assimilation of English principles, the Democratic party was inclined towards the support of the French. But such a course was bitterly resented by many, including the Federalists generally, and party feeling ran high. The French Revolution burst forth in all its fury and war ensued in 1793 between France and England. The most bitter difference of opinion arose in this country and in the Cabinet between the sections briefly described, as to the course to be pursued by the United States, some holding that the obligations of the treaty guaranties ceased with the cessation of the French monarchy, others holding that they were perpetual, whatever the form of government of France. The famous proclamation of neutrality of the United States was issued April 22d, 1793. (*Senate Doc. No. 102, 1826, p. 249.*)

Chief Justice Marshall, with the very best opportunities for correct knowledge, says that the proclamation was intended to prevent the French Minister from demanding the performance of the guarantee contained in the treaty of alliance. The French Minister reported to the French Government " that the Secretary of War, on my communicating the wish of the Windward Islands to receive promptly some firearms and some cannon, which might put into a state of defence, possessions guaranteed by the United States, had the front to answer, with an ironical carelessness, that the principles established by the President did not permit him to lend so much as a pistol."

The effect of the proclamation and of the resulting course pursued by this country was to annul the treaty, although all intention to annul it was denied at the time. Looked at from the point of view of the best political policy for this country to follow, this proclamation of neutrality takes high rank. Politically we were wise, but morally we were wrong. It would have been more honest to ask for the abrogation of the treaty. But the public and Congress were divided and distracted in opinion. Party feeling ran high, and bitterness and animosity reigned to an extent of which we can form no idea now except from critical study of the history and spirit of that time. We are told that a man would cross the street to avoid recognition of an acquaintance who was of the opposite side in politics, and men would not make their daily purchases except of shopkeepers of their own party!

None foresaw the results that followed, the estrangement between us and France, the mutual wrongdoing, until at last we stood upon the brink of war with that power without whose aid we might not have achieved our independence. None foresaw that the course entered upon was virtually an attempt to abrogate the treaties in the worst way a treaty can be abrogated, *i. e.*, by its repudiation by one of the contracting parties without the assent of the other party.

But blameworthy as was our conduct that of France was equally so. Only seventeen days after our proclamation of neutrality, and therefore before knowledge of it had reached France, the National Convention of France, on the 9th of May, 1793, issued a decree authorizing French ships of war and privateers to arrest and bring into the ports of the republic all neutral vessels laden either wholly or in part with neutral articles of provisions belonging to neutral nations and destined for an enemy's port, or with merchandise belonging to an enemy. This decree was issued in retaliation for the English attempt to starve the French by general blockade and seizure of neutral vessels with provisions on their way to France. So rigorously were these measures enforced by England that the English market was glutted with provision, while in France flour sold at forty dollars a barrel. It was admitted, in this decree itself, that it was a violation of the rights of neutrals, but the necessity of the case was urged as an excuse, and indemnity was promised to neutrals who might suffer by its operation. As the decree was a direct violation of the 23d article of our treaty of commerce, Mr. Morris, then resident minister of the United States at Paris, remonstrated and claimed exemption for American vessels from its operation, according to the terms of the treaty.

On the 23d of May, 1793, the National Convention formally declared that vessels of the United States were not to be included in the operation of this decree. Such was the instability of the French, however, that this decree of May 23d was abrogated by decree May 28th, and after various contradictory decrees, American commerce was left exposed to destruction under the first decree, that of May 9th. What with the consequent illegal acts of French privateers and the retaliatory acts of the British Government, many of our vessels were captured amidst excesses of all kinds, and a vast amount of American property was destroyed.

When information of these acts of spoliation reached the United States, the result was disastrous to confidence in maritime business. Merchants hesitated to expose their ships and cargoes to such risks. To restore confidence, our Government came forward with voluntary assurances of protection and redress, and Jefferson, then Secretary of State, issued a circular letter dated August 27th, 1793, in which he said:

"Complaint having been made to the Government of some instances of unjustifiable vexation and spoliation committed on our merchant vessels by the privateers of the powers at war, and it being possible that other instances may have happened, of which no information has been given to the Government, I have it in charge from the President to assure the merchants of the United States concerned in foreign commerce that due attention will be paid to any injuries on the high seas or in foreign countries, contrary to the law of nations, or to existing treaties; and that, on their forwarding hither, to the Department of State, well authenticated evidence of the same, proper proceedings will be adopted for their relief." (*Senate Document 102, 1826, p. 216.*)

President Washington, in his message of December 5th, 1793, also referred to these acts of spoliation, as follows:

"The vexations and spoliations understood to have been committed on our vessels and commerce by the cruisers and officers of some of the belligerent powers, appeared to require attention. The proofs of these, however, not having been brought forward, the description of citizens supposed to have suffered were notified that on furnishing them to the Executive, due measures would be taken to obtain redress of the past and more effectual provisions against the future." (*Senate Doc. 102, 1826, p. 253.*)

In commenting on these official declarations, Charles Sumner says:

"Here, then, was a double promise from the national government, under the influence of which our merchants continued their commerce and ventured once more upon the ocean. Their Government had tempted them, and on the occurrence of 'injuries on the high seas' these good citizens, according to instructions, made haste to lodge with the Department of State the 'well authenticated evidences of the same.' Their grandchildren and great-grandchildren are waiting, even now, the promised redress. (*Senate Report 10, 41st Congress, 2d session, 1870.*)

In response, our merchants lodged with the State Department their evidences of losses. The Department forwarded these papers to France, and strange as it may seem, kept no copies or records of them. They cannot be found now in Paris, and this accounts for part of the difficulty now met with in getting proof of these losses.

The French Minister to the United States, Fauchet, under date of March 27th, 1794, wrote to our Secretary of State:

"If any of your merchants have suffered any injury by the conduct of our privateers (a thing which would be contrary to the intention and express order of the republic) they may, with confidence, address themselves to the French Government, which will never refuse justice to those whose claims are legal." (*Senate Doc. 102, 1826, p. 265.*)

Mr. Morris, our Minister at Paris, wrote, March 6th, 1794:

"These captures create great confusion, must produce much damage to mercantile men, and are a source of endless and well-founded complaint. Every post brings me piles of letters about it from all quarters, and I see no remedy. * * * * In the meantime, if I would give way to the clamors of the injured parties, I ought to make demands very like a declaration of war." (*Senate Doc. No. 102, 1826, p. 77.*)

July 5th, 1794, the French Commissioner of Foreign Relations wrote to Mr. Morris:

"The sentiments of the Convention and of the Government towards your fellow-citizens are too well known to you to leave a doubt of their disposition to make good the losses which circumstances inseparable from a great revolution may have caused some American navigators to experience. (*Senate Doc. No. 102, 1826, p. 77.*)

We cannot stop to examine the history of the negotiations which led to the adoption of the treaty with Great Britain known as Jay's Treaty, dated November 19th, 1794. It was long held under advisement by our Senate, and was finally ratified in February, 1796. Historians relate at length the animosities aroused, already referred to, and the division in public opinion and sentiment of the time. The treaty was the culmination of the policy which amounted to the abrogation of our treaty obligations with France. The two treaties could not stand side by side. One or the other must be inoperative because they were contradictory. The treaty with England gave the same exclusive rights to her ships of war and privateers to shelter, etc., in our ports, and to sell their prizes, etc., that we had already given, also exclusively, to France. One of the articles of the treaty with England provided that prizes made by either England or the United States should be free to enter the ports of the other, and that no shelter or refuge should be given in the ports of either to such as should have made a prize upon the subjects or citizens of either. This was in direct contravention of our treaty with France.

Other objectionable articles in the British treaty were the surrender of the principle that "free ships make free goods" and the allowing English cruisers to capture goods or subjects of their enemies from our vessels, thus rendering French property and Frenchmen on board our ships liable to seizure, while the property and persons of the enemies of France, similarly situated, were protected by the 23d article of our treaty with France of 1778. Here we find the germ of the English doctrine afterwards asserted of "the right of search," one of the causes of our next war with her.

The list of contraband articles was also much extended in the Jay treaty as compared with the list in the French treaty. This was particularly injurious to France, then fighting against Europe generally, by increasing the difficulty of procuring articles of which she was then in great need. It helped to render more effective the English plan of starving the French into submission, by making more complete the English control of the high seas. Our Government immediately prohibited French privateers from fitting out vessels or from selling their prizes in our ports.

Upon deliberate examination of all these facts, the conclusion is inevitable that the course pursued by the United States was indefensible. The opportunity was given to us to negotiate a new treaty with France, but we declined it, and then deliberately violated the old treaty, and persistently maintained that course. The French Minister wrote, November 14th, 1793, to our Secretary of State:

" I beg you to lay open to the President the decree and the enclosed note, and to obtain from him the earliest decision, either the guarantee I have claimed the fulfilment of for our colonies, or upon the mode of negotiation of the new treaty I was charged to propose to the United States, which would make of the two nations but one family." (*American State Papers, 1 Foreign Affairs, p. 199.*)

The guarantee here referred to was the perpetual guarantee to the French of their possessions in America, before explained. At the time of the execution of the treaty these possessions were the islands of St. Domingo, Martinique, Guadeloupe, Ste. Lucie, St. Vincent, Tobago, Deseada, Mariegalante, St. Pierre, Miquelon, Granada, and, on the mainland, Cayenne. The occasion for the enforcement of this guarantee had already become urgent, for many of these islands were lost to the French in 1793, and, Alison says in his History, vol. iii., p. 396, "with hardly any loss to the victorious nation."

The news of the Jay treaty with England moved the whole French nation to indignation, as well it might. In conversation with Mr. Munroe, then our Minister to France, the French Minister said "that France had much cause of complaint against us independently of our treaty with England, but that, by this treaty, ours with them was annihilated." (*American State Papers, 1 Foreign Affairs, p. 731.*)

M. Adet, the French plenipotentiary to the United States, addressed our Government as follows:

"The undersigned, minister plenipotentiary of the French Republic, now fulfills to the Secretary of State of the United States a painful but sacred duty. He claims, in the name of American honor, in the name of the faith of treaties, the execution of that contract which assured to the United States their existence, and which France regarded as the pledge of the most sacred union between two people, the freest upon earth." (*American State Papers, 1 Foreign Affairs, p. 579.*)

In retaliation for our conduct the French Government passed three decrees. The first was to the effect that all neutrals would be treated in the same way as they might allow the English to treat the French. Under the second, the stipulations of the treaty of 1778 concerning the neutrality of the flags were suspended, and were altered in most essential points; and under the third decree the list of contraband of war was enlarged, Americans in the service of England were declared to be pirates, and certain documents were declared to be necessary to determine the national character of American ships. Among these documents a *rôle d' équipage* (a list of the crew in a particular form) was declared essential, although the 25th article of the treaty of 1778 specifically prescribed the form of sea letter to be used by the vessels of the two countries.

On the 30th of April, 1797, the French Minister of Marine was requested to declare officially whether American vessels not having a *rôle d'équipage* were good prize and whether the cargoes of such ships were also lawful prize. He decided that every American vessel without such a *rôle* was an enemy, and that therefore both vessel and cargo were subject to confiscation. The number of captures of American vessels now increased rapidly, and all remonstrances were in vain. The French, while admitting these decrees to be in conflict with the treaty, persisted in carrying them into effect. No matter what trade American vessels were engaged in, or with whom they were trading, they were seized and confiscated, against all law, under the color of law. Reprehensible as our conduct had been, that of the French was now equally so. In the remaining French islands in the West Indies the same spirit was manifested, and the plunder derived from this source formed the principal part of their revenue. In a report to the French Directory from their government it was stated: "That having found no resource in finance, and knowing the unfriendly disposition of the Americans, and to avoid perishing in distress, they had armed for cruising, and that already eighty-seven cruisers were at sea; and that for three months preceding, the administration had subsisted, and individuals been enriched, by the product of their prizes. They felicitated themselves that American vessels were daily taken, and declared they had learned, by divers persons from the continent, that the Americans were corrupt, perfidious, the friends of England, and that their vessels no longer entered the French ports unless carried in by force."

I have made thorough examination of all the registers, manifests and protests in the Custom Houses in Providence and Newport, and these records, of which I have minutes, show that a large proportion of the losses incurred in this State were incurred at this period in this way, our vessels having been captured and taken into the French ports in the West India islands and there condemned and sold. During the last summer all these records have been forwarded to the Department of State in Washington, in response to directions received from the Government, to be used as evidence, either by claimants or the Government, in the trial of petitions for indemnity before the Court of Claims, under the terms of the Act of Congress of last winter, which I will explain later.

Lest the statements made of the conduct of the French may be thought to be exaggerated, I will quote an extract from a report made by our Secretary of State to the President, in reply to a resolution of the House of Representatives, on the 21st of June, 1797. After mentioning the French decrees, the report says:

"Besides these several decrees, and others, which, being more limited, the former have superseded, the old marine ordinances of France have been revived and enforced with severity both in Europe and the West Indies. The want of or informality in a bill of lading, the want of a certified list of the passengers and crew, the supercargo being by birth a foreigner, although a naturalized citizen of the United States, the destruction of a paper of any kind soever, and the want of a sea letter, have been deemed sufficient to warrant a condemnation of American vessels and property, although the proofs of the property were indubitable. The West Indies, as before remarked, have exhibited the most lamentable scene of depredation. Indeed, the conduct of the public agents and of the commissioned cruisers there has surpassed all former examples. The American vessels have not only been captured under the decrees before mentioned, but when brought to trial in the French tribunals the vessels and cargoes have been condemned without admitting the owners or their agents to make any defence. This seems to be done systematically and for the obvious purpose of ensuring condemnations. By this monstrous abuse in judicial proceedings, frauds and falsehoods, as well as flimsy and shameless pretexts, pass unexamined and uncontradicted, and are made the foundation of sentences of condemnation."

The differences between the two countries had now assumed definite form, and we were on the verge of war. The French Government had valid claims against our Government for infraction of treaty obligations, and our citizens held valid claims against the French Government for acts of spoliation committed by her privateers upon our commerce. How were the two countries to extricate themselves from the dilemma?

In June, 1797, Messrs. Pinckney, Marshall and Gerry were appointed by the President of the United States Envoys Extraordinary and Ministers Plenipotentiary "to negotiate with the French Government on all subjects of difference between the two nations, and to make a treaty or convention for determining the same."

The Secretary of State, Mr. Pickering, in his letter of instructions to these envoys, dated July 15, 1797, said:

"Although the reparation for losses sustained by the citizens of the United States, in consequence of irregular or illegal captures or condemnations, or forcible seizures or detentions, is of very high importance, and is to be pressed with the greatest earnestness, yet it is not to be insisted on as an indispensable condition of the proposed treaty. You are not, however, to renounce these claims of our citizens, nor to stipulate that they be assumed by the United States as a loan to the French Government."

The envoys were also instructed to buy a release of our guarantee of the French islands, and they were authorized to offer to France a war subsidy in money or in provisions to the amount of two hundred thousand dollars annually.

But their mission was in vain. They were first indirectly asked to pay a bribe, under the pleasanter name of *a gratification*, of twelve hundred thousand francs! which, of course, they refused to pay. They were not allowed to hold official intercourse with the French Government. They remained some time in Paris on sufferance, and held informal interviews with Talleyrand and others, but could accomplish nothing, so they returned to America. Washington was called upon to be in readiness, for war with France was impending and was almost daily expected.

An Act of Congress of May 28th, 1798, authorized our navy to capture "armed vessels of the Republic of France which have committed or shall be found hovering on the coast of the United States for the purpose of committing depredations on vessels belonging to citizens thereof." An Act of June 13th, 1798, suspended all commercial intercourse between the United States and France "until the Government of France shall clearly disavow and shall be found to refrain from the aggressions, depredations and hostilities by them encouraged and maintained against the vessels and other property of the United States."

The next Act of Congress of June 25th, 1798, authorized merchant vessels of the United States to resist search or seizure by any armed French vessel, to repel assaults and to capture the aggressors until "the Government of France shall cause the commanders and crews of all armed French vessels to refrain from the lawless depredations and outrages hitherto encouraged and authorized by that Government against the merchant vessels of the United States."

Finally, by Act of Congress of July 7th, 1798, the treaties with France were declared to be annulled and no longer obligatory, the preamble stating "that the just claims of the United States for reparation of injuries had been refused, and their attempts to negotiate an amicable adjustment of all complaints between the two nations had been repelled with indignity." The treaties with France were thus declared to be annulled on the ground that France had violated them. It is true the treaty of amity and commerce had been violated by France. But it had never been alleged that France had violated the treaty of alliance; on the contrary, France had strictly and honorably fulfilled all her obligations under it. She helped us to win our independence at a cost estimated at two hundred and eighty millions of dollars in money and untold loss of priceless human lives. The only violation of the treaty of alliance was on the part of the United States in issuing the declaration of neutrality and in nullifying the treaty by the Act of Congress of July 7th, 1798, so far as such acts could effect its nullification. France, very naturally and very properly, denied the right or the power of either party to annul a treaty without the consent of the other party to the treaty. It is clear that where there are two treaties, as in this case, the violation of one of them does not affect the other; the treaty of alliance should have been held as still in force, even if the treaty of amity and commerce was legally annulled by the Act of Congress of July 7th, 1798. (See Vattel, p. 275.)

John Adams became President, and in 1799, desirous of a peaceful settlement with France, and upon her invitation, he appointed a new commission consisting of Chief Justice Ellsworth, Davie and Murray as Envoys to France. Their instructions were to secure indemnity for spoliation on our commerce, the cessation of the seizure of American vessels for want of the technical *rôle d'équipage*, the termination of our guarantee of the French West India islands, the abrogation of all the treaties between France and the United States, and the formation of a new treaty in which all obligations should be specified. From these instructions it is apparent that while our Government meant to do away with the burden of the national guarantee, it also meant to secure indemnity for the just claims of our citizens.

We have not time now to follow the negotiations that took place in Paris. Propositions and counter-propositions were made and rejected by both parties. It is enough for our purpose to know that France at last offered two propositions, one being the acknowledgment of the continuance of the old treaties by the United States, in which case France offered full indemnity for her illegal spoliations on our commerce, the other proposition being that a new treaty should be entered into, doing away with the perpetual guarantee to the French of their possessions in America and with the other provisions of the old treaties, France to be placed on an equality with the most favored nation by the United States, in which case no indemnity for spoliation would be made by France. This proposition, as stated by Webster in his speech on French

Spoliations in the Senate, January 12th, 1835, was, to quote his words:

"If you will acknowledge or renew the obligation of the old treaties, which secure to us privileges in your ports which our enemies are not to enjoy, then we will make indemnities for the losses of your citizens; or, if you will give up all claim for such indemnities, then we will relinquish our special privileges under the former treaties and agree to a new treaty which shall only put us on a footing of equality with Great Britain, our enemy." (*4 Webster's Works, p. 173.*)

Our envoys did not feel that they were authorized to accept either proposition. They wrote home August 15th, 1800, that it had now become manifest that negotiations must be abandoned or their instructions must be deviated from. Further negotiation ensued. At last our envoys determined it would be best to make some temporary arrangement which would extricate the United States from the situation in which they were involved, save the immense property of American citizens then awaiting adjudication before the French Council of Prizes, and secure, as far as possible, American commerce against the abuses of capture during the war then existing between France and England. Sept. 4th, 1800, the French Government proposed that the indemnities due by France to the citizens of the United States should be paid by the United States, France, in return, to yield the exclusive privileges secured to her under the 17th and 22d articles of the treaty of commerce and the rights under the guarantee of the 11th article of the treaty of alliance. Here was a distinct proposition of set off. The United States were to assume and pay the just claims of American citizens against France, and France was to relinquish her claims against the United States arising under the treaties, and also the guarantee and the exclusive rights thereunder. Our envoys declared these propositions to be inadmissible. The conferences continued through the month, and on September 30th, 1800, a "provisional treaty" was agreed upon. At the request of the

French, this title, which too plainly showed its temporary character, was subsequently changed to that of "convention," which name it still bears on our statute book.

Article 2 is as follows:

"The ministers plenipotentiary of the two parties, not being able to agree at present, respecting the treaty of alliance of 6th February, 1778, the treaty of amity and commerce of the same date and the convention of the 14th of November, 1778, nor upon the indemnities mutually due or claimed, the parties will negotiate further on these subjects at a convenient time; and until they may have agreed upon these points, the said treaties and convention shall have no operation, and the relations of the two countries shall be as follows:"

The next two articles provided for the mutual restoration of vessels and property captured, but not yet condemned: the fifth and last article provided that "the debts contracted by one of the two nations with individuals of the other, or by the individuals of the one with the individuals of the other, shall be paid, or the payment may be prosecuted in the same manner as if there had been no misunderstanding between the two States. But this clause shall not extend to indemnities claimed on account of captures or confiscations."

This convention was signed at Morfortaine, the country seat of Joseph Bonaparte, and the occasion was made a festival, which has been celebrated by the engraving of Piranesi. The First Consul, Lafayette and other notables were guests there, and Napoleon proposed as a toast, "The manes of the French and the Americans who died on the field of battle for the independence of the new world."

This convention, after it was signed by the ministers of the two countries, was sent to the United States, and submitted by the President to the Senate; and the Senate, on the 3d of February, 1801, consented to and advised its ratification, provided the second article be expunged and the following inserted: "It is agreed that the present convention shall be in force for the term of eight years from the time of the exchange of the ratifications," which change received the approval of the President, February 8th, 1801, by his proclamation announcing the ratification, " saving and excepting the second article, which is declared to be expunged, and of no force or validity." (*Statutes at Large, vol. viii., p. 192.*)

Mr. Murray, our Minister in Paris, wrote home his fear that the French Government would still press for an article of formal abandonment of our claims for spoliation, which he wrote he should evade. The French feared that the unconditional suppression of the second article would leave them still exposed to the claims of the United States without any chance to advance their counter-claims. They did not object to a mutual abandonment of claims, which, in the language of Mr. Murray, " would always be a set-off against each other."

At last, on the 31st of July, 1801, the convention was ratified by Napoleon, then First Consul, with the addition made by our Senate limiting it to eight years, and with the retrenchment of the second article by our Senate—the whole with the proviso added by the First Consul " that by this retrenchment the two States renounce the respective pretensions, which are the object of the said article."

It was again returned to the United States, and Jefferson, who meanwhile had succeeded Adams as President, again submitted it to the Senate, which, on the 19th of December, 1801, resolved " that the Senate consider the said convention as fully ratified, and return it to the President for promulgation." It was accordingly promulged by the President, December 21st, 1801, and thus became the supreme law of the land in France and in the United States. Both countries were well out of a most troublesome and dangerous difficulty.

The net result was that the United States assumed the claims of its citizens against France by thus using them in offset in settlement of the claims of France against her, and, in return, France released her treaty obligations, past, present and future, against the United States. The United States thus became absolved from that troublesome guarantee of the

French islands, from the grant of the exclusive privileges made to the French, and from all claims for damages arising from non-fulfilment of these obligations. Such was the opinion of the statesmen conducting the negotiations, and of most of the leading statesmen of that period and their successors to the present time. (See, for instance, the letter from the Hon. W. C. Preston, of January 29th, 1844, Appendix No. 3 to the speech of the Hon. John M. Clayton delivered in the Senate, April 23d and 24th, 1846; and the letter from the Hon. Timothy Pickering, Secretary of State under Washington, dated May 19th, 1824, Appendix No. 2 to the same speech.) The Emperor Napoleon at Saint Helena, dictating the events of his reign, said: "The suppression of this article" (the second article of the convention of 1800) " at once put an end to the privileges which France had possessed by the treaty of 1778, and annulled the just claims which America might have made for injuries done in time of peace." (*Gourgaud's Memoirs of the History of France*, vol. ii., p. 129.)

The case was clearly stated by Henry Clay, while Secretary of State, in the message of the President to the Senate on French Spoliations (*Senate Document No. 102, 1826, p. 7*):

"The two contracting parties thus agreed by the retrenchment of the second article mutually to renounce the respective pretensions which were the object of that article. The pretensions of the United States, to which allusion is thus made, arose out of the spoliations, under the color of French authority, in contravention to law and existing treaties. Those of France sprung from the treaty of alliance of the 6th of February, 1778, the treaty of amity and commerce, and the convention of the 14th of November, 1788. Whatever obligations or indemnities from these sources either party had a right to demand, were respectively waived and abandoned; and the consideration which induced one party to renounce his pretensions was that of the renunciation by the other party of his pretensions. What was the value of the obligations and indemnities so reciprocally renounced can only be matter of speculation. The amount of the indemnities due to citizens of the United States was very large; and on the other hand the obligation was great (to specify no other French pretensions) under which the United States were placed, in the 11th article of the treaty of alliance of 6th of February, 1778, by which they were bound forever to guarantee from that time their possessions to the crown of France in America, as well as those which it might acquire by the future treaty of peace with Great Britain : all these possessions having been, it is believed, conquered at, or not long after, the exchange of the ratifications of the convention of September, 1800, by the arms of Great Britain, from France."

Mr. Madison, then Secretary of State, in an official communication to our Minister, Mr. Pinckney, wrote :

"The claims from which France were released were admitted by France, and the release was for a valuable consideration, in a correspondent release of the United States from certain claims on them."

Mr. Pickering wrote, November 19th, 1824 :

"Then it seems clear that as our government applied the merchants' property to buy off those old treaties, the sums so applied should be reimbursed."

And Chief Justice Marshall, himself at one time one of the plenipotentiaries, as we have seen, and with the very best of opportunities for judging of this matter, said he was satisfied from his own knowledge our government was under the strongest obligation to compensate the sufferers by the French spoliations.

All through this century resolutions and reports of committees of many of the State Legislatures have recommended to Congress the payment of these claims. Memorials innumerable have been presented to Congress from claimants and their heirs. These claims have been acknowledged to be just claims against the United States by our statesmen all through the century, including Webster, Clay, Sumner and others illustrious in the annals of Congress and the history of our country. These memorials and petitions for redress have been referred to forty-two committees of Congress since 1800.

The first two committees (in 1802 and 1807) made no report. The next (in 1818, 1822 and 1824) reported adversely. But every report made since then, thirty-seven in number, has recommended the allowance of these claims. The first five reports were not favorable, because so little was then known about the matter, even to the committee or claimants themselves. In 1826 the President, in compliance with a resolution of the Senate, sent in a message to the Senate with copies of all the instructions to our ministers and envoys to France, and of all the correspondence and negotiations on the subject, making a thick volume of 840 pages. This is the Senate Document No. 102, 1826, to which I have often referred. Then for the first time did the country and the claimants themselves know the full strength and justice of these claims, and since then every committee of Congress to which this matter has been referred has reported favorably upon these claims and recommended measures for their adjudication and allowance; that is to say, since 1826, when this Senate Document No. 102 was published, committees of Congress have reported in favor of these claimants thirty-seven times and still their just claims remain unpaid. It would be difficult to find any parallel instance in history of such glaring and perverse injustice.

Several causes combined have prevented the acknowledgment and payment by Congress of these claims. As explained above, it was not until 1826 that they were really understood. The South, then in power, was jealous of the North, and of these claims; and Congress was always appalled by their magnitude. We must remember that before 1861 very different ideas obtained over what obtain now, as to our wealth and resources and ability to pay national claims, immense in amount.

Before the establishment of the Court of Claims there was no adequate tribunal to refer such claims to, for adjudication as to their merits and validity. A committee of Congress, sitting during the recess, as was sometimes proposed, was entirely incompetent for such work. And so these claims have dragged along, and we have all seen piteous accounts in the newspapers of the death in some almshouse or town poor-farm of the descendant of some merchant brought to ruin early in the century by acts of French spoliation, some poor creature whose life for fifty years was spent hoping for that justice from our Government he had a right to expect, but which never came.

In 1846 the bill recommended by the committee for the relief of these claimants passed both houses of Congress, but was vetoed by President Polk. In 1855 the bill recommended by the committee again passed both houses, but was vetoed by President Pierce. In brief, Polk argued that it was too late in the season and he had but little time to examine the matter; that the amount involved was large, while the country was in debt, that the claims were stale, that it was not proposed to pay them in full, &c., &c.

Pierce argued that the passage of such a measure would inculpate those who for fifty years had failed to pass the measure; that as the treaties were abrogated by one party, neither party had claims to release under them—as if one party can legally rescind a contract, or if it could, that it could annul all claims arising prior to such rescission—with other objections which we cannot stop to examine, but all of which were frivolous and wide of the mark.

The following is a list of the reports of committees of Congress upon these claims (from *Report No. 109, House of Representatives, 48th Congress, 1st session,*):

French Spoliation Claims.

Number.	Where reported.	By whom reported.	Committee.	Date.	Bills and reports.	Detailed reports.
1	House..	Mr. Giles (¹)......	Select......	April 22, 1802...		R.
2	House..	Mr. Marion (²).....	Select......	February 18, 1807.		R.
3	Senate.	Mr. Roberts.......	Claims......	March 3, 1818.....		R.
4	House..	Mr. Russell.......	Foreign Affairs..	January 31, 1822..	Adverse, No. 124..	R.
5	House..	Mr. Forsyth.......	Foreign Affairs..	March 25, 1824....	Adverse, No. 32...	R.
6	Senate.	Mr. Holmes........	Select......	February 8, 1827..	Adverse, No. 94...	R.
7	House..	Mr. E. Everett.....	Foreign Affairs..	May 21, 1828......	Favorable, No. 48.	R.
8	Senate.	Mr. Chambers......	Select......	May 24, 1828......	Favorable, No. 262	R.
9	Senate.	Mr. Chambers......	Select......	February 11, 1829.	Favorable, bill 206	R.
10	House..	Mr. E. Everett.....	Foreign Affairs..	February 16, 1829.	Favorable, bill 76.	R.
11	Senate.	Mr. E. Livingston..	Select......	February 22, 1830.	Favorable, bill 82.	R.
12	Senate.	Mr. E. Livingston..	Select......	December 21, 1830.	Favorable, bill 103	R.
13	Senate.	Mr. E. Livingston..	Select......	January 14, 1831..	Favorable, bill 31.	R.
14	Senate.	Mr. Webster (³)...	Select......	December 10, 1834.	Favorable, bill 32.	
15	Senate.	Mr. Wilkins.......	Select......	December 20, 1831.	Favorable, bill 5..	
16	House..	Mr. E. Everett.....	Foreign Affairs..	February 21, 1835.	Favorable, bill 9..	
16	House..	Mr. Cambreling....	Foreign Affairs..		Minority adverse statement. } 121	R.
17	House..	Mr. Howard.......	Foreign Affairs..	January 29, 1838..	Favorable, bill 452	R.
18	House..	Mr. Cushing (⁴)...	....	March 31, 1838....	Favorable statement.	R.
19	House..	Mr. Cushing.......	Foreign Affairs..	April 4, 1840......	Minority adverse statement. } 319	R.
20	House..	Mr. Pickens.......	Foreign Affairs..			
20	House..	Mr. Cushing.......	Foreign Affairs..	December 9, 1841..	Favorable, bill 57.	
21	Senate.	Mr. Choate........	Foreign Relations.	January 28, 1842..	Favorable, bill 148	
22	Senate.	Mr. Archer........	Foreign Relations.	January 5, 1843...	Favorable, bill 64.	
23	House..	Mr. C. J. Ingersoll.	Foreign Affairs..	April 17, 1844.....	Favorable, bill 339	

(¹) Favorable statement of facts, without coming to any conclusion.
(²) Favorable, including and adopting Mr. Giles's report of April 22, 1802.
(³) This bill was voted by the Senate, February 3, 1835; yeas 25, nays 20.
(⁴) Individual, by consent of the House.

Number	Where reported	By whom reported	Committee	Date	Bills and reports	Detailed reports
24	Senate	Mr. Choate	Foreign Relations	May 29, 1844	Favorable, bill 180	
25	Senate	Mr. Choate (⁵)	Foreign Relations	December 23, 1844	Favorable, bill 47	
26	Senate	Mr. Clayton (⁶)	Select	February 2, 1846	Favorable, bill 68	
27	House	Mr. Tru. Smith (⁷)	Foreign Affairs	July 16, 1846	Favorable, bill 68	R.
28	Senate	Mr. Morehead	Select	February 10, 1847	Favorable, bill 156	
29	House	Mr. Tru. Smith	Foreign Affairs	January 4, 1848	Favorable, bill 21	
30	Senate	Mr. Tru. Smith	Select	February 5, 1850	Favorable, bill 101	R.
31	House	Mr. Buel	Foreign Affairs	June 14, 1850	Favorable, bill 318	
32	Senate	Mr. Tru. Smith (⁸)	Select	January 24, 1851	Favorable, bill 101	
33	Senate	Mr. Bradbury	Select	January 14, 1852	Favorable, bill 64	R.
34	Senate	Mr. Hamlin	Select	February 15, 1854	Favorable, bill 36	
35	House	Mr. Bayly (⁹)	Foreign Affairs	January 4, 1855	Favorable, bill 117	
36	House	Mr. Pennington	Foreign Affairs	March 3, 1857	Favorable, bill 865	R.
37	Senate	Mr. Crittenden (¹⁰)	Select	February 4, 1858	Favorable, bill 45	
38	House	Mr. Clingman	Foreign Affairs	May 5, 1858	Favorable, bill 552	R.
39	House	Mr. Royce	Foreign Affairs	March 29, 1860	Favorable, bill 259	
40	Senate	Mr. Crittenden	Select	June 11, 1860	Favorable, bill 428	
41	Senate	Mr. Sumner	Foreign Relations	January 13, 1862	Favorable, bill 114	
42	Senate	Mr. Sumner	Foreign Relations	January 20, 1863	Favorable, bill 114	
		Mr. Frye		February —, 1882	Favorable	
		Mr. Walker		January 18, 1882	Favorable	

(⁵) This bill was ordered to be engrossed and read a third time, February 10, 1845; by yeas 26, nays 15, but not reached.

(⁶) This bill was voted by the Senate on the 9th of June, 1846; yeas 27, nays 23.

(⁷) This bill (being Mr. Clayton's bill as voted by the Senate) was voted by the House by yeas 94, nays 87. It thus passed both Houses, and was vetoed by President Polk as a Senate bill; and on the veto the Senate voted yeas 27, nays 15—not two-thirds.

(⁸) This bill was voted by the Senate; yeas 30, nays 26.

(⁹) This bill was voted by the House, y as 111, nays 77; and was voted by the Senate February 5, 1855, yeas, 28 nays 17, and was vetoed by President Pierce as a House bill; and the House vote on the veto was yeas 113, nays 81—not a two-thirds—so the bill was lost.

(¹⁰) This bill (Mr. Crittenden's, No. 45) was voted by the Senate on the 10th January, 1859; yeas 26, nays 20.

The General Assembly of Rhode Island has been equally persistent in asking for recognition of the justice of these claims and that provision be made for their payment. Upon examination of the schedules I find that action thereon has been taken as follows:

At the January session, 1832, p. 42, it was

" *Resolved*, that our Senators in Congress be instructed to use their exertions to secure for our citizens all the compensation for French spoliations, which, by treaty with France or otherwise, may be constitutionally provided and secured."

At the January session, 1844, (*Acts and Resolves, p. 57,*) on the report of the committee,

" *Resolved*, that prior to the convention between the United States and France in 1800, there were large and just claims due from France to citizens of the United States, for spoliations on their commerce, which claims were asserted as just by the Government of the United States, and were not rejected by France:

" *Resolved*, That by the ratification of said convention the Government of the United States released France from the payment of said claims, in consideration of a corresponding release from the claims of France against the United States, and from the obligations of the treaties which had before existed between the two nations: and that, in the opinion of this Assembly, the said mutual release has been of great advantage to the United States as a nation:

" *Resolved*, That this was such an appropriation of private property to public use as, in the opinion of this Assembly, entitles the said citizens to just compensation from the government of the United States.

" *Resolved*, That a copy of these resolutions and the accompanying report be transmitted by the Secretary to each of our Senators and Representatives in Congress, and that they be requested to use their exertions for procuring a just indemnification to said citizens."

These resolutions were adopted upon recommendation of the committee to which the subject was referred. Their report was full and lucid, and is one of the most clear, brief expositions extant, and is deserving of careful study. It is out of print, but ought now to be reprinted.

At the January session, 1846, (p. 92, *Schedules*,) we find that

"His Excellency the Governor having communicated to this General Assembly resolutions of the legislature of Massachusetts strongly urging on the United States Government payment of the claims of American citizens for spoliations committed on their commerce, under authority of the French Government, anterior to the year 1800, the indemnity for which was assumed by the United States, and France released therefrom, by the convention of that year, ratified in 1801; and this General Assembly concurring in the opinion expressed by the Massachusetts legislature, and reaffirming the report and resolutions adopted at the January session, 1844, and accepting the report made by the committee at the present session: do therefore

"*Resolve*, That the said claims are honestly due, and that a longer-continued refusal of payment, after many favorable reports have been made by committees to both houses of Congress, would be a denial of justice by that august body, highly derogatory to its character, and flagrantly injurious to our national credit:

"*Resolved*, That his Excellency the Governor be requested to transmit copies of these resolutions to the President of the United States, to the Governor of each State and to each of our Senators and Representatives in Congress, and that said Senators and Representatives be requested to use all honorable means and their most earnest efforts to procure the passage of an act which shall give full indemnity and ample justice to these long-delayed and much-injured claimants."

I have not been able to find the report of the committee here referred to. It was not published in the schedules of the General Assembly, and careful search in the vaults of the State House has been made for the original, but it cannot be found. I hope that anyone having a copy of it will make it known now, while all are so much interested in this subject.

In May, 1846, (*Schedules, p. 73,*) we find that the General Assembly again took action on this matter, as follows:

"Whereas, among the numerous class of American citizens who had just claims upon the Government of France for spoliations upon their commerce prior to the 30th of September, 1800, for which that government admitted its liability for adequate indemnities, are many citizens of this State: that, by the treaty of that date, the United States, in consideration of the release of the 'burdensome and onerous guaranties' stipulated in the treaties of 'alliance' and of 'amity and commerce' of 1778, fully exonerated and released the Government of France from such indemnities, and that, by subsequent conventions between the two Governments of April 30, 1803, for the cession and acquisition of Louisiana, the United States became legally and equitably obligated to their citizens for the aforesaid indemnities, yet they have not been satisfied in conformity to the conventions as aforesaid : and whereas, a bill appropriating five millions of dollars for the *pro rata* liquidation of said indemnities is now pending before Congress, therefore

"*Resolved*, That in the opinion of this General Assembly the aforesaid claims, with interest, are justly due and demandable of the Government of the United States;

"*Resolved, further*, That our Senators in Congress be, and are hereby instructed, and our Representatives be requested, to use their best exertions to procure from the government as full and adequate indemnities therefor as though said claims still existed against the Government of France, and to aid, by all proper means, the passage of any bill for the speedy liquidation thereof.

"*Resolved*, That his Excellency the Governor transmit copies of these resolutions to each of our Senators and Representatives, and request them to lay the same before their respective Houses."

There is a very prevalent belief that these spoliation claims were paid, or settled for with France at the time of the Louisiana purchase. But this is a mistake. Lest it may be thought that the resolution of our General Assembly, which I have just read, proves this belief to be correct, I will explain briefly that on the 30th of April, 1803, there was concluded at Paris a treaty and two conventions between France and the United States. The treaty ceded Louisiana to the United States for eighty millions of francs. The first convention provided for the payment of sixty millions of francs, part of the eighty millions, in United States stock. The second convention provided for the payment of the "debts" embraced in the fifth article of the convention of 1800, which we have already considered, these "debts" being specifically explained not to include prizes whose condemnation was confirmed, but to include only supplies and embargoes. To pay these "debts" the remaining twenty millions of the eighty millions of francs was agreed to be paid by the United States to these creditors upon satisfactory proof thereof. These spoliation claims proper, arising from illegal captures and sale of American vessels, were therefore not included.

The last resolution of our General Assembly on this subject was in January, 1872, (*Schedules*, p. 225,) as follows:

"Resolution instructing the Rhode Island delegation in Congress to use their best exertions to provide for the payment of claimants for French spoliations prior to the year 1800.

"*Voted and Resolved*, (the Senate concurring herein), That the Senators of this State in Congress be, and the same are, hereby instructed, and that the Representatives of this State in Congress be, and the same are, hereby requested, to use their best exertions to procure the passage of an Act of Congres granting indemnity to citizens of the United States for French spoliations on American commerce prior to the year 1800."

In 1799 these claims were estimated at twenty millions of dollars in amount. Senator Sumner in his valuable report on this subject (*Senate Report No. 10, 41st Congress, second session,*) deducted the payments made by France after that date, $728,000; for debts paid by France under the last-mentioned convention of 1803, $3,750,000; and payments made under the treaty of 1819 for vessels captured and sold in Spanish ports, $2,848,000, leaving a balance of $12,676,380. By a different method he arrived at nearly the same result, $12,572,000. This would assume that all the losses can be legally proved, which, unfortunately, is by no means the case. Many of the original papers are lost, mislaid or destroyed by fire or otherwise. Some were filed in Washington, sent to Paris by our government, and have disappeared. All the witnesses are dead, most of them leaving no legal evidence that can be used to prove these losses. It is doubtful if one quarter of these losses can be proved at the present day.

The act to provide for the ascertainment of these claims passed Congress, January 20th, 1885. It authorizes claimants for indemnity for acts of spoliation by the French prior to the convention of September 30th, 1800, to apply by petition to the United States Court of Claims. Thereupon the Court shall examine and determine the validity of the claims, their present ownership, and what assignment thereof, if any, has been made. The Attorney-General of the United States is directed to resist all claims presented by all proper legal defences. The Secretary of State is directed to procure all such evidence as can be procured from abroad as to these acts of spoliation, all of which, with all papers relating thereto on file in the Department of State in Washington, may be used by the claimants or by the United States. On the first Monday of December in each year the Court is directed to report to Congress the facts and conclusions reached in each case decided. All claims must be presented within two years from January 20th, 1885. The decisions of the Court are not final, however, as Congress expressly reserves the right under the act to pay or not to pay the claims, even after they are proved. But no doubt is felt that Congress will order the payment of claims found to be valid by the Court, especially if the amount prove to be small. The question is often asked whether Congress will pay interest also on the claims allowed. There can be no doubt interest should be paid, as the country has reaped the benefit for eighty-five years of the settlement then made for these claims; but the interest would amount to five times the principal, and should the claims allowed prove large in amount the sum total would prove appalling. Perhaps a low rate of interest may be allowed,—perhaps, if the amount finally proved turns out to be small, Congress, in a burst of generosity, may direct it to be paid with interest.

Acting under the authority conferred by the Act of Congress, the Secretary of State sent the Hon. James Broadhead to Paris last summer to procure copies of the decrees of condemnation of the captured vessels from the French courts, etc., but it is reported he found they had all been destroyed during the various revolutions the French capital has undergone. This winter he is to visit the Windward Islands for the same purpose, and it is hoped he may be more successful in his search there. I have in my possession one of the decrees of condemnation by the court in Guadeloupe of one of our Rhode Island vessels, the schooner " Betsey," the best possible proof of the validity of the claim. I am often asked what proof is necessary to make out a case to be submitted to the Court of Claims. In the Custom House in Providence and Newport we find, bound in books, the registers of the vessels. The manifests should also be on file there, but not having been bound some of them are lost. Upon the return home of the captain after the capture of his vessel, in order to account for her disappearance, his protest, under oath, was filed, stating the facts connected with the capture, when made, where and by what court the vessel was condemned, etc. Then an entry was made on the back of the register, " Captured by the French," with the date, and perhaps a statement showing what French port the vessel was taken into, and sometimes a memorandum is added, " Captain's protest on file." This protest is always valuable evidence, because made at the time and without reference to its ever being used as evidence in the recovery of the loss. It was made, as such protests, so called, are made now, to account for the disappearance of the vessel and to discharge the sureties from further obligation on their bond. Should our government be able to recover the decrees of condemnation of the French tribunals in the ports of the Windward Islands, their coincidence with the evidence found here would be conclusive.

Upon examining the registers the small tonnage of the vessels is remarkable. Our ancestors carried on trade and business generally in a small way compared with the present way. These captured vessels varied from 18 to 165 tons, the latter being the largest I find on my list. Last summer all the evidence in our Custom Houses relating to this subject was ordered sent to Washington for use by either side as evidence in the trial of these petitions, according to the terms of the act of Congress. Before they went I made memoranda of them. Among the vessels captured I find the Neptune, Happy Return, Betsey, Sally, William, Favorite, Ruth, Fanny, Ranger, Franklin, Becca, Peyton Randolph, Greenwich, Union, Lily, William, Betsey, Nancy, Polly, Reliance, Good Intent, Patty, Sophia, Gen. Greene, Commerce, Eliza, Industry, Mary, Agenoria, Brandywine, Alice, Nancy, Orange, Sukey, Sukey, Nancy, Henry, Ranger, Caroline, Peace, Lydia, Union, Columbia, Joanna, Friendship, Edward, Minerva, Betsey, Friendship, Friendship, Diana, Rover, Clementina, and others. Among the names of owners of these vessels I find the names of Simeon Martin, Peleg Clarke, Caleb Gardner, William Vernon, Benjamin Fry, Nicholas Peck, Thomas Church, Joseph Wardwell, Shearjashub Bourne, Samuel Wardwell, Ebenezer Cole, Walter Channing, Archibald Crary, George Gibbs, Frederic Crary, John Cook, Ebenezer Woodward, Jr., Anson Nye, Solomon Nye, Nathaniel Gladding, Daniel Gladding, Charles Collins, Jr., Isaac Manchester, Edward Church, Henry Munroe, Thomas Butler, Styles Phelps, Aaron Usher, Levele Maxwell, Robert N. Auchmuty, John W. Russell, Nathaniel Howland, Allen Munroe, William Champlin, James Maxwell, Constant Taber, Simon Davis, William Gardner, William Britton, Stephen Arnold, William Arnold, Perry G. Arnold, John Bullock, Lemuel Bishop, Thos. L. Halsey, James Atwood, John I. Clarke, Samuel W. Greene, Daniel Mathewson, Noel Mathewson, Benjamin F. Carlile, Samuel Carlile, Daniel Allen, Samuel Allen, Moses Lippitt, Thomas Jackson, Edward Dickens, Benjamin Clifford, Edward Dexter, Samuel Butler, Seth Wheaton, Richard Jackson, Zachariah Allen, Levi Bosworth, Samuel Aborn, Jr., Lowry Aborn, John A. Aborn, Cyrus Butler, Cyrus Northup, Jonathan Arnold, Eleazer Ellis, Joseph McClintock, Andrew Boyd, Rufus Williams, Wilson Jacobs, Thomas Sprague, Michael Anthony, Philip Peckham, Jr., Henry R. Cooper, Ebenezer Tyler, 3d, and others. I should be very glad to find out who are the heirs of many of these claimants, but I have not yet been able to. There are also claimants in Rhode Island for insurance losses paid by insurance companies. These claims can be preferred by petition signed by the company if still in existence, or by its assignee. The petition for the claim of an individual must be signed and preferred by his administrator.

I have two petitions signed by the original administrator, but generally speaking, an administrator *de bonis non* must first be appointed. As soon as one is appointed, but not until then, armed with his power of attorney and certified copy of his letter of administration I have the requisite authority to apply to the Department of State in Washington, and upon payment of the usual fees for copying, I am furnished with copies of whatever there may be on record there concerning the capture in question. This often supplements other proof already found here. I meet with some cases in which all the proofs of capture were retained here by the claimant, and in other instances they were all sent to Washington about the time of the capture, in response to the request of the Secretary of State. In some instances all the papers were placed in the hands of some member of Congress or of some lawyer, now dead, and no trace of them can now be found. The list of claimants and vessels published by the Government last winter (*Senate, Ex. Doc. No. 205*) is valuable and of great assistance, but is by no means exhaustive, because it includes only claims filed in Washington.

As to the bibliography of the subject, a list of books, articles, reports, speeches, &c., published in No. 71 of the Bulletin of the Public Library of Boston (vol. 6, No. 5) is of great value. And the message from the President of the United States to the Senate, May 20, 1826, (*Senate Doc. No. 102*) already spoken of, contains all the correspondence, negotiations, &c., relating to this interesting chapter in our history, although it cannot be said to be one that redounds to the credit either of the United States or of France.

To conclude, in the eloquent words of Sumner:

"Of all claims in our history, these are most associated with great events and great sacrifices. First in time, they are also first in character, for they spring from the very cradle of the republic and the trials of its infancy. To comprehend them, you must know first, how independence was won; and, secondly, how, at a later day, peace was assured. Other claims have been merely personal or litigious; these are historic. Here were 'individual' losses, felt at the time most keenly, and constituting an unanswerable claim upon France, which were employed by our Government at a critical moment, like a credit or cash in hand, to purchase release from outstanding 'national' obligations, so that the whole country became, at once, the trustee of these sufferers, bound, of course, to gratitude for the means thus contributed, but bound also to indemnify them against these losses. And yet these sufferers, thus unique in situation, have been compelled to see all other claims for foreign spoliations satisfied while they alone have been turned away. As early as 1794 our plundered fellow citizens obtained compensation, to the amount of more than ten million dollars, on account of British spoliations. Several indemnities have been obtained since from Spain, Naples, Denmark, Mexico, and the South American states, while, by the famous convention of 1831, France contributed five million dollars to the satisfaction of spoliations under the continental system of Napoleon. Spain stipulated to pay for every ship or cargo taken within Spanish waters even by the French, so that the French spoliations on our commerce within Spanish waters have been paid for, but French spoliations on our commerce elsewhere before 1800 are still unredeemed. Such has been the fortune of claimants the most meritorious of all.

In all other cases there has been simply a claim for foreign spoliations, but without any superadded obligation on the part of our Government. Here is a claim for foreign spoliations, the precise counterpart of all other claims, but with a superadded obligation, on the part of our Government, in the nature of a debt, constituting an *assumpsit*, or implied promise to pay; so that these sufferers are not merely *claimants* on account of French spoliations, but they are also *creditors* on account of a plain assumption by the Government of the undoubted liability of France. The appeal of these *claimant-creditors* is enhanced beyond the pecuniary interests involved when we consider the nature of this assumption, and especially that, in this way, our country obtained a final release from embarassing stipulations with France contracted in the war for national independence. Regarding it, therefore, as a *debt*, it constitutes a part of that sacred debt incurred for national independence, and is the only part remaining unpaid."

AN OLD BELL.—Considerable curiosity has been excited in this town by the factory bell which has been put up within a few days, recently purchased from among the celebrated Spanish bells in New York. The inscription we give below, and our readers can form their own opinions as to the antiquity of the bell. However that may be, its tone is certainly most melodious and musical, far more so than most of the bells of more recent manufacture.

```
            S E H I L O E S T A
            C A M P A P A S I E
            N D O G V A R D I A
            N E L M.  R P.  P R E D I
            C A D O R G E N E R
            A L.  E.  R.  R A E A E L
            A N T O N I O.  G A R C I A
            A N O D E I   8 2 8
     S A N.  R A E A E L  Y.  S A N.  E R A N
     S I S C O R O G A D.  P R O.  N O S O.
     T R O S.
```

The translation of which is said to be as follows:

"This bell, which God preserve, has been given by General F. R. Rafael Antonio Garcia, in the year of God 828.

"Saint Rafael and Saint Francisco pray for us."

—*Bristol Phenix, March 3, 1838.*

NOTE.—We print this in order to call attention to the fact that often escapes a careless reader, who reads this and at once leaps to the conclusion that this is one of the oldest bells in the country. The date is given 828. The word "General" is enough to attest the age, and then the Saints whose names are given and the General who presents it. These will call a student to a good cyclopedia for confirmation to which we refer. We think 1828 would be nearer its date than 828, and we would like to know where this bell is now.

A MYTHICAL PEDIGREE.

CONTRIBUTED BY RAY GREENE HULING, FITCHBURG, MASS.

FOR the following line of descent from Adam to the early Arnolds of Rhode Island no claim of accuracy is put forth. It is given merely for what it is worth, and, in the opinion of the author, that is very little. It occurred to him one stormy vacation week to follow back the well-known Arnold family tree, which has its root in Jestyn, King of Glaumorgan, so far as material should be available. Woodward's History of Wales, Powell's Caradoc's History of Wales, and an article in Penn. Historical Magazine, vol. iv. (1880), were examined in the course of the search. A printed statement underlies every step in the chain, but the author would prefer not to be responsible for the truth of all that is in print.

I think genealogists are agreed that the Arnold pedigree is correctly established to Roger Arnold of Llanthony, but differ as to the line of descent reaching back to Jestyn. It is not difficult to accept its probable accuracy from that point back to Cadwalladr, for it deals with historic names. Beyond this the Welsh Rolls are the authority. To these credence was given in former times, but is not now, I think, by reputable students of genealogy, though the funeral customs of the bards give some color of probability to the reported genealogies of the royal families. Of course, when the line leaves Britain and includes the names of classic story, it becomes purely mythical, although the Welsh explanation is at least interesting. The theory is that the classic heroes and gods were only heads of families who had become deified after death. At the very end of the line we become attached to the genealogy of the book of Genesis, though the names in coming through the Welsh have assumed a slightly unfamiliar form.

It is possible that some genealogists of a hypercritical turn will deem an apology due for having allowed this—macaronic genealogy, shall I call it?—to be dignified with a printed appearance. I have to offer only the urgent request of our genial Editor. Seeing him in serious doubt as to his descent from the "grand old gardener," I cannot refrain from giving him the comfort that arises from seeing one's ancestors named in print.

1 Adda (Adam),
2 Seth,
3 Enos,
4 Methusalem,
5 Lamech,
6 Noahen,
7 Japheth,
8 Javan,
9 Chetim,
10 Ciprius,
11 Coelus,
12 Saturnus,
13 Jupiter,
14 Dardan,
15 Ericthonius.
16 Iros,
17 Assaracus,
18 Capius,
19 Anchises,
20 Aeneas,
21 Ascanius,
22 Silvius,
23 Brutus,
24 Locrinus,
25 Medoc,
26 Membyr,
27 Evroc Cadarn,
28 Brutus Darianlas,
29 Lleon,
30 Rum baladr Cras,
31 Blenddut,
32 Lyn,
33 Regan,
34 Cunedda,
35 Riwallon,
36 Gorwst,
37 Seissylt,
38 Antonius,
39 Aedd Mawr,
40 Cynwarch,
41 Dodion,
42 Dyfnwall,
43 Beli,
44 Gurgan,
45 Cyhelyn,
46 Seissyll,
47 Dan,
48 Morudd,
49 Elidr mawr,
50 Geraint,
51 Caddell,
52 Coel,
53 Porrex,
54 Kerryn,
55 Andrew,
56 Uriew,
86 Genedawc,
87 Iago,
88 Tegid,
89 Padarn Perfrydd,
90 Adeirn,
91 Cynedda Weledig,
92 Eineon Irth,
93 Caffwallan Lawhis,
94 Maelgwn Gwynedd,
95 Rhun,
96 Beli,
97 Iags,
98 Cadfan, (603),
99 Cadwallan,
100 Cadwallar, (d. 688), Last King of the Britons;
101 Idwallo, (d. 720),
102 Roderick Moelwynoc (d. 755)

57 Ithel,
58 Clydawr,
59 Clydm,
60 Gorwst,
61 Muriawn,
62 Blenddut,
63 Caph,
64 Owain,
65 Seissylt,
66 Arthvael,
67 Eidiol,
68 Rytherich,
69 Saml Penissel,
70 Pyrr,
71 Cappoir,
72 Monogen,
73 Beli Mawr,
74 Affleth,
75 Owen,
76 Duve Brichwain,
77 Omwedd,
78 Amwerid,
79 Gorddufu,
80 Dufu,
81 Gwrtholi,
82 Doli,
83 Gwrgain,
84 Cain,
85 Genedawc,
103 Conan Dyndoethwy (d. 818),
104 Eisylht, (Queen of Wales),
105 Roderick Mawr, the Great, (d. 876),
106 Morgan Heu, or Mawr, (d. 972), King of Glaumorgan;
107 Owen, " "
108 Ithel Dhu, " "
109 Gwrgaut, " "
110 Jestyn, " "
111 Nestm. Ynir, King of Gwent,
112 Meiric,
113 Ynir Vichan,
114 Caradoc,
115 Dyfnwall,
116 Syssylth, (d. 1175),
117 Arthur,
118 Meiric,
119 Gwillim,
120 Arnholt,
121 Arnholt Vychan,
122 Arnholt,
123 Roger Arnold of Llanthony,
124 Thomas Arnold,
125 Richard Arnold,
126 Richard Arnold of Baghere, (d. 1595),
127 Thomas Arnold of Melcome Horsey.

This Thomas was father of William and Thomas who settled in Rhode Island, and who were the ancestors of most of the men in the State.   R. G. H.

NOTE BY THE EDITOR.—We are much obliged to our friend Huling for the trouble he has taken to run this line back to the "old gardener," and trust that our readers will be as much amused as we have been in reading the list. To continue the list to ourself, we have to add:

128 Thomas, b. 1599; d. Sept., 1674.
129 Richard, b. Mar. 22, 1642; d. April 22, 1710.
130 John, b.——, 1671; d. Oct. 27, 1756.
131 Seth, b. July 26, 1706; d. ——, 1801.
132 Seth, b. January 6, 1740; d.——.
133 Richard, b.——; d. Aug. 27, 1844.
134 James L., b. April 24, 1812.
135 James N., b. August 3, 1844.

Deed from Alexander to the Proprietors of Providence.

Recorded in old Book No. 3, Prov. Records, page 450.

CONTRIBUTED BY FRED A. ARNOLD.

PROUIDENCE 1. 12. 1661 (so calld)

Be it knowne vnto all men by these presents y^t I waumsittou or sepauqut Chiefe Sachim of paukanawqut doe by these presents for ye Consideration of one hundreth fath: of wampam and other Gifts Receaued make & pass ouer vnto Tho: Olny Senr· John Sayles: John Browne: Val. Whitman & Roger Williams all my right and interest Claime and Challenge vnto my Lands grounds or meadowes lying & being on ye west side of Secunk or pautuckqut riuer for the vse of the Towne of prouidence Excepting a trackt of land about fowre or fiue miles wch I gaue leaue to William or Quashawaunamut of massachuset to dispose of wch sayd land begins at the old field of wasquadomisk and whereas I have no interest in any land beiond that tract assigned to william aforesaid only some subiects of mine lay Claime to the next tract of land beiond y^t of william his tract Calld mashackquñt I doe promise to deale with my said subiects to treate and agree with prouidence men if they please before any other English in witnes of the premises I set to mine

in ye presence of

DANIELL WILLIAMS.

JOSEPH WILLIAMS.

JOHN SASUMAN

hand & Seale

ye m^{rk} of Alexander

alias Waumsittou & Sepauqut

the mark of Tom wachemoket

Enroled ye 22nd of Janeuary: 1667: p me SHADRACH MANTON Towne Clerke

When the purchase of and settlement at Providence was made in 1636, Massasoit had subjected himself and the tribes under him to the Narragansetts, and the original deed called the TOWN EVIDENCE was given by Canonicus and Miantonomi in their capacity of Chief Sachems of both tribes; but soon after, taking advantage of their relations with the Plymouth and Bay governments, they renounced their allegiance to the Narragansetts and were released from their subjection, and the petty tribes to the north and west of Providence adhering to Massasoit, laid claim to large tracts of lands thereabout. In 1646 a committee of the town was appointed to negotiate with them, and bargained with Massasoit for all his right in the lands between the town bounds at Pawtucket and Louisquiset; the deed having been drawn ready for signing, and an agreement having been made as to the amount of wampam and commodities to be paid, the committee proceeded to Portsmouth to procure the same; but on returning and tendering the agreed articles, Massasoit refused to sign the deed unless an increase in the amount of the gratuities be given him. This the committee refused, and so reported to the town, with a copy of the agreement and the unsigned deed.[1] Nothing further seems to have been done at this time; but in acknowledgment of this unsatisfied claim, there was inserted in most of the deeds of land in this locality given between the English settlers from 1640 to 1660 the following clause, "provided that if the town shall be put to any charge about Indians, that he or they that doth possess the land shall pay their share." (See deeds of William Reynolds,[2] John Sayles, William Blaxton, and others, of lands on the Pawtucket river.)

June 13, 1660, Massasoit being then dead, Wamsitta appeared at the Plymouth Court[3] with another Indian called William and laid claim to certain lands that had been sold by a Narragansett sachem, who, as they recite, "hath nor never had no interest in it." This claim was referred to Capt. Willett, and

[1] R. I. Colonial Records, I, 31-34.
[2] Providence Transcript, pp. 76-78.
[3] Plymouth Colony Records, III, 192.

no further action appears on Plymouth Records; but soon after, the deed now given was made, followed by one from the Indian, William.

Alexander, alias Waumsittou, Wamsutta, Sepauqut, and Mooanam, was the son of Massasoit and elder brother of King Philip, who succeeded him as Sachem. He first appears under the name of Mooanum in 1639, Sept. 25, when with his father Vssamequin (Massasoit) he renewed and ratified the ancient league between Plymouth Colony and the Wampanoag tribes.[1] His wife was Namumpam, alias Tatapanum, alias Weetamoo, squaw-Sachem of Pocassett, "as potent a prince as any round about her, and hath as much corn, land and men at her command."[2] When a prisoner at Plymouth in 1662, he was taken sick and allowed to return home, upon condition that his son should be sent as a hostage for his return upon recovery.[3] No name is given for this son, and I find no other mention of any children.

After the death of Alexander, Weetamoo married one Petonowowet, who deserted her at the outbreak of Philip's war and joined the English, whereupon, believing that the colonists had poisoned Alexander, her first husband, and seduced from her, her second, she now joined with Philip in the prosecution of the war, and crossing over to the Narragansett country she married Quianopen, alias Panoquin, a cousin of Canonchet and a leader in the war, who was captured and shot at Newport, Aug. 26, 1676. She was drowned about the 6th of the same month while attempting to cross to Pocasset. Her body was found at Mattapoiset by the English, who cut off her head and set it upon a pole at Taunton, when by the cries and lamentations of the Indian prisoners it was discovered to be the head of Weetamoo.

From 1639 to 1660, about which time his father died, Alexander appears to have been associated with him in the govern-

---

[1] Plymouth Colony Records, I, 133.
[2] Present State of New England, p. 3.
[3] Hubbard, I, 51.

ment of the tribe, much as Canonicus and Miantonomi were over the Narragansetts. He joined his father in various sales of land, and sometimes his name appears alone, to deeds that were afterwards ratified by Massasoit.

June 13, 1660, he appeared at the Plymouth Court,[1] and upon his petition the following action was taken: "Att the ernest request of Wamsitta, desiring that in regard his father is lately deceased, and hee being desirouse, according to the custome of the natiues, to change his name, that the Court would Confer an English name vpon him, which accordingly they did, and therefore ordered, that for the future hee shalbee called by the name of Allexander Pokanokett; and desireing the same in behalf of his brother they have named him Phillip." This action shows that Massasoit was dead previous to June 13, 1660, after which date but little appears in authentic records regarding Alexander.

April 8, 1661, he sold to Capt. Thomas Willett a tract of land called the "Rehoboth North Purchase," which included the present town of Cumberland, R. I., Attleborough, and parts of Mansfield and Norton, Mass. During the year 1661 he appeared at the Plymouth Court and "challenged Quabauke Indians to belong to him, and further said that he did warr against Vncas this summer on that account."[2] This was a tribe of the Nipmuck Indians, near the present town of Brookfield, Mass. Early in 1662 complaint was made that Alexander was contriving mischief against the English, and he was summoned to Plymouth to make answer. Not appearing at the appointed time, he was arrested, with some of his people, and hastily carried to Major Winslow's house, where he was held as a prisoner. Here he suddenly fell sick, and was allowed to return home, where in two or three days he died.

John Sasuman, or Sassamon, was by birth a Massachusett Indian, "his father and mother living at Dorchester, and both died Christians." (I. Mather.)

[1] Plymouth Colony Records, III, 392.
[2] Drake's Indians, II, 103.

He learned the English language, could read and write, had translated some of the Bible into the Indian language, and had been employed as a schoolmaster, to teach his countrymen at Natick. He left the English for some dislike, and went to live with Alexander, and afterward with Philip, by whom he was made a secretary. Becoming restless he returned again to the English, and was baptised and received into the Indian church, and becoming a preacher, was sent to the Nemaskets near Middleboro, whose chief, Watuspaquin, deeded him land in 1674 to induce him to remain among them, as he did also to his son-in-law, one Felix, who had married his daughter Assowetough, called by the English, Betty Sasemore. While living here, he learned of the intention of Philip to make war upon the whites, and communicated this information to the Governor at Plymouth, soon after which, his body was found in Assawomset Pond, as the English believed, murdered for the part he had taken in notifying them of the Indian plot. Three Indians were arrested, tried, and hung for this murder, and their hanging was the signal for the opening of the war, which was sooner than had been designed by Philip.[1]

Tom of Watchemoket, the last witness to this deed and the grantor in the preceding deed of December 10, 1661, was probably an under sachem of a tribe of the Wampanoags, and appears to have been a councillor and interpreter under Massasoit, Alexander and Philip. In the deed of August 9, 1646, made by Massasoit, but never executed, is the following clause, " I do hereby authorize Saunkussecit alias Tom of Wauchimoqut to mark trees and set the bounds of the land aforesaid."[2]

The deed of December 10, 1661, he signed as " Maugin calld Tom of Wauchimoqut." In 1667 he was witness to a deed made by Philip to Constant Southworth and others, which he signed as " Tom alias Sawsuett an interpreter."[3] Another deed of Philip's in 1668 he signs as " Tom Sansuwest, Inter-

[1] Drake's Indians, III, 8-12.
[2] R. I. Colonial Records, I, 31.
[3] Book of the Indians, III, 14.

preter."[1] Again in 1672 he signs as "Thomas alias Sanksuit."[2]

The country called Watchemoket was on the east side of the Providence and Blackstone rivers, and extended from about Watchemoket Cove, opposite Field's Point, northerly to the Ten Mile River, embracing the northerly part of the present town of East Providence. The point of land on the opposite side of the river where the westerly abutment of Red Bridge now stands was also called Wachamoquitt, as is shown by the following action of the town, December 17, 1664: "It is granted unto Arthur Fenner that he may have the Meere Bank beginning at the corner of his fence by his now dwelling house and so to go round the points unto a little creek or cove lying next unto Wachamoquitt point, and to have it upon this condition, laying down so much land in another place for the town use, and also to make three stiles, one by his house, another at the hollow *near Wachamoquitt point*, and another at the aforesaid creek or cove, and that people may have liberty to pass thro' on foot, or upon occasion to land goods upon the said land, &c."[3] This "Meere Bank" was the bluff or river bank from the vicinity of "What Cheer Rock" around the present location of Gano and Pitman streets to the point. The creek spoken of is crossed by Pitman street, and Waterman street has been filled across the "cove" in recent years.

In a deed dated April 14, 1641,[4] from the town of Providence to William Arnold, of several lots of land, one of them was described as "lying upon the neck of the town upon a point over against Wachamoquott." January 11, 1642–3, in making a deed to Thomas Olney, William Arnold reserves his lot of land "lieing upon the neck of the town before the poynt of Watchamoqut."[5] This lot he afterwards sold to Arthur Fenner, and describes it as "lieing upon the neck or point calld What Cheere."

---

[1] Book of the Indians, III, 14.
[2] Book of the Indians, III, 15.
[3] Providence Transcript, p. 175.
[4] Providence Transcript, p. 67.
[5] Providence Transcript, p. 43.

Joseph Williams, the youngest son of Roger and Mary (Warnard) Williams, was born, says the record, "At Providence about the beginning of December, 1643, (so called)." His father was then in England engaged in procuring the first Charter which was signed March 14, 1643-4, and did not return until Sept. 17, 1644, when Joseph was over nine months old.

His gravestone in the Williams burying ground at Roger Williams Park gives his birth as 1644, but a family memorandum book, once the property of Joseph Williams, Sen., and afterwards of his sons, Joseph, Jr., and James, gives the date as December 12, 1643,[1] which agrees with the record made by his father.

1661, February 24. He received "a purchase right" from the town,[2] as did also his brother Daniel.

1661-2. Received from town 19 acres on the neck on the east side of great swamp and near the place called the new fields.[3]

1665, February 19. Drew No. 43 in a division of lands.

1666, May 31. Engaged allegiance to King Charles II.

1669, December 17. He married Lydia, the youngest daughter of Thomas and Mary (Small) Olney, the brother of the bride, Thomas Olney, Jr., assistant, performing the marriage ceremony.[4] That he had already provided himself with a home is shown by a deed from the town dated May 27, 1670,[5] of 20 acres, on his purchase right "lying between the great pond called Mashapauge and the meadow called Mashapauge meadows *and near unto the now dwelling-house* of the said Joseph Williams and on the north side thereof;" the south bound of his land was the line between Providence and Pawtuxet, running from the head of Sasafrax Cove to Mashapauge.

The homestead upon which Joseph Williams appears to

---

[1] Rider's Book Notes, II, 25.
[2] Providence Transcript, p. 152.
[3] Providence Transcript, p. 7.
[4] Providence Transcript, p. 444.
[5] Providence Transcript, p. 8.

have been living in 1670, five years before Philip's war, and thirteen years before the death of his father, was south and south-east of Mashapauge pond, and a considerable portion of it is now called Roger Williams Park. This land was probably received by Joseph Williams from the town upon his own right, but no record evidence exists of this, nor is there any record to show that it ever belonged to Roger Williams, and given, or sold by him to his son. I think, however, it is safe to say that Roger Williams never owned this land, except in the sense that he owned all the town, until he made the deed to the proprietors in 1638.

1673. Laid out by the town 60 acres of land to Joseph Williams, it being part of his purchase right, bounded easterly on lot of Arthur Fenner, that he bought of John Lippitt, west with land of William Fenner and the common.[1]

1675, April 12. Was No. 41 in a division of lands on the west side of the seven mile line.

1679. Served in King Philip's war.

1679, July 1. Taxed 6s 3d.

1683-84-93-96-97-98 and 1713, Deputy.

1684-85-86-87-88-91-93-94, 1713-14-15, Town Council.

1685, November 17. Received from town[2] 56½ acres of land, about five miles north-west from Providence and adjoining on the east of other lands laid out to him.

1688. Rateable estate, 2 oxen, 1 horse, 1 steere, 6 cows, 4 three years, 4 two years, 3 yearlings, 1 colt, 10 acres pasture, 3½ shares meadow.

1697. John Sayles sells to his uncle Joseph Williams a piece of meadow called Many Holes.[3]

1698-99 and 1700 to 1707, Assistant.

1698, March 10. To receive a shilling from every person to pay for running their lines of lots on the west of the seven mile line.

1699, May 12 and September 20.[4] He bought from Stephen

---

[1] Providence Transcript, p. 276.
[2] Providence Deeds, I, 138.
[3] Providence Deeds, I, 254.
[4] Providence Deeds, I, 259; vol. ii., p. 326.

Cornell and Mary Strange, widow of Lott Strange, for £95, 400 acres of land at Rocky Hill, bounded east by Mashapauge Pond, west by Pauchaset river, and south by land of William Vincent.

1699, October 25. On a committee to inspect laws, &c.

1700, January 27. Sold to John Sayles for £70 a mesuage farm of 210 acres about seven or eight miles north-west from the salt water or harbour in Providence.[1]

1707, November 3. Bought of Joseph Carpenter of Musketo Cove, Oyster Bay, Queens County, Long Island, Province of New York, great-grandson of William Carpenter of Pawtuxet, all rights in one-half of that cove near the place called the landing-place cove in Pawtuxet.[2]

1711, August 6. Sold to James Whipple " a 40 foot lot that did of right belong to me from the town of Providence Shadrach Manton's lot on the south, Valentine Whitman's on the north and extending westerly 40 foot in width from the town street to the salt water."[3]

1715, September 17. Peleg Williams, son of Daniel, sells to his uncle Joseph all interest in lands in Pawtuxet Neck.[4]

1716–17, January 5. He sells the same to sons Thomas, Joseph, and James.[5]

1717, October 26. Signed will,[6] making his wife Lydia and son James, Adm. He gave his son Thomas 330 acres of land at Rocky Hill, "where he now dwelleth," and other small parcels and rights.

To son Joseph one-half of land at Masipauge, about 130 acres, to be taken on the westward side thereof, adjoining to his house where he now dwelleth, &c.

To son James he gave 200 acres of land at Rocky Hill adjoining land given to son Thomas. Also one-half of homestead farm at Masipague, being the east part adjoining " to

---

[1] Providence Deeds, I, 255.
[2] Providence Deeds, II, 82.
[3] Providence Deeds, II, 198.
[4] Providence Deeds, II, 472.
[5] Providence Deeds, III, 4.
[6] Providence Wills, II, 195.

my house," about 130 acres, with the dwelling house, &c. " But my loving wife Lydia Williams shall have the command, benefit and use of that Roome in my said House called the outward Roome wherein I now dwell, during the term of her natural life."

To his wife he gives the bed " wherein I vsally Lodg with all the furniture thereunto belonging."

All other moveables, together with all cattle, sheep, swine and horse kind he gives to son James, he to pay all debts, and provide for his mother during her life. This will was proved Oct. 12, 1724. Inventory £55 4s 2d.

1720, May 2. He made deeds to his sons of the lands given them in the above will.[1]

1721-2, February 3. He sells to his three sons equally, his purchase right in lands on the westward side of the seven mile line.[2]

His death occurred August 17, 1724, his oldest son Thomas dying the 27th of the same month, and his wife Lydia surviving him only 23 days, her death occurring Sept. 9. Her will was dated Sept. 3 and proved Oct. 12, all property to go to son James and he appointed Adm.[3]

JOSEPH WILLIAMS[2] (*Roger*[1]) b. in Providence December 12, 1643; d. August 17, 1724; m. December 17, 1669, Lydia, youngest daughter of Thomas and Mary (Small) Olney; b. 1645; d. Sept. 9, 1724. Children :

1. JOSEPH, b. Sept. 26, 1670, and on the second day of the week ; d. young.
2. THOMAS, b. Feb. 16, 1671-2 ; d. Aug. 27, 1724. (See Prov. Wills II., 195.) Married Mary, d. of James and Mary (Hawkins) Blackmar, who d. July 1, 1717. Children: 1 Joseph, 2 Thomas, 3 Stephen, 4 John, 5 Abigail, 6 Jonathan, 7 Mary.

---

[1] Providence Deeds, IV, 170-172-203-205.
[2] Providence Deeds, V, 134.
[3] Providence Wills, II, 199.

3. JOSEPH, b. Nov. 10, 1673; d. Aug. 15, 1752. (See Prov. Wills, III., 306.) Married Lydia, d. of Benjamin and Lydia Hearnden, who died 1763. Children: 1, Mercy, 2 Jeremiah, 3 Mary, 4 Lydia, 5 Martha, 6 Barbara, 7 Freelove, 8 Jemimah, 9 Meribah, 10 Patience.
4. MARY, b. June, 1676; d. ——; m. probably James, s. of Eleazer and Alice (Angell) Whipple, who died Oct. 3, 1731; m. (2d) John, s. of John and Wait (Waterman) Rhodes. Children: 1 Eleazer Whipple, 2 James Rhodes.
5. JAMES, b. Sept. 24, 1680; d. June 25, 1757; m. Elizabeth, d. of James and Mary (Hawkins) Blackmar, b. 1682; d. March, 1761. Children: 1 James, 2 Anne, 3 Sarah, 4 Joseph, 5 Mary, 6 Nathaniel, 7 Elizabeth, 8 Hannah, 9 Lydia, 10 Nathan.
6. LYDIA, b. April 26, 1683; died Aug. 17, 1725. Unm.
7. PROVIDENCE.

THE CHANGE FROM OLD TO NEW STYLE.—In early dates pertaining to the history of Rhode Island previous to 1752, all dates between the first of January and the twenty-fifth of March bore the date of two years—thus, "The first church was organized in Providence, March 16, 1638-39." March was called the first month notwithstanding the fact that the new year began on the 25th of March. This has led to much uncertainty concerning the precise date of many important events, the first month of the new year beginning twenty-five days before the year itself. But by an act of Parliament the calendar year 1752 began on the first of January, and the date January 1, 1752, is found in public documents instead of January 1, 1751-2. By an act of Parliament a correction of 11 days in the day of the month took place September 3d, 1752, that day being written September 14th. As a consequence, the month of September, 1752, has but nineteen days in it, the shortest month on record.

1812, March 1st. Married in Albany, N. Y., Seth Arnold, of Smithfield, R. I., to Magdalin Quackenboss, daughter of Isaac A. Quackenboss of Guilderland.—*Providence Gazette.*

ORIGIN OF NAME EAST GREENWICH.

WE believe the subjoined extracts relative to Greenwich in England afford a reasonable ground for believing that the town of East Greenwich in Rhode Island was named for Greenwich in England, and that some of the most prominent of its early settlers may have come from, or from the vicinity of, its namesake in our mother country.

The fact that our East Greenwich bore for a time the name of Dedford (a misspelling, perhaps, for Deptford), that the counties of both towns are alike named Kent, that the towns are similarly situated upon the water, and that both have Wickford and Kingston (or Kingstown) not far away strengthens the grounds for such a conclusion.

If anything stronger can be brought to support this theory it is the fact that when the town was incorporated in 1680 it was styled East Greenwich, when there was no West Greenwich in existence, which latter town was a creation of the last century, as can be seen by a reference to the "State Manual."

We would like to have an expression of opinion from those having information upon the subject.

We are under obligations to L. P. Spencer, Esq., of Washington, D. C., for copies of the following extracts and other valuable suggestions.

Extract from an old book entitled "A Perambulation of Kent," written by Wm. Lambard, and published in London in 1576:

"Greenwiche, in Latine, Viridis sinus: in Saxon ᴣnenaɾic [Grenawic]; that is to say, the Greene Town, In ancient evidences, East Greenwiche, for difference sake from Depforde, which in old instruments is called west greenwiche."

The following is from Ireland's History of County Kent, England, vol. iv., p. 692:

"Greenwich lies next to Deptford, eastward, on the bank of the Thames, Blackheath being situated on the upper or southern side. It was called in Latin *Grenovicum viridis* sinus a viridariis, in Saxon, Grenawic, that is the green town or dwelling on the bank of the river, which last syllable is now corrupted into *wich*; and in ancient evidences it was called East Greenwich, to distinguish it from Deptford, which was called West Greenwich."

EARLY HISTORY OF NARRAGANSETT.

R. I. Historical Society Collections, vol. iii., p. 307, 1885, etc.

CONTRIBUTED BY STEUBEN JENKINS, ESQ., WYOMING, PENN.

BULL—JENKINS.

HENRY BULL came, 1635, in the James from London, age 25, through Boston and Sandwich, Mass., to Narragansett, R. I. He was born in England, 1610. Came to R. I., 1637, and died 22nd of 2d mo. 1693-4, age about 84. Another authority says he came to London from South Wales.

He married Elizabeth ——, about 1636, who died 1st of 8th mo. 1665. He married for his second wife, 14th of 12th mo. 1666, Esther Allen, born 8th Dec. 1648, died 26th of 1st mo. 1676. She was daughter of Ralph and Esther Swift Allen of Sandwich. Ralph was brother of George Allen, Sr., and his wife daughter of William and Joan Swift, all of Sandwich, Mass. He married for his third wife Ann (Clayton), widow of Gov. Nicholas Easton, 28th March, 1677. She conveyed a lot of land in Newport (Ann Bull) in her own name and right in 1702, and died ye 30 of ye 11 mo. 1707-8.

Henry Bull was Governor of Rhode Island from May, 1685, to May, 1686, and from Feb. 1689, to May, 1690.

Gov. HENRY BULL[1] had by first wife, Elizabeth, a son Jirah,[2] (variously spelled Jireh, Jareth.) By his second wife Esther Allen had a daughter, Esther, born —, 1666, died —, 1676. No child by third wife Ann.

JIRAH,² born in Portsmouth, Sept. 1638; m. ——. They had children:

    HENRY³, b. —, 1658; d. —, 1690. He m. Ann Cole, dau. of John Cole, of Narragansett.
    JIRAH³, (of whom presently,) b. Sept. 26, 1659; d. 16th July, 1702.
    EPHRAIM³, (of whom presently.)
    EZEKIEL³, m. Elizabeth ——.
    MARY³, m. James Coggeshall, b. 17th Feb. 1660; d. 2nd April, 1712. She was b. 1661; d. 13th June, 1754, age 93 years.

JIRAH³, (*Jirah*², *Gov. Henry*¹,) m. Godsgift Arnold, dau. of Benedict. She died 23d April, 1691. They had children:

    JIRAH⁴, b. 1682.
    BENJAMIN⁴, b. 1685, Sept. 5.
    BENEDICT⁴, b. 1688.

EPHRAIM³, (*Jirah*², *Gov. Henry*¹,) of So. Kingstown; m. 1st Mary Coggeshall, dau. of John of Newport, 27th Oct., 1692. She was born 10th March, 1662. They had:

   i. MARY⁴, b. 30th July, 1693; m. Peleg Mumford.
   ii. REBECCA⁴, b. 27th July, 1697; m. Samuel Hayden.
   iii. CONTENT⁴, b. 24th Nov. 1699; m. Job Jenkins, 15th Nov. 1724.

He married for second wife Hannah Holloway, or Holway, 20th June, 1700. She was born 1st March, 1667. They had children:

   vi. EPHRAIM⁴, } m. Patience Rodman, of Thomas.
   v. HANNAH⁴, } Twins. Born 18th April, 1702.
   vi. MARY⁴,
   vii. AMEY⁴, m. Joseph Coggeshall.

JOB¹ JENKINS, son of Zachariah, was born in Sandwich, Mass., 5th June, 1699; died in West Greenwich in 1757. He married, 15th of 11th month, 1724, Content Bull¹, dau. of Ephraim³, of S. Kingstown. She was born 24th Nov. 1699; d. 6th May, 1752. They had a large family of children, of whom I know the names of but four:

JOB².
EPHRAIM², captain in Col. Holmes' Battalion, N. J., 14th June, 1780.
REBECCA², m. Thomas Sluman. Recorded 16th July, 1761.
MARY², N. Kingstown, b. 31st March, [year burned off.]

Job¹ married for second wife, 18th Jan., 1753, Prudence Ealy, of East Greenwich; Rebecca Jenkins, witness. Prudence, the widow, m. John Hall, 10th Aug., 1758. Job¹ in his will dated 25th Feb., 1757, gives to wife ——; to son Job, house and lands, and a bequest to daughter Rebecca. Inventory of estate, £630, 10, 0; books, £13, 10, 0.

I would like to know more about Job's family.

BULL—ALBRO.

HENRY BULL¹, Governor, m. Elizabeth ——. They had:

JIREH, born 1638-9.
HENRY, ESTHER, MARY.

JIREH², born 1638-9; m. ——. They had:

JIREH, HENRY, EZEKIEL,
EPHRAIM, m. 1700, second wife, Hannah Holway.

EPHRAIM³, by second wife, Hannah Holway, had:

HANNAH, MARY, AMEY,
EPHRAIM, born 1602-4-18; m. 1726.

EPHRAIM⁴, born 18th of 4th mo. 1702; m. Patience Rodman. They had, among others:

PATIENCE⁵, who m. Samuel Albro, b. 1751; who had

THOMAS ALBRO⁶, b. 5-9-1779; m. Ever Tice;
SAMUEL, WAITE, ALICE, HANNAH.

This Bull genealogy was furnished to John P. Albro by Charles A. Bull, of Lisle, Ill. I prefer the other, though possibly not perfectly correct.   J. S.

EDITORIAL NOTES.

ACKNOWLEDGMENTS.—We are very grateful to those of our readers that have sent in their subscriptions to us since our last issue, and we earnestly request all others who have not not done so will confer the like favor upon us. We urgently need all our dues, and as our circulation is limited, of course we feel all delays of this nature seriously.

No magazine can live unless the editor and his readers work together. The REGISTER feels that it has a generous class of patrons and readers that can see and appreciate an honest and persistent effort to compile and publish unwritten facts in regard to our State history. The REGISTER has labored long and patiently, and has done a grand work and is capable of doing still better and effective service in the future.

We entreat therefore that our friends will join us heartily and will aid us in every way possible in extending our circulation, and in providing us with funds in order to work to better advantage. The editor pledges himself to spare no pains on his part and entreats his friends to spare none on their part. Will they do this? Let each one do his part faithfully and not wait for another to do it for them. If each one will do his part then the future success of the REGISTER is assured.

THANKS.—We have received several letters speaking in very high terms of our historical paper in the last REGISTER and urging us to furnish more. It is really pleasant to know that our paper was so well received. We thank our readers for their pleasant words, and will try as soon as we can to gratify them with more matter of the variety asked for.

THE UNITED SERVICE MAGAZINE.—We are pleased to welcome this standard work to our exchange list. We have already received great pleasure in the perusal of its pages, and find several papers upon subjects interesting to Rhode Island. Such works as the *United Service* are truly an ornament and power in the literary world.

THE PROCEEDINGS OF THE WYOMING (PENN.) HISTORICAL AND GENEALOGICAL SOCIETY, VOL. II., PART 1.—We have received through the politeness of Sheldon Reynolds, Esq., the above. Its articles are timely and indicates that this society of historical students are energetic and enthusiastic in the pursuit of their chosen subjects. It is a pleasure to note such vigor, and we congratulate the society upon the great success of their enterprise.

SOCIETIES AND THEIR DOINGS.

RHODE ISLAND HISTORICAL SOCIETY. — Oct. 6, 1885. The most important piece of business transacted at this meeting was the appointing of a committee to act in connection with a committee appointed by the Veteran Citizens Historical Association, the two to act with a committee appointed by the city government to devise a plan for the celebration of the 250th anniversary of the founding of Providence, which occurs next year.

Nov. 3, 1885. The first historical paper of the season's course was read before the Society by its President, Professor William Gammell; subject, "The Huguenots and the Edict of Nantes."

Nov. 17, 1885. The second paper was read before the Society by Miss Esther Bernon Carpenter, of South Kingstown; subject, "The Huguenot Influence in Rhode Island."

Dec. 1, 1885. The third paper was read before the Society by Amasa M. Eaton, Esq., of Providence; subject, "The French Spoliation Claims and Rhode Island Claimants."

Dec. 15, 1885. The fourth paper was read before the Society by Carl W. Earnst, editor of the *Beacon;* subject, "International Law and the Labors of Henry Wheaton." Hon. Abraham Payne gave a brief sketch of Wheaton's life.

THE VETERAN CITIZENS' HISTORICAL ASSOCIATION.—Oct. 5, 1885.—The first meeting of the season was held in their lecture room, the meeting being addressed by E. H. Hazard, Esq. of South Kingstown, upon incidents in the Narragansett country, and by Hon. Abraham Payne on reminiscences of Providence. A committee was appointed to act with a similar committee appointed by the city government and the Rhode Island Historical Society to devise a plan for the proper celebration of the 250th anniversary of the founding of Providence, which occurs next year.

Nov. 2, 1885.—In absence of both the President and orator of the day, the Secretary made report of proceedings of the anniversary committee and made remarks relating to early history of Providence and also in regard to the Palatine light. Jas. N. Arnold, Esq., also made remarks upon the latter subject.

Dec. 7, 1885.—The Secretary, Rev. Frederic Denison, read a paper upon the "Israelites in Rhode Island." Myer Noot, the Jewish Rabbi, read a short essay and performed in Hebrew part of their divine worship.

THE PROVIDENCE FRANKLIN SOCIETY.—Sept. 15.—Prof. W. W. Bailey read a poem of welcome. An interesting exhibit of minerals and flowers were shown by the members.

Sept. 29.—Mr. T. P. Noyes read a paper on Meteorology, with incidents regarding cyclones, tornadoes, etc.

Oct. 27.—Mr. Samuel Austin read a paper on "Applied Science." A short talk on maples was had.

Nov. 10.—J. Tabot Pitman read a paper entitled "The Mechanical System of Natural Philosophy."

Dec. 10.—Dr. C. B. Johnson read a paper, "Lessons of Science as Read from the Heavens."

THE SOLDIERS' AND SAILORS' HISTORICAL SOCIETY. — Oct. 20. — Judge Pardon E. Tillinghast read a paper entitled "Reminiscences of the 12th R. I. Volunteers," and a memorial of Col. George H. Browne.

The November meeting was not held.

Dec. 15.—Dr. Wm. F. Hutchinson, in lieu of a paper, gave an address from his notes on "Farragut and his Times."

RHODE ISLAND ENTOMOLOGICAL SOCIETY.—This band of natural history students have not as yet commenced their season's work, but plans are now completed looking to the season's work before them, the nature of which we hope to report in future numbers of the REGISTER.

THE BARRINGTON HISTORIC ANTIQUARIAN SOCIETY. — This new and vigorous society, which was founded in May last, have not as yet commended their season's meetings for historical study. We are in hopes, however, to report in future numbers of the REGISTER the good work done by this band of earnest workers in historical pursuits.

THE NEWPORT HISTORICAL SOCIETY.—Oct. 20.—A paper was read which was prepared by the President of the Society, entitled "William Pitt" (Lord Chatham). Several valuable mementoes were contributed to the society's museum.

Nov. 17.—Dr. Henry E. Turner read a paper, "Newport Sixty years ago."

Dec. 15.—Valuable additions were made to the societies museum. A paper entitled "Newport Forty years ago" was read by John L. Dennis. A paper was read by Henry W. French, "Life and Writings of Washington Irving," and a paper by Miss Mattie Smith, entitled, "English Country Life as portrayed by the Sketch Book."

NEWPORT NATURAL HISTORY SOCIETY.—Dec. 3.—A paper was read by Rev. Charles G. Gilliot, entitled "Anthracite Coal." We understand that this society has a fine course of lectures and work in preparation and that it is doing a good work in its especial field for Southern Rhode Island.

THE Narragansett Historical Register.

VOL. IV.   PROVIDENCE, R. I., APRIL, 1886.   No. 4.

THE RECORD OF OLD SMITHFIELD FROM 1730 TO 1850.

From Records in Town Clerk's Office, Lincoln.

CONTRIBUTED BY THE EDITOR.

(*Continued from Vol. IV, page 211.*)

H.

MARRIAGES.

Hayes, George A., of Providence, and Abigail Weldon, of Smithfield; m. by Rev. John Risley, July 25, 1841.

Haynes Daniel, and Ellen Charlotte Alexander; m. by Rev. B. P. Byram, Feb. 6, 1848.

Hayward Hannah, and William Arnold, April 1, 1740.
    " Samuel, and Ruth Fish; m. by William Arnold, justice, July 13, 1743.
    " Gorton N., and Laura A. Peckham; m. by Rev. John Boyden, jr., Jan. 27, 1841.

Heath, Cyrus D., of Holliston, Mass., and Esther J. Staples, of Smithfield; m. by Rev. D. L. McGeer, March 13, 1848.

Heaton Nathaniel, and Harriet Jaqueth; m. by Rev. Stephen Gano, April 29, 1819.

Heavens William, resident of Smithfield, and Hannah Whipple, of David; m. by Valentine Whitman, justice, Jan. 14, 1732-3.

Hedden Alice, and Moses Man, May 4, 1773.

Hendrick Stephen, of Greenwich, son of Joseph, and Content Wing, of Benjamin, of Smithfield; m. by Caleb Aldrich, justice, June 13, 1773.

" Joseph, of Stephen, of Smithfield, and Ruth Capron, of Joseph, of Cumberland; m. by Levi Ballou, justice, Sept. 5, 1793.

" Stephen, of Dr. Stephen, and Mary Bennett, of Cumberland, daughter of Charles; m. by Thomas Man, justice, July 6, 1800.

" Wing, and Fannie Walker; m. by Daniel Thurber, justic, Nov. 27, 1823.

" Almira, and David Spear Wilkinson, March 29, 1842.

Herd Susan, and Joseph Almy, March 29, 1821.

Herendeen Sarah, and Edward Bishop, Sept. 11, 1733.

" Abram, and Abigail Chillson; m. by Thos. Sayles, justice, June 10, 1734.

" Francis, and Dorcas Brown; m. by Thos. Sayles, justice, Feb. 12, 1735-6.

" Ruth, and Job Phillips, Dec. 24, 1736.

" Joseph, jr., and Mary Shippee; m. by Thomas Sayles, justice, Nov. 12, 1738.

" Joshua, and Mary Truesdon, both of Boston; m, by David Comstock, justice, May 25, 1739.

" Merabah, and Joseph Wetherhead, Dec. 25, 1740.

" Elisha, jr., and Ruth Herendeen; m. by Thomas Sayles, justice, Jan. 4, 1740.

" Ruth, and Elisha Herendeen, Jan. 4, 1740.

" Bethiah, and Joseph Shippee, Aug. 2, 1744.

" Alice, and Benjamin Brown, Oct. 5, 1746.

Herendeen Zerviah, and Peter Phillips, Dec. 28, 1748.
" Zerviah, and Peter Shippee, Dec. 28, 1748.
" Obediah, and Annie Hows; m. by Thomas Sayles, justice, June 11 or 12, 1750.
" Amie, and Joshua Smith, July 5, 1750.
" Freelove, and Hezekiah Herendeen, Aug. 14, 1750.
" Hezekiah, of Smithfield, and Freelove Herendeen, of Gloucester; m. by John Smith, justice, Aug. 14, 1756.
" Elisha, jr., and Judith Herendeen; m. by Thomas Sayles, justice, Dec. 7, 1752.
" Judith, and Elisha Herendeen, jr., Dec. 7, 1752.
" Rufus, and Dorcas Man; m. by Thomas Steere, justice, Nov. 22, 1754.
" Martha, and Solomon Shippee, Dec. 11, 1755.
" William, and Bethiah Peters; m. by Stephen Sly, justice, April 5, 1756.
" Jane, and Jonathan Chillson, Feb. 9, 1757.
" Izreal, and Hetabel Shippee; m. by Stephen Sly, justice, March 19, 1759.
" Levi, and Mary Wilbur; m. by Stephen Sly, justice, Sept. 17, 1759.
" Dorcas, and Jonathan Bullard, April 27, 1760.
" Ezekiel, of Smithfield, and Esther Peters, of Cumberland; m. at C.; m. by Stephen Sly, justice, Sept. 5, 1761.
" Hannah, and Jones Dyer, Sept. 27, 1761.
" Waite, and Jeremiah Bullard, Dec. 15, 1761.
" Sarah, and David Balford, May 26, 1763.
" Nathan, and Huldah Dillingham; m. by Stephen Sly, justice, April 30, 1764.
" Oziel, of Smithfield, and Amie Hill, of Gloucester; m. by Stephen Sly, justice, April 29, 1765.
" Abigail, and Joseph Herendeen 3d, Dec. 5. 1765
" Joseph 3d, and Abigail Herendeen; m. by Daniel Smith, justice, Dec. 5, 1765.

Herendeen Elizabeth, and Hosanna Brown, Nov. 22, 1766.
" Stephen, and Martha Shippee; m. by Richard Sayles, justice, May 3, 1767.
" Kezia, and Fail Smith, Feb. 21, 1768.
" Rhoda, and David Shippee, Jan. 1, 1769.
" Daniel, of Francis, and Mary Joperson, of Douglass, Mass.; m. by Daniel Mowry, jr., justice, Sept. —, 1770.
" Martha, and Uriah Stone, Sept. 8, 1771.
" Alethere, and Oliver Smith, Feb. 21, 1779.
" Susannah, and Aaron Loge, April 1, 1779.
" Olive, and Henry Darling, Jan, 23, 1784.
" Abraham, of Obediah, of Adamstown, Mass., and Hepsebeth Callum, of John, of Gloucester; m. at Weathersfield, Conn., by Waters Phillips, justice, Aug. 2, 1786.
" Eliza, and Russell Smith, Aug. 26, 1839.
" Wanton, of Welcome, and Lucinda Brown, of Elisha; m. by Ephraim Sayles, justice, Jan. 3, 1841.
" Nancy R., and Joseph Holt, Feb. 7, 1842.
Herker Rosanna, and Guy Hancock, July 12, 1842.
Hester Fidelia, and Joseph Hoge, Dec. 12, 1741.
Hetock Hannah, and William Chambers, May 24, 1844.
Hewitt Rachel, and Joseph Orville Fairbanks, March 13, 1845.
Hicks Joseph, of Benjamin and Sarah, and Nancy T. Vose, of Seth and Elizabeth; m. by Rev. Joseph Smith, Dec. 3, 1840.
Hide Hannah, and Peregrine Mathewson, April 26, 1733.
" Patience, and Jeremiah Wilkinson, July 3, 1735.
Higgins, Abigail, and Benjamin Ray, March 24, 1816.
Hill Mary, and Jesse Thayer, March 8, 1749–50.
" Ruth, and Zephaniah Shepard, Sept. 20, 1754.
" Amie, and Oziel Herendeen, April 29, 1765.
" Samuel, of Providence, and Rhoda Phillips, of Smithfield; m. by Richard Sayles, justice, Jan. 8, 1767.

Hill George, of Samuel, and Mary Harris, of Jabez; m. by John Man, justice, Nov. 11, 1793.
" Lydia, and Christopher Almy, Oct. 9, 1774.
" Rufus, and Naomi Angel; m. by Benjamin Sheldon, Dec. 8, 1797.
" Barberry, and Benjamin Stone, Nov. 1, 1807.
" Ebenezer Allen, of Barnett, and Ruth Howland Slade, of Howland; m. by Stephen Mowry, justice, Nov. 4, 1819.
" Nancy, and James Carroll, March 3, 1831.
" Olive L., and Job S. Man, Oct. 13, 1831.
" Sarah Ann and Richard T. Bosworth, Sept. 24, 1840.
" Phebe R., and Freeman Clough, July 29, 1849.
" Anna Eliza, and G. Sullivan Woodbury, June 11, 1850.
" Olive L., and William H. Feltus, Jan. 15, 1852.
Hixon Samuel, jr., of Harwich, Conn., and Eliza Frost, of Smithfield; m. by Rev. D. L. McGeer, Dec. 22, 1846.
Hodgeson Samuel, of Thomas, and Mary Lever, of John; m. by Rev. Reuben Allen, Aug. 8, 1841.
Hoge Joseph, and Fidelia Hester; m. by William Arnold, justice, Dec. 12, 1741.
Hogg David, of Cumberland, and Mary Smith, of Smithfield; m. by Thomas Arnold, justice, April 15, 1759.
Holbrook Peter, and Sarah Clarke; m. by William Arnold, justice, Jan. 27, 1736–7.
" Samuel, and Lydia Staples; m. by William Arnold, justice, Sept. 26, 1750.
" Moses K., and M. B. Bradford; m. by Rev. John Borden, jr., Dec. 31, 1840.
" Alice Ann, and Abner Young, Aug. 15, 1843.
Holburton, Susan A., and Henry S. Smith, June 28, 1847.
Holden Joanna B, and Orace C. Aldrich, March 9, 1845.
Holley ———, and Thomas J. Harris, Jan. —, 1840.
" Rufus, and Katy Ann Pain Mowry; m. by Nicholas Shinson, justice, March 5, 1840.

Holley Amanda, and John W. Burkett, Oct. 3, 1843.
Holman Ansel, and Nancy W. Tabor; m. by Rev. T. A. Taylor, Feb. 28, 1848.
" Benjamin F., and Susan C. Ennis; m. by Rev. T. A. Taylor, July 20, 1848.
Holmes Samuel, of Samuel, and Mercy Winsor, of Eld. John; m. by Rev. Ezekiel Angel, Dec. 19, 1779.
" William, and Philena Stearns; m. by Rev. Pliney Brett, Feb. 27, 1816.
" Church, of Smithfield, son of Thomas, of Rochester, Mass., and Emily Maria Jenckes, of Smithfield, dau. of John 3d; m. by Simon A. Sayles, justice, Jan. 25, 1848.
Holoway Albert, son of Ichabod, and Sarah Streight, of Henry; m. by George F. Jenckes, justice, July 14, 1839.
Holt George W., and Lucy Dodge; m. by Rev. Timothy A. Taylor, Sept. 3, 1839.
" Lucy Ann, and Albert Mowry, Sept. 29, 1841.
" Joseph, and Nancy R. Herendeen; m. by Nicholas Shinson, justice, Feb. 7, 1842.
Hopkins, George E., of Foster, R. I., son of Simeon, and Eliza Cook, of William, of Gloucester; m. by Rev. Reuben Allen, Oct. 11, 1840.
" Minerva, and Benjamin Brown, Dec. 31, 1840.
" Lucy, and Joseph Phillips 2d, June 25, 1848.
Horswich James R., and Jane Critchley; m. by Rev. Edwin C. Brown, June 27, 1849.
Horton Simon, and Mrs. Abigail Hathaway, of Dr. Peleg; m. by Samuel Man, justice, June 30, 1811.
" Lydia A., and John Shaw, Nov. 27, 1845.
" Darius, of Benjamin, and Mary Crowell, of Nathan; m. by Rev. Charles Hyde, Dec. 16, 1845.
" Nathan S., and Abbie M. Martin; m. by Rev. D. L. McGeer, March 20, 1849.
Hotchkiss Edward, and Joanna Aldrich; m. by Henry S. Mansfield, justice, March 4, 1827.

Hough Louisa, and Nathaniel L. Parsons, June 13, 1843.
Howard Hannah, and John Arnold, Oct. 3, 1742.
" Sarah, and Ebenezer Cass, Feb. 14, 1747.
" William, and Nancy Johnston, of Solomon; m. by Henry S. Mansfield, justice, Feb. 20, 1825.
" James T., of Joseph, and Sally Arnold, of Whipple; m. by Thomas Man, justice, Jan. 3, 1830.
" Sarah, and Daniel Buxton, July 1, 1847.
" Sarah, and Henry M. Wheelock, March 25, 1847.
Howland Uranah, and William Smith, June 19, 1822.
Hows Anne, and Obediah Herendeen, June 12, 1750.
Hoyle Elizabeth S., and Perry D. Bailey, Nov. 14, 1839.
" Mary B., and George W. Pain, Nov. 14, 1839.
Hudson Mary, and Nathaniel Staples, June 23, 1734.
Hughes William, of William, and Margaret Read, of Andrew; m. by Simon A. Sayles, justice, Aug. 23, 1841.
Humes Alpheus, jr., of Mendon, son of Alpheus and Lucretia Cole, of Jonathan D., of Smithfield; m. by John Pain, justice, April 25, 1841.
" Abbie C., and George Cornell, Nov. 5, 1843.
Hunt John, and Keziah Darling; m. by Daniel Comstock, justice, June 6, 1738.
" Abigail, and Levi Aldrich, Feb. 27, 1745-6.
" Martha, and Ariel Man, June 25, 1815.
" Ann, of Darling, dec., and Joanna Sayles, of Richard; m. by Rev. Junia S. Mowry, Dec. —, 1849.
" A. C., of Smithfield, son of Abner and Minerva, of N. Y., and Mary Jane Booker, of Gardiner, Me., dau. of Nicholas and Sally; m. by Rev. I. J. Burguess, Feb. 3, 1850.
Hutchinson John, and Ruth Shippee; m. by Thomas Lapham, justice, April 23, 1760.
" Daniel, and Mercy Wilkinson; m. by Abram Mathewson, justice, Oct. 9, 1785.
" Orin, of Smithfield, and Polly Aldrich, of George; m. by George F. Jenckes, Oct. 11, 1840.

Hyndeman Edward, of Samuel, and Sarah McDanwell, of John; m. by Rev. Charles Hyde, May 18, 1847.

BIRTHS AND DEATHS.

Hall Jonathan, of Joshua and Susannah,				June 27, 1752.
" Hannah,	"		"	Sept. 12, 1763.
Harkness Nathan, of Adam and Mary,				Sept. 4, 1745.
"	Mary,	"	"	July 18, 1747.
"	Rachel,	"	"	Jan. 22, 1748.
"	Adam,	"	"	Dec. 16, 1750.
"	James,	"	"	Nov. 16, 1752.
"	Ruth,	"	"	Sept. 15, 1754.
"	Robert,	"	"	Nov. 4, 1756.
"	Anne,	"	"	Sept. 29, 1759.
"	Samuel,	"	"	Aug. 30, 1861.
Harris Mary, of Richard, jr., and Lydia,				March 5, 1725.
"	Jeremiah,	"	"	July 7, 1726.
"	Lydia,	"	"	Feb. 6, 1728.
"	Uriah,	"	"	Nov. 23, 1729.
"	Richard,	"	"	Aug. 21, 1732.
"	Amie,	"	"	Nov. 9, 1733.
"	David,	"	"	April 1, 1735.
"	Anthony,	"	"	June 5, 1736.
"	Amity,	"	"	June 5, 1736.
"	Tabitha,	"	Dorothy,	Oct. 2, 1738.
"	Uraniah, of Preserved and Martha,			April 2, 1745.
"	Izreal,	"	"	March 14, 1747.
"	Rufus,	"	"	Nov. 23, 1749.
"	Lydia,	"	"	May 8, 1752.
"	Elnathan,	"	"	Aug. 21, 1755.
"	Nathan,	"	"	March 23, 1758.
"	Jesse,	"	"	Aug. 6, 1760.
"	Martin,	"	"	Feb. 24, 1764.
"	Nathaniel,	"	"	Jan. 9, 1774.
"	Stephen, of Jabez and Mercy,			Oct. 24, 1758.
"	Mary,	"	"	Dec. 11, 1760.

Harris	Mary,	of Jabez and Mercy,		d. Nov. 10, 1778.
"	Benjamin,	"	"	Feb. 4, 1763.
"	Anna,	"	"	Sept. 14, 1764.
"	Mercy,	"	"	Dec. 8, 1767.
"	Jabez,	"	"	Oct. 17, 1771.
"	"	"	"	d. Nov. 17, 1778.
"	Joseph,	"	"	March 6, 1776.
"	William, b. Sept. 11, 1767.			
"	Barberry, (Allen) his wife, b. Jan. 18, 1767.			
"	Allen, of William and Barberry,			May 16, 1790.
"	Otis,	"	"	March 9, 1792.
"	Maria,	"	"	April 3, 1793.
"	Daniel,	"	"	July 3, 1795.
"	Avis,	"	"	May 25, 1797.
"	Wm. Brown,	"	"	June 15, 1799.
"	Welcome, of David and Abigail,			April 24, 1772.
"	Zerua Sayles, (of John and Abi.) his wife, April 26, 1778.			
"	Abigail, of Welcome and Zerua,			March 25, 1797.
"	"	"	"	d. April 20, 1809.
"	John,	"	"	Jan. 2, 1799.
"	David,	"	"	Feb. 2, 1801.
"	George,	"	"	March 1, 1803.
"	Rufus,	"	"	Oct. 14, 1805.
"	"	"	"	d. April 22, 1809.
"	Edwin,	"	"	June 2, 1808.
"	Ann Eliza,	"	"	Dec. 26, 1811.
"	Rachel,	"	"	Oct. 26, 1815.
"	Pearl,	of Rufus and Lucy,		May 8, 1774.
"	Martha,	"	"	Jan. 5, 1776.
"	Peter,	"	"	April 23, 1778.
"	Levi,	"	"	July 6, 1781.
"	Martin,	"	"	June 15, 1782.
"	Arthur,	"	"	Sept. 11, 1785.
"	Seth,	"	"	Feb. 11, 1788.
"	Betsey,	"	"	April 28, 1790.

Harris	Lucy,	of Rufus and Lucy,	May 1, 1792.
"	Polly,	" "	March 8, 1794.
"	Farnum, b. Aug. 4, 1778.		
"	Olive, his wife, b. Aug. 13, 1783.		
"	Achsah, dau. of Anne Mowry,		June, 22, 1781.
"	Keziah,	of Nicholas and Lucy,	May 12, 1794.
"	Thomas,	" "	Aug. 2, 1801.
"	Celaty,	" "	March 3, 1803.
"	Wescott,	" "	March 18, 1806.
"	Polly,	" "	July 1, 1808.
"	Lyman,	" "	Oct. 16, 1810.
"	Celia Ann,	" "	Aug. 7, 1812.
"	Laura Ann,	" "	Feb. 27, 1814.
"	Dinivius, (dau.)	" "	May 4, 1816.
"	Edward G., of David F. and Lydia,		Oct. 3, 1801.
"	Lucy,	of Farnum and Olive,	Nov. 20, 1810.
"	Abigail,	" "	July 5, 1812.
"	Susan Ann,	" "	April 22, 1817.
"	Dianna,	" "	April 22, 1817.
"	Elisha M.,	" "	June 11, 1821.
"	Wanton M.	" "	Sept. 8, 1823.

" Henry Sprout, b. July 17, 1829, son of Samuel B. and Adeline (Sprout).

" Sarah Ann, of Mason and Abbie S., Jan. 9, 1834.

" Benj. Wilkinson, " " Sept. 30, 1835.

" Alfred Bayles, of Samuel B. and Adeline (Sprout), May 8, 1838.

" Adeline (Sprout), wife of Samuel B. and dau. of Henry and Mercy (——) Sprout, of Taunton, Mass., d. March 20, 1843, aged 40 y., 0 m., 15 days.

" Orrin Jencks, ill. ch. of Maria Aldrich and Orrin Harris, b.——

" Welcome, died July 21, 1854.

Hendrick	Anne,	of Joseph and Ruth,	Feb. 8, 1794
"	William,	" "	Jan. 16, 1796.
"	Olive Thurber, of Wing and Fannie,		Aug. 4, 1824.

Hendrick Timothy Walker, of Wing and Fannie, Oct. 31, 1825.
" Ann Elizabeth, " " March 5, 1828.
" Julia Miranda, " " April 10, 1834.
" Benjamin Wing, " " Nov. 17, 1832.
" Ann Eliza, " " Aug. 9, 1835.
Henry Isaac H. P., ill. child of Nabby R. Paine and Joseph Henry, b. Aug. 15, 1825.
Herendeen Elizabeth, of Moses and Elizabeth, Sept. 12, 1732.
" Jane, of Aaron and Abigail, Dec. 30, 1734, or March 3, 1734.
" Elizabeth, of Aaron and Abigail, Jan. 17, 1838.
" William, " " Oct. 16, 1738.
" Aaron, " " June 10, 1752.
" Hannah, " " Nov. 20, 1754.
" Benjamin, of Benjamin and Hannah, May 6, 1735.
" Zachariah, " " Dec. 28, 1736.
" John, " " March 29, 1738.
" Abraham, " " Nov. 7, 1739.
" Izreal, of Joseph, jr., and Mary, March 7, 1740.
" Hart, of Hezekiah and Freelove, May 14, 1753.
" Mary, " " June 23, 1757.
" Freelove, " " Nov. 8, 1759.
" Susanna, " " Sept. 12, 1762.
" Olive, " " Feb. 6, 1765.
" Hezekiah, " " Feb. 6, 1768.
" Heber, " " May 11, 1770.
" Mercy, " " Aug. 19, 1773.
" Elijah, of Joseph and Abigail, May 30, 1763.
" Pennsylvania, of Nathan and Huldah, Jan. 13, 1765.
" Mercy, of Nathan and Huldah, Nov. 7, 1766.
" Welcome, " " April 18, 1768.
" Anne Savilla, of Abraham and Hepzabeth, born Springfield, Vt., Dec. 19, 1786.
" Obediah, son of Abraham and Hepzabeth, Oct. 25, 1789.

Herendeen Stephen, son of Abraham and Hepzabeth, Aug. 9, 1792.
Hill Samuel, of Samuel and Rhoda, Feb. 17, 1767.
Holbrook Benjamin, of Micah and Mary, Aug. 8, 1786
Holmes Salome, of Samuel and Mercy, May 5, 1780.
" Stephen, " " Aug. 8, 1781.
" John, " " Sept. 12, 1783.
" Cynthia, " " June 6, 1787.
" Harvey, of William and Philena, May 15, 1817.
" Lydia, " " Oct. 29, 1822.
" Mary, " " March 27, 1824.
" William, " " July 5, 1827.
Hotchkiss, Thomas Edward, of Edward and Joanna, Sept. 13, 1831.
" James Irwin, of Edward and Joanna, Feb. 20, 1842.
Howard Thomas Grundy, of William and Mary, Feb. 7, 1812.
" George Frederic, " " Aug. 27, 1814.
" Joseph, " " Oct. 5, 1827.
" Samuel, of William and Nancy, Aug. 26, 1825.
" Ellery, " " June 18, 1829.
Hutchinson William, of Daniel and Mercy, born No. Providence, July 18, 1785.

To be continued.

THE ANTIQUARY'S PUDDING.—From a manuscript book of household medicine compiled by Mr. John Rhodes, of Newport, shopkeeper, about 1720 :

To Make a Rice Pudding.—Take thin Creame or good Milk, of what Quantity you Please, boile it with a Littel cinamon in it and when it has boyled a while take out ye cinamon and put in Rose water and Sugar Enough to make it sweet and good ; then haveing ye Rice redy beaten as fine as flower and Sarched as some do it ; Strew it in till it be of ye thickness of hasty-Pudding then Pouer it into a Dish and Sarve it.

ANCIENT NORTH END LANDMARKS OF THE TOWN OF PROVIDENCE.

BY AN OLD RESIDENT.

No. I.
THE BRICK HOUSE AS BUILT BY DEPUTY GOVERNOR ELISHA BROWN ABOUT THE YEAR 1760.

LAPSE of time tends to produce erroneous impressions relative to the construction and uses of old buildings prominent to an observer on account of peculiar architectural or other features indicating age; and tradition, built upon conjecture or idle gossip, assumes the rôle of authentic history, furnishing a theme for comment to those who care more for sensational effect than for an honest and truthful exhibit when dealing with subjects pertaining to the antique. Thus any structure of a century's existence, if a knowledge of its origin and its uses are observed by many changes of ownership, and particularly if dilapidation rests upon it by lack of the fostering care of watchful and thrifty proprietors, is doomed to become the reputed theater of traditionary events that have not a particle of foundation in fact. The old brick house in question has not escaped this destiny, but has had the reputation of a diversified experience, which may readily be recalled by those who are familiar with the current newspaper literature of the times. So far as can be authoritatively determined, its history for the past fifty years, which is well understood, is but a continuation in its uses as existed from the beginning, except for a short period, at first, when the two basement rooms at the north and south ends, as originally constructed, were devoted to mercantile purposes.

This original construction has of late been a study for many who have been interested in ascertaining its extent on the street line. It is known that a part of the building on its north end was taken down many years ago on account of an insecure foundation which threatened a collapse, and the little cottage now standing there, built upon or removed to its site, leaving the present brick structure, with its arrangement of doors and windows as shown on its front, as a basis of calculation or conjecture of its original length, in the absence of positive knowledge as to the fact.

Working from this data it has been generally conceded that the center of the three north windows was the center of the street line. This seemed a reasonable conclusion and was acquiesced in by those who sought to solve the problem. But recent investigation has resulted in a definite knowledge of its extent, and shows that the portion yet standing is a counterpart of the portion taken down, thus giving its entire length as about seventy-two feet. This is shown by real estate records ranging in point of time from 1790 to 1794, noting reference to three forty-feet lots laid out on the Elisha Brown estate, " commencing three feet north of the brick house " and extending north on the street line. The first of these lots is the one on which stands the stone house built by Benjamin Lewis about the year 1822. The north line of the Lewis lot can be easily determined, and that seems to be the initial point in fixing the northern boundary of the brick house, namely, thence forty-three feet south. This comes to a point about the same distance north of the house yet standing as the length thereof, and evidences the fact that the original in its full proportions was a double house, the remaining portion fairly representing the northern part, and the whole combined giving a building as represented by the cut at the head of this article. The perpendicular line shown in the cut represents the line of separation between the part yet standing and the part demolished.

The lack of confidence then felt in the stability of a building built of brick is shown by the means taken to strengthen it by letting the floor joists extend through the walls, as is shown by a photograph of the front, taken before the reconstruction of the basement a few years since, when this feature was covered by a wooden projection; and by a timber tie built into the wall about half way up between the floor above the basement and the windows above, which is now clearly outlined though covered by a coating of cement.

It was built by Deputy Governor Elisha Brown about the year 1760. An advertisement in the Providence *Gazette* of April 23, 1763, offering it for sale, represents it as being "a new brick dwelling house, conveniently built, and well situated towards the upper end of the town street of Providence." A purchaser was not found until August 21, 1770, when Mr. Brown sold it to Paul Bunker, of Nantucket, Mass., subject to a mortgage held by Thomas Owen. Bunker held it until April 12th, 1786, when he sold it to Thomas Jenkins, also of Nantucket. As Jenkins became a resident of Providence about that time, it is fair to presume that he occupied the house as a home, at first, although subsequently he resided at the south end of the town, where he acquired by purchase other real estate. Under Jenkins the estate became divided, and November 12th, 1782, the southern half part was bought by Samuel Hamlin, pewterer, of Providence. Mr. Hamlin was father of Samuel E. Hamlin, who succeeded him as pewterer and brittania ware maker, pursuing the vocation many years in a building that stood where the south end of the Lonsdale Block is located opposite the Friends Meeting House, on North Main street; also the father of William Hamlin, mathematical instrument maker on South Water street, who died in 1869, aged 97 years. The next owner was Esek Aldrich, innkeeper, and if he set up a tavern there and Lafayette, as tradition has it, was a guest there, Aldrich was probably the General's host. Aldrich was afterwards proprietor of the Aldrich tavern, on Weybosset street, later known as the Washington Hotel.

The next purchaser of the south end was Capt. James Westcott, mariner, who bought it of Aldrich, January 3d, 1787. And here it loses its shifting proprietorship and settles down to a quiet homelike habitation where families are reared and attachments to the homestead inaugurated, which seem to have descended to a present generation that loves to look over the ancestral home in its time-worn aspect, and cherish as keepsakes photographic representations of it now so easily attainable. After more than twenty-two years as owner and occupant, Capt. Westcott sold it September 15th, 1809, to Benjamin Taylor, and after the lapse of nearly seventy-six years it can hardly be said to have passed from the control of his descendants, being now owned by Lewis F. Hubbard, whose wife was a granddaughter of Benjamin Taylor.

To go back to the time of Thomas Jenkins's disposition of the north division of the estate, September 22, 1784, he sold it to Deborah Jenkins, who was a widow of his brother Benjamin, and joined with his family on their removal from Nantucket to Providence. Thomas was then living at the south end of the town, and Deborah's home was probably on her purchase at the north end. Her family consisted of a son, Alexander, a daughter Eunice, and perhaps others. June 4th, 1791, being then a resident of Hudson, N. Y., she sold the property to James Graves, whose wife Hope owned the forty foot lot north, heretofore mentioned as the Lewis lot, and back land on the east to the extent of about 1½ acres. It may be well in this connection to note that on the unfortunate breaking up of Deputy Governor Brown's estate through insolvency, Richard Borden, of Freetown, Mass., became the owner of the Brown homestead with adjoining lands, also of lands in other localities in Providence. These estates he parted with by gift deeds to his three daughters, namely, Patience Butler, wife of Abner Butler, mariner, of Martha's Vineyard; Elizabeth Valentine, wife of William Valentine of Freetown and Hope Graves, wife of James Graves. This disposition brought these three families into Providence as residents. The "Butler house," a name yet retained for the old homestead, derives its name from the daughter Patience who received as her portion the west end of it which was held as a home for the family of her son Thomas until about the year 1835. These circumstances tend to the belief that James Graves lived in the north end of the brick house as long as its condition warranted a safe habitation. At the time of the sale of the south end by Capt. Westcott to Benjamin Taylor in 1809 it was evidently standing, as his northern boundary was then stated as at the partition dividing the two parts, but at the time of Graves's sale of the whole estate, comprised of his purchase of Deborah Jenkins and his wife Hope's property, to Earl D. Pearce, April 5, 1817, its destruction must have been complete, as no mention is made of it in the deed of conveyance.

The period of twenty years which terminates in 1765 was an era that promised well for the growth and prosperity of the North End. Particularly in the neighborhood now under consideration was this evidenced by the erection of several large buildings, mostly of the type of architecture pertaining to the one prompting the writing of this paper. There was what is called the Arnold Whipple house, at the junction of North Main and Hewes streets, built by Dr. Joseph

Hewes; the large gambrel roof house at the foot of Olney street, built by Capt. Joseph Olney, father of Col. Jeremiah Olney; the one of similar size and construction built by another Joseph Olney, father of Capt. Stephen Olney, on the east side of the street, which was demolished for the purpose of affording an entrance of Lippit street to North Main street; the large double house, or two houses combined, directly opposite the old brick building, familiarly called "Noah's Ark," the northern part of which was built by John Foster, blacksmith, in 1755, and recently taken down by Mr. Pitman, to enable him to place upon its site the more modern structure recently erected, and the southern part built about the same time by William Wolcott, jr., shop-keeper, and yet standing, which was bought by Noah Smith, chaise-maker, December 1st, 1785, and only recently passed from the ownership of his descendants, after a possession of nearly one hundred years; and the Elisha Brown homestead, yet standing a little back of the Church of the Redeemer, built by Mr. Brown in 1749. This last, though not of the gambrel roof pattern like the others named, was an imposing structure and is now called the "Butler house," as before noted.

At this period the rivalry between the North End and the central region was at its height. The first, striving to maintain its ascendancy in point of mercantile importance and political influence that had hitherto been its lot, and the central and southern region, to wrest from its neighbor the prestige of these important auxiliaries to advancement in prosperity. The advantages of the latter, through proximity to marine facilities, tended to strengthen its chances, and gradually the tables were turned, and what had been from the inception of the settlement of the town noted as the "court end" and leading section, lapsed into a lethargic condition, and much of its territory became the possessions of those whose homes and leading interests were in another section.

A LIST OF THE BIRTHS OF SOUTH KINGSTOWN.

From Records in Town Clerk's Office.

CONTRIBUTED BY THE EDITOR.

(*Continued from page 177.*)

S.

Sands	Wm. Case, of Robert G. and Anne,		June 27, 1785.
"	Anne Maynard, " "		April 15, 1787.
Seager	Abigail,	of John and Abigail,	March 7, 1787.
"	John, " "		Nov. 15, 1788.
"	Elizabeth, " "		April 3, 1790.
"	Sarah, " "		Jan. 18, 1792.
"	Francis Brayton, " "		Feb. 24, 1794.
"	Joseph Taylor, " "		April 11, 1796.
"	David Anthony, " "		March 12, 1798.
"	Alice, " "		June 17, 1802.
"	Hannah, " "		Dec. 27, 1805.
Sheffield	George,	of Joseph and Mary,	July 12, 1718.
"	Martha Tefft, " "		Sept. 29, 1719.
"	Ezekiel, of Edmund and Sarah,		Jan. 31, 1720–1.
"	Elizabeth, " "		March 16, 1722–3.
"	Jeremiah, of Deborah,		May 8, 1729.
"	William, of Nathan and Dorcas,		Jan. 23, 1730.
"	Christopher, " "		Nov. 18, 1732.
"	Elizabeth, " "		Aug. 8, 1734.
"	Susannah, " "		Feb. 29, 1736.
"	Nathan, " "		Oct. 23, 1737.
"	Dorcas, of William and Lois,		May 12, 1753.
"	Sarah, " "		May 7, 1755.
"	Edmund, of Joseph and Mary,		June 21, 1749.
"	Prudence, " "		June 12, 1751.
"	Joseph, " "		Jan. 19, 1754.
"	John, " "		Jan. 24, 1757.

Sheldon	John,	of John and Horred,	Feb. 10, 1706–7.
"	Dorcas,	" "	Jan. 4, 1707–8.
"	George,	" "	May 25, 1709.
"	Samuel,	" "	Jan. 15, 1713–14.
"	William,	" "	March 27, 1714.
"	Elizabeth,	" "	March 31, 1720.
"	Sarah,	" "	Feb. 26, 1721–2.
"	Thomas,	of Isaac and Susannah,	Feb. 18, 1708–9.
"	Roger,	" "	Dec. 15, 1710.
"	Elizabeth,	" "	Nov. 8, 1713.
"	Isaac,	" "	March 4, 1715–16.
"	John,	" "	Aug. 21, 1718.
"	Susannah,	" "	Oct. 23, 1720.
"	Joseph,	" "	March 17, 1721–2.
"	Palmer,	" "	May 16, 1724.
"	Benjamin,	" "	March 4, 1727.
"	Sarah, of Isaac and Sarah,		Jan. 3, 1735.
"	Herodias, of John and Sarah,		May 21, 1729.
"	John,	" "	May 21, 1729.
"	Dorcas,	" "	Feb. 12, 1732.
"	Abigail,	" "	March 3, 1734.
"	Sarah,	" "	May 22, 1736.
"	George,	" "	Dec. 17, 1738.
"	James, of Isaac and Sarah,		April 11, 1743.
"	Samuel, of Isaac and Abigail,		June 30, 1747.
"	Lydia,	" "	Aug. 23, 1749.
"	Sarah,	" "	Aug. 17, 1751.
"	Isaac,	" "	July 22, 1755.
"	Benjamin,	" "	July 28, 1758.
"	Palmer, of John and Elizabeth,		Jan. 28, 1745.
"	Mehitable,	" "	July 20, 1746.
"	John,	" "	April 29, 1748.
"	Isaac,	" "	May 11, 1750.
"	Nathan,	" "	March 29, 1752.
"	Jonathan,	" "	May 4, 1755.
"	George,	" "	Oct. 11, 1757.

Sheldon	Joanna, of John and Elizobeth,		April 10, 1760.
"	Augustus, of James and Hannah,		Feb. 23, 1763.
"	Henry, " "		March 30, 1765.
"	Sarah, " "		May 7, 1767.
"	Hannah, " "		July 17, 1770.
"	Dorcas, " "		Sept. 17, 1773.
"	William J., " "		July 15, 1776.
"	Waite, of James and Elizabeth (2d wife), Oct. 13, 1782.		
"	Elizabeth, " "		Sept. 20, 1784.
"	William, of Jonathan and Dorcas,		March 27, 1785.
"	Susannah, " "		Aug. 24, 1786.
"	Hannah, " "		Aug. 12, 1788.
"	Samuel, " "		May 2, 1790.
"	Elizabeth, " "		April 29, 1792.
Sherman	Daniel, of Daniel and Susannah,		Aug. 28, 1735.
"	Mary, of Josiah and Mary,		Aug. 1, 1727.
"	Abigail, of Jonathan and Mary,		Oct. 25, 1737.
"	Jonathan, " "		Oct. 14, 1731.
"	Gideon, " "		Oct. 25, 1741.
"	Mary, " "		Nov. 5, 1745.
"	Robert, " "		Sept. 14, 1752.
"	Amie, of Abiel and Susannah,		June 1, 1746.
"	Nathaniel, of Henry and Ann,		Aug. 15, 1748.
"	John, " "		Oct. 24, 1750.
"	Mary, " "		March 11, 1753.
"	Charles, " "		Feb. 1, 1756.
"	Henry, " "		March 31, 1759.
"	Martha, " "		March 9, 1762.
"	Sarah, " "		March 29, 1765.
"	Josias, of Benjamin and Mary,		Sept. 21, 1745.
"	Waite, of Jonathan, Jr., and Sarah,		Jan. 11, 1755.
"	Elizabeth, " "		Aug. 12, 1757.
"	Gideon, " "		Feb. 22, 1763.
"	Jonathan, of Robert and Honor,		July 20, 1779.
"	Catherine Greene, of John R. and Margaret, March 5, 1801.		

Sherman David, son of David, April 18, 1786.
" Hannah, wife of David, Feb. 3, 1785.
" David, of David and Hannah, Sept. 2, 1805.
" Lydia B., " " April 24, 1808.
" Ruth B., " " Jan. 7, 1811.
" George Washington, of David and Hannah, Jan. 9, 1815.
" Susannah E., " " Aug. 16, 1817.
" Nehemiah K., " " May 14, 1820.
" Arnold S., " " April 28, 1823.
" Horace Dunn, " " Sept. 5, 1826.
" Abner O., of David and Salome (2d wife,) Jan. 3, 1839.
" Jane E., " " Dec. 28, 1841.
" Clarissa A., " " Feb. 12, 1843.
" Joseph, " " March 5, 1846.
" Mary C., " " March 5, 1846.
Smith John, of John and Mary, July 26, 1712.
" Mary, " " July 17, 1715.
" Mary, 2d, " " Aug. 5, 1717.
" William, " " Oct. 9, 1719.
" Phillis, " " Sept. 29, 1723.
" Arnold, of Ephraim and Mercy, June 30, 1739.
" Stafford, " " March 11, 1740.
" Elizabeth, of Abigail, of Ephraim and Mercy, Dec. 19, 1743.
" James Alexander Seabury, son of Wm. and Magdalen, baptized by Bishop Seabury, born May 29, 1788.
Stanton Latham, of David and Martha, Jan. 13, 1744-5.
" Benjamin, of Benjamin and Sarah, June 21, 1800.
" Daniel, " " April 3, 1802.
" Abigail, " " April 24, 1804.
" Wm. Knowles, " " Nov. 6, 1806.
" Ann Hoxsie, " " Jan. 8, 1809.
" Sarah Sheffield, " " July 9, 1811.
" Hannan Sherman, " " July 10, 1811.

Stanton James Sherman, of Benjamin & Sarah, Jan. 20, 1814.
" Mary, " " Oct. 6, 1816.
" John Sherman, " " March 23, 1820.
Steadman Daniel, of Thomas and Hannah, Oct. 10, 1728.
" Thomas, " " Oct. 10, 1730.
" Enoch, " " Nov. 5, 1734.
" Hannah, " " Feb. 6, 1736.
" James, " " March 3, 1738.
" Sarah, " " Aug. 30, 1742.
" William, " " May 4, 1745.
Sunderland George, of Wm. and Penelope, Dec. 29, 1754.
" Augustus, " " Dec. 19, 1758.
Swain Elizabeth, of John and Hannah, Sept. 28, 1731.

T.

Tanner Nathan, of William and Elizabeth, Feb. 20, 1709.
Taylor Mary, of Joseph and Experience, Nov. 1, 1749.
" Ann, of William and Ann, April 26, 1741.
" Sarah, " " June 2, 1744.
Tefft Samuel, of Samuel and Abigail, Jan. 19, 1711–12.
" Daniel, " " June 14, 1714.
" Stephen, " " Oct. 5, 1718.
" Tennant, " " Sept. 29, 1720.
" Ebenezer, " " Feb. 14, 1723–4.
" James, of John and Joanna, April 21, 1715.
" Abigail, of Samuel and Mary, Dec. 24, 1731.
" Mary, " " Jan. 28, 1732.
" Mercy, " " April 24, 1735.
" Hannah, of Tennant and Tabitha, June 28, 1741.
" Caleb, " " Oct. 11, 1743.
" Sophia, of Samuel, Jr., and Mary. ———
" Samuel, " " June 20, 1742.
" Oliver, " " March 22, 1743.
" Alexander, " " July 30, 1746.
" Stanton, of Nathan and Isabel, July 9, 1744.
" Isabel, " " March 14, 1745.

Tefft Mercy, of Nathan and Isabel,	Dec. 14, 1749.
" Nathan, " "	Aug. 28, 1752.
" John, " "	March 24, 1756.
" Mary, " "	May 2, 1758.
" Sarah, " "	Aug. 14, 1762.
Torrey Elizabeth, of Joseph and Elizabeth,	July 19, 1731.
" Joseph, " "	Feb. 4, 1732–3.
" Oliver, " "	Feb. 14, 1734–5.
" Ann, " "	May 13, 1737.
Totten John Levi, of Levi and Martha,	July 30, 1790.
" Eliza, " "	March 26, 1791.
" Henry Morris, " "	March 9, 1794.

U.

Underwood John, of Joseph and Ruth,	Dec. 24, 1732.
" Joseph, " "	April 12, 1734.
" Anne, of William and Susannah,	June 26, 1743.
" Joseph, " "	Oct. 21, 1744.
" Henry, " "	Jan. 25, 1752.
" Alice, " "	Aug. 24, 1753.
" Samuel, " "	Jan. 29, 1756.
" Anne E., of Perry G. and Mary E.,	Sept. 20, 1855.

W.

Waite Dorcas, of Matthew and Mercy,	Sept. 25, 1816.
" Benjamin Case, " "	April 10, 1819.
" John, " "	April 10, 1821.
" Samuel, " "	June 16, 1823.
" William, " "	Sept. 12, 1826.
Walmesley Thomas, of Thomas and ———	Jan. 2, 1706.
" Mary, " "	Nov. 16, 1708.
" Patience, " "	Jan. 5, 1710.
" James, " "	July 17, 1713.
" Sarah, " "	Nov. 6, 1715.
" Joseph, " "	Dec. 27, 1717.
" Samuel, " "	Dec. 29, 1720.
" Benjamin, " "	Dec. 27, 1723.

Watson	Hannah,	of Jeffrey and Bathsheba,	June 2, 1733.
"	Jeffrey,	" "	Oct. 16, 1734.
"	Elisha,	" "	July 10, 1736.
"	Mercy,	" "	July 10, 1740.
"	Dorcas,	" "	June 5, 1741.
"	Sarah,	" "	Jan. 11, 1743.
"	William,	" "	April 25, 1745.
"	Bathsheba,	" "	Sept. 16, 1748.
"	John,	of John and Isabel,	May 23, 1737.
"	Hannah,	" "	Sept. 28, 1738.
"	Bridget,	" "	Dec. 24, 1741.
"	Job,	" "	Aug. 7, 1744.
"	Mary,	" "	Sept. 3, 1746.
"	Elisha,	" "	Aug. 5, 1748.
"	Isabel,	" "	May 7, 1753.
"	Walter,	" "	May 7, 1753.
"	Robert,	of Benjamin and Sarah,	March 27, 1750.
"	Avis,	" "	July 10, 1752.
"	Isabel,	of Job and Sarah,	Sept. 22, 1766.
"	Job,	" "	Oct. 25, 1767.
"	Robert Hazard,	" "	Feb. 28, 1769.
"	Walter,	" "	June 10, 1770.
"	Borden,	" "	Feb. 9, 1772.
"	John,	" "	Nov. 1, 1774.
"	George,	of John and Desire,	Dec. 16, 1783.
"	Mary,	of Elisha, Jr., and Miriam,	April 6, 1775.
"	Elisha,	" "	Oct. 1, 1776.
"	Joseph Dennison, of Elisha, Jr., and Miriam, Aug. 30, 1778.		
"	Asa,	" "	" May 24, 1780.
"	George,	" "	" Mar. 24, 1782.
"	William,	" "	" Dec. 26, 1783.
"	Freeman, of Elisha, Jr., and Susannah, May 16, 1787.		
"	Susannah,	" "	March 13, 1789.
"	Elizabeth,	" "	June 24, 1790.
"	Miriam,	" "	Oct. 30, 1793.

Webb, Margaret, of John and Joanna,	Aug. 21, 1721.
" Elizabeth, " "	March 27, 1724.
Weeden, Mercy, of Caleb and Lydia,	Sept. 24, 1750.
" John, of Daniel and Martha,	April 16, 1754.
" Judah (a dau.), " "	Jan. 18, 1756.
Weir, James, of Daniel and Phebe,	Nov. 9, 1749.
Welch, Henry, of William and Catherine,	Oct. 1, 1735.
Wells, James, of Peter, Jr., and Ann,	Sept. 30, 1706.
" Ann, " "	Oct. 20, 1708.
" Rebecca, " "	Dec. 30, 1710.
" Peter, " "	May 4, 1713.
" John, " "	April 14, 1716.
" Samuel, " "	Feb. 2, 1725.
" James, of James (of Westerly) and Mary,	Nov. 1, 1732.
" Barbara, " "	Aug. 1, 1734.
" Peter, " "	Aug. 29, 1737.
" Barker, " "	May 16, 1750.
" Joshua, " "	Aug. 24, 1753.
Wilcox, Mary, of Robert and Sarah,	June 4, 1727–8.
" Robert, " "	Sept. 9, 1729.
" Arnold, " "	June 7, 1731.
Williams, McCoon, of Thomas and Thankful,	Aug. 15, 1735.
" Henry, " "	Feb. 11, 1736.
" Thomas, " "	June 10, 1742.
" Daniel, " "	April 2, 1744.
" Mary, " "	Feb. 2, 1745.
" Martha, " "	April 5, 1747.
Wilson, Mary, of Jeremiah and Mary,	Nov. 13, 1721.
" Samuel, " "	March 23, 1723.
" Jeremiah, " "	May 11, 1726.
" John, " "	May 11, 1726.
" James, " "	Sept. 2, 1728.
" George, " "	Feb. 7, 1730.
" Alice, " "	June 15, 1733.
" Samuel, of Samuel and Hannah,	Jan. 16, 1746.
" Samuel, 2d, " "	Jan. 16, 1747.

Wilson John,	of Samuel and Hannah,			Jan. 25, 1849.
"	John, 2d,	"	"	March 29, 1752.
"	James,	"	"	May 20, 1754.
"	Hannah,	"	"	Oct. 5, 1756.
"	George,	"	"	Dec. 20, 1758.
"	William,	"	"	Oct. 2, 1761.
"	George,	of Jeremiah and Abigail,		Nov. 26, 1754.
"	William,	"	"	Feb. 24, 1756.
"	Mary,	"	"	Dec. 6, 1759.
"	John,	of John and Hannah,		July 24, 1763.
"	Hazard,	"	"	Not given.
"	Arnold,	"	"	Not given.
Worden, Phebe,		of Samuel and Abigail,		June 30, 1724.
"	Benjamin,	"	"	June 7, 1726.
"	Penelope,	"	"	March 24, 1728–9.

(THE END.)

THE STORY OF THE TABLETS.

IV.

CONTRIBUTED BY JAMES L. SHERMAN, ESQ., PROVIDENCE, R. I.

From the North Burial Ground, Providence.

THOMAS HARRIS
TILLINGHAST,
Son of
William and Delana Tillinghast.
Born April 5, 1805.
Died March 14, 1879.
"The memory of the just is blessed."

DELANA,
Wife of
William Tillinghast.
Daughter of

Capt. Thomas Atwood, of Pawtucket.
Born Feb. 6, 1778.
Died April 8, 1808.
Interred in the Tillinghast Family Burial Ground
on Benefit street.

Here are entombed the remains of
Mr.
WILLIAM TILLINGHAST,
son of William Tillinghast
who was born Dec. 1, 1775,
and died March 29,
1851.
He sought no popularity
but in the discharge of his duties he was
Ever faithful,
His home was the sphere of his active
Humility and amiability
Were predominant traits in his character,
The needy never asked in vain,
He calmly yielded his spirit to the Giver.
For He that respected Isael shall neither
Slumber or sleep.

"Yea though I walk through the valley of the shadow of death, I will fear no evil, for thou are with me: thy rod and thy staff they comfort me."

Here are entombed the remains of
Mrs.
PHEBE TILLINGHAST,
consort of
William Tillinghast,
and daughter of
Luke Arnold, Esq. & Phebe his wife,
of Smithfield.
She was born Aug. 4, AD 1782,
and died March 12, 1847.

She was a woman of uncommon energy of character;
Endowed with sound judgment, originality of wit,
and powerful thought.
She gave a beautiful example that the mind may be
brilliant and capable of imence feeling,
and yet the highest exercise of it may be performed
in the family circle.
Self culture lent a charm to her character.
Amenity of manners, a high flow of spirits, and a firm
yet elastic disposition, blended with her other virtues,
She had a high sense of Duty,
and nothing could swerve her from its path.
In every relation of life,
she acquitted herself nobly & honorably,
sealing the purity of it with the
serenity of its close.

" He came with shadowy step, who turns
The breathing from the clay—
He came, and from the whitened lip
Kissed the sweet soul away."

Ever will the buds of affection bloom with unfading lives,
and shed their undying fragrance around thy holy
Memory.

Sacred
To the Memory
of
COL. KNIGHT DEXTER.
He was born in Providence, R. I.
the 10th of July
A. D. 1734
and died 8th February, 1814
in the 80th Year
of his Age.

Also, of his Wife
ANNE DEXTER
Daughter of

Andrew Brown,
of Glocester.
She was born 18th July,
A. D. 1734,
and died 4th February, 1759
in the 25th year
of her age.

Sacred
To the Memory
of
MRS. PHEBE DEXTER,
Wife of
Col. Knight Dexter
and Daughter of
the Hon. Joseph Harris
of Cranston.
She was born 4th November
A. D. 1735
and died 25th June, 1813.
in the 77th Year
of her Age.

Sacred to the Memory
of
EBENEZER KNIGHT DEXTER, ESQ.
Who departed this life
August 10, A. D. 1824,
Aged 51 years.
Having sustained through life
The character of
An Upright Man and Useful Citizen,
He was in death resigned to the will of that
Adorable Being,
Who gives and receives again to Himself
The spirit of Man.
The deceased received many tokens of public confidence,
For many years, and until his death, he sustained the office of

Marshall of the United States for the Rhode Island District,
And by a happy union of vigilance with humanity,
In the discharge of his official duties,
Conciliated the esteem of the Government
And of the publick.
His memory is endeared to his fellow citizens
of this, native place, as well by his many virtues, as by the
Munificent Donation
Of a large portion of his Ample Estate
To the Town of Providence,
To constitute a Permanent Fund
For the comfortable and respectable support
of
The Unfortunate Poor.
This Fund, with other valuable property devised to the Town
Will remain a
Lasting Monument
Of his
Publick Spirit
And
Benevolence.

Sacred to the Memory
of
Mrs. Waitstill Dexter
Wife of
Ebenezer K. Dexter,
and Daughter of the
Hon. David Howell.
She was born 27th June, AD. 1776
and died 15th May, 1819
in the 43d Year
of her Age.

Pure and polished was the mind,
Whose earthly temple slumber here,
Her's were the choicest traits combined
To win respect, to charm endear.

The Christian faith, the Christian hope,
Were also her's—she put her trust
In Him, who by his blood did ope
Redemption's way to sinful dust.
Her's was a spirit, stainless pure,
As ever soared to realms of light;
And duty's sphere, unerring sure,
Proclaimed its course was peerless bright.
Sweet is the memory of the just.
"Yea, saith the spirit, for they rest,"
And oh! how sweet to feel, to trust,
That worth like her's will sure be blest.

Sacred
to the memory of
Mrs.
ABIGAIL ROSSITER,
wife of
Nathaniel Rossiter, Esq.
and daughter of
Col. Knight Dexter.
She departed this life July 23.
A. D. 1826:
Aged 51 years.

In her life were strikingly exemplified
all those virtues
which adorn the female character.
She lived deservedly beloved,
and
died sincerely lamented.

"Blessed are the Pure in Heart;
For they shall see God."

WILLIAM EYRE LYON
Was born in Northampton
Virginia

September 23, 1803.
and died in Providence
May 31, 1826.
He was the son
of Doctor James Lyon
a native of Carlisle,
Pennsylvania,
and of Sarah Eyre
of Northampton County,
Virginia.

Here lie entombed the remains
of
WILLIAM EARLE,
an experienced nautical commander.
Son of
Benjamin & Rebecca Earle,
of Warwick.
Born Feby. 12, 1727.
Died in
Providence,
December 30, 1804,
Aged 77 years, 10 months
& 18 days.

MARY,
Wife of
Capt. WILLIAM EARLE,
& daughter of
George Brown, Esq. and Esther
his wife,
of Providence.
Born Jan. 21, 1734.
Died Aug. 22, 1800,
Aged 66 years, 7 months
& 1 day,

Deed from Wesauamog to the Proprietors of Providence.

Recorded in old Book No. 3, Providence Records, page 451.

CONTRIBUTED BY FRED A. ARNOLD.

PROUIDENCE 24. 4 mon: 1662 (so calld)

This witnesseth y^t I wesauamog Sachim & Inhabitant of mishoaskit doe by these presants for good consideration in hand Receaued with wch I Acknowledge my selfe fully Satisfied I Giue & Surrender vp all my Right interest & Claime in the land aforesaid vnto Tho: Olny Senr John Browne Val: Whitman: & Roger Williams. in the Name & for the vse of ye men of prouidence and their heires & Assignes for Euer and doe promise to keepe a leage of friendship and loue with them & to Endeauer y^t all the Natives of Mashovsakit shall so doe & y^t the English may freely Cutt the meadowes build houses feed Cattell & plant ye ground in peace & safetie the bounds of this land he saith is Southward from the pond of mishovsakit about thre miles to a pond Cald Nanipsick Northward joyning to wayvnkege: Eastward neere Sakesakit & westward about seuen miles.

in witnes of y^e premises I Subscribe
    my marke   y^e m^{rk} of WESAUAMOG

Witnes   OBADIAH: HULLMES

    MARKE LUCAR   y^e m^{rk} of   GEORGE

Calld pigs eyes.

Enrolled y^e 22nd of Janeuary 1667:

p me  Towne Clerke

3 of March 65 / 66 (as Calld

MEMORANDUM y\{t} pepewashim y\{e} Son of Askwhut Deceased did before vs Consent and Subscribe willingly vnto the Contents made by wesauamog on y\{e} other side

ROGER WILLIAMS
JOHN BROWNE

y\{e} m\{ke} of   pepewahim

This deed is the last in the series made to the proprietors of the Town of Providence in their corporate capacity. They may be divided into three classes—the first being the original grant from Canonicus and Miantonomi; then three from their successors, called deeds of confirmation, in which were provisions for satisfying the Indians actually residing on the lands; and, third, four deeds from these resident Indians. Of the Indians, parties to this deed, I find no other record; and this remark applies as well to some of the names in deeds heretofore given.

The larger part of the land covered by this deed was probably in the northern part of the present town of Scituate, extending perhaps a little over the bounds of that town, on the north and east, into the present towns of Glocester, Smithfield and Johnston. The northeastern corner bound was the country called Wayunkege, about Greenville in Smithfield: directly south of which, in Johnston, is Sakesakit, which is generally described in early deeds as between four and five miles west of Providence and about two miles east of Moswansicut Pond. This pond was perhaps one of those spoken of as the eastern line of this land, and from which line it extended westward seven miles.

OBADIAH HULLMES, or HOLMES, as more generally written, was in Salem, 1639, with wife Catherine, where he was admitted to the Church, March 24th.

They came from Preston in Lancashire. He is spoken of in Salem records as a glassman or glassworker..

In 1646 he was excommunicated from Salem Church and removed to Rehoboth, of which place he had already become one of the proprietors, his name appearing as early as 1643 on a list of taxable estates, rated at £100; and in 1644 on a list of those who drew house lots. Here he joined the church of the Rev. Samuel Newman.

In 1649, disliking the tenets and discipline of the Rehoboth Church, he with eight others withdrew themselves and established a new one under Baptist principles, and Mr. Holmes was chosen their pastor. They were re-baptised, it is supposed, by the Rev. John Clarke of Newport.[1] Mr. Newman excommunicated them; and June 30, 1650, the General Court at Plymouth ordered them to desist from meeting, and Mr. Holmes was bound over in the sum of £10 for his appearance at Court. At the next Court the following bill of indictment was presented against them :

"Att a Generall Court holden att New Plym the 2coned of October
Before William Bradford, Gent. Gouer",

Tho Prence,	Timothy Hatherly
William Collyare,	William Thomas and
Captaine Miles Standish	John Alden

Gent Asistants

October the 2coned, 1650. Wee, whose names are heer vnder written, being the grand inquest, doe present to this Court John Hazaell, Mr· Edward Smith and his wife, Obadia Holmes, Joseph Tory and his wife, and the wife of James Man, William Deuell and his wife, of the towne of Rehoboth, for the continewing of a meeting vppon the Lords Day from house to house, contrary to the order of this Court enacted June the 12th, 1650."[2]

1651, July 20. Mr. Holmes and two others were arrested in Lynn for holding a meeting at a private house, carried to Boston, and thrust into jail. After the farce of a trial, Mr. Holmes was fined £30, or to be well whipped. Arriving at the place of execution, he refused to disrobe, saying "that

---

[1] Bliss's Rehoboth, p. 206.
[2] Plymouth Col. Records, II, 151.

for all *Boston* I would not give my bodie into their hands to be bruised upon another account, yet upon this I would not give the hundredth part of a *Wampon Peaque* to free it out of their hands, and that I made as much conscience of unbuttoning one button, as I did of paying the £30 in reference thereunto." [1] Whereupon the thirty lashes were administered in such an unmerciful manner, says Governor Joseph Jenckes, " that in many days, if not some weeks, he could take no rest, but as he lay upon his knees and elbows, not being able to suffer any part of his body to touch the bed whereon he lay." [2] " Those who have seen the scars on Mr. Holmes' back (which the old man was wont to call the marks of the Lord Jesus,) have expressed a wonder that he should live." [3]

1652. He was elected Pastor of the First Baptist Church in Newport in place of the Rev. John Clarke, who had been sent by the Colony to England.

1656. His name appears on ye Roule of Freemen of Newport.

1656–58. He was Commissioner for Newport.

His will is dated April 9, 1682.

He died in Newport, October 15, 1682, aged 76,[4] and was buried in his own field, where a tomb was erected to his memory.

This homestead is situated in what is now Middletown, R. I.

He had a brother Robert, and sisters, to whom he writes, living in the Parish of Manchester, Lancashire; [5] and speaking of his honored parents, he says they brought up three sons at the University of Oxford.[6]

Mr. Holmes is said to have brought the first pendulum clock to America. This timepiece, one of the first of the kind ever

---

[1] Letter of Obadiah Holmes in Ill News from New England, p. 50.
[2] Benedict's History of the Baptists, p. 376, note.
[3] Morgan Edwards, in R. I. His. Col., VI, 367.
[4] Backus, I, 506.
[5] Ibid. 256-261.
[6] Ibid. 208.

constructed, is still doing duty in the cabinet of the Long Island Historical Society, Brooklyn, having been presented to them by John Holmes Baker, Esq., a descendant of the reverend gentleman, whose memory it serves to keep green.[1]

OBADIAH HOLMES, b. about 1607; d. at Newport, Oct. 15, 1682, aged 76; m. Catherine ———, who survived him. Children :

1. MARY, b. ———; d. after 1690; m. John, s. of Rev. Chad and Elizabeth Brown, of Providence—b. 1630; d. about 1706. Children :
    1, Sarah; 2, John; 3, James; 4, Obadiah; 5, Martha; 6, Mary; 7, Deborah.
2. MARTHA, bapt. at Salem, May 30, 1640; d. after 1682.
3. SAMUEL, bapt. at Salem, March 20, 1642; d. 1679: m. Oct. 26, 1665, Alice, d. of Nicholas and Ann (Van Dyke) Stillwell, of New York. Children :
    1, Samuel; 2, Ann; 3, Joseph; 4, Catherine; 5, Henry; 6, Mary.
4. OBADIAH, bapt. at Salem, June 9, 1644; m. ——— Cole, and removed to New Jersey. Children :
    1, Obadiah; 2, Samuel; 3, Jonathan; 4, a daughter; 5, a daughter; and perhaps 6, John. (See below.)
5. LYDIA, b. ———; m. John, s. of William and Ann Bowne. Children :
    1, John; 2, Obadiah; 3, Deborah; 4, Sarah; 5, Catherine.
6. JONATHAN, b. ———; d. at Newport about Nov., 1713; m. Sarah, d. of Richard and Joan Borden of Portsmouth; b. May, 1644; d. after 1705. Children :
    1, Obadiah; 2, Jonathan; 3, Samuel; 4, Sarah; 5, Mary; 6, Catherine; 7, Martha; 8, Lydia; 9, Joseph.
7. JOHN, b. 1649; d. at Newport, Oct. 2, 1712; m. (1st.) Dec. 1, 1671, Frances, eldest d. of Randall and Frances (Dungan) Holden, of Warwick—b. 1649; d. 1679. Children :
    1, John; 2. Catherine.
    Married (2d.) Oct. 12, 1680, Mary, d. of John and Mary (Williams) Sayles, widow of William Greene. Children :
    3, William; 4, Mary; 5, Frances; 6, Ann; 7, Susannah; 8, Deborah; 9, Phebe.

---

[1] Appleton's Journal, XV, 726.

(This son John, called Ensign, and after 1696, Lieut., was Treasurer of the Colony from Feb. 1690, to May, 1709; Deputy from Newport, 1704-5, and Treasurer again from 1708 to 1709; and could not have been the Judge, spoken of by Benedict, as at Philadelphia in 1692. That John, as well as the Jonathan who appears at Middletown, N. J., in 1688, were probably sons of Obadiah, Jr.)

8. HOPESTILL, b. ——— ; m. ——— Taylor.

MARKE LUCAR, the second witness, was one of the associates of Dr. John Clarke in the formation of the First Baptist Church at Newport about 1644.[1] Mr. William Hubbard, who joined this church in 1648, has preserved a roll of its members at that date, in which he is called a "Ruling Elder."[2] In 1649 he accompanied John Clarke to Seekonk and assisted in a religious work, of which, in a letter to Gov. John Winthrop, dated Dec. 10, 1649, Roger Williams writes as follows: "At Seekonk a great many have lately concurred with Mr. John Clarke and our Providence men about the point of a new baptism, and the manner of dipping: and Mr. John Clarke hath been there lately (and Mr. Lucar) and hath dipped them. I believe their practice comes nearer the first practice of our great founder Christ Jesus, than other practices of religion do, and yet I have not satisfaction neither in the authority by which it is done nor in the manner."[3] . . . Among those baptized at this time were Obadiah Holmes, Edward Smith and Joseph Torrey, who were afterwards members of the Church at Newport.

1655. His name appears on "ye Roule of ye Freemen of Newport."

He seems to have been the life-long friend of Dr. John Clarke, and is mentioned in his will of April 20, 1676,[4] as follows: "Item, unto my well beloved friend Mark Luker I

---

[1] Morgan Edwards, R. I. His. Soc. Col., VI., 324.
[2] Barrow's History of the First Baptist Church in Newport, p. 15.
[3] Bartlett's Letters of Roger Williams, p. 188.
[4] Foster Papers, VI, 4.

give and bequeath Fifty shillings a year in provisions at prices current for and during the term of his natural life." He did not survive to long enjoy the bounty of his friend, as his death occurred the same year, December 26, " at an advanced age, and leaving the character of a worthy walker."

It is not known that he had any family, and aside from his, the name does not occur on any R. I. records. His name appears as one of the purchasers of Monmouth County, N. J., between 1667 and 1670.[1] This county was settled chiefly by people from about Newport, R. I., but many of those whose names appear upon the list of purchasers did not actually remove there.

SHADRACH MANTON, the recorder of this deed, was the son of Edward Manton, whose home lot was on the town street near the head of Constitution Hill, between the lots of John Whipple and Gregory Dexter. He (Edward) was one of the signers of the first compact of 1640; on the Roule of Freemen, 1655; received lands from the town at or near "Venter" on the Wanasquatucket river, and about Neutecontenaut Hill; and died before May 13, 1682.

Shadrach Manton was admitted a freeman of Providence, May 18, 1658, which was probably soon after his marriage, his oldest child being born Dec. 11 of that year. In several deeds he is called a cooper.

1658, May 15. The town gave him a piece of meadow above Wanskuck and a house share next Epenutus Olney toward the great swamp.[2]

1660-1, Feb. 4. The town gave him a full purchase-right of lands as follows: A house lot or home share and a six acre lot in one parcel, lieing in the Neck—bounded west on the highway, north on land of Lawrence Wilkinson, south with land of Robert Pike, and east with the common. Also a share of meadow on the southerly and westerly side of the Wanas-

---

[1] Newport His. Mag., III, 202.
[2] Prov. Transcript, p. 108.

quatucket river, about a mile up the stream from "Venter," and bounded on land of his father Edward. Another share on the north and east side of the same river; another on both sides of West river about half a mile above Wanskuck fields; also 60 acres of land on the hill called Neotaconckanitt, bounded on Edward Manton; also 25 acres of land lieing northwest of "Ventor" about a mile, and lieing on two small streams which run into Wanasquatucket river.[1]

He lived near the present village of Manton and on the west side of the river, where, after the death of his father, he owned a very large tract of land. The Killingly road, after crossing the river at Manton, passes through this land.

1661-65-69-75. He was elected Juryman.
1664. Town Constable.
1667, May 30. Engaged allegiance.
1667 to 1670. Town Clerk.
1667 to 1671. Deputy.
1669, April 2. He bought of Henry and Waite Brown the home lot on the town street adjoining the home lot of his father on the north,[2] [near the head of Constitution Hill.]
1675. The town laid out to him about 25 acres, about two English miles west of "Cawcaunchewatchatt," and bounded southerly on land of Arthur Fenner and Joseph Williams.[3]
1679, July 1. He was taxed with son Edward, 1s. 3d.
1683. Surveyor of Highways.
1687. Overseer of the Poor.
1695. Bought of Nathaniel and Susannah Waterman 65 acres about four and a half miles west of the town, and lieing near and upon the hill called Sekesakit hill.[4]
1703, May 31. He bought 36 acres of Nicholas and Mercy Power adjoining the above.[5]

---

[1] Prov. Transcript, p. 253.
[2] Prov. Transcript, p. 273.
[3] Prov. Deeds, I, 25.
[4] Prov. Transcript, p. 335.
[5] Prov. Transcript, p. 379.

1709, July 15. The town laid out to him 20 acres in exchange for the land bought of Nicholas Power, "lieing within the swamp which lieth a small distance norwestwardly from Sekesacutt hill, and is called the pine swamp."[1]

1712-13. He bought lands of Andrew Harris.

1713-14, Jan. 27. He was found dead upon the road not far from his house. No will appears, nor any probate proceedings on his estate—his only son Edward succeeding to the property.

"Here followeth the Record of the Coroners inquest on the death of Shadrach Manton.

The jury impanilled by Richard Waterman Assistant.

You Richard Clemence foreman, Mr. John Browne, Mr. Edward Hawkings, Leif^t. James Olney, Mr. John Steere Junr, Mr. Silas Carpenter, Mr. Epenetus Olney, Mr. Benjamin Smith, Mr. John Angell Junr, Mr. Joseph Place, Mr. John Sheldon, Mr. James Browne.

You being upon a jury of inquest to enquire into & after the death of Mr. Shadrach Manton of Providence in the Colony of Roade Island & Providence Plantations, who was found dead upon the Roade this 27th day of January 17$\frac{13}{14}$ betwixt his dwelling & Wanasquatucket River.

You do promise true & faithfull alegiance to her Majesty and on the Trust comitted to your Equal justice & Right to do to all persons both poore & Rich without partiallity and make Returne in writing under your hands, that so her Majesty may know how shee came to loose her subject.

We find according to the best of our judgement & the best information that wee can gett, that his time being come hee died a naturall death."

Recorded Feb. 18, 1713-14.[2]

SHADRACH MANTON[2] (*Edward*[1]), b. about 1637 ; d. Jan. 27, 1713-14 ; m. Elizabeth, d. of John and Alice (———) Smith, (Miller). Children :

---

[1] Prov. Deeds, II, 137.
[2] Prov. Town Council Book, III, 156.

1. EDWARD, b. Dec. 11, 1658; d. Aug. 14, 1723 (see Prov. Wills, II., 153,); m. Dec. 9, 1680, Elizabeth, d. of John and Sarah (——) Thornton, who d. after 1723. Children:
    1, Shadrach; 2, Edward; 3, John; 4, Anne; 5, Catherine; 6, Mary; 7, Elizabeth; 8, Sarah.
2. ANN, b. ——; d. 1728; m. Sept. 18, 1682, John Keese, of Portsmouth, R. I., who d. Dec. 10, 1700. Children:
    1, Alice; 2, William; 3, Patience; 4, John; 5, Shadrach; 6, Ann.
3. ELIZABETH, b. ——; d. before 1695; m. before 1683, Henry, s. of Thomas and Ann (——) Estance, or Esten, of Providence—b. Jan. 11, 1651; d. March 23, 1711. Children:
    1, Elizabeth; 2, Amey.
4. A son; d. young.
5. A son; d. young.

RHODE ISLAND VETERAN CITIZENS HISTORICAL ASSOCIATION.

A MEETING DEVOTED TO THE HEBREWS, DECEMBER 7, 1885.

THIS meeting, by the suggestion and special efforts of the President, B. B. Hammond, Esq., and the Secretary, Rev. Frederic Denison, was arranged and conducted to secure as far as possible a record of the Jews in Rhode Island and their manners of worship. To this end suitable papers were prepared by the movers of the design, and invitations were extended to the Orthodox Rabbi at Newport, A. P. Mendez, and the Acting Reformed Rabbi in Providence, Mr. Myer Noot, to give addresses and exemplify parts of the Jewish service. Mr. Noot responded with a portion of the choir, of his synagogue. These unique exercises, showing such regard to the Hebrews as was never before manifested in christendom, but in perfect keeping with the spirit and principles of Rhode Island, are here reported, that they may have in our State the historical niche that they so richly deserve.

The meeting of the Association—being its regular monthly session—was held in Franklin Lyceum Hall, No. 62, Westminster street, Providence, December 7, 1885. After the usual opening and reading of records, on motion of Hon. J. N. Arnold, it was

Resolved, That the President be requested to appoint a committee to inquire into the introduction of the first steam engine into the State—who was its builder, who purchased it, and to what uses it was put; said committee to report at the next meeting.

The Hon. Elisha Dyer was so appointed.

President Hammond then made the following

ADDRESS.

Ladies and Gentlemen:

Through the courtesy of the Rev. Frederic Denison and Mr. Myer Noot, Acting Rabbi of the Israelites in this city, you are to-day to hear somewhat of the Hebrews in this State, and witness an illustration of a portion of their religious service as conducted in their synagogues. These people "*outwardly* are the descendants of Jacob and professors of the Jewish religion, but *inwardly* they are believers in, and the servants of God." The very name of Jew has been associated in our minds with the idea of "wanderer"—a people away from home—scattered among many nations—not mixing with any, but ever preserving their distinctive characteristics, and maintaining with unexampled faithfulness the faith and worship of their fathers in all lands and under all circumstances. Anciently honored, as the chosen people of God, they have ever appeared as his champions, bearing on their banners the mystic words—talismanic with them every where—"Hear, O Israel: The Lord our God is one Lord."

To-day we shall hear these words as they were once uttered in their solemn assemblies; and as we listen, may we catch some of the atmosphere and inspiration that once filled their temples and proclaimed their God " the God and Father of us all."

The President then called upon the Secretary, Rev. Frederic Denison, who read the following paper prepared by him on

THE ISRAELITES IN RHODE ISLAND.

While for thousands of years the world has been variously endeavoring to exterminate the descendants of Abraham, that remarkable people still preserve their identity and in both flesh and spirit manifest even a nationality, and are evidently reserved by Divine Providence for some important mission in the great economy of the ages. They present a historic problem to be devoutly studied. By them the history of the world has been greatly colored. Whatever relates to their career, of old or of late, is invested with large interest.

They have a good record on our continent and in our republic. We here seek to present a part of that story. We propose what, singularly enough, with the exception of a small monograph on the Jews in Newport, by Mr. Mason of that city, never before has been undertaken, namely, to collect and put together all obtainable facts, from their widely scattered sources, for a chapter of their life and doings in Rhode Island.

By the Jewish Cemetery and the Jewish Synagogue in Newport, so reverently cherished and studied in that "queen of summer resorts," large historical and religious credit are reflected upon the city and indeed upon the whole State. These preserve strange and rich memories of a people whose large commercial activities and sacred assemblies once gave importance to our colony and great honor to our religious freedom.

From fragmentary notices gleaned from various quarters, from all known personal records and incidental allusions, we have aimed to reproduce that by-gone and influential life. Unfortunately the records proper of the Newport Jews, particularly those of the Synagogue, have in main perished, having been lost probably with other valuable Newport papers in the disasters of that city during the Revolution. The Scrolls of the Law belonging to the Synagogue were however finally entrusted to the keeping of the Portuguese Synagogue in New York City.

The persecutions of the Middle Ages, often animated by race-hatred, bore so heavily upon the children of Israel that they were driven to whatever refuges could be found. The exiles from the Spanish Peninsula, driven out by the cruel expulsion of 1492, turned their feet to all lands where sympathy might be found.

Many of them were afterwards found in Holland. Not a few of those were distinguished for wealth, culture and intelligence. Indeed the Portuguese Jews regarded themselves and were regarded by others as the aristocracy of their race.

Soon after the unique colony founded by Roger Williams and John Clarke became known as a sanctuary for persecuted consciences, certain Jews from Holland, whose ancestors were from Spain, sought refuge and abode on these, then the only religiously free, shores of the world. Some it is thought came from Curaçoa. And some, it is known came by the way of New Amsterdam (New York) having been expelled in 1654 by Governor Stuyvesant. It is thought that the first Jews reached New York near 1650.

It seems evident that some reached Newport while John Clarke was in England securing the second charter of the colony. Of the names of the most of these who first came, or the exact dates of their coming we are not positively informed.

As with the other settlers, their worship for a long time was in their private dwellings and was somewhat informal. Entering into trade, which of late centuries has been the passion of their race, they steadily increased in numbers and in resources, and thereby added both to the reputation and wealth of the colony.

When death invaded their ranks they sought a Machpelah all their own where they might lay their dead. Two of their number, Mordecai Campannall and Moses Peckeckoe, Dec. 28, 1677, bought of Nathaniel Dickens the ground, since enlarged and improved, now so well known as the Jewish Cemetery, at the junction of Kay and Touro streets. The early graves in their place of sepulture present no inscribed stones, and, like the graves of other early settlers, are now indistinguishable.

That these children of Abraham were kindly received in Rhode Island is shown by the action of the General Assembly under date of June 24, 1684, reading as follows:

"Voted: In answer to the petition of Simon Medus, David Brown, and associates, being Jews, presented to this Assembly, bearing date June the 24th, 1684: We declare that they may expect as good protection here as any strangers, being not of our nation residing among us in this his Majesty's Collony, ought to have, being obedient to his Majesty's laws."

When they qualified themselves and sought the privilege, they were admitted freemen of the colony, like others, by vote of the General Assembly. (See Colony Records.) Their enjoyment of civil and religious freedom, so rigidly and bitterly refused them throughout the world, but so freely granted in this cradle of soul-liberty, and their unrestrained participation in commercial and civil affairs, were a happy illustration of the spirit and principles of the colony, and constitute a pleasing chapter in the history of the State. Indeed they were here always treated according to their manhood and their worth.

Prior to 1750 some distinguished Spanish Jews by the name of Lopez appear in the affairs of Newport, and soon we find associated with them a number of their kindred. All these, in intelligence as in estate, were of a superior class, as their after career testified. Here they entered largely upon marine and mercantile pursuits and were greatly prospered in their enterprises. Their learning and skill in practical sciences became an aid and adornment to the life of the colony. Moses Lopez effectively served the colony as a translator of the Spanish language, for which service he received certain legislative favors. In 1750 the Colonial Assembly granted him "a patent," or exclusive right, for "the art and mystery" of making potash, a process then "known to very few in the kingdom" of Great Britain. At the same time the colony forbade the sale of ashes beyond its limits that Mr. Lopez might have the more advantage.

Aaron Lopez, also eminent for ability, seems to have here introduced important trade with foreign ports. At the opening of the Revolution, Aaron and Moses Lopez owned not less than twenty-seven square-rigged vessels engaged in foreign voyages and in the whale fishery. For that day this was an immense business for two men. Nearly if not quite all these vessels were lost during the war. Moses had a brother Jacob, whose record we are now unable to trace. Certainly Newport's early advantages from trade with distant lands were derived largely from these Israelites.

Jacob Rodrigues Riviera introduced into Newport, and so into our country, the process of manufacturing spermaceti.

On account of the terrible earthquake at Lisbon, in Portugal, Nov. 1, 1755, other Jews of that country were scattered abroad.

Among these was a regular orthodox Hebrew Rabbi named Isaac Touro. He reached Newport, R. I., as early as 1758; probably a little earlier. Here he found enough of his countrymen to be gathered into a regular orthodox congregation. Being a man of talents, broad education and ardent Hebrew devotion, he became a leader among his people and thoroughly organized them for established worship. The congregation appears in regular form in 1758, and was named Yeshuat Israel, signifying the "Strength of Israel," the name ever after found in all the notices of the assembly and even on some of the tombstones of the members. The Rev. Mr. Touro then proceeded to secure a house of worship for his flock. With the generous contributions of his people and their friends he finally raised the necessary funds for the erection of the solid and beautiful Synagogue now so valued in Newport, located midway on the north side of Touro street. The builder was the famous Peter Harrison, who was assistant architect of Blenheim House, England, and builder of the Colony House—now the State House—in Newport, in 1742, as also of the Redwood Library Building, in 1748-50. The wealthy Jews were resolved upon a house worthy of their ancient faith and of their large pecuniary resources. The edifice was begun in 1762, and was "consecrated Dec. 3, 1763, (Tebet, A. M. 5524, in Hebrew chronology,) being the Feast of Dedication in the Jewish calender. The Ritual (Minhag) was in the Portuguese tongue, but the Scrolls and reading of the Law were, as always, in Hebrew. The day of dedication (called Hanneah) was the Jewish festival in commemoration of the rededication of the Temple at Jerusalem by Judas Maccabees, B. C. 163, (See 1. Maccabees IV. 59). That was a historic day in Newport when for the first time, under Rhode Island's ægis of religious liberty, was devoutly and fully celebrated that ancient Jewish feast, and the children of Abraham joyfully entered their new and elegant Synagogue. Then "was there very great gladness among the people."

The structure is of brick and stone, measuring 48 by 40 feet on the ground, and has a wing on the north side; both parts two stories in height; a fine portico on its front to the west; the whole, both exterior and interior, in chaste Roman Doric style of architecture; a really superb edifice for its day, and still justly admired. Its front is not to the street but to the west, as all regular synagogues are built, that the worshippers may turn their faces directly toward Jerusalem. The assembly room has galleries on the north, west, and south. Near the front entrance is the large, square reading desk that faces eastward. On the east wall is the cabinet to contain the Scrolls of the Law and other precious articles. No permanent seats were ever provided; only chairs and benches were occasionally introduced. Usually the worshippers stood, all with their heads covered, and in acts of worship turned their faces to the east. In the lower story of the wing were the means for preparing the unleavened bread for the Passover. The women enter the wing and ascend by stairs to the galleries, the only part of the building assigned to them. Among the Orthodox Jews the men and women are apart in the synagogue service. This custom is not followed by the Reformed Jews.

In this sanctuary in Newport the Hebrews, while they grew in numbers and opulence, joyfully met to celebrate their rites and festivals with holy chantings. For thirteen years, undisturbed, they kept their Sabbaths, the Feast of Passover, the Feast of Pentecost, the Feast of the New Year, the Feast of Tabernacles, the Feast of the Eighth Day of Solemn Convocation, and the Feast of the Day of Atonement. The synagogue had a Minister, a President, a Board of Directors, a Treasurer and a Secretary.

That some youths of the stock of Abraham studied in Brown University is concluded from the fact that the college authorities instituted a regulation excusing Jews from attending collegiate duties on their Sabbaths (Saturdays).

Among the Newport worshippers were some wealthy Spanish and Portuguese families from the adjacent colonies, as Newport, then having a population of about six thousand, was the leading commercial port in this country, and in culture was deemed "the Athens of America."

Among the notable Hebrew families were found such names as Benjamin, Elizar, Hart, Hays, Lucena, Levy, Lopez, Oliveyra, Polok, Riviera, Seixas, and Touro.

These were Orthodox Israelites (Sephardim), in distinction from what are known as Reformed Israelites (Ashkenarim). As an indication of their learning it may be mentioned that Dr. Ezra

Stiles, then a preacher in Newport and afterwards President of Yale College, took lessons in the Hebrew tongue of these Israelites.

In 1760 these Jews reported above sixty families. When Dr. Stiles reported "seventy souls" as constituting the church he must have meant heads of families, a Jewish mode of counting. Prior to the Revolution, says a Newport annalist, "upwards of three hundred attended the synagogue." As they were religiously opposed to a "numbering of the people" they did not give their names and numbers when the families of Newport were counted in 1774.

"The able and faithful Rabbi," Isaac Touro, married Reyna Hays, a sister of Moses Hays then of Newport, and afterwards a resident of Boston. Isaac and Reyna had three children: Abraham, born in 1773; Judah, born in 1775; Rebecca, born in 1779. Occasion will appear hereafter for speaking of Abraham and Judah. Rebecca married Josiah Lopez who lived on the north side of the Parade, a part of Newport containing numerous Jewish dwellings.

Just as Newport was reaching a wonderful pitch of commercial prosperity the storm of the Revolution gathered and broke. It swept sea and land. Ships and shops, merchandise and merchants were scattered. Rabbi Touro and his people were obliged to flee. He finally went to the West Indies, where at Kingston, Jamaica, while laboring for his people, he died Dec. 8, 1783, aged forty-six years. We infer that he was buried where he died. Rhode Island, in view of his character and labors owes him an enduring record.

His sons, Abraham and Judah, were placed with their uncle, Moses Hays, in Boston, with whom they learned to be wise and successful importing merchants. Their mother, at her death, was laid with solemn service in the Newport cemetery.

While the British occupied Newport, confiscation and plunder, camp fires and army exactions, left but little of the large Hebrew property. "The north side of the Parade was once covered with Jewish residences which were destroyed." The Synagogue was spared though its doors were closed. For half a century thereafter, except for certain funerals of Jews, no reading of the Law, no intoning of the Prophets, no chanting of the Psalms, were officially performed within the sacred walls. It was a veritable dispersion. The harps were on the willows hung. And but few of the old congregation ever returned to Newport to remain.

By a custom among the Orthodox Jews, it requires ten persons present on any given occasion in the synagogue to form the proper number to offer acceptable prayer; a usage suggested by the mention in Moses' writings of the "ten righteous men" required to effectually intercede for Sodom. Obedience to this custom explains in part the long closing of the Newport Synagogue.

The Jews were friends of the colonies in the Revolutionary struggle. They gave liberally of their means to sustain the patriot cause. In some cases they served in the continental armies. The address they delivered to Gen. Washington on his accession to the Presidency of our nation was one of great beauty of expression and pertinency of sentiment. The reply they received was equally complimentary, felicitous and just. Always the Jews have stood on the side of liberty.

Abraham Touro, educated and established in Boston, became a man of high reputation, large trade and enviable fortune. He acquired his wealth as an importer, trading particularly with ports on the shores of the Mediterranean. At his death in October, 1822, in the forty-eighth year of his age, his direct bequests amounted to more than sixty-thousand dollars, not including goods, stores, merchandise and a balance to his brother Judah and his sister Rebecca.

We may mention the chief these bequests:

"$10,000 to the Legislature of Rhode Island for the purpose of supporting the Jewish Synagogue in that State, in special trust, to be appropriated to that object in such manner as the said Legislature together with the municipal authority of the town of Newport from time to time may direct and appoint."

"$10,000 to the Trustees of the Jewish Synagogue in New York."

"$10,000 to the Massachusetts General Hospital."

"$5,000 to the Trustees of the Asylum for Indigent Boys in Boston."

"$5,000 to the Female Asylum for orphans in Boston."

"$5,000 to the municipal authorities of Newport" "for repairing and preserving the street leading from the burying ground (Jewish Cemetery) to the main street."

"$5,000 to a Humane Society."
"$5,000 to Moses Myers in trust."
"$2,000 to Moses L. Moses."
"$2,000 to Miss Juliet Lopez of New York."
"$1,000 to Miss Frances Bruner."
"$500 to Nathan Cobb, a yellow servant."
"$500 to William B. Proctor."

From the avails of one of his bequests, in 1843, the Synagogue grounds were enclosed with heavy, cut granite walls and massive iron palings, and adorned with a beautiful Quincy granite gateway, the cap of which bears his name and the Jewish date of erection A. M. 5603.

His body was brought and devoutly laid in the cemetery that was so dear to him; and in view of his active, enterprising life and his many and large benevolences, it is no wonder that his name here

"Smells sweet and blossoms from the dust."

Judah Touro, educated in like manner to trade, also became a man of opulence and of very wide reputation. He pursued his business career chiefly in the south, particularly in New Orleans, where he settled before Louisiana was purchased, in 1803, by the United States. While an eminent merchant he was alive to all benevolences and all patriotic endeavors. In the last war with England he served with Gen. Jackson in the defense of New Orleans and received Jan. 1, 1815, a severe wound in battle. He became famous by his deeds of kindness and his munificent gifts. His wealth became immense.

In 1843, at an expense of about $12,000, he erected heavy cut granite walls and strong iron palings around the Newport Jewish Cemetery, where his kindred sleep, and adorned the entrance with a superb Quincy granite gateway in pure Egyptian style of architecture, a style peculiarly rich in memorial associations. The cap of this gateway is embellished with a winged globe while the posts bear inverted torches.

Judah died in New Orleans Jan. 4, 1854, in his seventy-ninth year, leaving bequests to institutions and persons to the amount of $459,000, not including large gifts of real estate and property to the Hebrew congregation in New Orleans and to found a Hebrew Hospital in that city, with a residue to his "dear old friend," Rafer Davis Shepherd, of Virginia, "to whom, under Divine Providence he was indebted for the preservation of his life when he was wounded" in battle.

We may mention the principal bequests:

$80,000 for establishing an Alms House in New Orleans.

$50,000 to Per Moses Montefiore, of London, to be used for the relief of Jews in the Holy Land.

$20,000 to the Hebrew Education Society, Philadelphia, Penn.

$20,000 to the Jews Hospital Society of the city and state of New York.

$13,000 to the Talmuth Torah School Fund of the city of New York.

$10,000 to the city of Newport, R. I., for the purchase of the Old Stone Mill property as a Public Park and promenade ground.

$10,000 to the North American Relief Society for indigent Jews of Jerusalem and Palestine, in the state and city of New York.

$10,000 to the Massachusetts Female Hospital.

$10,000 to pay the salary of a reader or minister to officiate in the Synagogue in Newport, R. I., and to endow the ministry of the same, as well as to keep in repair and embellish the Jewish Cemetery in Newport aforesaid.

$10,000 to Aaron Reppell Josephs, of New Orleans.

$10,000 to Gershom Kurshudt, of New Orleans.

$10,000 to Pierre Andre Destrae Carenaœ, of New Orleans.

$7,000 to the three daughters of Moses M. Myers, of Richmond, Va.

$7,000 to the surviving children of the late Samuel Myers, of Richmond, Va.

$5,000 to the Hebrew Benevolent Association, of New Orleans.

$5,000 to the Congregation Shangaria Chased, of New Orleans.

$5,000 to the Ladies Benevolent Society, of New Orleans.

$5,000 to the Hebrew Foreign Society, of New Orleans.

$5,000 to the Orphan Home Asylum, of New Orleans.

$5,000 to the Society for the Relief of Destitute Orphan Boys in the Fourth District of New Orleans.

$5,000 to St. Armas Asylum for the Relief of Destitute Females and Children.

$5,000 to the New Orleans Female Orphan Asylum.

$5,000 to St. Mary's Catholic Boys' Asylum.

$5,000 to Milsie Asylum, of New Orleans.

$5,000 to the Fireman's Charitable Association, of New Orleans.

$5,000 to the Seaman's House in the First District of New Orleans.

$5,000 to the Hebrew Congregation Chachay Shalome, Boston, Mass.

$5,000 to the Hebrew Congregation, Hartford, Conn.

$5,000 to the Hebrew Congregation, New Haven, Conn.

$5,000 to the Hebrew Benevolent Society, Mashebat Nafesh, of New York.

$5,000 to the Hebrew Benevolent Society, Gimeleet Chased, of New York.

$5,000 to the Hebrew Congregation, Beth Shalome, of Richmond, Va.

$5,000 to the Hebrew Congregation, Sheareth Israel, of Charleston, S. C.

$5,000 to the Hebrew Congregation, Mikoe Israel, of Savannah, Ga.

$5,000 to the Jews Hospital, of Cincinnati, Ohio.

$5,000 to the Asylum of Orphan Boys, Boston, Mass.

$5,000 to the Female Orphan Asylum, Boston, Mass.

$5,000 to Miss Catharine Hays (his cousin), of Richmond, Va.

$5,000 to supply Clapp Twing, of Boston, Mass.

$5,000 to Mistress Ellen Brooks, wife of Gorham Brooks, of Boston, Mass.

$3,000 to the Rev. Theodore Clapp, of New Orleans.

$3,000 to the Redwood Library, of Newport, R. I., for books or repairs.

$3,000 to the Educational Institution of the Hebrew Congregation, Briai Jeshurum, of New York.

$3,000 to the Hebrew Congregation, Shangarai Tefila, of New York.

$3,000 to the Ladies' Benevolent Society, New York city.

$3,000 to the Female Hebrew Benevolent Society, of Philadelphia, Penn.

$3,000 to the United Hebrew Benevolent Society, of Philadelphia, Penn.

$3,000 to the Hebrew Congregation, Ashabat Israel, of Fells Point, Baltimore, Md.

$3,000 to the Hebrew Congregation, Adas Israel, of Louisville, Ky.

$3,000 to the Hebrew Congregation, Briai Israel, of Cincinnati, Ohio.

$3,000 to the Hebrew School, Talmud Yeladin, Cincinnati, Ohio.

$3,000 to the Hebrew Congregation, Tifereth Israel, Cleveland, Ohio.

$3,000 to the Hebrew Congregation, Briai el Israel, St. Louis, Mo.

$3,000 to the Hebrew Congregation, Beth el Israel, Buffalo, N. Y.

$3,000 to the Hebrew Congregation, Beth el Israel, Albany, N. Y.

$3,000 to the Rev. Isaac Leeser, of Philadelphia, Penn.

$3,000 to the Rev. Moses N. Nathan, and his wife, of London.

$2,500 to Mrs. M. D. Josephs, of New Orleans.

$2,500 to Mrs. Rebecca Kurshudt, of New Orleans.

$2,000 to the Hebrew Congregation, of Memphis, Tenn.

$2,000 to the Hebrew Congregation, of Montgomery, Ala.

$2,000 to the Hebrew Congregation, Shangarai Shamoyen, of Mobile, Ala.

Surely Judah was a princely giver. His remains were brought to Newport and with fitting solemnity and ceremony, June 6, 1854, laid in the cemetery that he had adorned. Over his remains stands a substantial granite monument. At his burial there was placed with his remains a small portion of earth that had been brought from Palestine.

In this last named particular, we meet with an old custom, followed as far as possible by the Orthodox Israelites. Persons have been known to give $20 for a handful of such earth to be used in a burial service. Many Hebrews, on visiting the Holy Land, bring home with them portions of earth to be thus used on burial occasions. This usage is not so generally observed by the Reformed Jews. Both Orthodox and Reformed have a custom of putting earth of some kind into the pillow under the head of the deceased when the body is laid in the grave, thus signifying "dust thou art, and unto dust shalt thou return"; at the same time placing the hands of the deceased by the sides of the body with open palms, to express the truth that we "brought nothing into the world and can carry nothing out."

It is traditionally told of Judah Touro that he cherished a special affection for his cousin, Catharine Hays, of Richmond, Va., mentioned in his will with a bequest of $5,000, "as an expression of the kind remembrance in which that esteemed friend" was held by him. She reciprocated the tender regard and, it is said, remembered him in her will for a like amount and in similar language of esteem. Forbidden to marry by Jewish law, they both lived single, but always mindful of each other's welfare. Judah annually sent a trusted agent from New Orleans to Richmond to inquire after Catharine's happiness. She responded through the same confidential lips. They did not trust their pulsing hearts to paper. While Judah gave his hands to trade and to all good causes, his inner heart was with Catharine. She also was devoted to all good deeds. Singularly, she died two days before him— Jan. 2, 1854—at the age of seventy-seven, two years younger than he. Tradition further says "his name was the last word she uttered," and of him it is said "in his delirium, before death called him, he talked of walking in a beautiful garden with Catharine Hays, his first and only love." They both rest together in the Jewish Cemetery in Newport. On Judah's monument we read: "The last of his name, he inscribed it in the book of philanthropy, to be remembered forever." Surely, in view of his many and great deeds of beneficence, his name survives "like sweet perfume." He and his brother Abraham left funds in the keeping of the State of Rhode Island that now amount to about thirty-nine thousand dollars.

Let us now visit the Jewish Cemetery. Entering by the beautiful granite gateway, passing through the well kept walks, among the solemn pines, the wreathing vines, the love-planted shrubs and rare flowers,—all like a sacred garden—we tenderly study the pious records carved on large headstones, broad horizontal slabs and variously shaped monuments. The memorials are of slate, marble and granite. The inscriptions are in both Hebrew and English. We have indicated some of the names here found. Let us read a few others.

"Moses Michael Hayes, died May 9, 1805, aged 66 years." He was born in New York, but resided in Boston the last twenty-four years of his life, and was distinguished "for the probity of his dealings, the philanthropy of his nature, and the noble frankness of his manners." Said the Boston Centinel, "He walked abroad fearing no man, but loving all. Under his roof dwelt hospitality ;—it was an asylum for friendship, the mansion of peace. He was without guile, detesting hypocrisy as he detested meanness." Having a dispensation from the Masonic Order in New York, he founded, near 1790, King David's Lodge in Newport, a Lodge that was afterwards incorporated with St. John's Lodge.

"Moses Lopez died 1767."

"Aaron Lopez died May 28, 1782, in his 51st year."

Aaron was "a man of eminent probity and benevolence," "whose bounties were widely diffused" and "not confined to creed or sect." He and his nephew, Moses Lopez, on the breaking out of the Revolution, moved to Providence and afterwards to Leicester, Mass. He built in East Greenwich a two-storied gambrel-roofed brick house, with a store in one corner below. The edifice is still standing (1882) on the corner of Main and Long streets. This was probably one of his branch trading houses. He was drowned May 28, 1782, being thrown from his sulky into Scott's Pond, a few miles north of Providence.

"Isaac Polok died May 23, 1764, aged 63 ys. 9 mo. 6 days."

"Moses Seixas died Nov. 28, 1809, aged 66 years." He was the first cashier of the Bank of Rhode Island, the first bank established in Newport, in 1805.

Perhaps it may suffice to simply mention some of the remaining names: David Lopez, Abraham Lopez, Rebecca Lopez, Benjamin Levy, Judith Levy, Moses Levy, Myer Benjamin, Isaac Jacobs Polok, Isaac Mendes Seixas. These and others are worthy of long remembrance.

The Rivieras removed to Boston.

Joseph Lopez, son of Aaron, returned to Newport after the war and resumed business.

Jacob Rodrigues Riviera, after the war, returned, but did not re-enter upon business.

Abraham Rodrigues Riviera, an importer of dry goods before

the war, won the title of "the honest man," because after all his heavy losses, having no underwriters in that day, he at last paid all his creditors, principal and interest. He finally died in possession of a fortune.

Between 1810 and 1820, two Jewish youth, Samuel and Jacob Lopez, were in Providence and attended the school on Meeting street. Jacob lived with Mr. Knight Dexter. Samuel became a jeweller and married the daughter of Benjamin Tallman, Jr.

Newport now counts none of the old Jewish families of Portuguese and Spanish blood. Samuel Lopez, who lived on Pelham street, moved to New York, near 1820. The last of the old stock and faith, living on the north of the Parade, removed to New York in the spring of 1822. When some of these sold their residences, they made a reservation in the deeds that they should have the privilege, on occasion of bringing their dead to Newport for burial in their cemetery, of occupying their old homes for a few hours in the performance of funeral ceremonies. Instances of such reoccupancy occurred.

Except for rare funeral occasions the doors of the Synagogue were not ceremonially reopened till 1850, when a few Jews from New York and other cities, in official robes and with covered heads, re-entered the sacred walls and repeated the ancient ritual. Another similar service was observed in the autumn of 1877. Still another kindred service was conducted in 1881. Latterly the worshippers represent remnants of the old families and some families of later immigration. Of the ancient stock we recognize members of the Hays and Lopez families.

The Synagogue was again opened for the Portugues ritual (Minhag) August 4th and 5th, 1882, and a full Jewish Sabbath was observed, the services beginning on Friday evening. The officiating Rabbi was the Rev. H. P. Mendez, the minister of the Nineteenth Street Portuguese Synagogue of New York City. He was assisted by the President of his synagogue, Mr. J. Blumenthall. Many visitors of rank were present, and some clergymen of other denominations. During the evening service, while the old candelabra threw over the room its "dim religious light," it seemed as if a by-gone age had returned. The reading, the chanting, all the associations of the service seemed to reach back more than two thousand years. The scene was exceedingly impressive and suggestive. The chants however were recited in Spanish melodies or tones arranged more than four centuries ago, but the reading was from texts dating back more than three thousand years. Rabbi Mendez delivered an appropriate and forcible address from the words, "Ye are my witnesses."

Since 1882 a Jewish school, called The Touro Institute, has been conducted in Newport, by an Orthodox Rabbi, A. P. Mendes, who also leads weekly service in the Synagogue for about a dozen Hebrew families.

After the Spanish and Portuguese Jews were driven from Newport by the British army, a few of them came to Providence, but not a sufficient number to organize public worship and establish a synagogue.

In the present century, and within the past fifty years, with the growth of the trade of Providence appeared a number of Hebrews from central and northern Europe. These German, Polish and Russian Jews, with some from other regions, have at last become quite a factor in certain kinds of trade and in some crafts in the city.

The Russian and Polish Jews claim to be Orthodox, holding the old forms of ritual, remaining covered in worship, and requiring the separation of the sexes in the place of worship. To them the Hebrew tongue is pre-eminently sacred. Their prayers are in Hebrew; their discourses in German. In 1875 they organized a small Congregation, named "Sons of Zion," meeting at first on Canal street. Their minister was the Rev. Lazarus Finsilever. They afterwards leased rooms in the Wayland Building. They next removed to No. 42 Canal street.

The German Jews, in main, count themselves Reformed, taking greater liberty than the Orthodox, in ritual, dress, discourse, and in allowing females to sit with the males in their public assemblies. Their prayers are in both Hebrew and German. Like the Orthodox, however, they worship with their faces toward Jerusalem. But, in general, they are more free, open and progressive than the old school, endeavoring to be in harmony with the spirit of our age. Their discourses are in English.

They organized their Congregation, named "Sons of Israel," in 1878. For four years they had their synagogue—a leased building—on the corner of Pine and Page streets. They then removed to No. 98 Weybosset street.

The Jewish Cemetery in Providence was opened in 1857, but was not ceremonially dedicated till Sept. 14, 1882. It is on Reservoir avenue. The ministers for the "Sons of Israel" have been, Rev. Dr. Jacob Voorsanger, Rev. M. Moses, Rev. M. Rottenberg, and Mr. Myer Noot. This congregation numbering perhaps fifty active members (1882) and an assembly of perhaps two hundred, sustains quite a vigorous Sabbath School.

At the expense of being episodical, I shall here venture to present some historical facts, gleaned in my researches, that have never been put in print, relative to the first settlement of Israelites in three other important cities of our country where they have acted a conspicuous and effective part in trade and in society.

They first appear in the city of New York near 1650, where their first Congregation, named "Shearith Israel," was organized near 1700, as its records reach back clearly to 1706. These records are in the Spanish language, and they contain certain names that afterwards appear in Newport, such as Levy and Riviera. These New York Hebrews secured their first burying ground in 1681, and built their first Synagogue in 1729, and consecrated it in 1730 on Mill street. Their second house was erected, on the same street, in 1817, and consecrated in 1819. In 1833 they removed to Crosby street and consecrated their third house in 1834. In 1860 they removed to their present location on Nineteenth street. "There was but a single synagogue in New York city until 1825, when the first synagogue of the German Jews was erected." That city now (1882) reports about a dozen able Jewish preachers.

In Philadelphia the first Orthodox Synagogue was dedicated Sept. 13, 1782, and bore the name of the previously existing Congregation, "Mikve Israel"—Hope of Israel. This congregation was composed of Portuguese whose ancestors had been exiled from their country. Among the organizers of their worship was the Rev. Gersham Mendes Seixas, from New York, who became their first Rabbi. He afterwards became Rabbi of the Synagogue, Shearith Israel, in New York, in 1816. Their next Rabbi in Philadelphia was the Rev. Jacob Raphael Cohen, who died in 1811.

Of the worship of the Israelites in Boston, the Rev. Alexis

Alexander says: "The first Jewish prayer meeting met in Warrenton street, opposite Bennett street, in 1852, and consisted of about fifteen members. Two years later they bought a house on Warrenton street and converted it into a synagogue. The Congregation was named Ohabei Shalom—Love of Peace. The first Rabbi was named Socks." From this, other congregations have gone out; some of them being of the Reformed school. There are now (1882) eight congregations in the city, having about five hundred members.

Perhaps we shall be pardoned for one more digression, as the facts have fallen under our notice and are not in print, though they are of importance to the Jews and to all our people.

In this country the Israelites organize themselves into great friendly societies, such as B. nai Berith (Sons of the Covenant), Free Sons of Israel, Kisher shel Barzel (Iron Link), and Improved Order Free Sons of Israel. They have a "Union of American Congregations" that counts one hundred and eighteen bodies in its membership. These congregations have differing ways of interpreting Scripture. Some keep Sabbath on Sunday. The Orthodox however adhere to the old Jewish Sabbath. Some pray in English, asserting this to be a right in their Reformed practice. At present (1882) it is claimed that there are in the United States two hundred and seventy-eight congregations with twelve thousand five hundred and forty-six members.

We cannot close these brief notes and notices of the Hebrews in Rhode Island and this country without thinking of the almost miraculous tenacity of life manifested in that nation, and recalling the vast indebtedness of the world to this divinely chosen and defended people for the great part they have acted in receiving and preserving that richest of volumes—the Old Testament—the Law and the Promises of Almighty God. In themselves they are a historic proof of the Bible—a bulwark that no infidelity can destroy.

And as we look upon the guarded Jewish Cemetery and the solid, well preserved Synagogue in Newport, we almost feel that they, with the Jerusalem in Palestine, are a prophecy of the day when, the fullness of the Gentiles having come in, "All Israel shall be saved."

Acting Rabbi, Myer Noot, of the Reformed Synagogue, "Sons of Israel," in Providence, then made the following

ADDRESS.

Mr. President, Members of the Rhode Island Veteran Citizens Historical Association:

LADIES AND GENTLEMEN.—It having pleased your society to set apart this day devoted to the Israelites of this State, and being cognizant of the appreciation of the same, I have prepared a short essay to speak upon this subject, although I feel that this task might have been placed in better and more competent hands in order to do justice to the occasion.

When I look around and see in this assemblage men of intelligence, men of character and prominence, I feel that my People in Judaism should feel themselves highly flattered that this society should have so far given us an opportunity to show what the Israelites have done towards furthering the social and commercial interests of little Rhode Island. As far as the social interests are concerned we as Israelites claim we are contributing our share in this respect. We are law abiding people, ever willing and ready to stand by any and all laws which have been promulgated from time to time for the good government of all classes. And while we do not aspire to seeking for public offices we contribute our mite in giving evidence of our willingness to co-operate with our Christian brethren in matters relating to the interest of our city and State.

Commercially speaking we have been engaged in various pursuits and have endeavored to become with our sister merchants men who are toiling in various branches of industry striving hard to gain a livelihood.

The question though of to-day's gathering, my friends, does not give me full scope to speak at any great length on the purpose that has brought us here, and if I deviate from that particular point in order to speak on a subject which will vie with the other, I hope I may not be considered out of order, for it is done with a view of showing what progress we have made, how much is Judaism understood both by Jew and Gentile, and to what extent we Israelites have worked towards commanding the respect as a religious sect from those who do not believe as we do. I have only to go back ten years to rehearse before you how things were in this city as far as the mode of worship was concerned. A mere handful of people composed the congregation at that time; the service was entirely in the Hebrew language, and to have introduced English in the synagogue at that time would have been considered an innovation, so to speak. It was a rare thing to see children or young men attend the synagogue. If a non-Israelite happened to enter the synagogue it was so much Greek to him, to comprehend what was going on. Then the additional days which were observed, which were however contrary to the Mosaic command, neither to add or diminish from the tenor of the Law.

How we as Israelites have been benefited by this great turn in the affairs of our religion words cannot express. Our doors are open now to any one who is desirous of hearing our service. The young and old of people congregate there to hear the Word of God expounded in language suited to the present time; they can readily follow the reader or minister and understand what they are saying.

Our Christian brethren have access to our place of worship, can understand what we are doing and may perchance become interested in what might be termed a Jewish worship. While reform in the mode of worship is no thing of a recent date still we as Israelites of this city have only come to our senses within the last eight years, and have realized the dire necessity of establishing for ourselves such recompense in this respect, so that the younger element may have the benefit therefrom, and that they may find in the synagogue a place where they may supplicate to their Father in Heaven in a language best suited to their present condition and the land that gives them the right to worship as they may best see fit.

In this direction, my friends, we have done much to diffuse among our people and the community at large a certain amount of respect which must ultimately give rise to a better feeling for the Israelites of this city.

I fear in my remarks I may have merged too much on religious matters, but the opportunity has presented itself and our people have not been understood during the past twenty-five years, that a few words touching upon this subject will not be out of place.

There are in this city over one hundred and fifty Jewish families numbering probably five hundred people, employed in various kinds of mercantile pursuits. We have also two synagogues, one strictly Orthodox and the other Moderate Reform. The former are composed chiefly of Russian Jews, and the latter principally Germans, and a few who claim this country as their birthplace. The Orthodox Jews in this city adhere strictly to all the forms and ceremonies as practised years ago. The Reformers, however, have always believed that a change in the mode of worship was necessary (for reasons stated before) and the result has been that from a congregation of eighteen we number to-day sixty members of the male sex.

While we do not believe as they do as regards the old forms and ceremonies in the synagogue, we respect them as Israelites, and are at all times willing and ready to affiliate with them on all occasions. When God said to Moses we shall be a peculiar people, and that peculiarity has been manifest in all these years. We admit being a distinct people, and therefore hold together as such as far as our religious identity is concerned.

There are in this city three Jewish Orders, the various Grand Lodges of which are in New York. The aims and objects are alike in all and are strictly Jewish so far as not to admit any but Israelites, as the name would denote—Sons of Covenant. The inconsistency of admitting non-Israelites is self-evident to any fair minded person. There is also a Jewish Benevolent Association composed of females only. They administer to the wants of those who need aid and consequently there is no need of going out of our precincts in that direction. In fact, my friends, we Israelites of this city and State are alike all our other cities, ever willing and ready to dispense charity and benevolence to our own people and to others who do not believe as we do.

We cannot boast of having a synagogue of our own, but a fund has been established for that purpose, and it is to be hoped the time is not far distant when this worthy project will have been made a success.

When I look back but a short time and see how we Israelites have been blessed in this country with the right of Religious Liberty;

when in this very State our people have been honored at least by one Israelite who has held the position of Representative in the General Assembly, a distinction that would have been laughed at years ago, I feel, my friends, that we must have done something, or at least our people who have lived here years ago, to merit such an act.

And to what can we attribute the kindly feeling that is slowly being made manifest towards our people? The Israelites lived in this city in oblivion, our Christian brethren could not find out anything about them. If in years gone by the question was asked, Where is your synagogue or house of worship? they would shrink from telling you, and under some pretense or other would evade the question. But how different are things now. Ask our people that you would like to hear our services, they will only be too glad to take you to our synagogue. Is this not, my friends, an improvement? Should we not feel proud to think that time has wrought for us a miracle in this enlightened age of progress, and that we can be good Israelites if we do not believe as our Orthodox brethren do.

Another change which has worked wonders in our mode of worship was the introduction of music in the synagogue, something which the Orthodox Jews do not tolerate. And right here I desire to place myself on a right footing in regard to this question. I hope, however, it will not be taken amiss if I am expressing myself in terms Orthodox too much. My sole aim is, and will be in this discussion, to show to what extent Judaism has fared much better than in the days of Orthodoxy especially in this city, and when I mention this city I mean the State of Rhode Island.

Before, however, I quote my authority on the question of music in the synagogue, I feel as though the time has arrived that our Christian brethren should know something more of my people than they do. We have for the past fifteen years been in darkness, and our people have only of late years endeavored to come to the front and show their willingness to co-operate with other cities as to what was actually necessary in this city to give them prominence as a religious denomination. We as Israelites of Providence and vicinity have felt that in order to command the respect of our fellow man, we must give evidence of something tangible as to our distinctive religious identity. Everybody is aware that there are Israelites living here, have lived here for many years, but how have they lived? *in obscurity, so to speak.*

What has time wrought for our people, however, during the past ten years? Wonders, if I may use the term. *Miracles.* You may ask in what manner; in what particular? I will answer thus wise.

The Israelites of Rhode Island to-day as a religious class are respected. We have proved that there is material in our midst that can be utilized, and if given the opportunity in the right direction have the intelligence to hold positions of honor, provided they are aspirants for the same.

There is a bright future in this city for our people. Although few in numbers compared with other cities, we have the satisfaction of knowing that we command the respect due from one to the other notwithstanding what his belief may be.

Judaism to-day stands on a solid foundation. Judaism is the same as it always was, and like the unchangeableness of God, was, is, and ever will be a beacon light to all who may walk the path thereof, illumined by the rays of Divine light, spreading in all directions.

While we have at all times believed in a reform as to the service in the synagogue we have never deviated from the spirit of the Mosaic Law. This is our stronghold, our banner, which has been carried through thousands of years. We cannot be assailed although fanatics, so to speak, have tried to tamper with the same, but the results will not have benefited them to any great extent. The very most important question which the so-called conference of radical Rabbis in Pittsburgh endeavored to embody in their platform the question of the regulation of diet. This important matter is sufficient to show their unfitness in attacking a question of the sanitary laws of the Jews,—a question which is conceded by men of all creeds to be a matter which cannot be excelled.

We Israelites of the 19th century, and especially in this city, have known for some years the need of a proper service. Our people have fallen into error on this question, and we have endeavored to rectify this evil as far as it relates to our religious worship. That we have considered it a duty we owe ourselves and to our brethren at large, to declare that it is not our desire for innovation, not a want of respect for those institutions which our more immediate ancestors obeyed, but an obligation, a deep sense of right, which nothing can weaken; a conviction resulting from long, cool, and serious reflection, that impelled us to those measures which in our hearts we considered the only means of arousing our people in this city from that state of indifference and erroneous thoughts into which they were sinking, and to save our religion from criticism and self-respect from other denominations.

When we consider how things have changed among our own people it is hardly possible to recognize it ourselves.

The time in years gone by that it was necessary to hold divine services on the Sabbath's was such to keep them from attending the synagogue. Imagine 4.30 P. M. as an hour to gather people in the synagogue. Imagine a multiplicity of prayers entirely in the Hebrew, and an occasional Chaldaic poem, which I question was not understood by any of the congregation. Again the observance of double festivals, a practice which originated before the astronomical calculations of the calender was introduced, has nevertheless been rigorously upheld in days when we were enabled to determine the months, even to the fraction of a minute.

It was, my friends, to remedy these great evils that we Israelites of this city brought about a reform in our service, and which up to the present time has proved a blessing to our people. The time appointed now for divine service is such as to enable the entire congregation, men, women and children to assemble prior to the commencement of prayer.

The prayers are said by the minister aloud. Appropriate psalms and hymns are chanted by the choir, and responses made by the congregation.

And now, my friends, to go back as to the question of organ music in our synagogue. A fondness for music and melody is clearly traceable amongst the Israelites as early as the times of Samuel, (x. 5,) and no one can attentively read the biblical records of that age without noting the idea then taking root that music tends to kindle the imagination, to warm the heart, and to awaken the liveliest sentiments of piety. Abundant evidences exist to establish the fact that music was employed during the administration of Samuel in connection with some of the most important offices of religion.

We find in Is. vi.; Chron. xxv., 5th and 6th verses, after the recovery of the possessions which the Philistines and other enemies had wrested from the Hebrews, and when Israel found itself in the enjoyment of peace and prosperity, David, the reigning sovereign, brought the public worship into unison with the improved social condition of the people, and introduced into the sanctuary instrumental music on a most extensive scale. He instituted twenty-four classes of musicians and singers, and placed them under the direction of two hundred and eighty-eight leaders, the most renowned of whom are Asaph, Heman and Jeduthum. And they did not consist of males only, since the three daughters of Heman are mentioned in the list of performers.

I have merely brought this matter before your notice to show that the reform in this respect was based upon a usage which had its origin thousands of years ago. Hence the introduction of organ or instrumental music into the synagogue at the present day is not an innovation, so called, as pronounced by our Orthodox brethren. Anything that would in a measure tend to improve the services, have been adopted in this country in all the synagogues of the Moderate Reform Platform.

Thus, my friends, have I as time would permit, endeavored to explain the motives that have brought me before your honorable society, and have given evidence to what extent we, as Israelites of this city, have progressed in our religious workings. If I have not spoken at length on the question of commerce and manufacturing interests among our brethren, and if I have not adhered closely to the subject for which this meeting was called together, it is because my Brother Denison has exhausted the subject and has been better informed on this question than I have been, and has left no room for me to dwell upon. I have considered the true objects of this meeting and the sentiments of both the Israelites and my Christian brethren. I have long examined into the question of how little Judaism and our people in this city have been understood as a religious creed, and have therefore endeavored to place them on a proper footing.

That henceforth this exposition will fully exonerate us from the imputation of entertaining the wild speculations which have attributed to us that of having our services held in private, and we feared non-Israelites being present at our synagogue, I trust will be removed from the minds of those who have the intelligence to know better.

Every effort we have made for the improvement in our devotion to Almighty God we have striven to confine strictly to the spirit of the immutable law of God, and before closing my remarks I desire to give this assemblage a little information which no doubt will interest you all, on the question that has so often been asked, Why we Israelites do not uncover our heads when attending divine worship, or when engaged in prayer? It appears, my friends, to be nothing more than an original custom, for in Asia this day, it is a mark of respect toward a superior to keep his head covered in his presence, whereas in western countries our customs are just the reverse of all this, since the recognized mark of social intercourse and to superiors, is to keep the head uncovered, and there can be no doubt but that the deepest marks of reverence and respect that any human being can pay are due to God.

But the fact is that this keeping our heads covered is not because of any custom in any part of the world, but because of a positive commandment which renders it a duty incumbent upon us of the House of Israel. According to the thirteen articles of the creeds, we Israelites believe that the Creator is one, and that he alone is God, who was, who is, and who will be, everlastingly. While the third art declares that God is not corporeal, or material, and not subject to accidents of bodies or matter, He consequently is altogether independent of time, place or custom; and as God's law and precepts are the spiritual food or sustenance of the soul, it follows that they must also be immutable and that our intercourse with God is, or should be, the embodiment and practical carrying out of this law, and therefore unaltered whether it be in the East or in the West. Now the command of God, through Moses, His servant, in Leviticus 16th chapter, 3d and 4th verses, directs: Thus shall Aaron come into the holy place, a holy linen coat shall he put on, and with a linen mytre (called in Hebrew Mitznefes,) turban or head covering, he shall be attired. Thus God commanded the Priest to perform divine service with his head covered. So long as the Temple of Jerusalem and the Levitical ritual remained in their glory this precept was always observed; but now that we have no altar, and the Priest can offer no sacrifices, sacred Scripture instructs us to compensate for the offering of bullocks, "with our lips." Or, in other words, that prayer is to replace sacrifice, (Hosea xiv. 2). Accordingly, every Israelite during divine worship officiates as a Priest, offering in lieu of sacrifice, his prayers in his place of worship, which Scripture declares to be Mikdosh, Holy Place of minor holiness, but still Holy, and which replaces the altar in the Temple. And as each Israelite thus performs the function and service of the Priest, and as he must in all things and to the utmost of his power conform to the law of God, he is bound to keep his head covered during divine worship even as the Priest was commanded to do when engaged in the sacred service appertaining to his office.

This, then, concludes my remarks to-day. If what I have said has in any way interested you I am pleased to think that in my humble capacity as a private individual, that I have added something that may reflect with credit upon the Israelites of Providence and vicinity. Our people will ever remember this day as something never to be forgotten in the history of this State, that we should have been allowed this privilege and honor of having a special day set apart whereon to give them prominence as a religious sect. God grant that such feelings of brotherly love may at all times be evinced towards us, and that we may merit at all times what has been advanced here this day. The Israelites of this city will have the satisfaction of knowing one thing, that they have entered upon a new era of usefulness, and the ultimate results thereof must be beneficial to them and the community at large. With my best wishes for the future prosperity of this venerable and honorable institution, accept my thanks and those of the Israelites of this city for the honor conferred.

Mr. Noot then proceeded, with the aid of members of the synagogue, to explain and exemplify portions of both Orthodox and Reformed Hebrew service. The Rabbi wore his cap, and the voices were supported by an organ. The recitations and chantings by the Rabbi, and the psalms and songs of the responding choir, were rendered with admirable pathos and purity, holding the assembly in rapt attention, and awakening a truly catholic religious spirit, alike among Gentiles and Jews. Altogether, the day was emphatically historic in our State, giving prominence to a peculiar and valuable portion of Rhode Island records, and cultivating in an unusual manner that charity and brotherhood which should be felt by the children of the Great All-Father.

IS AMERICA ONLY EAST GREENWICH.

SIR JAMES MARRIOTT, in a speech made in the House of Commons in 1782, as an argument in favor of the right of Great Britain to tax American Colonies, after maintaining that the American War was just in its origin, pointed out that, although it had been frequently pretended that the inhabitants of the colonies were not represented in the British Parliament, yet the fact was otherwise, for they were actually represented. The first colonization by national and sovereign authority was the establishment of the colony of Virginia. The grants and charters made of these lands, and of all the subsequent colonies, were of one tenor, and expressed in the following terms:

"To have and to hold of the King's or Queen's majesty, as part and parcel of the manor of East Greenwich, within the county of Kent, *eddendum* a certain rent at our castle of East Greenwich, etc."

So that the inhabitants of America were in fact by the nature of their tenure represented by the Knights of the Shire for the county of Kent in Parliament.

This, it must be remembered, was the opinion of a high legal authority, Sir James Marriott being the Judge who presided in the Court of Admiralty, and therefore not likely to make a mistake on a matter of no slight interest and importance.

From this rendering, our English cousins hold that the whole of America is but an appendage of an English Shire; nay, worse, a borough of the manor of East Greenwich, so that every American citizen is necessarily a resident of East Greenwich, in the county of Kent, and this fact our English cousins would have us believe is a higher honor than that of an American citizen. There are two opinions about that, of which our own is, that if the first is a high honor, we have added a higher one to it, and if our fathers did a grievous thing in effecting a separation, it was no more than what other subjects had done and unsuccessfully.

We are much pleased to have this English opinion brought to our notice by our East Greenwich patron, and feel that the genius that presided over the place at the time of its naming was desirous of bestowing an honored name, and we are pleased that the good people of the town have worn the name with honor.

A RHODE ISLAND MAN THE ORIGINATOR OF OUR POSTAL SYSTEM.—In —— Benjamin Franklin was appointed Deputy Postmaster for America and organized the postal system for the Colonies upon a remunerative basis. But in 1773 Franklin had presented at the English Parliament the petition to remove Governor Hutchinson and Chief Justice Oliver, and when the news of the Boston Tea Party reached England, the feeling against America became intense, and Franklin was removed. But William Goddard, formerly printer of the *Providence Gazette* and then engaged in publishing papers in Philadelphia, traveled through the Colonies and consulted with the people upon the matter of a postal system, and upon the 26th of July, 1775, the Continental Congress adopted his plan and Benjamin Franklin was appointed Postmaster General.

ANCIENT HIGHWAYS.—Some of the highways in North and South Kingstown have been in use many years, as at the autumn session of the Assembly, held at Warwick, 1705, the highways in Kingstown recently laid out were received and confirmed. The line between Greenwich and Kingstown was established by the Assembly in 1705.

SOCIETIES AND THEIR DOINGS.

RHODE ISLAND HISTORICAL SOCIETY.—Dec. 29, 1885.—Geo. C. Mason, Jr., of Newport, read a paper entitled "Our Apprenticeship and the Manual Labor Schools."

Jan. 12, 1886.—Annual Meeting. The President read his annual address, which proved to be a thoughtful paper and very practical. The President reported the affairs of the Society in a flourishing condition. The election of officers resulted as follows: President, William Gammell; Vice-Presidents, Francis Brinley and Charles W. Parsons; Secretary, Amos Perry; Treasurer, Richmond P. Everett. The regular committees were then re-elected with few changes.

Jan. 26.—Dr. Charles W. Parsons read a paper on "Town Names in Rhode Island." Edward Field 2d, read on "The Fortifications in and around Providence."

Feb. 9.—Rev. Dr. Wm. F. B. Jackson read a paper, "Trial of Anne Hutchinson."

Feb. 23.—Prof. William Matthews read a paper on the "Battle of Waterloo."

Mar. 9.—James Burdick, of Providence, read a paper "Reminiscences of a Forty-niner in California."

Mar. 23.—Rev. James P. Root read a paper, "Captain Arthur Fenner and His Times." Hon. Charles H. Denison, of Westerly, read a paper, "The Romance and History of the South County."

April 6.—Quarterly Meeting. A number of interesting communications were made. The evening being very stormy rendered the attendance slim.

April 20.—Rev. W. R. Bagnall, of Wilbraham, Mass., read a paper on "The Textile Industries of our Country Prior to 1800." This paper is the final one of the winter's course.

VETERAN CITIZENS HISTORICAL ASSOCIATION.—Jan. 4, 1886. —This meeting was omitted.

Feb. 1.—A paper was read by Andrew B. Patton, Esq., on

"The Early Land Titles of Providence." President Hammond then read a paper written by Welcome A. Greene, Esq., "A New Theory Regarding the Origin of the Palatine Light."

Mar. 1.—Rev. F. Denison read a paper on "Old Schools and Teachers." A short paper on "Zerviah Mason's School" by A. H. was read by President Hammond. Ex-Mayor Jabez C. Knight read his "Reminiscences of Providence" in rhyme.

April 5.—Judge J. Russell Bullock, of Bristol, read a paper upon "Stuteley Westcott and His Times."

May 3.—C. S. Scarborough, Esq., read a paper, "The Taverns of Providence and their Relations to the Business of the Town." A paper prepared by an old resident was read by Welcome A. Greene, Esq., "The Stampers Hill School, 1696." The Treasurer read a paper, "The Old Sabin Inn and its Relation to the Gaspee Affair, 1772."

PROVIDENCE FRANKLIN SOCIETY.—Dec. 22, 1885.—James N. Arnold read a paper upon "Prehistoric Rhode Island."

Jan. 5, 1886.—Annual Meeting. The following officers were elected: President, Levi W. Russell; Vice-President, D. W. Hoyt; Secretary, C. M. Salisbury; Treasurer, A. L. Calder; Standing Committee, George Hunt, Dr. W. O. Brown, Thomas Battey; Cabinet Keeper, T. H. Shurrucks; Librarian, W. M. Knowles. The annual reports showed the society to be in a very flourishing condition.

Jan. 19.—No meeting.

Feb. 2.—Mr. Thomas Battey gave a description of the marl beds of New Jersey and exhibited specimens, and also specimens from Rhode Island beds. Mr. D. W. Hoyt made remarks. Several valuable additions were made to the cabinet for which the society returned thanks to the donors.

Feb. 16.—An informal talk was had upon meteoric showers. References were made to the recent floods, and it was stated the rainfall was nine and a quarter inches, an unprecedented record.

Mar. 2.—Mr. William H. Williams, of Brown University,

read a paper, "Personal Reminiscences During a Residence in Brazil."

Mar. 16.—Mr. E. H. Burlingame read a paper upon "The Hudson River Tunnel."

Mar. 30.—A paper was read by Prof. Winslow Upton, of Brown University; subject, "A Visit to the Volcanoes of the Sandwich Islands, with especial mention of Kilahea."

April 13.—Prof. L. W. Russell read a paper; subject, "The Forest Trees of Rhode Island." The subject was illustrated with the stereoptican from views made by Mr. Charles F. Janes.

April 27.—James N. Arnold read a paper, "The Evidences of the Mound Builders in Narragansett."

April 24.—The society made an excursion to Burial Hill and Fort Ninigret in Charlestown. At this meeting a vote of thanks was given to the Hon. George Carmichael, Jr., and his son, Mr. William F. Tucker, and Mr. George W. Hoxie, for their efforts in making the excursion a success.

SOLDIERS AND SAILORS HISTORICAL SOCIETY.—Jan. 19.—Annual Meeting. The following officers were elected: President, Capt. J. M. Addeman; Vice-President, Dr. George B. Peck; Secretary, Dr. W. H. Hutchinson; Corresponding Secretary, Col. George N. Bliss; Treasurer, Col. Philip S. Chase; Cabinet Keeper and Librarian, Col. Theodore A. Barton. Col. George N. Bliss read a paper, "Reminiscences of the First Rhode Island Cavalry in connection with the Cavalry Fight at Kelly's Ford." This battle is considered by some to be the first action of the Rebellion which could be called strictly a cavalry fight.

Feb. 16.—Prof. E. B. Andrews read a paper, "Reminiscences of a Private the First Year of the War."

Mar. 16.—Capt. Albert R. Greene, of Warwick, read a paper, "From Bridgeport to Ringgold, by way of Lookout Mountain."

April 20.—Major John K. Bucklin, of Mystic Bridge, Conn., read a paper upon the "Humors of the War."

BARRINGTON HISTORIC ANTIQUARIAN SOCIETY.—Dec. 30, 1885.—Rev. S. Bourne, Rev. William House, and Hon. L. B. House made short addresses. Rev. G. H. Tilton invited the society to be present at the dedication of a Historical Museum, in Rehoboth, in May next. Miss Mary S. Bradford presented a pair of knee buckles that once belonged to Dr. John Clarke.

NEWPORT HISTORICAL SOCIETY.—Jan. 19.—F. G. Harris read a paper upon "Liberty and Liberty Trees." Several valuable additions were made to the library. Dr. F. H. Rankin presented in behalf of the Newport Medical Society a handsome mural tablet of Dr. John Clarke, inscribed: "John Clarke, Physician, 1609, 1676; Founder of Newport and of the civil polity of Rhode Island. Erected by the Newport Medical Society, December, 1885." Dr. Rankin, in presenting the tablet, expressed a hope that the citizens of Newport would erect, at no distant day, a suitable memorial to Dr. Clarke.

Feb. 16.—Col. William Gilpin read a paper upon "Religion." President Brinley paid an eloquent tribute to the memory of Miss Ellen Townsend, a liberal friend and benefactor of the society.

Mar. 16.—Thomas Nichols read a paper upon "The Friends of Newport."

Mar. 18.—Annual Election. The following officers were elected for the ensuing year: Francis Brinley, President; William Gilpin and Henry E. Turner, Vice-Presidents; R. H. Tilley, Librarian; H. R. Storer, Treasurer; G. W. Carr, Assistant Treasurer; H. B. Wood, Recording Secretary; F. G. Harris, Corresponding Secretary; H. R. Storer, Curator of coins and medals. The society was reported in a very flourishing condition.

THE NEWPORT NATURAL HISTORY SOCIETY.—Jan. 14, 1886.—Professor Wm. W. Bailey read a paper "On certain Curious Relations of Insects to Flowers."

Feb. 11. (Evening for short communications).—A paper

was read by Mr. Amos Parmenter on "The Birds of Newport and Vicinity." A paper was read by Mr. C. H. Lawton, Jr., on our "Winter Birds."

Mar. 11.—Rev. F. F. Emerson read a paper on "Ants."

EDITORIAL NOTES.

With this issue we publish the REGISTER from Providence, R. I. We do this in order to save expense in transportation and to avail ourselves of the advantages of the great State libraries and other favors now accorded us, which has not been heretofore in our power to enjoy. We have always had a pride in publishing from Narragansett, and have decided to make this change only after becoming convinced that we could serve the interests of our patrons to better advantage here than in our former place. We have no desire, nor do we in any way intend to neglect Narragansett history, and shall give in future numbers as much matter as we can possibly find room for and not neglect other portions of our State. The REGISTER intends to do its utmost to compile and publish the unwritten history of the State, and entreats its readers to stand by and aid us by all means in their power to bring about this desirable consideration. The present number is only a foretaste of what we have in the future for our readers. We intend to make our new volume worthy of every scholar's attention.

The REGISTER has always felt that its efforts in the cause of historical knowledge would win appreciation and support as fast and as far as its productions were brought into notice.

We are pleased to be able to announce that such appreciation has extended further than we had dared to hope.

The General Assembly of the State of Rhode Island has recently made an appropriation to furnish all the FREE PUBLIC LIBRARIES in the various towns of the State with copies of the REGISTER so far as issued. That this action is primarily in the interests of education we recognize, but we cannot help feeling a sentiment of personal satisfaction that our labors are thus appreciated, and we shall endeavor to press forward the work so that the future numbers shall exceed in interest and value our past production.

The libraries so benefited will, we think, find it a marked advantage to them to have so much historical matter that has hitherto been inaccessible to the majority of the readers thus placed upon their shelves.

Our list of contributors is larger than ever before, and embraces some of the most talented and industrious workers in the historical field in this and neighboring States.

Altogether we feel that the General Assembly has made a wise and prudent movement in thus encouraging the growth of historical learning, and are deeply gratified at finding our magazine the recipient of its attention.

HISTORY OF PROVIDENCE PLANTATIONS.—Messrs. J. A. & R. A. Reed, the publishers of Providence, R. I., have in press, and will issue in August next, a historical work entitled "THE PROVIDENCE PLANTATIONS FOR 250 YEARS," with a graphic description of the city at the present time. The editor and principal author is Welcome Arnold Greene, Esq., well known to our readers as author of the interesting article on "RHODE ISLAND PAPER CURRENCY," published in our number of July last. All who have read that article will be satisfied that any work by Mr. Greene will be ably and carefully done.

From a careful perusal of the advance sheets of the work, we can assure our readers that it contains much matter that is the result of original research and reflection which is so woven into the detail of the well known historical facts as to present a concise and clear description of the origin and growth of Providence Plantations.

Mr. Greene will hereafter contribute interesting articles for the REGISTER. We congratulate the Messrs. Reid upon obtaining such an able editor for the above work.

THE GENEALOGICAL DICTIONARY OF RHODE ISLAND.—We take pleasure in announcing that this excellent work is progressing favorably and that it now bids fair to be published next summer. Mr. Austin, the author, has chosen a happy time in placing his great work before the public, namely, on the 250th anniversary of the settlement of the State. It will be one of those historic milestones that mark the annals of the State's progress.

NEW ENGLAND MAGAZINE AND BAY STATE MONTHLY.—With the January (1886) number of this excellent monthly the management have decided to embrace the six New England States in the range of subjects within its province—an excellent idea; and, we should judge from the inital numbers were in a fair way to be successfully carried out.

GENEALOGICAL NOTES RELATING TO NEW YORK AND NEW ENGLAND FAMILIES.—Mr. Talcott writes us that before the edition is exhausted he would like to have more of his Rhode Island friends secure a copy. We are pleased that the author is so thoughtful for his friends, and we would esteem it a great favor to have his work more generally purchased here. The price (six dollars) is very cheap when we take into consideration the great amount of labor bestowed on its eight hundred pages. Please secure a copy therefore while you can.

QUERY.—George Belford and his wife, members of St. Paul's Church, Narragansett, were buried under their own pew. Dr. McSparren and his successor, Dr. Fayerweather, were buried under the altar. When the memorial was erected to the memory of the Doctors in 1868, instead of erecting it over them, it was placed over that of Mr. Belford and wife. This is an interesting theme to ponder over, and we would like some of our Episcopal friends to inform us more about Mr. Belford. Also upon what authority was that memorial placed in its present position.

DESCENDANTS OF WILLIAM HANNUM, who emigrated from England to Massachusetts in 1630, are requested to correspond with C. S. Hannum, P. O. Box 501, Westfield, Mass., who is preparing a genealogy of the family.

HISTORICAL NOTES.

THREE FACTS REGARDING RHODE ISLAND.—Of the 36 cities and towns in Rhode Island 20 of them border on water that is navigable. Railroads cross every town on the main land except three, Foster, East Greenwich and Little Compton, and surveys for new roads cross the centre of these three. Foster is the only town whose water shed is such that nearly half of its water flows into another State. With this exception and a small part of western Coventry, the rest of the State retains its water fall and empties it into the ocean together with much water collected in southern and central Massachusetts.

USQUEPAUG PATENTS.—It is not generally known that several very important inventions originated here. Grant invented the felt hat body from which he soon realized a fortune of a quarter of million of dollars. Slocum's solid headed pin brought its inventor another cool quarter of million of dollars. Silas Mumford invented a burr picker from which parties realized handsome fortunes. J. G. Perry's sausage meat cutter realized twenty thousand dollars, and its sales are now a handsome income.

FIRST INTERMENT IN RIVERSIDE CEMETERY, WAKEFIELD.—Stephen C. Fiske was one of the original incorporators of this cemetery and took a great interest in its promotion. He was the first one to choose his lot, and then went home in his usual health. Three days afterwards he was buried on the site he had selected only a few days before he died.